Hands-On Network Programming with C# and .NET Core

Build robust network applications with C# and .NET Core

Sean Burns

BIRMINGHAM - MUMBAI

Hands-On Network Programming with C# and .NET Core

Commissioning Editor: Richa Tripathi
Acquisition Editor: Sandeep Mishra
Content Development Editor: Digvijay Bagul
Technical Editor: Aniket Iswalkar
Copy Editor: Safis Editing
Project Coordinator: Ulhas Kambali
Proofreader: Safis Editing
Indexer: Pratik Shirodkar
Graphics: Tom Scaria
Production Coordinator: Saili Kale

First published: March 2019

Production reference: 1280319

Published by Packt Publishing Ltd.
Livery Place
35 Livery Street
Birmingham
B3 2PB, UK.

ISBN 978-1-78934-076-1

`www.packtpub.com`

mapt.io

Mapt is an online digital library that gives you full access to over 5,000 books and videos, as well as industry leading tools to help you plan your personal development and advance your career. For more information, please visit our website.

Why subscribe?

- Spend less time learning and more time coding with practical eBooks and Videos from over 4,000 industry professionals
- Improve your learning with Skill Plans built especially for you
- Get a free eBook or video every month
- Mapt is fully searchable
- Copy and paste, print, and bookmark content

Packt.com

Did you know that Packt offers eBook versions of every book published, with PDF and ePub files available? You can upgrade to the eBook version at www.packt.com and as a print book customer, you are entitled to a discount on the eBook copy. Get in touch with us at customercare@packtpub.com for more details.

At www.packt.com, you can also read a collection of free technical articles, sign up for a range of free newsletters, and receive exclusive discounts and offers on Packt books and eBooks.

Contributors

About the author

Sean Burns is a software engineer and author dedicated to craftsmanship and quality in his work. His professional career began while attending Virginia Commonwealth University in 2012. Leaving school to pursue his career full-time, he has accumulated 7 years of experience as a professional software engineer, working in a wide range of industries. Over the course of his career, he has developed and released software for every layer of the application stack. His projects include feature-rich and high-performance frontend user interfaces exposed to millions of consumers, as well as high-performance web services and APIs. Since it began, his career has been driven by an innate curiosity and a continued passion for software and technology.

First and foremost, I want to thank my amazing and supportive wife, Megan. She is a constant source of inspiration, and I owe the success of this book to her. Thanks to my parents and sisters for their unwavering confidence in me. I also owe a great deal to my friend and technical reviewer, Drew. Finally, I would like to thank those friends who supported me throughout this process, including Majid, Johnny, Joe, Alex, Hannah, Gigi, Brendan, and others.

About the reviewer

Andrew Brethwaite is a professional full stack software engineer currently working in the financial services sector. He graduated from Virginia Polytechnic Institute and State University in 2012 with a degree in mechanical engineering. Early on in his career, Andrew was able to pivot and pursue his passion for developing software full-time. Since then, he has devoted his time to learning new technologies and architectural patterns in an effort to create scalable, extensible, and maintainable technical solutions.

I would like to thank the author of this book, Sean, for including me on this project. I would also like to thank my family, especially my wife, Emily, for her support in helping me to get where I am today.

Packt is searching for authors like you

If you're interested in becoming an author for Packt, please visit `authors.packtpub.com` and apply today. We have worked with thousands of developers and tech professionals, just like you, to help them share their insight with the global tech community. You can make a general application, apply for a specific hot topic that we are recruiting an author for, or submit your own idea.

For Lady Godiva, who taught me mindfulness and gratitude.

– Sean Burns

Table of Contents

Section 2: Communicating Over Networks

Section 3: Application Protocols and Connection Handling

Section 4: Security, Stability, and Scalability

Section 5: Advanced Subjects

Preface

Network programming is a complex undertaking, with the potential for an extremely high impact on the performance and scalability of the software it supports. Learning to leverage the high-level language constructs and features of C# and the .NET Core libraries can help engineers to fine-tune their network applications to the performance modern users have come to expect. This book is written to serve as a comprehensive exploration of the concepts of network programming, as viewed through the lens of the .NET Core framework. It seeks to explain every aspect of computer networks, and the software that makes those networks possible. Using little more than the .NET Core SDK and a code editor, the contents of this book demonstrate how to implement flexible, stable, and reliable software to facilitate large-scale computer networking.

Who this book is for

If you have any experience with object-oriented programming languages, and would like to learn more about how C# and .NET Core can facilitate network and web programming, this book is for you. Additionally, if you administer or manage network resources and would like to develop the skills to manage or customize your network with the tools available in .NET Core, this book is an excellent resource. And finally, if you have any experience with network programming, but would like to take a closer look at the .NET Core framework, this is the book for you.

What this book covers

`Chapter 1`, *Networks in a Nutshell*, introduces readers to the fundamentals of computer networks, and the challenges of writing software for use on distributed systems.

`Chapter 2`, *DNS and Resource Location*, explores the basics of resource location and the origins of the DNS.

`Chapter 3`, *Communication Protocols*, investigates the OSI network stack and the variety of communication protocols designed for each layer of that stack.

`Chapter 4`, *Packets and Streams*, looks at how data is encapsulated in packets and how groups of packets are consumed by your software as a stream.

`Chapter 5`, *Generating Network Requests in C#*, takes a deep dive into the request/response model of network communication and how that model is implemented in C#.

`Chapter 6`, *Streams, Threads, and Asynchronous Data*, looks at how C# programs can be designed to consume data streams from remote resources asynchronously, thereby improving performance and reliability.

`Chapter 7`, *Error Handling over the Wire*, looks closely at how to design and implement error-handling strategies in network software.

`Chapter 8`, *Sockets and Ports*, examines how logical connections are established between network hosts by mapping a socket in your application code to a port on your network interface.

`Chapter 9`, *HTTP in .NET*, takes a thorough look at how every aspect of HTTP is implemented within the context of C# and .NET Core. It looks at implementing HTTP clients and server applications using ASP.NET Core and the `System.Net.Http` library.

`Chapter 10`, *FTP and SMTP*, looks at some of the less commonly leveraged protocols of the application layer of the OSI network stack, implementing a fully functional FTP server in the process.

`Chapter 11`, *The Transport Layer – TCP and UDP*, takes a close look at the transport layer of the OSI network stack, exploring the distinction between connection-based and connectionless communication protocols, and looking at how to implement each in C#.

`Chapter 12`, *The Internet Protocol*, explores the backbone of the modern internet by looking at how the **Internet Protocol** (**IP**) provides for device addressing and packet delivery.

`Chapter 13`, *Transport Layer Security*, looks at how the SSL and TLS were designed to provide security for data transmitted over global, unsecured networks, and how to implement TLS in .NET Core applications.

`Chapter 14`, *Authentication and Authorization on Networks*, considers how you can validate the identity of users of your network software and restrict access to different features and resources based on your users' permissions.

`Chapter 15`, *Caching Strategies for Distributed Systems*, looks at the various benefits of caching different resources in your network software for performance and reliability improvements.

`Chapter 16`, *Performance Analysis and Monitoring*, takes a close look at how to monitor the health and performance of your network applications, and how to respond to, and reduce the impact of, network unreliability in relation to your software.

`Chapter 17`, *Pluggable Protocols in .NET Core,* looks at the .NET concept of a pluggable protocol, and how you can use it to define your own custom application layer network protocols, and incorporate those protocols seamlessly into your .NET applications.

`Chapter 18`, *Network Analysis and Packet Inspection,* examines the tools and resources available in the .NET Core framework for investigating network traffic and the state of network devices on your host machine. It looks at how you can investigate the content of network traffic being processed by your host with packet inspection, and how you can use the information gained by packet inspection to respond to security risks.

`Chapter 19`, *Remote Logins and SSH,* looks at the origins of the SSH protocol and how it enables secure access to remote resources over an unsecured network. It looks at the most popular C# library for interacting with remote hosts via SSH and considers the range of applications you might build on top of the SSH protocol.

To get the most out of this book

This book assumes a basic knowledge of the principles of object-oriented programming, and an ability to at least read and follow along with C# source code. A basic, high-level understanding of networking concepts and principles is also assumed.

To leverage this book, you will need to at least download and install the latest version of the .NET Core SDK and command-line interface. You should also take the time to familiarize yourself with a C# source code editor, such as Visual Studio Community Edition, or Visual Studio Code, both of which are free to use.

Download the example code files

You can download the example code files for this book from your account at `www.packt.com`. If you purchased this book elsewhere, you can visit `www.packt.com/support` and register to have the files emailed directly to you.

You can download the code files by following these steps:

1. Log in or register at `www.packt.com`.
2. Select the **SUPPORT** tab.
3. Click on **Code Downloads & Errata**.
4. Enter the name of the book in the **Search** box and follow the onscreen instructions.

Once the file is downloaded, please make sure that you unzip or extract the folder using the latest version of:

- WinRAR/7-Zip for Windows
- Zipeg/iZip/UnRarX for Mac
- 7-Zip/PeaZip for Linux

The code bundle for the book is also hosted on GitHub at `https://github.com/PacktPublishing/Hands-On-Network-Programming-with-CSharp-and-.NET-Core`. In case there's an update to the code, it will be updated on the existing GitHub repository.

We also have other code bundles from our rich catalog of books and videos available at `https://github.com/PacktPublishing/`. Check them out!

Conventions used

There are a number of text conventions used throughout this book.

`CodeInText`: Indicates code words in text, database table names, folder names, filenames, file extensions, pathnames, dummy URLs, user input, and Twitter handles. Here is an example: "Note the inclusion of the `System.Net.Security` namespace in our `using` directives. This is where the `AuthenticationLevel` enum is defined."

A block of code is set as follows:

```
var httpRequest = WebRequest.Create("http://test-domain.com");
var ftpRequest = WebRequest.Create("ftp://ftp.test-domain.com");
var fileRequest = WebRequest.Create("file://files.test-domain.com");
```

When we wish to draw your attention to a particular part of a code block, the relevant lines or items are set in bold:

```
if(!WebRequest.RegisterPrefix("cpf://", new CustomRequestCreator())) {
    throw new WebException("Failure to register custom prefix protocol
handler.");
}
```

Any command-line input or output is written as follows:

```
$ mkdir css
$ cd css
```

Bold: Indicates a new term, an important word, or words that you see on screen. For example, words in menus or dialog boxes appear in the text like this. Here is an example: "Select **System info** from the **Administration** panel."

Warnings or important notes appear like this.

Tips and tricks appear like this.

Get in touch

Feedback from our readers is always welcome.

General feedback: If you have questions about any aspect of this book, mention the book title in the subject of your message and email us at `customercare@packtpub.com`.

Errata: Although we have taken every care to ensure the accuracy of our content, mistakes do happen. If you have found a mistake in this book, we would be grateful if you would report this to us. Please visit `www.packt.com/submit-errata`, selecting your book, clicking on the Errata Submission Form link, and entering the details.

Piracy: If you come across any illegal copies of our works in any form on the internet, we would be grateful if you would provide us with the location address or website name. Please contact us at `copyright@packt.com` with a link to the material.

If you are interested in becoming an author: If there is a topic that you have expertise in, and you are interested in either writing or contributing to a book, please visit `authors.packtpub.com`.

Reviews

Please leave a review. Once you have read and used this book, why not leave a review on the site that you purchased it from? Potential readers can then see and use your unbiased opinion to make purchase decisions, we at Packt can understand what you think about our products, and our authors can see your feedback on their book. Thank you!

For more information about Packt, please visit `packt.com`.

1
Section 1: Foundations of Network Architecture

Part one of the book will start by exploring the various network architectures that make distributed programming possible in the first place. It will examine the standards adhered to by hardware and software vendors to allow communication across networks, including the DNS naming system, IPv4 and IPv6 standards for device addressing, and local hardware-level APIs and data structures that allow users to program for those networks, with basic examples of C# software that leverage or demonstrate these concepts.

The following chapters will be covered in this section:

`Chapter 1`, *Networks in a Nutshell*
`Chapter 2`, *DNS and Resource Location*
`Chapter 3`, *Communication Protocols*
`Chapter 4`, *Packets and Streams*

1
Networks in a Nutshell

It's hard to imagine that anyone reading this book doesn't have some intuitive idea of what a network actually is. As I write this introduction, I'm surrounded by no fewer than six distinct, network-connected devices within arm's reach. Even before I began a career in software engineering, I could have given a reasonably accurate description of what constitutes a network. However, no amount of intuition about what networks are or what might run on them, nor the use of software running on distributed systems, can account for the impact of a distributed architecture on your code. It's that impact on your software design and implementation decisions that we'll cover in this chapter.

We'll try to nail down a concrete definition of a network, and we'll consider the new problems you'll need to solve when writing software for them. This book assumes a fair amount of general programming skills within the C# language from its readers. I won't take any time to explain the use of native language structures, types, or keywords, nor will I discuss or explain the common general algorithms used throughout. However, I will stop short of making any assumptions of the reader's knowledge of networks, inter-device communication, or how those problems are solved in .NET Core. As such, this chapter will start from the most basic first principles and seek to provide a stable foundation from which anyone with at least some programming skill can proceed competently through the rest of the book.

The following topics will be covered in this chapter:

- The unique challenges of distributing computational or data resources over a network, and how those challenges manifest in software
- The different components of a network, and how those components can be arranged to achieve different goals
- The impact of the variability of devices, latency, instability, and standardization of networks on the complexity of applications written for network use

- Common concepts, terms, and data structures used for network programming, and how those concepts are exposed by .NET Core
- Understanding the scope of applications that are made possible by networked architectures, and the importance of developing skills in network programming to enable those kinds of applications

Technical requirements

This being an introductory chapter, there will be no meaningful code samples, as we'll be covering the high-level concepts and vocabulary of networks to establish a clear foundation for the rest of the book. However, in this chapter, we'll be discussing the `System.Net` class library provided by .NET Core. While this discussion will be happening at a very high level, it would be a good opportunity to familiarize yourself with the development tools made available to you by Microsoft Visual Studio Community edition. This is free to use, and provides a rich feature suite out of the box, with broad support for .NET Core project management and administration provided out of the box. As we discuss some of the libraries provided within the .NET Core tools, I encourage you to investigate using the Visual Studio IDE to include those libraries into your project and begin exploring them through the IDE's IntelliSense.

Expanding the scope of software – distributed systems and the challenges they introduce

The first step to understanding programming for networks is, of course, understanding networks. Defining what they are, clarifying the aspects of networks we are concerned with, addressing how network architecture impacts the programs we write, and what kinds of software solutions networks need to be effective.

What is a network?

At its most basic, a network is nothing more than a physical implementation of an undirected graph; a series of nodes and edges, or connections, between those nodes, as demonstrated in the following diagram:

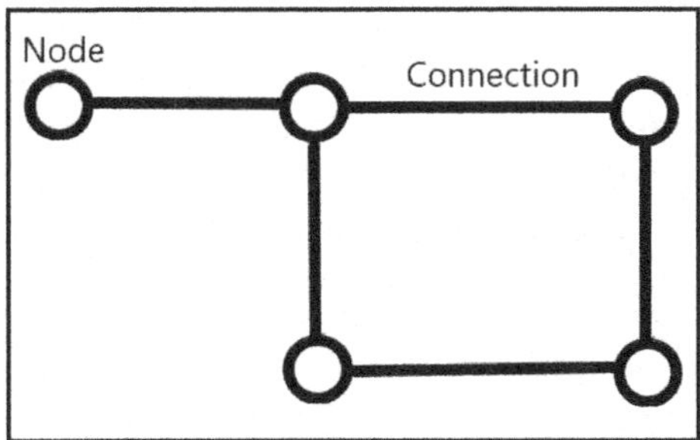

A basic, undirected graph

However, the preceding diagram doesn't quite capture the full picture. What constitutes a node, and what is sufficient for a connection are all very pertinent details to clarify. An individual node should probably be able to meaningfully interact with other nodes on the network, or else you might have to concern yourself with programming for a potato connected by two wires to a network of routers and servers. It's safe enough to say that potatoes very obviously aren't nodes, and that an active and stable Azure server very obviously *is*, so the line delineating nodes from non-nodes on a network falls somewhere between those two poles. Likewise, we can easily identify that the cables from the power supply of a computer to the outlet in a wall don't constitute a network connection, but that a CAT-5 cable from our computer to a router obviously does. The dividing line probably falls somewhere between those two, and it is important that we take care to draw that line accurately.

We'll start with a workable definition of networks for the purposes of this book, unpack the definition, and examine why we chose to make the specific distinctions we have, and finally, consider what each essential property of a network means to us as programmers. So, without further ado, the definition of a computer network is as follows:

> *A computer network is, for our purposes, an arbitrarily large set of computational or navigational devices, connected by channels of communication across which computational resources can be reliably sent, received, forwarded, or processed.*

On the surface, that might seem basic, but there is a lot of nuance in that definition that deserves our consideration. So, let's take a deeper dive.

An arbitrarily large set

What do we mean when we say arbitrarily large? Well when you're writing software for a router (accepting that you would realistically be bound by the maximum size of physically-addressable space), you would not (and should not) care about how many devices are actually connected to your hardware, or how many routes you need to reliably pass resources or requests along. Suppose you are writing the system software for a wireless router. While doing so, you tell your product owner that their marketing copy should specify that this router can only connect a maximum of four computers to the internet. Can you imagine any product owner would take that news kindly? You would be looking for a new job in no time! Networks must be able to scale with the needs of their users.

A basic property of almost all computer networks is device-agnosticism, which is to say that any device on a network should assume no knowledge of the number or kind of other devices on that network at any given moment. Indeed, a program or device might need to discern whether or not a specific device or piece of software exists on the network, but nothing about the network connection it obtains will convey that information. Instead, it should be equipped to send and receive messages in a format that is typically standardized for the communication protocol over which the messages are sent. Then, using these standardized messages, a device can request information about the availability, configuration, or capabilities of other devices on the network, without actually knowing whether or not the devices it expects to be available on the network are, in fact, available on the network.

Ensuring that the receiving end of any given outgoing connection from a device is properly connected, or that the receiving devices are configured accordingly, is the concern of the network engineers who support your software. Supporting and responding to requests sent by your software is the responsibility of the authors of the receiving software. Obviously, if you're working in a sufficiently small software shop, both of those roles may well also be filled by you; but in a sufficiently mature working environment, you can likely rely on others to handle these tasks for you. However, when the time comes to deploy your software to a networked device, no information about whether or not those responsibilities were handled properly is available to you simply by virtue of being connected to a network.

Device-agnosticism means that a network has no idea what has connected to it, and, accordingly, cannot tell you as much. A corollary attribute of networks is that other devices on the network cannot and will not be notified that your device or software has connected and been made a resource.

Ultimately, this is what is meant by an arbitrarily large set of devices. Technically, a single computer constitutes a network of one node, and zero connections (though, for the purposes of this book, we'll only be considering networks with at least two nodes, and at least one connection between any given node and any other node on the network), but there is no fixed maximum value of nodes beyond which a network ceases to be a network. Any arbitrary number of nodes, from one to infinity (or whatever the maximum number of physically possible nodes may be), constitutes a valid network, so long as those nodes have some valid connection between themselves and the rest of the network.

Computational devices

Now that we know we can have an arbitrarily large number of computational devices as nodes in our network, it bears further scrutiny to discern what exactly a computational device is. While this may seem obvious, at least initially, we can quickly identify where it becomes unclear by way of an example.

As per our definition of a network, the device I'm using to draft this book right now might well qualify as a self-contained network. I have a keyboard, mouse, monitors, and computer, all connected by standardized channels of communication. This looks awfully network-like at a conceptual level, but intuitively, we would be inclined to say that it is a network of one, and so, not really a network at all. However, while the what of the non-network status of my computer seems obvious, the why might be less clear.

This is where we benefit from clearly explicating what constitutes a computational device for the purposes of our definition of a network. Simply being able to perform computation is insufficient for a network node. In my example, I can tell you that my mouse (a relatively high-end gaming mouse) certainly performs a number of complex calculations transforming a laser-sensor signal into directional inputs to pass to my computer. My monitors certainly have to do a fair amount of computation to transform the raw binary data of pixel color values into the rendered screens I see 60 or 120 times per second. Both of these devices are connected by way of reliable, standardized communication protocols to my machine, but I wouldn't necessarily be inclined to consider them nodes on a network. My computer, when connected to the internet, or my local home network, surely constitutes a node, but its individual peripherals? I'm inclined to say no.

So, if peripherals aren't network devices, then what essential property is it that they're missing? Open communication. While a monitor and a keyboard can communicate over a connection with a wide variety of other devices, the manner in which they can communicate is restricted to a very specific and limited range of possible signals. This highlights an important distinction to be made between distributed systems and networks. While a network is always a distributed system, a distributed system may not necessarily always constitute a network.

My computer is a distributed system; its components can function independently of one another, but they operate in a coordinated fashion to perform the responsibilities of a computer. However, my computer is very obviously not a network. It lacks device-agnosticism, as each component is explicitly configured to communicate its presence to the next node in the graph, so that it can be used to service the needs of the end user. It is also not arbitrarily scalable. I can only have, at most, three monitors connected to my machine at any given time, and only under very specific conditions of connection interfaces and organization. While being connected to a network, my computer and each of its peripherals can instead be conceptually considered a single, atomic computational device. Thus, on a network, we can specify that a computational device is something that can facilitate the requirements of the network. It accepts and communicates openly over device-agnostic channels of communication to provide or leverage computational resources on that network.

Navigational devices

In our definition of a network, I specify computational or navigational devices. For the sake of this book, a navigational device is a valid network device, and constitutes a node on our network. The meaningful difference between a computational and navigational device (or resource) is that a navigational device provides no resources of its own, and instead exists only to facilitate the successful communication of other devices on the network. A simple switch or router would fall under this category. These devices are still programmed to operate successfully on a network, but are typically done at the system level in C or C++, with on-board firmware. The concerns of programming these intermediary devices will generally fall outside the purview of this book, but I wanted to note the distinction for the sake of clarity and completeness.

Channels of communication

Within the context of networks, what constitutes a channel of communication is merely a shared interface for data transmission between any two devices on a network. There are no constraints on the physical implementation of a channel of communication, or the format in which data must be transmitted over a channel, simply that at least two devices can communicate across that channel.

The software impact

When writing software meant to leverage or be leveraged by other devices on a network, there are a number of new considerations and constraints that developers are shielded from when only writing code for local systems. How these issues are best dealt with will be addressed more thoroughly in subsequent chapters, but for now it is worth considering what the impact these aspects of general computer networks might have on the software we write.

The impact of device-agnosticism

When we talk about device-agnosticism, we assume our software is not given information about which resources we expect to be available are actually available. So, going back to the example of my computer as a distributed system that is not a network, I can reliably write local programs that print or draw information to a screen. Because the program is executed locally, I can trust that my operating system will take responsibility for acquiring the connection to my monitor and transmitting the data from my program's stack frame to the monitor's display port connection.

The monitors are resources that are not inherent to the distributed system; I can technically execute any series of commands on my computer without a monitor. It's not essential for the system to function, even if it is essential for the system to function in a way that is decipherable to me. However, I can reliably assume that if the monitors are present on the system, my software will have access to them, because my operating system acts as an intelligent broker of requests between those peripherals. It will always have, and be capable of delivering, information about the status of any peripherals that my software needs to use.

As soon as my software needs to access resources distributed on a network, however, I can no longer make assumptions about the availability of those resources. That's the crux of device-agnosticism and how it impacts networked programs. Where the operating system of my computer served as an intelligent broker, we cannot assume the same of a network. So, verifying the presence of resources, and our ability to access them, becomes a key component in the design of our software. And I'll note that this task becomes more challenging when we have multiple devices on our network that could provide the resources we're looking for.

In that case, it's the responsibility of some software on the network to determine which specific device ultimately services our software's request for that resource. Whether that work is done by our own program as part of its communication algorithm, or handled by some other intelligent broker deployed to the network to facilitate this situation, the work needs to be done for our software to behave reliably on such a network.

Writing for open communication

When we talk about open communication on networks, we're talking about collaboration between different devices or software components. This collaboration puts some responsibility on every developer who intends to leverage the resources of another; the responsibility to agree upon some standard for communication, and to respond according to that agreed upon standard. There may be a functionally infinite number of ways to format data to send and receive over a pipe, but unless someone else on the network has agreed to receive your data in the format you've decided to send it, none of it can be considered valid. You are, essentially, screaming into the void.

The broad range of possibility creates a need for standardization that is met by an equally broad number of organizations, including the **World Wide Web Consortium** (**W3C**) and the **International Standards Organization** (**ISO**). What this means for you is that you will ultimately be responsible for understanding what standards your software should adhere to in order to meet the functional requirements of your projects, and to provide the most value to other users of your product. Common standards you'll learn about in this book include communication protocols, such as TCP, UDP, and HTTP, as well as addressing and naming standards such as the IP addressing standard and the domain naming system.

Topologies and physical infrastructure

Having spent a sufficient amount of time discussing what a network is, we should now consider how networks are actually implemented. This section will consider the various solutions that the engineers have arrived at to build systems that meet the definition of a network. We'll discuss the distinction between a logical and a physical topology for a network, and then examine the most common examples of the former.

Physical and logical topologies

In the same way that the topology of a geographic region describes how the features of that region are arranged over the area of the region, the topology of a network describes how the components of that network are arranged relative to one another. There are two ways to think about the organization of networks. As should be obvious, having read the header for this subsection, they are the physical topology and the logical topology.

The physical topology describes how a network is physically connected and organized in real space. It describes the medium by which connections are established, the medium of the connections themselves, the location of devices in physical space, and the layout of the connections between nodes. It is determined, in part, by the specific networking devices of the network and the connections those devices allow (I can't use coaxial cabling to connect to a router with only Ethernet ports). Separately, the physical topology itself determines the maximum capabilities of the network in terms of performance, resilience, and, in some cases, even security. Imagine that all incoming network traffic trying to access a **local area network** (**LAN**) I own must be funneled through a firewall for security purposes. If I only expose one physical device to act as that firewall, my network won't be very fault tolerant. However, if I expose multiple firewall devices, with each servicing requests from different regions, I can increase my fault tolerance considerably. Especially if each is capable of serving as a backup in the event that one of the others is taken offline for any reason. The physical topology of one firewall provides less fault tolerance than the physical topology of several.

The physical topology also describes the variety of network devices I use on the network at any point in time. This is where our high-level abstractions of communication channel and node or computational device is brought down into concretions. Instead of a link or connection, a physical topology characterizes a connection as wired or wireless. A robust topology may even specify the type of wire used as coaxial or fiber optic cables, as is typical of most high-speed home internet connections, or as twisted-pair copper wire, like what's used for telecom networks.

This is also where our network nodes get nailed down to a concrete, specific device. Instead of a computational device, we have switches, routers, bridges, and **network-interface controllers** (**NIC**). Each of these devices is responsible for a different task or service on a network, and some, or all, of them may be present on any given implementation. For example, I have no need for a bridge on my home wireless network, but it would be impossible to imagine how the entire internet could exist without the use of each and every device I listed, and dozens more that I haven't.

Meanwhile, the logical topology of a network explains the conceptual organization of relevant actors on the network, and the connective paths over which they can, or must, communicate with any other actors on that network. One important consideration to make, though, is that physical topologies do not necessarily map directly to the logical topology. Looking back at our earlier example of a physical topology with one firewall as compared to a physical topology of multiple firewalls, we can illustrate the distinction between physical and logical. First, let's take a look at the initial, naive implementation of an internal network with a single physical firewall device to restrict access to our server resources:

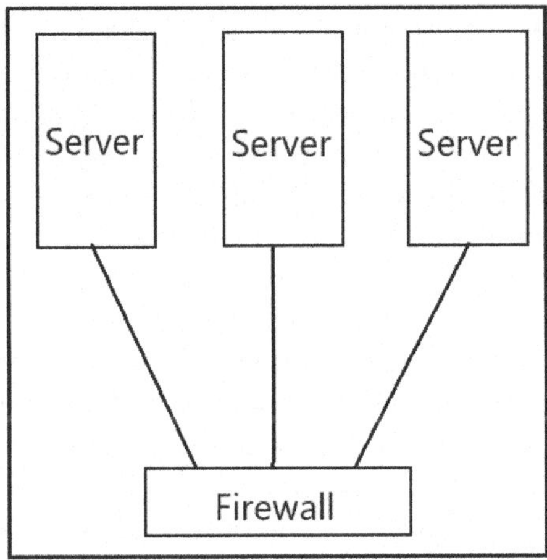

Initial, single-firewall physical topology

While a complete physical topology would define and describe the type of connection supported, and perhaps even define the model of the physical devices represented in the preceding diagram, this will be sufficient for our purposes. Next, let's look at the more resilient physical topology with multiple firewalls and a failover strategy for unresponsive firewalls:

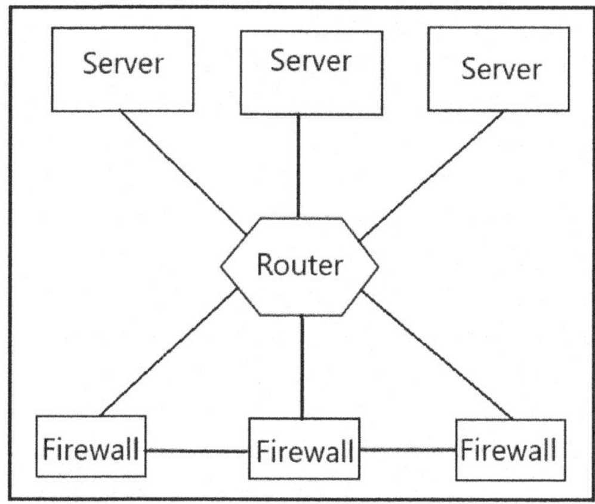

It's easy to see why the physical topology diagram would be different, because there are different physical components in play. What's more, for as simple a difference as it is between them, the physical difference between the two is non-trivial, as the second topology has a meaningful impact on the owner of the network in terms of cost, reliability, and performance.

The point we want to make with this, however, is that in both physical implementations, the logical topology remains the same. If we think of the single firewall (in the case of the first physical topology) and the multi-firewall along with requesting the brokering router (in the case of the second physical topology) as being, conceptually, a single secure access point into our internal network, then we can easily see how both physical topologies map to the following logical topology:

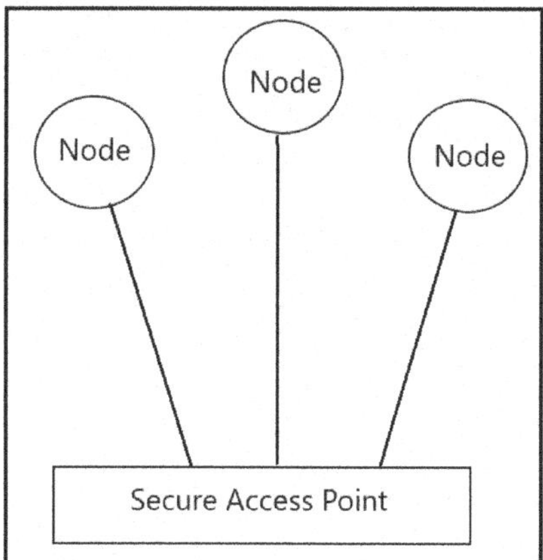

Looking at this diagram, you might also notice that it bears a striking resemblance to the physical layout of the first diagram, but looks wholly different from the second. This serves to illustrate the fact that a logical topology might map one-to-one to its physical counterpart, but does not necessarily map one-to-one with its physical implementation.

For the remainder of this book, we'll exclusively be concerned with the logical topology of a network, as this abstraction defines the interactions we'll be processing in the software we build. Device manufacturers can deal with the hardware components, and network engineers can work to meet the physical performance constraints. We'll just think about what resources we need, or need to provide, and how we can meet those needs. The logical topology will be sufficient for that.

The specific organization of the logical topology of our network may well have an impact on our software implementation, however, and there is a variety of common topologies with their own strengths and disadvantages we'll want to consider, so we should take some time to do so now.

Point-to-point topology

Let's start with the most basic. A point-to-point topology is exactly what it sounds like. A single logical connection between two nodes on a network. This topology is how we would define a minimum complete network, which is to say, at least one connection between at least two nodes. It is the lowest cost in terms of implementation, and has the lowest impact on the engineering considerations for software meant to be deployed to such a network. Point-to-point networks can maintain a dedicated connection between the two relevant nodes, or establish that connection dynamically as needed. Any direct peer-to-peer communication is an instance of a point-to-point network on your system, even if that peer-to-peer connection is established over a more complicated logical network topology, the communication session itself is an instance of a logical point-to-point topology.

While the cost of a point-to-point connection might be exceptionally low, the benefits you can possibly reap from those costs are also extremely low. The kinds of problems solved by a point-to-point network design are limited in scope, and are usually specific to an immediate problem.

Linear topology (daisy-chaining)

A linear topology is exactly what it sounds like – a line! It is the most primitive extension of the point-to-point topology, one of the simplest logical topologies conceptually, and often one of the cheapest in terms of a corresponding physical implementation. In a linear network topology, we extend our point-to-point model in such a way as to only ever have one node connected to at most two other nodes at a given time. The benefit here is obviously in the physical implementation cost (even with high resiliency, this configuration can only ever get so complicated). The drawback, however, should be similarly obvious. Communication from one node to any node other than one of its nearest neighbors will require the intermediary nodes to do some work investigating the target of the inbound request and determine if they are suitable to process the request, and if not, know to pass the request along to the neighbor that didn't originate the request.

Note that specification to not return the request to the neighbor that originated the request in the first place. If the nodes responded by simply submitting the request back out to both of your neighbors blindly, you would end up in an infinite loop of submitting and re-submitting the request between the two nodes. At least one of the nodes in any pair has to be aware enough to not re-submit a request to its originator. This highlights the most important drawback of this topology. Specifically, that it requires a tight coupling of nodes to their conceptual position in the network structure.

While none of this is particularly complicated, you can already see how the logical organization of your network can impact the design of your networking code. That will only become more apparent as the complexity of the topology increases.

Bus topology

A bus topology is one in which every single node on the network is connected to every other node on the network by way of a single channel of communication, as seen in the following diagram:

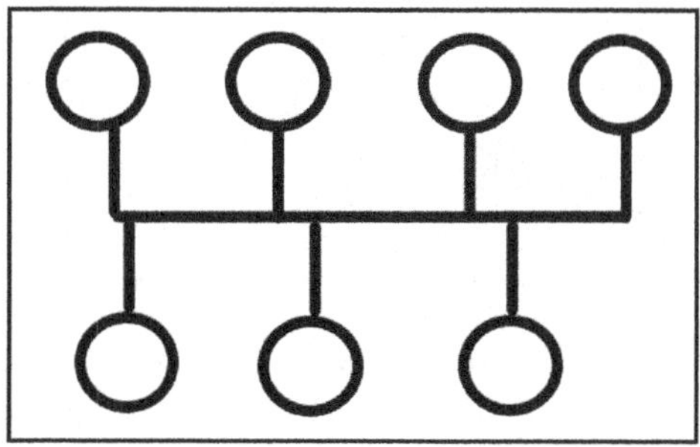

Each connection coming off of a node is joined to a shared connection between all nodes by way of a simple connection interface. Any packets sent by a node on a bus topology will be transmitted on the same bus as every other packet transmitted over the network, and each node on the bus is responsible for identifying whether or not it is the most suitable node to service the request carried by that packet. Similar to the linear network previously described, packets on a bus topology must contain information about the target node for the request.

As is the case with each of the topologies of lesser complexity, the bus topology has the obvious benefit of a low upfront cost of implementation, and relatively low overheads for orchestration. Hopefully, however, the previous description I provided helps to characterize the particular challenges associated with this particular network topology. Because all network communication happens over a single channel, all traffic, even under ideal circumstances, is limited by the bandwidth of that channel. Especially chatty software doesn't do well on a bus topology, as it tends to monopolize the link between nodes.

Additionally, because there is only a single channel of communication across the whole of the network, that channel serves as a single point of failure for the network. If the central bus comes offline, then each node is isolated simultaneously.

Star topology

Finally, we begin to consider network topologies more common in enterprise networks. The star topology is arranged in such a way as to produce an asterisk-like star shape, with each peripheral node connected by a single channel to a central hub-node, as demonstrated in the following diagram:

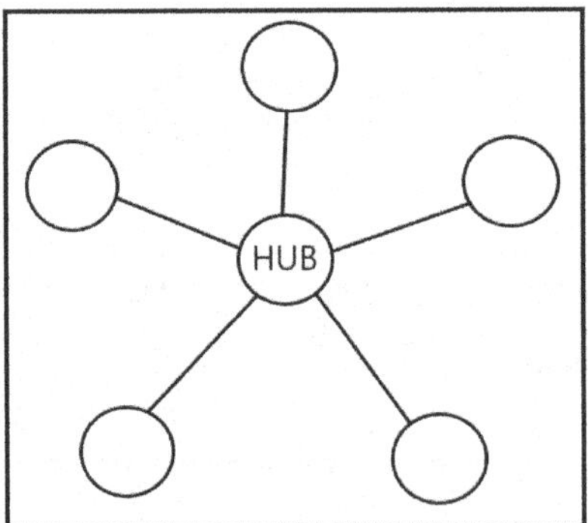

The **hub** of a star topology serves as a broker of communication between all peripheral nodes. It receives and forwards requests from each of its peripheral nodes by way of a direct, point-to-point connection.

This topology provides the benefit of isolating the failures of peripheral nodes or their connections to the hub to those nodes specifically. Each of the other nodes can maintain their connections to all the other nodes in the network with any one of them going down. It is also, at least conceptually if not physically, infinitely scalable. The only task necessary to add a node to the network is to add a link between the new node and the hub node.

Hopefully, by this point in the discussion of network topology, you'll already have identified the obvious downside to this approach. If the hub-node goes offline, the entire network is eliminated. From the perspective of any one peripheral node, loss of the hub means a loss of the entire network, since everything can only ever communicate with the hub.

In reading my description, you may have also realized that some network topologies can be decomposed into sub-networks of completely different topologies. A network defined by any given peripheral node and the hub node of a star topology is itself a single instance of a point-to-point network. Likewise, a network defined by any two peripheral nodes and the hub node of a star topology is technically a linear topology (which is itself a specialized implementation of the bus topology). By logically extending these simple diagrams into larger compositional topologies, we can describe any kind of network you could possibly write software for.

Ring topology

A ring topology is very similar to a linear topology (which, as I noted before, is technically an implementation of the bus topology) except that, in the case of a ring topology, the endpoints are ultimately connected, and communication is unidirectional, as shown in the following diagram:

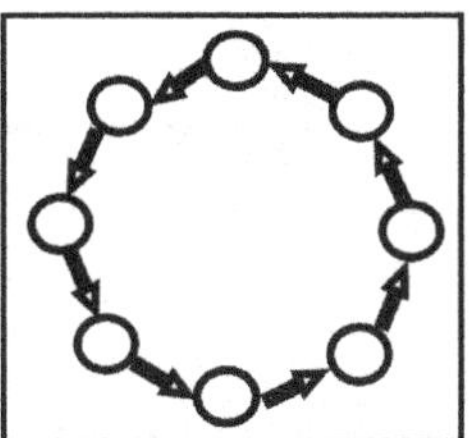

The benefit of this particular network topology might not be immediately apparent, but with each node in the network serving as a peer of the previous node in the chain, there's no need for any request broker, or communication specific software or hardware. This can lower your network management costs substantially.

The drawbacks are similar to each of the previous implementations in that, once a link in the chain is broken, the network is essentially rendered useless. Technically, because of the unidirectional communication pattern of a ring topology, the node residing immediately after the broken link in the chain can still communicate with every other node in the network, and maintain some degree of operation. However, since any responding device would be incapable of transmitting their response back to the originating node, communication would be one-way for all nodes on the chain. I'm having an extremely hard time imagining a scenario in which a device on a network can meaningfully interact with a distributed system via strict one-way communication.

Another less obvious downside to this is that the maximum performance of the whole network would be limited by the lowest performing link between any two nodes in the network. This is the case because any round-trip communication of request-response between two nodes would necessarily traverse the whole chain.

Mesh topology

The mesh topology is one of the most resilient and common network topologies in use today. And the reason for that is that it is almost entirely arbitrary in how it is organized. A mesh topology simply describes any non-formal topology of connectivity in which some nodes are connected by way of a single point-to-point connection to some other nodes, and some may have multiple connections to multiple nodes. The original graph diagram from the beginning of this chapter, shown as follows, is technically a mesh network topology:

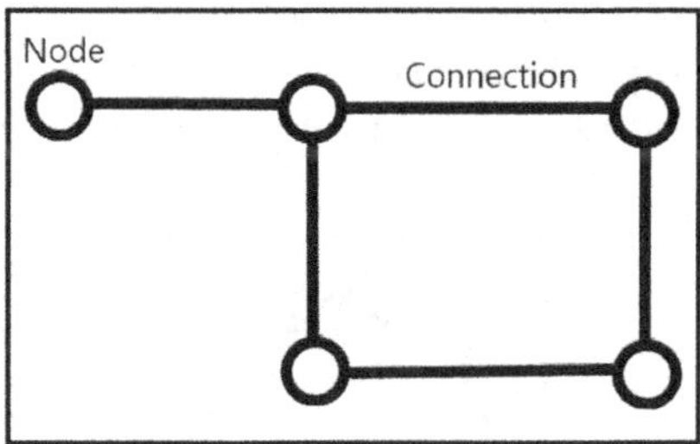

In case you forgot.

You'll note that the nodes in the preceding diagram have anywhere from one to three direct connections to other nodes in the network. This can provide some of the resilience of other network topologies where necessary, without incurring their costs. Since there is no obvious specification for a mesh network other than that it does not fully implement any of the other network topologies we discussed, it can include networks with an arbitrary degree of connectivity between nodes up to, and including, a fully-connected mesh network.

Fully connected mesh network

A fully connected mesh network is one in which every node has a direct connection to every other node in the network, as demonstrated in the following diagram:

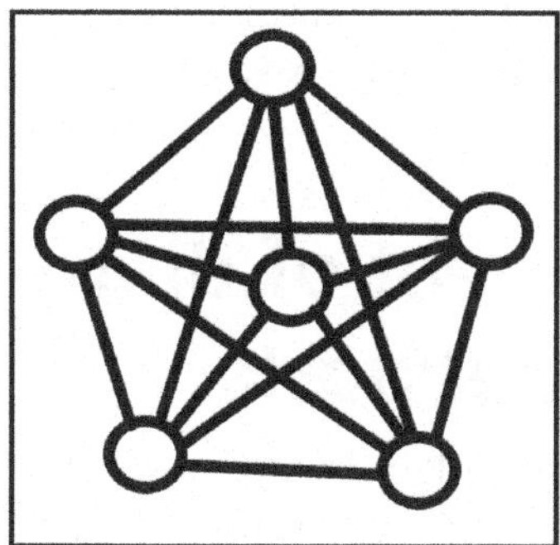

If this diagram looks a bit crowded to you, you've already noticed the single biggest drawback of a fully-connected mesh network. It's nearly impossible to scale beyond a certain point, because each new node on the network requires a connection for each previously connected node on the network. The math works out to a quadratic increase in connections for each new node to be added. Moving past a few nodes on the network becomes physically impossible very quickly.

The incredibly high cost of a fully connected mesh network, however, brings with it the most stable and resilient topology possible. No node has to be responsible for packet-forwarding or request switching, because there should be no context in which two nodes are communicating with each other indirectly. Any one node or connection between nodes can go down, and every other node on the network has full connectivity with no loss of performance. A single weak connection between two nodes has zero impact on the performance of any other two nodes. As topologies go, a fully connected mesh is bulletproof. It's also often prohibitively expensive, and so not common in anything but the smallest and most trivial contexts.

Hybrid and specialized topologies

As I mentioned before, most larger networks over which you might need to access resources are composed of multiple topologies joined together into what are typically called **hybrids**. A star topology, in which one of the peripheral nodes is also a link in a linear topology, would be an example of such a hybrid.

Other kinds of topologies are actually variants of the topologies we've discussed here. For example, a scenario where a node of a linear network topology is also the access point to a secondary linear topology constitutes a tree topology, simply a hierarchical linear topology. The specifics of these structures are less important than knowing that they exist and that, depending on the nature of the software you intend to deploy onto a network, you know that there are costs and considerations to be made for them. And speaking of those costs...

The software impact of distributing resources on a network

All this talk of device-agnosticism and open communication might sound extremely abstract up to this point. You may well be reading this and wondering yeah, so what? I don't have to code a network switch, which is probably true. It is certainly true that you won't have to code a network switch in C# using .NET Core, since that is quite a bit beyond the scope and capabilities of the framework, and thus, this book. The impact of the unpredictability of a network on your software, however, will be pretty substantial, and that will be true no matter what part of the network stack you're programming for. So, let's look at some of the ways your code should be prepared for distributed systems.

Security

I've gone to the most obvious and complicated issue first, because I personally find it to be the most interesting. Writing software in a professional context will, across the board, require you to code your applications to be secure. Even if your job doesn't explicitly require it, I would argue until I'm blue in the face that, as an engineer, you have an ethical obligation to write secure software regardless. That can be a daunting task. Especially since having secured software is always a moving target. It's important that you keep this in mind, though, because making your software useful as a resource to a wide variety of benevolent consumers inherently opens you up to malicious intent.

This is where device-agnosticism and open communication become hugely important. Device-agnosticism means you can't reasonably be sure that a malicious actor hasn't gained access to a network that you may have assumed was secured upstream from your hosting environment. You will only ever see and process requests on the access points to your software. And open communication means you may end up getting a number of requests that are malformed that you'll attempt to parse initially, before determining that you can't, and disposing of them. This need to first read the messages you're given, in order to know, if they're something you care about, as that ultimately exposes you to malicious commands or code.

Thankfully, as we'll explore later, the .NET Core libraries provide a wide array of strong security components right out of the box, and the leg-work of getting and leveraging the encryption libraries and request sanitizing algorithms is just a matter of knowing what `using` statements to include at the top of your source files.

Communication overhead

The other, most obvious concern you face with networked programming is dealing with the openness of open communication. That property means that you'll have to spend a substantial amount of time familiarizing yourself with the specific messaging standards of different communication protocols (which I'll cover in depth in this book). There's an immense amount of organization necessary to cram data into well-formed packets, with appropriate header information to tell your software when to start and when to stop reading from your connection to get the full, uninterrupted binary stream and convert that back into meaningful data structures in your code. It's a headache just describing the process.

In locally hosted code, you have the benefit of sharing DLLs of your libraries among consumer applications to facilitate a shared contract for data structures. You could communicate with other software on your system through the filesystem itself. You could just use the systems, file-access APIs to expose all the nuts and bolts of how much data exists in your message, what the encoding of that data is, and expose it through random access into the file.

With a network, you have to give enough context for someone else to make sense of your message with the message itself. And you have to communicate that context in a way that a consumer could understand it before they have that context. Once again, the .NET libraries will come to your rescue here, providing easy-to-use classes exposing standardized headers and message formats to keep your code clear of that overhead.

Resilience

I mentioned this concept a few times talking about network topologies, but it bears special mention here, because you'll be responsible for maintaining resiliency of your application on a network from both ends of a connection. If your application leverages any resources on a network, you'll have to account for the very likely possibility that there will be times at which those resources aren't actually available on that network. You'll need to write your code so that it still responds to its users in a reliable and stable manner in the event of such an outage.

Likewise, if your software is a dependency for other systems on your network, and it goes down, the best thing for you to do is have a strategy in place for rebounding from such an outage. There are a number of viable solutions in place for notifying your downstream consumers that you've recovered from an outage, each with their own strengths and costs in terms of resource usage or development time, and we'll discuss several of them later in this book. For now though, it is sufficient to consider this as you design your solutions and adjust those designs accordingly.

Asynchrony

Tying in somewhat closely with the notion of resiliency and open communication is the concept of asynchronous communication. This is a hugely important concept for maintaining any semblance of reliable performance on a networked program. Put simply, it's the concept of processing the result of a request that is not provided by the code internal to your system when that result becomes available.

When your program needs to request some resources from another node on its network, there is a round-trip time associated with sending your initial request and then receiving some meaningful response. During that time, you program technically could lock and wait for the response to come back, but realistically, there is no reason why it should lock and wait. However, even after our program may have moved on, deciding not to wait on the response to our initial request, we typically want to take a step back and handle the response whenever it does come back over the network. This process is asynchronous programming, and it's a major key to developing reasonably performing network software.

One obvious case of asynchronous programming you may have encountered separately from the context of network programming is in programming responsive user interfaces (UI). Typically, a UI component needs to actively listen and respond to user inputs whenever that user chooses to engage with it. Since the programmer can't ever know precisely when a user might want to press a button they've been presented with, they must respond to the input at the earliest moment that resources that can respond to the input without keeping those resources on hold while they wait to respond.

Network objects and data structures in .NET Core

It may sound like a daunting task to start writing network code from scratch, and in some cases, it absolutely is. There is help, however, in the form of the .NET Core class libraries. With these libraries, you'll be well positioned to start working with clean abstractions for complicated, and often frustrating, network protocols and standards to start producing valuable components on a distributed network.

Using System.Net

The `using` statement might be one of the most important statements you can include in source files containing any sort of networking code. The `System.Net` namespace is a suite of general-purpose .NET Core classes and utilities for programming most protocols and networked system behaviors. It is the root namespace for the most common networking classes you'll use as we move through this book.

The namespace includes classes for the following:

- Domain name resolution and DNS access
- The abstract base `WebRequest` and `WebResponse` classes, as well as common implementations of those classes, including `FtpWebRequest`, and `HttpWebRequest`
- **Internet Protocol** (IP) resolution and definition
- Socket utility class definitions
- Many others

The classes in this namespace will be your bread and butter as you begin to develop more complex and powerful software, and you should spend a fair amount of time familiarizing yourself with the features and functionality the System.Net namespace encapsulates.

Getting specific with sub-namespaces

While the System.Net namespace encapsulates a wealth of useful classes for network programming, there are a number of useful sub-namespaces under the System.Net package hierarchy that you should also be familiar with, as follows.

- `System.Net.Http`: A utility class used to provide HTTP standards-compliant messages and interactions within your .NET Core app
- `System.Net.NetworkInformation`: Provides traffic data, address information, and other details about the host node on the network
- `System.Net.Security`: Provides reliably secure networked communication and resource sharing and accessing
- `System.Net.Sockets`: Exposes netcore managed access to the WinSock interface

Each of these namespaces and the classes they expose will be explored in much greater detail over the course of this book, but for now, I wanted to expose you to some of the most commonly used, and most broadly valuable, network classes provided out of the box by .NET Core.

Their software is open source and described by robust and reliable documentation here:

`https://docs.microsoft.com/en-us/dotnet/api/?view=netcore-2.1`

It would certainly be worth the time of anyone considering a career in network web development to examine the classes in their fullest.

A whole new computing world

The maximum value a piece of software can deliver is limited by the number of downstream consumers of that software who have the ability to leverage it. Deploying your software on a widely available network can increase the overall impact it has on your organization or community of consumers. This last section takes a look at the kinds of applications opened up by this transition.

Long – distance communication

Thanks to communication protocols such as **File Transfer Protocol** (**FTP**) and **Simple Mail Transfer Protocol** (**SMTP**), it is possible to write to, or receive a letter from, someone on the entire other side of the globe within a few seconds of them having sent it. This feat of engineering is made possible by a robust, resilient physical infrastructure supporting the internet as a whole, and by the end of this book, the target is for you to have the skills necessary to develop these kinds of applications.

With peer-to-peer communication protocols, we can build systems of networked multiplayers for real-time, high-intensity, high-action games.

Share functionality, not code

With well-defined standards such as the RESTful API design and the messaging format of HTTP, you can write stable, clean, well-isolated web API projects that allow a variety of consumers to request functionality you've written on demand. Instead of sharing code directly, you can keep your abstractions abstract and allow only conceptual access to the business process you own through well-documented channels of communication.

Summary

This chapter took a very deep dive on a small handful of subjects. We delivered a carefully considered definition of a network, and then considered how the key components of that definition impact our development strategies for network programs. We considered the distinction between a physical and logical network topology, and then explored the most common logical topologies we'll be working with. Lastly, we considered what kinds of new design decisions and strategies we'll have to make as we start to write our first network programs, as well as the .NET classes that will help us implement those strategies easily and cleanly.

In the next chapter, we'll take the first steps into programming for networks, as we look into resource location and addressing.

Questions

1. What is the definition of a network?
2. What is the difference between a physical and logical topology?
3. Which was the only network topology discussed in this chapter that is not exposed to a potential single point of failure?
4. What are some of the physical devices that implement channels of communication on a network? What physical devices serve as nodes?
5. What is the root namespace for the most common networking libraries and classes provided by .NET Core?
6. Name at least four classes exposed by the System.Net namespace.
7. What are the four other most commonly used namespaces provided by .NET Core for reliable and stable network programming?

Further reading

For additional general information on networks, check out *Building Modern Networks* by *Steven Noble,* which is available through Packt Publishing. It's a great resource for understanding the challenges facing modern network engineers, and a good, deep dive into the applications of the concepts discussed in this chapter.

2 DNS and Resource Location

The last chapter was spent dissecting networks to such a degree that most readers will likely never think about them again. In this chapter, we'll take those concepts and look at their real-world implementations. We'll start with a look at how the problem of resource allocation is solved at the scale of the internet. Distributing resources is useless without being able to access them from across your network, and this chapter will introduce you to the systems and standards that make doing so possible. As we investigate these topics, we'll finally get our hands dirty with some code. Throughout this chapter, we'll look at software examples to get you familiar with leveraging the tools available with the .NET Core framework.

The following topics will be covered in this chapter:

- How data and services are exposed and made available on everything from your home Wi-Fi network to the internet
- The specific standards used to identify resources at different levels of your network, from URLs and domain names, to devices names and local directory access
- Using the DNS class in .NET Core to access external resources and resolve requests for data within your network

Technical requirements

To follow this chapter, you'll need to have either Visual Studio Code, or Visual Studio Community Edition. Both are free downloads available at the Visual Studio website, at `https://visualstudio.microsoft.com/`.

Check out the following video to see the code in action: `http://bit.ly/2HVSHad`

We'll also be using the .NET Core **command-line interface (CLI)**. This will give us access to a series of programs we can call directly from the command prompt. To follow along, you'll need to make sure you have the .NET Core SDK installed locally, which can be downloaded from `https://www.microsoft.com/net/download`.

The source code is available at `https://github.com/PacktPublishing/Hands-On-Network-Programming-with-C-and-.NET-Core`.

Needles in a haystack – data on the internet

The first step to using the resources exposed on a network is finding them. While this problem is easily solved on a LAN with only four computers, you can imagine how daunting a challenge it becomes when your context grows to the several billion devices actively connected to the internet. To ensure reliable delivery of requests broadcast on a network, each device on that network must be uniquely addressed, and any software that wants to communicate with a device must know the address of the target device. With this in mind, let's look at how the problem has been solved at scale and consider how we can apply that solution to our more locally-relevant use cases with .NET Core.

The first network addresses

As I mentioned, every device on a network must be uniquely identifiable so that, at any given time, requests intended for a specific device can be delivered. Likewise, unique addressing means that any responses can be reliably returned to the originating device, no matter how many network nodes lie between the two. If someone has written a service that solves a problem you have, it's only useful to you if you can actually use that service. This means either knowing the address of the device hosting that service, or, at the very least, knowing who to ask for the address.

Thankfully, this is a problem that was solved long before even the earliest incarnations of the modern internet. I am, of course, referring to telecommunication networks, and their well-established system for addressing and address look-ups. With early telecom networks, engineers needed to solve problems for a large set of devices that needed to be uniquely addressed. Whatever system they came up with, though, would need to exhibit the following characteristics in order to remain viable in the long term:

- Usability: The system would be used by anyone who wanted to communicate over the telecom network, and so the system could not have been prohibitively complex.

- Scalability: The ultimate goal was to connect every home in the nation with a single, unified network. The solution for adding nodes to that network would need to grow with the population and the geographic region that it would ultimately support.
- Performance: If a telephone call took as long as the postal service to deliver messages back and forth, no one would use it. And, while that was never going to be the case, there would certainly be a limit to what customers would tolerate in terms of speed and reliability.

Thankfully, what they came up with was a sustainable solution that has scaled and functioned for decades.

The system that telecom engineers devised was that of phone numbers. By assigning 10-digit addresses to each phone on a telecom network, engineers guaranteed a network capable of uniquely addressing up to 9,999,999,999 devices. Add two digit country codes to that, and you've got a network that can theoretically support up to a trillion devices, or over 100 unique addresses for each human on the planet, with approximately another 240 billion to spare.

You might have noticed that I specified that the phone numbering system only theoretically supports up to a trillion devices. However, there are certain limitations of the addressing system of telecoms that make reaching the theoretical maximum difficult. As most of you will be well aware, the first three digits of a US telephone number are known as the **area code**. Those digits were originally determined by the specific geographic location in which the phone was located. This helped route numbers quickly, but means that the total number of possible devices supportable by telecom networks is limited by the distribution of those devices across geographic regions. Within an area code, there is only a theoretical maximum of 9,999,999 possible devices; barely more than the total population of New York.

I'm over-simplifying the solution here, but what this trade-off provided for telecom engineers was a simple mechanism for narrowing down the possible field of physical phones to which an address would resolve as quickly as was reasonably possible. Calls could be routed to a substantially restricted region by examining only the first three numbers. This provided an obvious performance benefit by applying semantic meaning to a syntactic standard. The telephone numbering system simply specifies that a physical phone is addressed by a 10-digit address. That is a syntax requirement. However, the geographic information conveyed by the first three digits of that address is a semantic standard. There is an underlying meaning baked into those first three numbers that conveys how the entire address should be handled.

The scalability of this numeric addressing system helps network devices direct traffic accurately. For a human user, though, an arbitrary series of seven to ten numbers can be difficult to remember, and are error-prone to use. Those who grew up in the time before smartphones and built-in contacts lists may remember the need to have a Rolodex, or contact book, to keep frequently needed, but difficult to remember, phone numbers organized and on-hand at all times. However, it was often the case that you'd need to call someone whose number you didn't have conveniently stored. This is where the phone book comes in. It served as a simple way of mapping easily-remembered unique identifiers for a person (specifically, a full name and street address) to their corresponding network-friendly address (their phone number).

All of these features, taken together, provided telecoms with the hallmarks of a successful network implementation: usability (through the simplicity of phone books), scalability (with the extensive range of valid addresses), and performance (with improved routing speeds achieved by embedding semantic meaning into the syntactic standards of the address). By now, though, you've likely correctly guessed that we won't be programming for telephone networks in C#. So, let's see how the design decisions made by telecom engineers translate to modern computer networks.

DNS – the modern phone book

As I have alluded to, engineers designing modern computer networks faced the same problem as telecom engineers: defining a standardized syntax with which they could create unique addresses for each device on their network. Thankfully, though, there were already giants on whose shoulders those computer network engineers could stand (to paraphrase Sir Isaac Newton).

The phone numbering system demonstrated that a simple system of fixed-length numeric addresses could be quickly parsed and routed. Moreover, strictly numerical addresses can be represented in binary. This meant no additional standards needed to be applied for consistently representing non-numeric characters. However, this was a trade-off in usability. The software written to use those addresses would still need to be written by humans. As is often the case, the easier (and more performant) solution for computers to use was the more difficult solution for humans. This meant that computer network engineers would need to devise a phone book of their own. Thankfully, they rose to the occasion.

On all modern computational networks, the fixed-length numerical address by which you can reliably locate an external device is the **Internet Protocol (IP)** address. Meanwhile, the system from which you can reliably ask for the address of a given device is the **Domain Name System (DNS).** This, the DNS, is the computer network's phone book. It's essentially an elaborate, distributed mapping of human-readable domain names to their underlying IP addresses.

Every device on the internet (or any local networks) will have their own IP address. However, the specifics of how that IP address is determined, and the strengths and limitations of the syntax for those addresses, will be discussed later in this book. For now, what we're concerned with is specifically how those addresses are resolved by their more meaningful, human-readable domain names. In this next section, we'll explore fully how that happens every time you look up a resource by its URL.

URLs, domain names, and device addresses

With a solid understanding of the primary concerns that must be addressed for resource location on networks, let's look at how they've been addressed in more detail. First, let's consider how the much less error-prone URL naming convention allows easier access to remote resources. Then we'll look at how the DNS provides a bridge between the usability of URLs or domain names, and the speed and reliability of IP addressing.

URLs – user-friendly addressing

I've been taking a very basic approach to explaining the nature of locating resources so far. I'm certainly aware, though, that most of you probably have at least some idea of how that happens in, at the very least, a high-level context. Hell, you likely used a web browser to find this book in the first place, and had a pretty solid idea that the long string of seemingly random words and letters strung together in your browsers address bar was, in fact, a URL. However, I have certainly met my fair share of developers who were surprised to learn exactly how URLs are constructed and used. So, much as we've done so far, we're going to start with a very basic explanation of what exactly URLs are, and how we can use them to find what we need.

Uniform Resource Locator (**URL**) is a universally agreed-upon standard for (unsurprisingly) locating resources on the web. It does so by specifying the mechanism by which to retrieve the resource, as well as the specific route over which to retrieve it. It does so by specifying the order of, and delimiters between, specific components that collectively define the specific physical location of any resource. The specification will initially seem complicated, but will become more intuitive as we elaborate on the components and the responsibilities they hold.

URL components

Every URL begins with the scheme by which a resource should be located. This specifies the transport mechanism, or location type, that should be used to find what you're looking for. There is a finite list of universally valid schemes that you can specify, including http, ftp, and even file for locally hosted resources. The scheme is always followed by a colon (`:`) delimiter. After the scheme specification, a URL could contain an optional authority specification, which itself contains a small handful of sub-components.

The authority component

The authority has a designated prefix: the special delimiter of two consecutive forward slash (`//`) characters, whose presence indicates that characters that follow should be parsed according to the specification for a URL authority. This prefix is optionally followed by access credentials, or user information, which transmits an optional user ID and/or password to the destination host. These values, if included, will always be separated from one another with a colon (`:`) as a delimiter, and will be separated from the rest of the authority component with an at sign (`@`) delimiter.

Whether access credentials are included as part of the authority or not, it will always include a host domain. This always follows either the double forward slash (`//`) prefix, or, in the event of access credentials, the (`@`) delimiter. The host domain specifies the physical address of the hardware hosting the resource being located. It can be specified as either a registered domain name, or the underlying IP address for the hardware.

Finally, an authority might specify a listening port on the host. This is delimited from the host domain name or IP address by the colon (`:`) character, and indicates the only ports on the hardware to which requests for the specified resource should be sent.

The path component

The path component specifies a series of path segments over which requests must travel to arrive at the searched for resource. Each segment of the path is individually delimited with a forward slash (/) character. It's technically valid to have an empty segment as part of your path, resulting in two consecutive forward slash characters (//).

The query component

After the final segment of the path, the URL may contain an optional query component, indicated by the presence of the question mark character (?) delimiter. The query component allows users to specify additional parameters for more specific results from the requested resource. Each different query comes in the form of a parameter, the equals sign (=) delimiter, and the requested value of the query parameter. Finally, each parameter is delimited by either a semi-colon (;) or ampersand (&) delimiter between any two query parameters and their values.

The fragment component

The final piece of a URL, at least ordinarily, is the fragment component. It's an optional piece of the URL string, and its presence is indicated by the reserved pound, or hash (#) prefix. The fragment component is often used to identify a sub-component of the eventually-returned resource, and is typically used by web browsers to navigate to a specific fragment of the HTML document that was searched for.

Putting it all together

Having clearly enumerated all the relevant components of a URL, we can simplify things with a basic syntax specification. Every URL ultimately breaks down to the following structure, where optional components are designated with square brackets []:

```
scheme:[//authority/]path[?query][#fragment]
```

So here, we see plainly that the only required components of a URL are the scheme and subsequent colon delimiter, and a path. Everything else is optional, and you'll note that each optional component has its presence in the URL indicated by its unique prefix character. And we can, of course, expand on the following components.

Authority specification

The authority, as we already specified, can be broken down as follows:

```
//[access_credentials][@]host_domain[:port]
```

So, if an authority component is present, it will always be prefixed with a (`//`) delimiter, and will always contain the host domain. Meanwhile, the access credentials component is also broken down as follows:

```
[user_id][:][password]
```

Here, only one component is required. However, if either component is present, then the (`@`) character separating access credentials from the host domain becomes a requirement. And, if both the `user_id` and the `password` functions are present, then the colon (`:`) delimiter between the two components will be required.

Query specification

Finally, the last component that has a well-defined specification for how it can be composed is the query component. It can be broken down as follows:

```
?[parameter=value][(;|&)parameter=value]...
```

The sequence of additional delimiters and key-value pairs can extend all the way to the maximum allowable length of a valid URL.

By following these syntax specifications, you can decompose any URL you are presented with into its component parts, and meaningfully leverage it to access the resource it identifies.

The URL as a sub-type of the URI

We've spent the bulk of this section discussing URLs specifically. What you may not have realized, however, is that a URL is actually a single, specific kind of something known as a **Uniform Resource Identifier** (**URI**), which is a string of characters adhering to a well-defined syntax that universally and uniquely identifies a resource on a network.

The distinction between a URL and a URI is subtle, and almost entirely conceptual. The simplest way to characterize that distinction is to note that, by using a URL, we are guaranteed to be able to identify and locate a requested resource. The only thing we are guaranteed, given a simple URI, is an ability to identify it that is to distinguish the resource from any other arbitrary resource.

In practice, however, the terms URL and URI are frequently used interchangeably. This is because, since URL is a specific kind of URI, it's always valid to characterize a URL as a URI. Meanwhile, it is often sufficient to characterize a URI as a URL since knowing the specific identity of a resource within the context of a network is usually enough to then locate that resource.

If you're wondering why I brought up a subject of such apparent triviality, it's for clarity's sake. Over the course of this book, I'll consistently talk about resources as being identified by their URL. However, the class exposed by .NET Core for constructing, decomposing, and leveraging these addresses is named for the more generic URI specification. In fact, let's take a quick look at that class now.

The System.Net.UriBuilder class

If you've made it all the way through this elaborate definition of the URL specification, you might be wondering how on earth you can leverage this in your code to access a resource, when you already know specifically where to look for it. Enter, dear readers, the `UriBuilder` class!

Living in the `System.Net` namespace, the `UriBuilder` class is a factory class for generating instances of the `Uri` class. It provides users with several overloaded constructors to allow the specification of more of the components of a valid URL progressively. It also provides accessors to properties representing each of those components individually. Finally, it provides a function to produce the well-formed instance of the `Uri` class from the component parts.

Let's start with a very simple example. We'll use `UriBuilder` to compose an instance of `Uri` with only the `Scheme` and `Host` components as follows:

```
public Uri GetSimpleUri() {
   var builder = new UriBuilder();
    builder.Scheme = "http";
    builder.Host = "packt.com";
    return builder.Uri;
}
```

With this method, we can see how the `UriBuilder` class composes a well-formed and syntactically correct `Uri` out of the component parts we specify, as demonstrated in the following code snippet:

```
using System;
using System.Net;
using System.Threading;
```

```
namespace UriTests {
    public class TestUriProgram {
        public static Uri GetSimpleUri() {
            //...
        }

        public static void Main(string[[ args) {
            var simpleUri = GetSimpleUri();
            Console.Warn(simpleUri.ToString());

            Thread.Sleep(10000);
        }
    }
}
```

By running this program, you should see the `http://packt.com` output while your console is open for ten seconds, before it closes and the application terminates.

Here, we didn't need to specify that the `http` component of the URL should be followed by a colon character. We didn't say anything about the host we specified being prefixed with the `//` prefix characters. The `UriBuilder` class did that for us. This factory class gives us a clean way to incrementally construct a more specific desired location, without us, as the developers, having to keep the nitty-gritty details of delimiters, prefixes, and suffixes in our heads all the time.

In this example, we leveraged the fact that the `UriBuilder` class provides public `get` access to all of the properties that it has to encapsulate each component of a `Uri`. However, you can also apply many of those properties through a series of overloaded constructors, if you know their values at the time of construction.

The `UriBuilder` class has seven overloaded constructors. We've seen the default constructor, taking no parameters, but now let's look at a program that leverages each of the constructors and see what they provide. Given that we know the transport scheme and domain name we intend to look up, we can simplify our initial method for a simple `Uri` as follows:

```
public static Uri GetSimpleUri_Constructor() {
    var builder = new UriBuilder("http", "packt.com");
    return builder.Uri;
}
```

With that change, the output from our `TestUriProgram` will print the exact same string we saw before, but the code to produce that output is one-third of the size. Whenever possible, I recommend using the constructor overloads to instantiate the `UriBuilder` class. Doing so shrinks our code height and makes our intentions explicit when instantiating the class. Always be more explicit in your code when possible.

Hosts – domain names and IPs

In my description of the host component of a URL, I specified that the host domain could be either a domain name, or an IP address. As I mentioned before, an IP address is the underlying numeric address used by routing hardware and software to navigate to a resource on a network. It's the unique ID, specific to a piece of hardware at a specific location. A domain name, however, is the human-readable string of words and alpha-numeric characters used to make addressing easier and more consistent. It is more consistent, easily remembered, and less prone to error than a raw IP address. What's interesting, however, is that domain names and their IP addresses are actually functionally interchangeable. In any context in which you can use one, you can always safely substitute the other.

Given that IP addresses can be resolved directly by the network transport layer, and don't need to be resolved before they can be serviced by any node in the routing process, we'll ignore them for now. We'll explore the syntax, limitations, and advantages gained by using the IP address of a device later on in this book. For now, though, we're more concerned with how we can find the IP address in the first place. That's why, for this chapter at least, we're only concerning ourselves with domain names and how they're resolved by the DNS.

I'd bet that among everyone reading this book, there isn't a single person who knows a single other person who hasn't typed `google.com` or `en.wikipedia.org` into their browser's address bar. Our use of domain names is ubiquitous, and yet most of us have no idea how, exactly, they are created or used. Even for me, it wasn't until I was explicitly tasked with writing software for resolving those domain names on an internal network that I finally took the time to understand what made that system work. At that time, I learned how the web of DNS servers facilitated network usage by human users. While I only mentioned it previously, it's time to consider just what the DNS is more deeply, and how we can use it.

The DNS is a distributed, decentralized network of authoritative servers that hosts a directory of all sub-domain servers, as well as any domain names that can be resolved by that authoritative server. Any domain name that has been registered with a certified domain name registrar, and which meets the syntax standards of a domain name (and which hasn't already been registered), is considered valid. Valid domain names are added to the distributed registry hosted by authoritative servers. Between your computer and any other network node you hope to interact with using a valid, registered domain name, your request will have to interact with one or more of these name servers.

Each server will inspect the domain name given, and look up the domain in its own directory of names and IP address mappings. Naturally, the server will first determine if the given name can be resolved by that server, or at least by one of its subordinate servers. If so, the authoritative server simply replaces the domain name in the request with the IP address to which it maps, and forwards the request along accordingly. If the current server cannot resolve the domain name, however, it will forward it along up the hierarchy of name servers to a more general, parent domain. This process continues up to the root name server, or until the name is resolved.

The DNS in C#

It is occasionally necessary to identify the underlying IP address for a domain name from within the context of our software. For that, .NET Core provides the static `Dns` class as part of the `System.Net` namespace. With the `Dns` class, we can access directory information as returned by the nearest downstream name server capable of resolving the given name. We can request an instance of the `IPHostEntry` class, containing all of the relevant directory information of a DNS entry, or simply an array of IP addresses registered to resolve requests against the domain name.

To see this in action, simply invoke any of the methods exposed by the static `Dns` class in a sample program as follows:

```
using System;
using System.Net;
using System.Threading;

namespace DnsTest {
    public class DnsTestProgram {
        static void Main(string[] args) {
            var domainEntry = Dns.GetHostEntry("google.com");
            Console.WriteLine(domainEntry.HostName);
            foreach(var ip in domainEntry.AddressList) {
                Console.WriteLine(ip);
```

```
            }
            Thread.Sleep(10000);
        }
    }
}
```

With this program, we should see the following output:

```
google.com
172.217.10.14
```

Of course, the IP address that is resolved when you look for a host entry that resolves the `google.com` domain name will likely be different. Google's servers are widely distributed, and the specific server slice (and its associated IP address) that is nearest your network location will be what resolves a lookup of that domain name.

If you want to validate that the IP address returned is in fact what is registered for that domain name, you can actually intercept the host entry lookup locally by modifying your computer's hosts file. On a Windows OS, that file will live at the `C:\Windows\System32\drivers\etc\hosts` directory, and will have no file extension. On macOS and *nix systems, it simply lives at `\etc\hosts`.

This file serves as the first stop on any outbound requests for a network resource addressed by a host name. It is, technically, your computer's internal name server, and you can use it to direct traffic any way you'd like. To demonstrate this, add an entry to your hosts file as follows:

```
127.0.0.1    fun.with.dns.com
```

Now, opening your command prompt, navigate to an empty folder, and spin up a new .NET Core Web API project with the following CLI command:

```
dotnet new webapi
```

Your console should print information about .NET Core, telemetry, ASP.NET Core, and finally, finish execution with the following line:

```
Restore succeeded.
```

Assuming that this worked, you can immediately run the application by executing the following command from within the same directory that you created the project:

```
dotnet run
```

After this, you should see that your application is running and listening, as seen in the following screenshot:

```
C:\Users\shurns\Desktop\dns_test_app>dotnet run
info: Microsoft.AspNetCore.DataProtection.KeyManagement.XmlKeyManager[0]
      User profile is available. Using 'C:\Users\shurns\AppData\Local\ASP.NET\DataProtection-Keys
' as key repository and Windows DPAPI to encrypt keys at rest.
info: Microsoft.AspNetCore.DataProtection.KeyManagement.XmlKeyManager[58]
      Creating key {786611bf-465d-40de-8b96-da841314b9f8} with creation date 2018-10-31 01:43:18Z
, activation date 2018-10-31 01:43:18Z, and expiration date 2019-01-29 01:43:18Z.
info: Microsoft.AspNetCore.DataProtection.Repositories.FileSystemXmlRepository[39]
      Writing data to file 'C:\Users\shurns\AppData\Local\ASP.NET\DataProtection-Keys\key-786611b
f-465d-40de-8b96-da841314b9f8.xml'.
Hosting environment: Development
Content root path: C:\Users\shurns\Desktop\dns_test_app
Now listening on: https://localhost:5001
Now listening on: http://localhost:5000
Application started. Press Ctrl+C to shut down.
```

Pay attention to the specific port your application is listening on.

If we look inside the blank Web API application, we can see that .NET Core stood up a single controller, named `ValuesController`, and that it exposes a number of REST endpoints. The only things that we're concerned with for now is the route specified for the API, and the endpoint listening for HTTP GET requests, listed as follows:

```
[Route("api/{controller}")]

...

[HttpGet("{id}")]
public ActionResult<string> Get(int id) {
    return "value";
}
```

This tells us that we should expect to see the `"value"` result if we navigate to the `/api/values/{id}` path on the listening port of our local machine.

Sure enough, if you open your browser of choice and type the application's URL into your address bar, appending the path specified in the controller, you should see the **value** string displayed in your browser, as shown in the following screenshot:

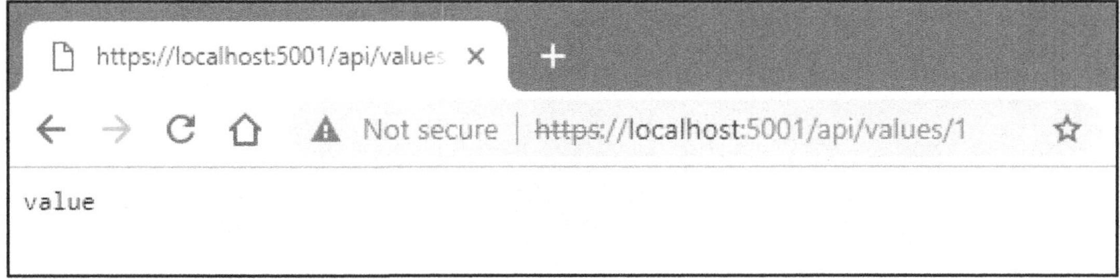

What's interesting, though, is that localhost is itself an alias for the `127.0.0.1` IP address. By convention, that address always resolves to the current local machine. Since we modified our hosts file, however, we should be able to replace `localhost` in our URL with the `fun.with.dns.com` as new domain name. Make the change in your browser, and you'll see the same response!

Now that we've seen how to set up our own domain name entries locally, we can use our hosts file to explore the `Dns` class in more detail, and validate the responses.

First, add an additional entry to the hosts file with a new IP address, but the same fake domain name as before. Your new hosts file should read as follows:

```
127.0.0.1    fun.with.dns.com
1.0.0.127    fun.with.dns.com
```

Here, it doesn't actually matter what the addresses are, since we won't be looking for resources at those locations. What matters is that there are two. With those entries in place, you can see more concretely how the `Dns` class in .NET exposes a host entry from the nearest domain name server that can resolve it. We can modify our program from before as follows:

```
using System;
using System.Net;

namespace DnsTest {
    public class DnsTestProgram {
        static void Main(string[] args) {
 var domainEntry = Dns.GetHostEntry("fun.with.dns.com");
 Console.WriteLine(domainEntry.HostName);
 foreach(var ip in domainEntry.AddressList) {
 Console.WriteLine(ip);
 }

 var domainEntryByAddress = Dns.GetHostEntry("127.0.0.1");
 Console.WriteLine(domainEntryByAddress.HostName);
 foreach(var ip in domainEntryByAddress.AddressList) {
```

```
    Console.WriteLine(ip);
    }
    Thread.Sleep(10000);
    }
        }
    }
```

We can now see the following output:

```
fun.with.dns.com
1.0.0.127
127.0.0.1
fun.with.dns.com
1.0.0.127
127.0.0.1
```

This demonstrates how we can access host information for a given domain name or IP address using the `Dns` class. Note that the instance of the `HostEntry` class returned by the methods of the `Dns` class always contain all of the IP addresses for which there is a record in the naming server. Even when we looked up the `HostEntry` class by a specific IP address, the `Dns` class still resolved and returned every other IP address registered for the domain name that matched the IP address of the original lookup. This provides the flexibility of being able to access and leverage alternative hardware resources for a given request in the event that one of the registered addresses is unresponsive. The extent to which you'll leverage this class in your work may vary, but I hope you see now that it can be a useful tool to keep in your belt.

Summary

In this chapter, we examined the primary characteristics network engineers identified as necessary to make networks viable. We considered the trade-off of usability for routing hardware versus readability for humans when defining a standard syntax for network addressing. With that consideration in mind, we looked at how the work of the telecom engineers of previous generations contributed hugely to the solutions that were ultimately standardized on all modern networks today.

Within that context, we looked at how IP addresses are used by network hardware to locate resources, and how the DNS facilitates the more memorable, human-readable addressing schemes of URLs and URIs. We learned how those domain names are explicitly mapped to their underlying IP addresses by implementing a domain name server of our own, using the hosts file of our operating system. Using the sandbox of our self-contained DNS server, we explored the C# classes provided by the System.Net namespace to facilitate building syntactically correct URLs, and leveraging the DNS to lookup the underlying IP addresses of a given URL, or resolve requests to do the same.

With this foundation in place, we'll use the next chapter to explore the communication protocols that allow for data transmission from one host to another. We'll look at how a standardized model facilitates communication between entities, and take a close look at some of the most common protocols used in that communication.

Questions

1. What are the three characteristics network engineers seek to achieve for long-term viability of a network addressing standard?
2. How did telecom engineers sacrifice the maximum possible scale of telecom networks to achieve higher routing performance?
3. What are the phone number and phone book of the modern internet?
4. How does a URL locate resources on the web?
5. What are the valid components of a URL? Which of them are optional?
6. What is a fully qualified domain name?
7. How is a device given a domain name?

Further reading

For more information on URLs, domains, and resource location on networks, consider *Managing Mission-Critical Domains and DNS* by *Mark E. Jeftovic*. It provides a deeper and more considered analysis of working with the DNS, and strategies for leveraging that system to your advantage when constructing networks of your own.

3
Communication Protocols

We've spent the first two chapters of this book discussing what makes networks hard to program for open communication and device agnosticism. These aspects of networks demand standardization, and in this chapter, we'll examine how standards provide a common language that the network software can communicate through. First, we'll learn about the governing body that defines those standards. We'll learn a bit about who they are and what objectives they sought to achieve. Once we understand who defined the common architecture of networks, we'll take a deep dive into the way they've organized and categorized each tier of the hierarchy of network layers.

The following topics will be covered in this chapter:

- The origin of the current standard for network architecture and a brief history of it, as well as some background on the organization that is responsible for it.
- How application code interacts with networked resources through the application layer and what communication standards are provided for that layer.
- How data is communicated out to, or read from, the network on the transport layer of the network architecture standard.

Technical requirements

As with `Chapter 1`, *Networks in a Nutshell,* this will be more of a conceptual examination of the standards defined for networks. There is no specific technology as such that is required for this book. We'll be using the same technology for this chapter as we have in others: NET Core 2.1 SDK and either Visual Studio Code, or Visual Studio Community Edition to use as an IDE.

Check out the following video to see the code in action: [Placeholder link]

The Open Systems Interconnection network stack

There are several steps in the process of sending or receiving a resource from a remote source over a network, and each of those steps has been deeply considered by the network engineers tasked with executing them. In this section, we'll look at who those network engineers were, and how they defined a general pattern for implementing each step in that process. This section will be all about the OSI, and how that specification defines the network stack of a given network device.

What exactly is the Open Systems Interconnection?

In order to talk about communication protocols, we need to understand how each protocol fits into the larger picture of network connectivity, and to do that we need a common model for thinking about each step in the process. To that end, we have the OSI model for computer and telecommunication networks. This model seeks to organize the different steps of standardized communication to or from a given device into a tiered model of abstraction layers. Much like the logical topologies of a network, which we discussed in `Chapter 1`, *Networks in a Nutshell,* the OSI model exists on a purely conceptual and abstract level.

As the name suggests, it was defined in such a way as to be useful as a reference while remaining entirely agnostic as to how any of the tiers defined in the model are ultimately implemented at the physical level. In fact, many implementations of communications protocols or standards do not cleanly map to the OSI network model. However, the model is broadly considered the gold standard, and has been since it was formalized in 1984. So, let's take a look at how that came to be.

The origins of the OSI

The need for a standardized model for network implementations became apparent almost as soon as networking became possible. To that end, back in the late 1970s, two different organizations for governing standardization in computing set out to define such a model. The first of these organizations was the **International Organization for Standardization** (**ISO**). The other organization that set out to solve the same problem, at roughly the same time, was the **International Telegraph and Telephone Consultative Committee** (**CCITT**, initialized from the French translation of the name).

Interestingly, the shortened name for the International Organization for Standardization, ISO, is not an initialism of the name of the organization. Instead, since the name of the organization would be initialized differently in each language that it is recognized, the members chose to shorten the name to ISO. This is in reference of the Greek isos, which means equal, and speaks to the goal of the organization to bring about equal understanding.

The fact that two organizations sought to define their own model at roughly the same time as one another isn't entirely surprising. The problem was faced by engineers across a wide array of disciplines, and the lack of standardization was quickly becoming a bottleneck to progress in those disciplines. What is surprising, however, is how similar the solutions were to one another. Like Leibniz and Newton independently inventing calculus, these organizations incidentally arrived at a common solution to their common problem. However, this happy coincidence helped to expedite the standardization process, since the similarity of their solutions served to validate both models as being highly likely to be correct.

Given the success of both organization's efforts, it took only a handful of years before both models were merged into a single standard. Thus, in 1983, the Basic Reference Model for OSI was born. Over time, the name has, of course, been shortened to the OSI model. By 1984, each organization had published this new shared model under their own official reference documents, canonizing the model, and its specific protocols, within the international community. So, let's take a look at what that model entails.

The Basic Reference Model

The Basic Reference Model was formalized by ISO as standard ISO-7498 (and as standard X.200 by the ITU, the successor to the CCITT). The model could be cleanly broken into two parts. The first part is the abstract Basic Reference Model for networking. The second is the list of protocols the organizations saw fit to standardize for use by systems that implement the reference model.

The reference model defines network communication streams, as implemented by a compliant device on a network, in a hierarchy of seven distinct conceptual tiers, or layers, organized in a stack. This stack is defined as far down as the transmission of raw bits over physical media, and all the way up to the high-level application software that might use any resource distributed over a network.

For our purposes, as we describe these layers, when we say a layer is higher in the stack, we mean farther away from the hardware-level transmission of bits across a physical medium.

The model defines a strict mechanism of unidirectional interaction between layers. According to this communication standard, a given layer can only ever communicate with the layer directly beneath it through an abstract interface exposed by that lower layer. This interface is known as the **service definition** of a layer, and it defines the valid operations by which a higher layer can interact with any lower layers. The interaction model between layers of the OSI network stack shows the same:

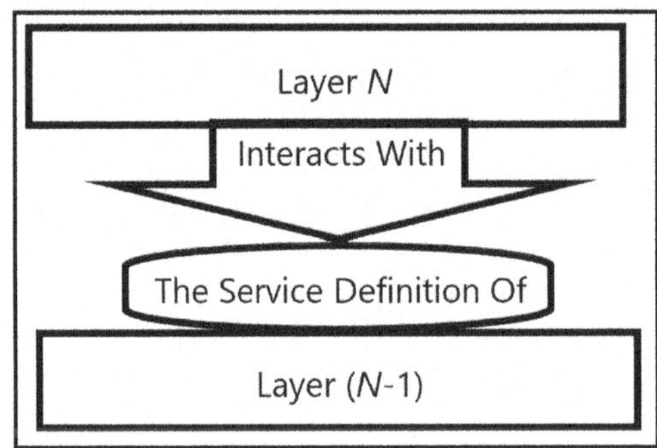

As data moves through the layers of the stack, each lower layer wraps the packet in its own series of headers and footers to be parsed by the recipient device. This contains information about what layer in the stack the data originated from, as well as how to parse it. The data packet that gets passed down, layer-to-layer, through the network stack, is known as a **Protocol Data Unit** (**PDU**).

While service definitions provide an interface for interaction from one layer to the layer beneath it, **protocols** provide standardized interaction for an entity at a given level in the network stack to interact directly with a corresponding component at the same level on a remote host. These protocols assume smooth interaction down the stack of the originating host, and then back up the stack on the remote host. Once it has bubbled up the stack to the target layer of the remote host, the protocol determines how the receiving entity should process the data.

So, we can describe the entire process of data transmission through the OSI stack, as follows:

1. An entity on the originating host creates a data packet, known as a PDU, at a given layer in the network stack, **N**.
2. The originating layer passes it down the stack by leveraging the service definition of the layer immediately beneath it.
3. Lower layers receive the PDU, each wrapping it in a set of headers and footers, to be parsed by the corresponding layer on the remote host.
4. Once the PDU has been wrapped in headers and footers by the bottom most layer of the stack, it is transmitted to the remote host.
5. Each layer of the stack on the remote host removes the headers and footers applied by the corresponding layer of the originating host, bubbling the PDU up through the stack.
6. The PDU is received by layer **N** on the remote host. The receiving layer then parses the data of the PDU according to the specifications of a protocol for layer **N**, as specified by the originating host.

And just like that, our data is transmitted, reliably, over the network. That is the complete, if abstract, process of using protocols to transmit data units through the service definitions of each layer in the network stack. I know, it's a lot to take in at once, but it will become slightly more clear as we build up the picture more completely. So, with that, let's look at what the individual layers of the stack are, why they're ordered the way they are, and what they're ultimately responsible for.

The layers of the network stack

As we examine each layer of the network stack and what it is ultimately responsible for, there are some key things to bear in mind. First, remember that the model is abstract at its core, and is only meant to serve as a reference. For this reason, there may be times where it's not obvious which layer a given responsibility or task belongs to. Second, bear in mind that as we discuss the responsibilities of each layer in the stack, we're speaking specifically about the responsibilities of that layer with respect to the successful transmission of data over the network. So, the responsibilities of the session layer in the context of the network stack are completely independent of, say, the management of a user session in the context of a web application.

Finally, it's useful to remember that the farther down the stack we go, the closer we get to the physical transmission of data over a physical medium. We'll be numbering the layers in our stack in descending order, from top to bottom, so that the smaller the number, the closer we are to the signals on the wire. This will be helpful when considering why one layer is lower than another, and how its responsibilities are distinct from those of the layer above it. With all of this in mind, let's dive in, top to bottom, through the OSI network stack.

The Host/Media distinction

The first thing to understand about the network stack is that there are different levels of abstraction that you can view. The higher up, conceptually, that you look at network interactions, the fewer layers there are, and the easier it is to distinguish between the responsibilities of those layers. Meanwhile, when you build a model closer to its concrete implementation, you see the distinctions between more subtle roles and responsibilities of each entity in that model. We're going to be looking at the full, lower-level model provided by the OSI reference model, but I want to take a moment to consider the higher-level distinction between entities on a network, which breaks down into two fundamental layers.

The first of these layers is the Host layer. This encapsulates the four higher levels of the OSI stack and describes entities or responsibilities specific to a given host trying to communicate on a network. In the most basic context of two-way communication between two hosts on a network, each host is responsible entirely for its own implementation of the OSI layers that aggregate up under the Host layer (hence the name). Bundling application data, specifying encoding and reliability expectations, and the methods for sending out a PDU to a given target all fits, loosely, under the Host layer.

The second layer in the higher-level view of networks is the Media layer. These layers describe the physical implementation of the network components between two hosts. This provides the expected functionality specified or requested by entities in the Host layers. Entities of this layer are typically implemented either on the hardware level, or in a low-level systems language such as C or C++. For this reason, entities of this layer will generally fall outside the scope of this book. However, C# provides abstractions that encapsulate and represent the functionality of entities in this layer, so it's important to understand how the layers that fall under the Media layer actually work on a basic level.

With that high-level distinction made, let's take a look at the full OSI model for networks, starting from the top.

The application layer

The top most layer of the network stack is also the layer that most developers will interact with over the course of their careers. The application layer provides the highest-level interface for interaction with network communication. This is the layer that business application software uses to interact with the rest of the stack. There are a number of protocols leveraged by entities on the application layer, and we'll discuss them later in this chapter. For now though, it's only important to remember that the application layer serves as the access point between actual end user applications and the OSI network stack.

The presentation layer

While it may sound like a way of visually representing the data, the presentation layer is actually a way of defining how the data is to be interpreted by any consumer that wants to look at it. This layer provides context for application-layer entities from different hosts to mutually interact with a PDU. Entities in the presentation layer are responsible for describing how data passed from the application layer should be interpreted on the other side of a given data transaction. It does the work of abstracting away the encoding or serialization of PDUs from the higher-level business logic of application layer entities.

The session layer

Entities on the session layer are responsible for establishing, maintaining, resuming, and terminating an active communication session between two hosts on a network. The entities at work on this layer provide communication mechanisms such as full-duplex interactions, half-duplex interactions, and simplex interactions, as specified by the constraints of the protocol used.

Full-duplex, half-duplex, and simplex communication

When a session is established between two hosts, there are a handful of ways that communication can happen over that session. The two most common are the full and half-duplex implementations. These simply describe a communication session that both connected parties can communicate over.

In a full-duplex session, both parties can communicate with one another simultaneously. The typical example for this kind of communication is a telephone call. On a phone call, both parties can talk and hear the other talking at the same time. The extent that someone can listen to what is being said to them while also speaking allows for much more efficient data transfer, and can facilitate reliable communication systems.

A half-duplex system is one where both parties can communicate over the session, but only one party can communicate at a given time. A common example of this is a two-way radio or walkie-talkie. On these systems, engaging the microphone of one radio will lock the channel and prevent the other radio from transmitting until the first microphone has disengaged. This can allow more reliable communication over a limited bandwidth, since there is less opportunity for signal interference.

Finally, a simplex communication session is one where only a single party can actually transmit data. That is, there is a sender and a receiver. A common example of this is network television; there is a single broadcast source, with multiple receivers actually accepting the transmitted signal. This is uncommon in most modern communication networks, since the additional cost of implementing a duplex communication session is often trivially small in relation to a simplex connection. However, it should be noted that a duplex communication system is simply a system of two simplex connections with one connection going in each direction between the hosts.

The transport layer

Entities in the transport layer use protocols specifically designed for interacting with other hosts and the network entities in between. It might seem redundant given our description of the presentation and session layer; however, there's an important role to be played here. The presentation layer is concerned with character encoding, or the mapping from platform-specific data representations to platform-agnostic descriptions of that representation. The transport layer, though, looks at the full block of encoded data that was passed down by the presentation layer, and determines how to break it apart. It's responsible for cutting the data into segments of otherwise useless streams of binary. And, importantly, it breaks those segments up in such a way that they can be reassembled on the other side of the connection. The transport layer is also responsible for error detection and recovery, with different protocols providing different levels of reliability.

This layer is the lowest layer in the Host layers umbrella previously described. Determining what transport mechanism can and will be supported by a host remains the responsibility of that host. However, it is the lowest boundary of a given host's responsibility in successfully implementing network interaction. Everything below this layer falls into the Media layer, and is the responsibility of the engineers who support the network that the host has been deployed on.

The network layer

Entities on the network layer manage interactions over the network topology. They're responsible for address resolution and routing data to target hosts once an address has been resolved. They also handle message delivery based on constraints or the resource availability of the physical network. So, while the transport layer determines the interactions between host-level tiers of the network stack on either side of a connection, the network layer is responsible for applying the transport protocol across the chain of devices that form the route between two hosts. The distinction between adjacent layers can be subtle, and we'll discuss some of the responsibilities specific to the network layer later in this chapter. So, if the distinction between transport and network layers is unclear, trust that we'll (at least, attempt to) clarify that distinction later.

The data-link layer

The data-link layer falls very clearly into the Media layer's grouping, as entities in this layer provide the actual transfer of data between nodes in a network. It's responsible for error detection from the physical layer, and controls the flow of bits over physical media between nodes. So, for example, in a half-duplex communication setup, an entity in the data-link layer is responsible for restricting the transfer of data in one direction while data is being transferred in the other direction. Entities in this layer almost serve as the traffic lights directing traffic over the roads of a node-to-node connection. The data-link layer is broken down even further into two sub-layers by the **Institution of Electrical and Electronics Engineers** (**IEEE**) standard 802. These two sub-layers are as follows:

- The **Medium Access-Control** (**MAC**) layer: This sub-layer controls who can transmit data through the data-layer entity, and how that data can be transmitted.
- The **Logical Link Control** (**LLC**) layer: This sub-layer encapsulates the logical protocols of network interaction. It is essentially the interface that provides the entities links as a set of abstract protocol operations.

Driving home how narrowly specific the data-link layer is in terms of its responsibilities on a network, its most common protocol is the **Point-to-Point Protocol** (**PPP**). This just highlights that entities of the data-link layer really are only concerned with facilitating the connection between two points.

The physical layer

Finally, we've arrived at the bottom of the stack, with the simplest layer to understand. The physical layer encapsulates the entities that are responsible for transmitting raw, unstructured data from one node in the network to another. This is the layer responsible for sending electrical signals that correspond to the strings of bits in a data packet. It encapsulates the devices responsible for modulating voltage, timing signals, and timing the frequency of wireless transmitters and receivers. Entities on this layer are explicitly outside of the scope of this book, but are an interesting concern regardless.

Putting it all together

Now, we've seen how the OSI model organizes the responsibilities of transmitting data. Hopefully, by this point, it should be clear how each layer in the stack is intended to provide a reliable abstraction for the layer above it. However, the process of communicating with a remote host, in its entirety, may still seem a bit vague. So, let's consider a concrete example and address each of the concepts that we talked about as they arise through the process of data transmission.

First, let's assume that an entity on layer 5 of our host (the session layer) wants to establish a session with an entity on **Layer 5** in a remote host. I haven't said so explicitly until now, but we can always assume that an entity on a given layer on one host only ever communicates directly with a corresponding entity on the same layer in the remote host. So, for our example, an entity in layer 5 will communicate with a remote entity that also resides in layer 5.

Communicating with remote entities will always happen through a protocol. Given this, the first responsibility of any entity seeking to communicate with a remote host is to wrap the transmitted data in the headers and footers appropriate for that protocol. For our entity in the session layer, let's assume they are hoping to establish a session using the **Session Control Protocol** (**SCP**). This means that our local entity will produce the data necessary to establish a session, then wrap that data in SCP headers and footers, creating a well-formed PDU (hopefully, this makes it clear why the name describes this package). This ensures that the recipient host will be able to unwrap the data based on the information stored in the headers and footers of our PDU.

Since entities that reside on any layer above the physical layer cannot communicate directly with one another, we have to pass our PDU down the stack. In our example, we can reliably pass the PDU down to **Layer 4** by taking advantage of its service definition and trusting that the logical operations exposed through that definition are accurately implemented by all of the responsible entities below **Layer 5**. So, we don't need to know how **Layer 4** implements transport mechanisms. Instead, we simply ask it to use the appropriate transport mechanism for this particular instance and trust that it will do so appropriately.

This pattern of trusting that lower layers in the stack will correctly implement the operations being requested by higher layers in the stack continues all the way through to **Layer 1**. Over the course of this process, each layer in the stack will wrap the PDU in its own headers and footers. These standardized chunks of data give each intermediary layer on the receiving host enough information to know to pass the PDU up its own stack. By continuously wrapping the data in well-formed, well-understood chunks of binary data, each layer on the remote host can trust that the inner segment of data that is passed up the stack is exactly what should move up.

This process of wrapping the PDU in deeper and deeper layers of metadata continues down the stack until we reach **Layer 1**. **Layer 1** holds the physical connection from our host to the remote host. Once we've reached this level, we can step across the expanse of the network and start looking at how our PDU moves back up the network stack until it reaches our target entity on **Layer 5**. Entities on each layer of the remote host will diligently remove and read the headers and footers applied by the corresponding layer of the originating host. The information in those wrappers will indicate that the PDU is destined for a layer above the current layer, and so entities will simply strip their headers and bubble the rest of the data up the network stack.

Once the data has reached layer 5 on the remote host, an entity on that layer will read the headers and footers of the PDU that were applied on **Layer 5** of the originating host. This metadata will indicate that layer 5 is, in fact, the target layer for this particular PDU. The metadata will also indicate what protocol should be used to parse the data passed to the remote host. Using this information, the recipient host will have enough data to properly read the data in the PDU, and construct its own response PDU.

Once that response is received by the originating host, a session will be established, and be open for use by any entities above the session layer in the originating or remote host. This whole process is captured in the following diagram of the full life cycle of data transmission through the OSI stack:

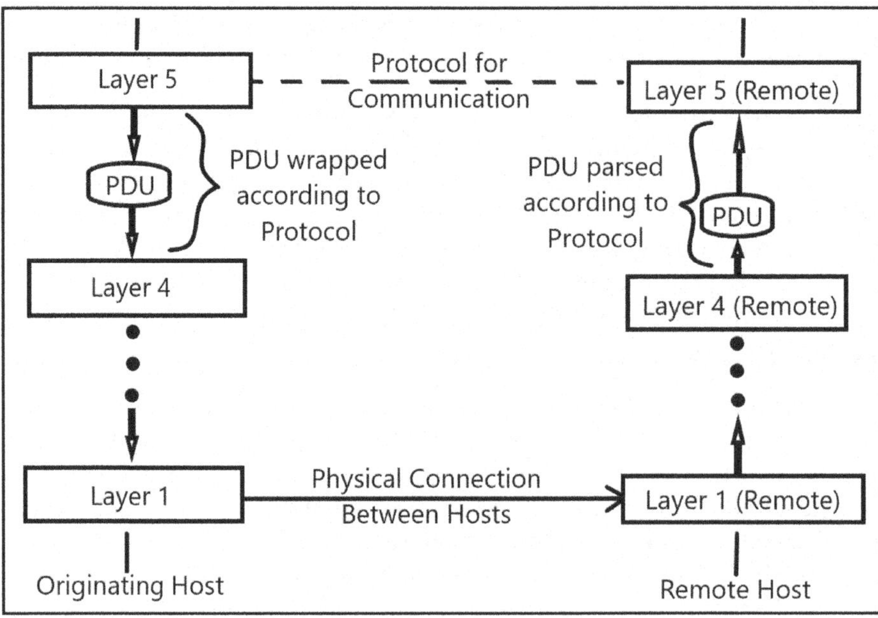

With this diagram in mind, is easy to see how the standardization provided by the OSI model makes it easier for engineers to program software for networks. The clean separation of concerns and the explicit pattern for passing data through the stack allows for well-formed contracts, against which all interested parties can design and develop. Engineers programming entities on the application layer can ignore the details of transporting data. They simply pass down a well-formed PDU through the stack.

Hopefully, this description clarifies how entities on specific layers expose their abstractions through a service definition, and how entities operating on the same layer of the network stack on different hosts reliably communicate through protocols. With this perspective in mind, let's take a closer look at the layers of this stack that we'll be programming for most frequently, as well as looking at some of the classes that C# provides to represent the entities of these layers.

The application layer

I mentioned it before, but it bears repeating, application layer is where the vast majority of day-to-day network programming will take place. This is especially true within the .NET Core framework, since the libraries provided by that framework deliver a wide array of clean, easy-to-use abstractions for entities or responsibilities that must be programmed lower in the stack. So, first, let's see why we should be so concerned with the responsibilities of the application layer. We'll look at the kinds of responsibilities that are typically delegated to entities in the layer, and see how frequently those responsibilities overlap with the requirements faced by everyday .NET Core developers. Then, given the extensive range of use cases for entities in the application layer, we'll take a look at some of the common protocols used by entities at that tier of the stack. We'll seek to understand them on a fundamental level. We'll look at what classes and libraries we have available to us for each of those layers; however, after this chapter, my hope is that you'll have a deep enough understanding to be able to reconstruct those classes yourself.

The most common layer in the stack

This might feel redundant at this point, but it really is worth driving home that the application layer is where the vast majority of .NET developers are going to be doing their network programming. Since that accounts for most of you, we're going to keep talking about it. But *why* is the application layer so important?

The crux of it is that the application layer serves as the gateway to network activities for your business logic. This becomes very apparent as you explore how thoroughly .NET has hidden the implementation details of any of the responsibilities of lower levels of the network stack. Essentially, if there is something that you need to specify about how your application should behave anywhere below the stack, you'll be doing so through a .NET library class.

I really can't stress enough how important it is to understand how the protocols behave under the hood. Knowing how the libraries are implemented will leave you better equipped to actually use them in the future. It's like learning to drive a stick shift. If you only ever learn the steps you have to perform to change gears, you'll likely get rusty without consistent practice. Over time, you'll have forgotten enough to not be able to drive a manual transmission anymore. However, if you learn *how* the steps you take serve to allow your car to drive, you'll never forget the steps themselves. Even if it's been years since you last drove a stick shift, you'll be able to reconstruct the steps you need to execute based on your understanding of what those steps actually accomplish. By this same measure, understanding exactly what the .NET core libraries are doing for you will enable you to use them more efficiently and correctly. You'll find yourself looking up the documentation less frequently and be better able to find the methods or properties you need through IntelliSense. That said, let's look closely at some of the most common protocols in the most common network layer.

HTTP – application to application communication

Welcome to the bread and butter of almost every .NET Core developer working today. HTTP is by far the most common and useful protocol for applications to interact over networks currently in use today. Why is that? Because HTTP is the protocol that almost every single web page on the internet is served up on by remote hosts, and requested by local clients. That alone is reason enough to call it the most common protocol in use. If you want more evidence, though, consider that most native mobile applications that serve up web-hosted data request this data from APIs that are exposed via HTTP. It almost feels ridiculous to have to make a case for the importance of understanding HTTP, since I'm certain there won't be a single person reading this book who *doesn't* have at least some experience with, or understanding of, HTTP.

So, why bother covering it so thoroughly if most of my readers are assumed to have some basic understanding of it? The answer to that is twofold. First, it's because it is so common as a communication protocol! HTTP is so prevalent that it would be criminally negligent not to give it due consideration in a book purporting to teach network programming fundamentals. And the second reason is because, at least in my own personal experience, most developers, and even engineers who work with it daily, only have a passing or surface-level understanding of what the specification provides. My hope is that by the end of this book, anyone who has read it, cover to cover, can and will go forth and program software that leverages every aspect of their target networks confidently and competently. It wouldn't be possible to do that without a deep, thorough understanding of what HTTP is, why it was defined, and how it is used by thousands of applications every second of every day. With that in mind, let's take a look at the protocol.

What is HTTP?

As almost every reader of this book is likely to be shouting at its pages already, let's go on to HTTP. As should already be obvious, HTTP is a protocol implemented and leveraged by software that lives in the application layer of the OSI network stack. It's the primary mechanism of communication for applications exposed through the internet, and is designed for the transfer of hypermedia over a network. Hypermedia typically refers to hypertext documents that contain multimedia information, as well as hyperlinks that can be used to navigate to and load additional resources from other remote hosts.

The transfer component of HTTP is, fundamentally, a request/response protocol that assumes a client-server relationship between hosts in an active HTTP session. To understand how this is done, let's start with the notion of a client-server relationship.

The client - server model in HTTP

Throughout this chapter, we've been referring to communication over a network as simply happening between originating and target hosts, as if the two were functionally identical, depending on which was sending a packet. In the client-server model, however, the two hosts actually perform distinct and specific duties, and so they are not conceptually interchangeable. A client entity is one who requests, and is granted, use of the services or resources provided (or served) by the server entity. Servers do not make active requests of clients, except when necessary to complete a service request already made by the client (for example, requesting additional login information from the client, when the client has initiated the transaction by requesting protected data). Likewise, clients are not expected to serve any specific resources to the server, except the information necessary for the server to sufficiently process and respond to a request.

Today, it's not uncommon for two applications to use HTTP to interact with one another in such a way that, depending on the interaction, either application could be considered the client or the server. For example, a desktop finance application might be responsible for storing local user data, while also using a remote API to access live data feeds about current interest rates on different kinds of loans. Now suppose the authors of that desktop application want to periodically access information about users of their software. In the case of a user logging onto their application to look up market rates for mortgages, the desktop application will request information from the remote API; so the desktop application is the client, while the API is the server. However, when the remote software decides to query instances of its desktop application for user data, the roles are reversed. The remote software will request the data from known hosts of the desktop application; the remote software is the client, requesting information from computers running the desktop applications, which are the servers in this scenario.

Alternatively, an application or host might be the client of one remote host, while simultaneously operating as the server for a different remote host. Consider the case of an API that responds to requests by aggregating information from a number of other APIs. In the act of servicing requests by their downstream consumers, the application in question is very obviously a server. However, when the application requests information from other APIs upstream, it is acting as the client.

I bring these examples up to highlight the fact that the client-server relationship is mostly conceptual. The assignment of client or server roles to a given host is specific to a given interaction context. If that context changes, so too might the conceptual role of the hosts involved. It's important that we avoid confusion by only referring to clients and servers within the context of a specific interaction.

Request/response

In describing the nature of the client-server relationship, we've also touched on the nature of the HTTP request/response protocol. This protocol, as a way of serving up information, is fairly intuitive to understand. When a client makes a request of a server (the request part of request/response), the server, assuming it meets the specifications of the protocol, is expected to respond with meaningful information about the success or failure of that request, as well as by providing the specific data initially requested.

Sometimes, the complete process of requesting information and receiving a meaningful response requires several intermediary round-trips between the client and server to establish initial connections, determine the ability of the server to service the request, and then submit the information necessary to initiate the request. This entire process, however, will be considered a single request/response session from the perspective of application-layer software. This leads us nicely onto the subject of just how those sessions are initially established in the first place.

HTTP sessions

So far, we've talked about the back and forth of the request/response communication patterns of HTTP, but we've neglected the context that allows that chatter to happen so seamlessly. This fluid interaction is facilitated by an underlying session established prior to satisfying the first request made by a client. Historically, this session has been provided by a **Transmission Control Protocol** (**TCP**) connection established against a specific port on the host server. This port can be specified in the URI when designating your target host, but typically will use default ports for HTTP, such as `80`, `8080`, or `443` (for HTTPS, which we'll cover later in this book). Once the connection is established, round trips of HTTP communication can proceed freely until the session is terminated.

You might have noticed that I specifically said that TCP is historically used for HTTP. This is because, for each of the current versions of HTTP (1.0, 1.1, and now HTTP/2), TCP has been the standard transport layer protocol supporting it. However, in the current proposed specification for HTTP/3, the protocol is being modified to take advantage of alternative transport protocols, including the **User Datagram Protocol** (**UDP**), or Google's experimental **Quick UDP Internet Connections** (**QUIC**) protocol. While there are trade-offs associated with these alternate transport protocols, the underlying sessions they provide are the same from our point of view. Each of these protocols serve to establish a connection with a listening host and facilitate the transmission of request and response messages. Next, let's take a look at some of the operations a client might request of a server, and how those operations are specified through the HTTP standard by way of request verbs.

Request methods

When a client wants to make a request of a server, it must specify the method by which the server will be expected to respond to the given request. These method specifications are typically called **HTTP verbs**, since most of them describe an action to be taken by the server when processing a request sent by the client. The standard methods are as follows:

- **OPTIONS**: This returns the list of other HTTP methods supported by the server at the given URL.
- **TRACE**: This is a utility method that will simply echo the original request as received by the server. It is useful for identifying any modifications made to the request by entities on the network while the request is in transit.
- **CONNECT**: CONNECT requests establish a transparent TCP/IP tunnel between the originating host and the remote host.
- **GET**: This retrieves a copy of the resource specified by the URL to which the HTTP request was sent. By convention, GET requests will only ever retrieve the resource, with no side-effects on the state of the resources on the server (however, these conventions can be broken by poor programming practices, as we'll see later in the book).
- **HEAD**: This method requests the same response as a GET request to a given URL, but without the body of the response. What is returned is only the response headers.
- **POST**: The POST method transmits data in the body of the request, and requests that the server store the content of the request body as a new resource hosted by the server.

- **PUT**: The PUT method is similar to the POST method in that the client is requesting that the server store the content of the request body. However, in the case of a PUT operation, if there is already content at the requested URL, this content is then modified and updated with the contents of the request body.
- **PATCH**: The PATCH method will perform partial updates of the resource at the requested URL, modifying it with the contents of the request body. A PATCH request will typically fail if there is no resource already on the server to be patched.
- **DELETE**: The DELETE method will permanently delete the resource at the specified URL.

A server will not respond to a request method invoked against a given location unless the server has been configured to do so. This is because some of the methods defined by the HTTP standard can permanently impact the state of resources on that server, and so should only be invoked and processed when it is safe to irrevocably update that state. There are, however, a number of methods designated as safe, by convention. This simply means that they can be processed by a server without having any side-effects on the state of the resources on that server. HEAD, GET, OPTIONS, and TRACE are all conventionally designated as safe.

Status codes

Even when an application has constructed a valid HTTP request object, and submits that request to a valid path on an active host, it's not uncommon for the server to fail to properly respond. For this reason, HTTP designates, as part of a response object, a status code to communicate the ability of the server to properly service the request. HTTP status codes are, by convention, 3-digit numeric codes returned as part of every response. The first digit indicates the general nature of the response, and the second and third digits will tell you the exact issue encountered. In this way, we can say that status codes are categorized by their first digits.

When you're writing software that responds to HTTP requests, it's important to send accurate status codes in response to different errors. HTTP is a standard that must be adhered to by developers in order to remain useful.

There are only five valid values for the first digit of an HTTP status code, and thus, five categories of responses; they are as follows:

- **1XX:** Informational status code. This indicates that the request was in fact received, and the processing of that request is continuing.
- **2XX:** Success status code. This indicates that the request was successfully received and responded to.
- **3XX:** Redirection. This indicates that the requesting host must send their request to a new location for it to be successfully processed.
- **4XX:** Client Error. An error that is produced by the actions of the client, such as sending a malformed request or attempting to access resources from the wrong location.
- **5XX:** Server Error. There was a fault on the server preventing it from being able to fulfill a request. The client submitted the request correctly, but the server failed to satisfy it.

Status codes are returned by servers for every HTTP request made against the server, and so can be very useful for building resiliency into your client software.

The HTTP message format

Requests and responses in HTTP are always sent as plain text messages. Those plain text messages consist of a well-ordered, and well-structured, series of message segments that can be reliably parsed by the recipient. In requests, messages consist of three required message components and one optional component:

- The request line consists of the method, the path to the requested resource, and the specific protocol version that should be used to determine the validity of the rest of the message; for example, `GET /users/id/12 HTTP/1.1`.
- A series of request headers and their values, for example, `Accept: application/json`.
- An empty line.
- (Optional) A request message body. This consists of content headers that provide metadata about the content type, as well as the content itself.

Each segment is delineated by a `<CR>` carriage return character and an `<LF>` line feed character; these are special white-space characters whose specific **American Standard Code for Information Interchange** (**ASCII**) values allow them to reliably be used to indicate the breaks between segments in a message stream.

Meanwhile, an HTTP response consists of its own series of almost identically structured segments, each also delimited by the `<CR><LF>` characters. Just as with the request message, it contains three required segments and one optional message body segment, as follows:

- A status line consisting of the specific protocol, the HTTP status code, and the reason phrase associated with that status code:
    - `HTTP/1.1 401 Bad Request`: A response containing the 401 client error status code (indicating that the client sent an improper request message for the resource that it was looking for).
    - `HTTP/2.0 201 Created`: A response indicating the 201 success status code, meaning that the desired resource has been created on the server.
- Headers, as with the request message segment, providing metadata about how the response should be parsed.
- An empty line.
- An optional message body.

Those simple segments fully define every valid HTTP message sent across the internet. This accounts for millions of requests per second, between millions or billions of devices. It's the simplicity of the message specification that makes that kind of scale possible.

HTTP in C#

Remembering the proper character delimiters and order for segments in an HTTP message, anyone should be able to build a request from scratch. Thankfully though, you don't have to remember those details; .NET Core has you covered with the `System.Net.Http` namespace. We'll explore this namespace in much greater detail later in the book, but for now, just trust that any feature or detail you find yourself needing to leverage HTTP communication in your application is exposed through that namespace. This namespace exposes enum types for status codes and header values, and an `HttpMethod` class to specify your message verb. As a library, it's rich with out-of-the-box features while remaining flexible and extensible enough to be leveraged in any use case.

FTP and SMTP – the rest of the application layer

While we have developed a deep understanding of HTTP due to its prominence in the daily lives of network programmers, we must also take the time to mention and briefly look at some of the other common application-layer protocols in use today. In this section, we'll look at the **File Transfer Protocol** (**FTP**) and **SSH File Transfer Protocol** (**SFTP**), which allow for remote file copy operations and filesystem navigation; and the **Simple Mail Transfer Protocol** (**SMTP**), which is used for email transmission over networks.

Interestingly, with each of these protocols operating on the application layer, it's not uncommon to see one protocol provide the functionality that has historically fallen under the domain of another protocol. For example, the data-agnostic nature of HTTP's plain-text message structure makes it trivially simple to use HTTP to transfer complete file data over an HTTP session. It's as simple as writing software on the server to transmit files through the message body of the response. For this reason, FTP, and to a lesser degree, SMTP, have fallen out of favor with network programmers in recent years, in favor of implementing their responsibilities in HTTP-aware software hosts. The protocols remain, however, and it will benefit us to consider what their flaws and advantages are.

FTP and SFTP

FTP (and SFTP) leverages a client-server model similar to the one used by HTTP, but its connection specification is slightly more complicated than we saw before. Where HTTP sent messages over a single connection by way of a series of stateless request/response transactions, FTP maintains two connections between the client and server over the course of a stateful session. One connection establishes a stateful control pipeline that tracks the current state of the directory exposed by the FTP server and submits the commands necessary to execute the desired file transfers. The other connection is stateless, and facilitates the transfer of the raw file data between hosts. Establishing both of these connections for a single FTP session introduces the benefit of reliability at the cost of latency and complexity. Moreover, the limited nature of tasks that can be reliably executed through FTP as a communication protocol has only served to limit its popular use as time goes on. Thankfully though, as was the case with HTTP, much of the details of implementing an FTP server or client is taken care of by way of the `System.Net` namespace in .NET core, and we'll explore those tools later on in this book.

SMTP

Similar to FTP, the feature set supported by the SMTP is quite limited and narrowly tailored to performing a few specific tasks. However, the need to implement email servers is actually fairly common, and understanding the complexity of sending or receiving messages through SMTP remains a relevant and useful skill; certainly more so than with FTP these days. SMTP is a connection-oriented protocol for sending mail messages to remote servers that are configured to receive them. It leverages a client-server model leveraging reliable sessions, over which a series of commands and data-transfer processes transmit email, unilaterally, from the client to the server. The back-and-forth of an SMTP session is actually quite a bit more complicated than we saw with HTTP and FTP, and that complexity is beyond the scope of this chapter. For now though, it's sufficient to say that any network programmer worth their salt will have a sound understanding of HTTP, FTP, and SMTP.

The Transport layer

While the application layer is the layer of the OSI model that the vast majority of .NET developers work with in their daily lives, it would be useless without sound, reliable protocol implementations on the transport layer. It's on this layer that the connections are made and the data is streamed. It's the lowest layer in the stack that an individual host is directly responsible for, and in the transport layer, TCP and UDP reign supreme. Each provide their own mechanisms for delivering streams of data to their destination, and each present their own trade-offs, to be considered when choosing a transport protocol for your network services. As with all of these protocols, we'll take a closer look at them later in this book, but for now let's learn what they are and why they came to be.

TCP

Developed in 1974 by engineers in the IEEE, the TCP is defined as a connection-based communication protocol that provides the reliable delivery of ordered packets. It's used to facilitate communication between hosts of all kinds from the internet, to SMTP clients and servers, **Secure Shell** (**SSH**) connections, FTP clients and servers, and HTTP. It is ubiquitous as the transport layer protocol of choice for almost all modern applications.

The broad adoption of TCP as the transport layer supporting most application-layer requests is primarily due to the reliability of a TCP connection. By convention, entities that implement TCP are written to detect packet loss and the out-of-order delivery of data streams, to re-request lost data, and to reorder the out-of-order streams. This error correction is resolved prior to returning that data back up the stack to the application layer entities making use of the TCP connection.

Of course, the obvious cost incurred by this error handling is latency and performance. Multiple round-trips to fetch, essentially, the same data two or three times can add substantial downtime to the client application. The reliability of TCP is ensured by leveraging a round-trip chain of request, acknowledgements of the receipt of a request, then another request, and so on. All the chatter incurred by this consistent back-and-forth makes TCP far from ideal for real-time applications, such as for gaming, video streaming, or video conferencing. Instead, where reliability or guaranteed ordering can be sacrificed in favor of performance, UDP or a similar protocol should be used as the transmission layer of choice.

UDP

If the reliability of TCP is not strictly required for an application, then UDP begins to look like a very attractive option for its simplicity and performance. UDP is a simple, unreliable, and connectionless communication protocol for transmitting data over a network. Where TCP provided robust error handling through its pattern of repeated requests and acknowledgments, UDP has no handshaking or acknowledgment signals to indicate whether a packet was properly transmitted from host to host.

While UDP does not provide robust error-handling in the case of lost or unordered packets, it does, at the very least, provide error-checking on the packet level. It does so by using a checksum value stored in the header of the packet. The difference being that when an error is detected in a packet, the packet is simply dropped by the UDP entity, and no request is sent out to try to retrieve the packet again in a valid state.

This packet-delivery-oriented model of sending out individual packets without regard for their successful delivery also means that UDP data requests can be sent without any prior establishment of a connection between hosts. This lack of an initial round-trip greatly reduces overhead in software systems that need to make frequent, real-time connections between many hosts. In fact, this lack of an initial handshake is one of the primary distinguishing factors between connection and connectionless communication protocols, and that is a distinction that warrants elaboration.

Connection versus connectionless communication

The idea of connectionless communication might seem like an oxymoron at first. How could two entities possibly communicate if they haven't connected first? How would one even know that the other exists to communicate with?

The underlying principle is that in a connection-based communication protocol, both hosts must first establish a line of communication before the transmission of any application-specific data can begin. The handshake sequence in TCP is the most obvious example of this. There is a complete round-trip of sent/received messages that must succeed before the connection is considered established, and data can be transmitted between hosts. That established line of communication is the 'connection' in this context. It consumes time and bandwidth, but provides reliability and error correction, and in almost all cases, the value of the reliability and error correction is worth far more than the costs incurred.

Meanwhile, in connectionless communication, data could be transmitted, and the communication terminated, without even a single complete round-trip from the client to the server, and back to the client again. The packet has sufficient information in its own headers to be properly routed to a listening host. Provided that host has no follow-up to the initial request, that communication will stop with only a one-way packet delivery. The low-latency of this transmission pattern could be a major benefit in certain application contexts.

There's still so much more to explore with both of these protocols, going forward, but that is the concern of a later chapter in this book. For now though, I hope this makes it clear why the transport layer and its protocols serve such a major role in designing and implementing high-performance and highly-reliable network software.

Summary

In this chapter, we learned everything there is to know about the OSI network model. First, we learned about the governing bodies that defined the standard reference model, including when and why they set out to solve the problem of unified network modeling. Then, we took a close look at the model they defined, including looking at every layer in their stack, and what responsibilities entities in those layers assume. We learned about how protocols define standardized communication patterns for entities operating on the same level in the network stack, but on separate hosts on a network. We saw how service definitions allow entities to pass data through the network stack and deliver messages to remote entities.

We also took a close look at some of the most common communication protocols, which we'll be interacting with in the rest of this book. We started with the king of all network protocols, HTTP. We looked at how HTTP sessions are established to allow communication between clients and servers. We saw how HTTP operates through a series of requests and responses using well-defined verbs to specify the operations to be performed in servicing those requests. We looked at TCP and UDP, and how the transport layer serves as the bus through which all application-layer network interactions must travel. Finally, we looked at how the network layer facilitates this communication through the IP addressing system, and discrete packet transmission.

With this foundation in place, we're well positioned to take a close look at how data is broken down into discrete packets and transmitted over the network through data streams in the next chapter.

Questions

1. What does OSI stand for, and what is the name of the organization that standardized it?
2. What is the abstraction layer via which layers of the OSI network stack communicate with layers beneath them?
3. How many layers are in the OSI network stack, and what are they?
4. What is the name of the standardization mechanism by which entities on the same layer of the network stack on different hosts communicate?
5. What does HTTP stand for? For which network layer is HTTP used as a communication protocol?
6. Name all of the HTTP verbs that a request can be sent from.
7. What are some of the primary differences between the TCP and UDP transport protocols?

Further reading

For more information about the OSI Reference Model, see *Building Modern Networks*, by *Steven Noble, Packt Publishing*.

Additionally, you can refer to *Computer Networking: Beginner's Guide for Mastering Computer Networking and the OSI Model* by *Ramon Nastase's*, and *The OSI Model for Network Engineers: Improve Your Network Troubleshooting*, by *Al Rivas*. Both are available in e-book form on `amazon.com`, and will provide a much more thorough examination of the OSI stack than I had time or space to cover in the context of this chapter.

4
Packets and Streams

This chapter will build upon the discussion in `Chapter 3`, *Communication Protocols,* of network architecture to trace the flow of data across a network, and break down the software you will write in C# to handle the data at each step in the process. We will explain the encapsulation of data into minimal packets for network transmission, and how that encapsulation helps to ensure that packets are delivered to the correct destination and are decoded properly. We will explain the concept of a data stream as a serialized sequence of discrete packets, and demonstrate the various ways that serialization can be executed in C#. Finally, we will demonstrate a variety of abstractions exposed by the `System.IO` namespace for handling streams.

The following topics will be covered in this chapter:

- Understanding how data moves through a network, and how the various layers of network-stack metadata are unwrapped at each step in the transmission process to ensure proper delivery
- A deep dive into the structure of a packet delivered over a network
- Understanding the concept of a data stream as a collection of discrete packets, and how to leverage it to abstract away the process of receiving and parsing packets using C#'s many `Stream` classes

Technical requirements

For this chapter, we'll be looking closely at network communication. To that end, I'll be using the *Wireshark* packet sniffing tool to demonstrate some of the concepts we discuss. If you want to follow along and explore the network traffic on your own machine, Wireshark is a free download, available at `https://www.wireshark.org/`.

Whether you plan to use it to follow along with this chapter or not, I absolutely recommend familiarizing yourself with it as a tool. If you are at all serious about doing any meaningful network programming with C#, low-level traffic inspection will be a major key to your success and the earlier you learn the tool, the better off you'll be.

Leveraging networks – transmitting packets for use by remote resources

To understand specifically what a packet is, we should first understand the constraints of a network that necessitates packets in the first place. To do that, we'll need to understand the limitations of bandwidth, latency, and signal strength. Each of these constraints plays a key role in determining the maximum size of an atomic unit of data that can be transmitted over a given network. These limitations demand that pieces of data transmitted over the network include a number of attributes to ensure any measure of reliability. Data packets sent between nodes in a network must be small, and contain sufficient context to be properly routed. With that in mind, let's look at the ways a network's physical limitations can inform and drive the software solutions written for them.

Bandwidth

Anyone with an internet connection is probably fairly familiar with the concept of **bandwidth**. The monthly rates for an internet service are typically (at least in the US) tiered by the maximum bandwidth provided. In professional programming vernacular, the term bandwidth is often used, somewhat loosely, to refer to the amount of time or mental capacity a team or team member can dedicate to new tasks. Each of us should have a somewhat intuitive understanding of the concept. Put simply, it's the maximum rate of data transmission over a given network connection.

While that definition might seem basic, or even trivial, the way that bandwidth drives the standards for packet size and structure may be less obvious. So, let's consider more thoroughly what bandwidth describes and how it impacts data transmission. There are two things to consider when we're discussing bandwidth: the speed of throughput and the channel's maximum capacity.

The easiest way to conceptualize these concepts is through the analogy of a highway. Imagine that you're the operator of a tollbooth on this hypothetical highway. However, for this analogy, let's say that, instead of collecting a toll, you're responsible for counting the total number of cars that move past your booth over a given period of time. The cars on your highway represent individual bits of data. Every time a car crosses your toll booth, you tally it. The total number of cars that cross your booth in any given time represents the bandwidth of your highway over that time period. With this analogy in place, let's see how the throughput and channel capacity can impact that bandwidth.

In this characterization, the speed of throughput is analogous to the speed limit of your highway. It's the physical maximum velocity that a signal can travel over a connection. There are a number of factors that can impact or change this speed, but in most cases, the physics of electrical or optical signals traveling over their respective media render the impact of those changes negligible. Speed will ultimately boil down to the physical limits of the transmission medium itself. So, for example, fiber-optic cables will have a much higher throughput speed than copper wire. Fiber-optic cables transmit data at speeds approaching the speed of light, but copper wire introduces resistance to electrical current, slowing and weakening any data signal traveling over it. So, in the context of our highway analogy, fiber-optic cable networks have a much higher speed limit than copper cables. Sitting in your tollbooth over a single shift, more cars will pass by on a highway with a higher speed limit. Given this fact, it can be trivially simple to increase the bandwidth of a network by taking the basic step to upgrade your transmission media.

While the speed of throughput is a strong determinant of bandwidth, we should also take a moment to consider the maximum **capacity** of a given channel. Specifically, this refers to how many physical wires can actively carry an individual bit at any given moment along a channel. In our highway analogy, the channel capacity will describe the number of **lanes** on our highway that a car could travel. So, imagine that instead of a single-file line of cars moving down a single lane of our highway, it's been expanded to four lanes in one direction. So now, at any given moment, we could have four cars, or four bits of data, moving through our tollbooth at any given moment.

Obviously, it's the responsibility of system programmers writing firmware for network interface devices to write support for properly handling multiple simultaneous channels. However, as I'm sure you can imagine, variable channel capacity can demand very specific optimizations for the network entities responsible for breaking your data into atomic packets.

Latency

Bandwidth limitations are only one consideration for the efficiency of a network. The next most common limitation for which engineers must design, and that most users are at least intuitively familiar, is **latency.** Put simply, latency is the time between the initial moment a signal is sent, and the first moment a response to that signal can be initiated. It's the delay of a network.

There are two ways to think about latency. Simply put, you can measure it as one-way, or round-trip. Obviously, **one-way latency** describes the delay from the moment a signal is sent from one device, to the time it is received by the target device. Alternately, **round-trip latency** describes the delay between the moment a signal is sent from a device, and the moment a response from the target is received by that same device.

One thing to note, however, is that round-trip latency actually excludes the amount of time the recipient spends processing the initial signal before sending a response. For example, if I send a request from my software to an external API to provide some calculations on a piece of input data, I should reasonably expect that software to take some non-trivial amount of time to process my request. So, imagine first that the request spends 0.005 seconds in transit. Then, once received, the request is processed by the API in 0.1 seconds. Finally, the response itself spends another 0.01 seconds in transit back to my software. The total amount of time between my software sending the request and getting a response is $0.005 + 0.1 + 0.01 = 0.115$ seconds. However, since 0.1 seconds was spent processing, we will ignore this when measuring round-trip latency, so the round-trip latency will be measured as $0.115 - 0.1 = 0.015$ seconds total.

It's not uncommon for a software platform to provide a service that simply **echoes** the request it was sent without any processing applied in response. This is typically called a **ping service**, and is used to provide a useful measurement of the current round-trip latency for network requests between two devices. For this reason, latency is commonly called **ping**. There are a number of factors that confound the reliability of a ping request in any given scenario, so the response times for such requests are not generally considered accurate. However, the measurements any ping service provides are typically considered to be approximate for a given network round-trip, and can be used to help isolate other latency issues with a given request pipeline.

As I'm sure you can imagine, a constraint as generically defined as a **network delay** can have any number of contributing factors to its impact on network performance. This delay could come from just about any point in the network transaction, or on any piece of software or hardware in between the originating and target devices. On a given packet-switched network, there may be dozens of intermediary routers and gateways receiving and forwarding your package for any single request. Each of these devices could introduce some delay that will be nearly impossible to isolate when performance monitoring or testing. And, if a given gateway is processing hundreds of simultaneous requests, you could experience delays just by virtue of being queued up behind a number of requests that you had nothing to do with and of which you might have no direct knowledge.

Mechanical latency

The different contributing factors to latency are sometimes categorized slightly differently. Mechanical latency, for instance, describes the delay introduced into a network by the time it takes for the physical components to actually generate or receive a signal. So, for instance, if your 64-bit computer has a clock speed of 4.0 GHz, this sets a physical, mechanical limit on the total amount of information that can be processed in a given second. Now, to be fair, it would be a lot of information to be processed by such a system. Assuming the CPU is processing a single byte per clock cycle, it's 4 billion 64-bit instructions per second being processed; that's a ton. But that clock speed constitutes a mechanical limit that introduces some measurable latency to any transaction. On such a system, a 64-bit instruction cannot move onto the network transmission device any faster than at least 0.000000128 seconds, assuming a bit is processed and delivered to the transmission stream at every interval of the clock cycle.

Operating system latency

The preceding example describes a somewhat unrealistic system, in that 64 bytes of data can be sent directly to the transmission media uninterrupted. Realistically, an **operating system** (**OS**) will be handling requests from the application and system software to send over that hypothetical packet, and it will be doing so while simultaneously processing thousands of other requests from hundreds of other pieces of software running on the host machine. Almost all modern OSes have a system for interlacing operations from multiple requests so that no one process is unreasonably delayed by the execution of another. So really, we will never expect to achieve latency as low as the minimum mechanical latency defined by our clock speed. Instead, what might realistically happen is that the first byte of our packet will be queued up for transport, and then the OS will switch to servicing another operation on its procedure queue, some time will be spent executing that operation, and then it might come back and ready the second byte of our packet for transport. So, if your software is trying to send a packet on an OS that is trying to execute a piece of long-running or blocking software, you may experience substantial latency that is entirely out of your control. The latency introduced by how your software's requests are prioritized and processed by the OS is, hopefully very obviously, called **OS latency.**

Operational latency

While I did state earlier that latency typically describes only the time that a packet spends in transit, it is often useful for you, as a network engineer, to consider the impact of latency on your end user experience. While we would all like to, no engineer can get away with ignoring a negative user experience by claiming that the causes are out of your control. So even though your software may be performing optimally, and deployed to a lightning-fast fiber-optic network, if it is dependent on an upstream resource provider that is slow to process requests, your end user will ultimately feel that pain, no matter how perfect your own code is. For this reason, it's often useful to keep track of the actual, overall window of time necessary to process a given network request, including the processing time on the remote host. This measurement is the most meaningful when considering the impact of network operations on your user's experience, and is what's called **operational latency.** So, while most of the contributing factors to the operational latency of a task are, typically, out of your control, it is often important to be aware of its impact and, wherever possible, try to optimize it down to a minimum.

Ultimately, what each of these individual metrics should tell you is that there are dozens of points throughout a network request at which latency can be introduced. Each of them has varying degrees of impact, and they are often under varying degrees of your control, but to the extent that you can, you should always seek to minimize the number of points in your application at which external latency can be introduced. Designing for optimal network latency is always easier than trying to build it in after the fact. Doing so isn't always easy or obvious though, and optimizing for minimal latency can look different from either side of a request.

To illustrate, imagine we are writing an application that is responsible for collecting one or more transaction IDs, looking up the monetary value of those transactions, and then returning a sum of them. Being a forward-thinking developer, you've separated this transaction aggregation service from the database of transactions to keep the business logic of your service decoupled from your data-storage implementation. To facilitate data access, you've exposed the transaction table through a simple REST API that exposes an endpoint for individual transaction lookups by way of a single key in the URL, such as `transaction-db/transaction/{id}`. This makes the most sense to you since each transaction has a unique key, and allowing individual-transaction lookup allows us to minimize the amount of information returned by your database service. Less content passed over the network means less latency, and so, from the data-producer perspective, we have designed well.

Your aggregation service, though, is another story. That service will need multiple transaction records to generate a meaningful output. With only a single endpoint returning a single record at a time, the aggregation service will send multiple, simultaneous requests to the transaction service. Each one of those requests will contribute their own mechanical, OS, and operational latencies. While modern OSes allow for multithreaded processing of multiple network requests simultaneously, there is an upper limit to the number of available threads in a given process. As the number of transactions increases, requests will start to become queued, preventing simultaneous processing and increasing the operational latency experienced by the user.

In this case, optimizing for both cases is a simple matter of adding an additional REST endpoint, and accepting `POST` HTTP requests with multiple transaction IDs in the request body. Most of us reading this will have likely already known this, but the example is useful as an illustration of how **optimal performance** can look very different on either side of the same coin. Often, we won't be responsible for both the service application and the database API, and in those cases, we will have to do the best we can to improve performance from only one side.

No matter what side of a request you're on, though, the impact of network latency on application performance demands your consideration for minimizing the size of atomic data packets that must be sent over the network. Breaking down large requests into smaller, bite-sized pieces provides more opportunities for every device in the communication chain to step in, perform other operations, and then proceed with processing your packets. If our single-network request will block other network operations for the duration of an entire 5 MB file transfer, it might be given lower priority in the queue of network transactions that your OS is maintaining. However, if our OS only needs to slot in a small, 64-byte packet for transmission, it can likely find many more opportunities to send that request more frequently, reducing your OS latency overall.

If our application must send 5 MB of data, then doing so in 64-byte packets gives your application's hosting context much more flexibility in determining the best way to service that requirement.

Signal strength

The last major constraint of network communication that we'll look at is variable **signal strength.** Over any non-trivial network, the strength of a given signal can be impacted by anything from the distance between wireless transmitters and receivers, to just plain distance between two gateways connected by a wire. This isn't much of a concern on modern fiber optic networks, since those rely on the transmission of visible light through glass or plastic fiber, and are thus not subject to many of the confounding factors that interfere with older physical network standards. However, reliable signal strength can be a major concern for wireless networks, or wired networks that use electric signals over copper wiring.

If you're at all familiar with the impact of resistance on signal strength (for those of you who remember your college physics or computer hardware classes), you'll know that the longer the wire over which you want to send a signal, the weaker the signal will be at the receiving end. If you're defining a bit as being a 1 whenever the voltage on a wire is above a given threshold, and the resistance of your wire reduces the voltage of a signal over time, there's a non-zero chance that some bits of your packet will be rendered indeterminable by your target due to the interference of your signal. A weak signal strength means a lower reliability of transmission.

And mere resistance isn't the only thing that can weaken your signal strength. Most electrical signals are subject to interference from any other nearby electrical signals, or simply the electromagnetic fields that permeate the earth naturally. Of course, over time, electrical engineers have devised innumerable ways to mitigate those effects; everything from wire insulation to reduce the impact of electromagnetic interference, to signal relays to reduce the impact of resistance by amplifying a signal along its route. However, as your software is deployed to wider and wider networks, the extent to which you can rely on a modern and well-designed network infrastructure diminishes significantly. Data loss is inevitable, and that can introduce a number of problems for those responsible for ensuring the reliable delivery of your requests.

So, how does this intermittent data loss impact the design of network transmission formats? It enforces a few necessary attributes of our packets that we'll explore in greater depth later, but we'll mention them here quickly. Firstly, it demands the transmission of the smallest packets that can reasonably be composed. This is for the simple reason that, if there is an issue of data corruption, it invalidates the whole payload of a packet. In a sequence of zeroes and ones, uncertainty about the value of a single bit can make a world of difference in the actual meaning of the payload. Since the payloads are only segments of the overall request or response object, we can't rely on having sufficient context within a given packet itself to make the correct assertion about the value of an indeterminate bit. So, if one bit goes bad and is deemed indeterminable, the entire payload is invalidated, and must be thrown out. By reducing the packet size to the smallest reasonable size achievable, we minimize the impact of invalid bits on the whole of our request payload. It's much more palatable to re-request a single 64-byte packet due to an indeterminable bit than it is to restart an entire 5 Mb transmission.

Astute readers may have already identified the second attribute of packets that are driven by unreliable signal strength. While variable signal strength and external interference could simply render a single bit indeterminable, it could also very well flip the bit entirely. So, while the recipient might be able to determine its received value with certainty, it ultimately determines the **incorrect value**. This is a much more subtle problem since, as I mentioned before, packets will likely contain insufficient information to determine the appropriate value for a specific bit in its payload. This means packets will have to have some mechanism for, at the very least, **error detection** baked into the standard headers. So long as the consuming device can detect an error, it can know, at the very least, to discard the contents of the erroneous packet and request re-transmission.

It's worth noting that the benefits of decomposing a request into smaller and smaller packets reach limits beyond which it ceases to be beneficial for network performance. Subject this line of thinking to reduction ad absurdum and you'll quickly find yourself with a full-fledged packet for every single bit in your payload, error-detection and all. With our imagined request payload of 5 Mb, that's 40,000,000 packets being sent simultaneously. Obviously, this is an absurd number of packets for such a small request. Instead, network engineers have found a reliable range of sizes for packets being sent according to a given protocol as falling somewhere between a few hundred bytes and a few kilobytes.

Now that we know why network communication is done with small, isolated packets, we should take a look at what those are.

The anatomy of a packet

While I've touched on some features already in this chapter, here we'll take a closer look at the attributes that a network packet must exhibit in order to actually be useful as a piece of information. We'll look at how the standard for network packets is defined and the minimum amount of features that all network packets will contain in some form or other. Then we'll take a brief look at how different transmission protocols implement their own standards for packets, and how some of the required attributes are expanded on to provide more reliable data transmission, or higher performance. This will ultimately lay the foundation for later in this book where we look at network security, diagnostics, and optimization.

What is a packet?

So, to start off with, we should engage in a bit of nit-picking. The term I've been using throughout this chapter-packet-is not, strictly speaking, the most accurate term for what I've been describing. Until now, I've been using the word packet to describe the most atomic unit of data transmission over a network. However, for the sake of accuracy, I should note that the term packet refers specifically to the most atomic piece of data transmitted by the network layer of the **Open Systems Interconnection** (**OSI**) network stack. In the transport layer, where we'll be most concerned with it (since that is the lowest layer in the stack we'll directly interact with through C#), the atomic unit of data transmission is actually called a **datagram.** However, I'll note that it is much more common to refer to data units of the transmission layer as packets than datagrams and so will continue with this colloquial use of the term throughout the chapter and throughout the rest of the book. I did, however, want to take the opportunity to point out the distinction between the two terms in case you encountered either being used elsewhere in different contexts. With that in mind, what exactly is a datagram, or packet?

We already know quite a bit about what a packet must be in order to be useful, so let's formalize it into a definition. A **packet** is an atomic unit of data, encapsulated with sufficient context for reliable transmission over an arbitrary network implementation.

So basically, it's a **payload** (unit of data) with a **header** (sufficient context). This shouldn't be surprising by this point, but let's look at how this translates to an actual array of bytes passed from our transport layer to the network layer. To do so, we'll use Wireshark to examine the actual data packets being sent to and from my own Ethernet port, and look at how each part of that definition translates to actual datagrams.

Setting up Wireshark

As a tool for network engineers, Wireshark is immeasurably useful, and I strongly encourage you to familiarize yourself with its features and start to think about how you could leverage it in your own development tasks. For now, though, we'll be using its most basic packet sniffing functionality to examine every packet that comes through our open internet connection. So, once Wireshark is installed, simply open it up and select your Ethernet connection as your target for packet sniffing, as seen in the following screenshot:

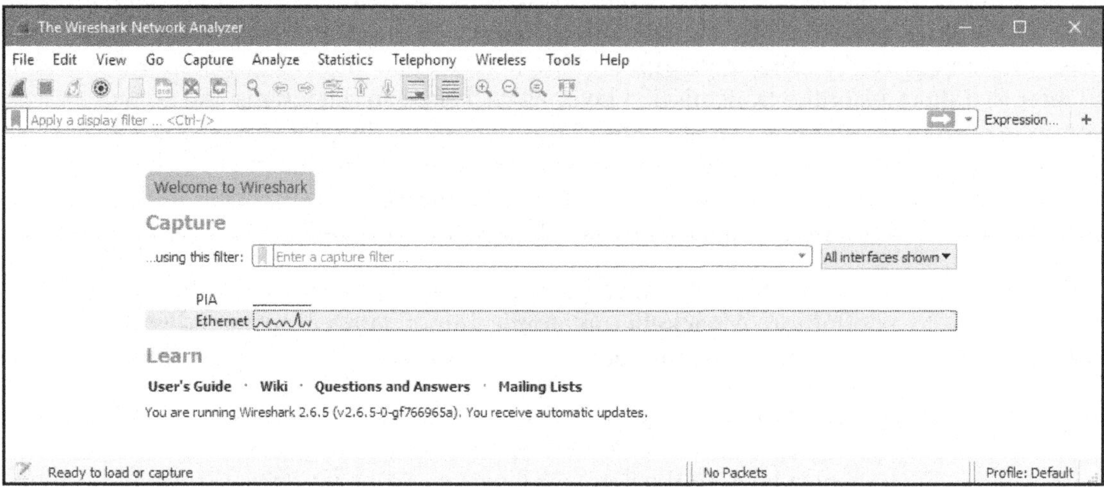

When you open it on your own machine, take a second to watch the graph growing out to the right of the traffic source. This actually provides a quick view of the relative activity on the given source over time. Once your primary internet source is selected, start capturing by clicking the capture button on the top-left of the toolbar, or simply double-clicking the desired source. Allow the tool to capture traffic for a few minutes just to get a good range of sample data and then start exploring on your own. If you've never used a tool such as Wireshark or Fiddler before, you'll likely be surprised by how much chatter is actually happening, even with no input from you directly.

With the tool installed and running, let's take a look at some of the features of a packet specified by our definition and see how it translates to real-world implementations.

Atomic data

If you have any experience with database design, you might already have a pretty clear idea of what constitutes **atomic data**. Typically, it means the smallest components into which a record can be broken down without losing their meaning. In the context of network communication, though, we're not really concerned with the payload of a packet losing its meaning. It would recompiled into the original data structure by the recipient of the payload, and so it's fine if the small chunk of data that moves over the network is meaningless on its own. Instead, when we talk about atomic data in the context of network transactions, we're really talking about the minimum size that we can truncate our data into, beyond which we will stop seeing the desired benefits of shrinking our data into smaller and smaller chunks. Those chunks may well splice double-precision decimal values in two, sending one half over in one packet and the other half in an entirely separate packet. So, in that case, neither packet has enough information to make sense of the data in its original form. It wouldn't be considered atomic in the same way that a `FIRST_NAME` field will be the most atomic way to store the first name of a user record in a database. But if that decomposition results in the most efficient distribution of packets for transmission over the current network, with minimum latency and maximum bandwidth utilization, then it is the most atomic way to represent it in a network packet.

For an example of this, just look at any arbitrary packet you recorded in your Wireshark capture. Looking at a packet in my data stream, we've got this arbitrary **Transmission Control Protocol** (**TCP**) packet (or datagram), as follows:

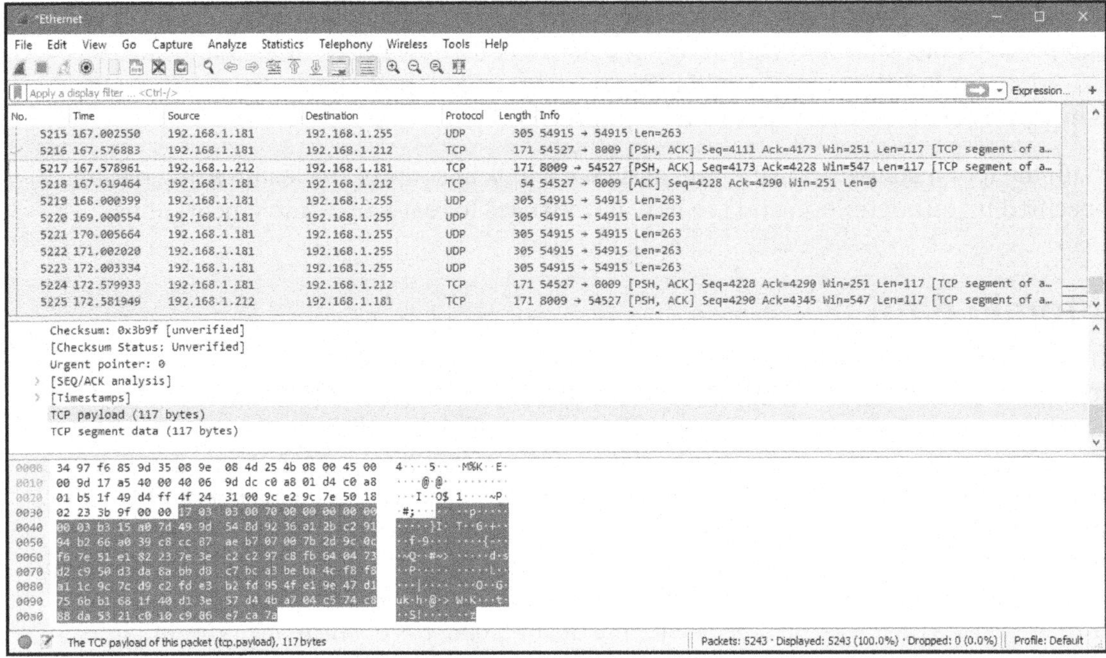

As you can see in the selected text of the raw data view on the bottom of my Wireshark panel, the payload of that particular packet was 117 bytes of nonsensical garbage. That might not seem very useful to you or me, but once that specific TCP request is reassembled with the rest of the packets in that request, the resulting data should make sense to the consuming software (in this case, the instance of Google Chrome running on my computer). So, this is what is meant by an **atomic unit of data**. Fortunately, that's not something that we'll have to concern ourselves with, since that's handled directly by the hardware implementation of the transport layer. So, even though we can implement software that directly leverages a transport layer protocol of our choice, the actual act of decomposing and recomposing packets or datagrams will always be out of our hands when we're working on the .NET Core platform.

Encapsulated with sufficient context

This aspect of our definition is actually the real meat of it, and is the real reason we're messing about with Wireshark in the first place. What exactly does it mean to encapsulate a packet with sufficient context? Let's start with the context that a datagram must have. This refers to the information that any device in between the source and destination hosts will need to route the packet accordingly, as well as any information necessary for the destination host to properly read and process the packet once received. For obvious reasons, this information is contained at the very front of a packet (which is to say, it composes the first bits that will be read by a receiving device), and is what constitutes the header of a packet. The **context** is the information necessary to either forward or process a packet correctly.

So what, then, constitutes **sufficient context**? Well, that actually depends on the specific protocol under which the packet was constructed. Different protocols have different requirements and expectations, and thus, different requirements to be serviced properly. What constitutes sufficient context for one might be grossly insufficient for another.

The two most commonly used transport layer protocols are TCP and **User Datagram Protocol** (**UDP**), and each of them have different service contracts for the application software that leverages them. This means that both of them have very distinct header specifications. TCP seeks to provide sequential, reliable, error-checked transmission service for packets traveling between hosts. Meanwhile, UDP, as a connection-less protocol (we'll discuss specifically what that means later in this book), doesn't explicitly aim to provide the reliability of transmission or a guarantee of the ordering of data. Instead, it seeks to provide light weight communication with a minimal protocol definition to enforce. As such, the sufficient context for UDP is actually substantially less than for that of a TCP packet.

A UDP packet header consists of a mere 8 bytes of data, broken up into 4 individual fields that each are 2 bytes in length; those fields are as follows:

- **Source port:** The specific port of the socket connection on the source machine generating the request.
- **Destination port:** The port of the connection on the destination machine.
- **Length:** The exact length of the packet, including the payload that immediately follows the 8-byte header.
- **Checksum:** A simple value used to verify the data integrity of the payload.

Using Wireshark, we can see this in action. With a simple UDP packet, the full contents are captured by those few relevant fields, as seen in the **Packet Details** view in the middle of my Wireshark window:

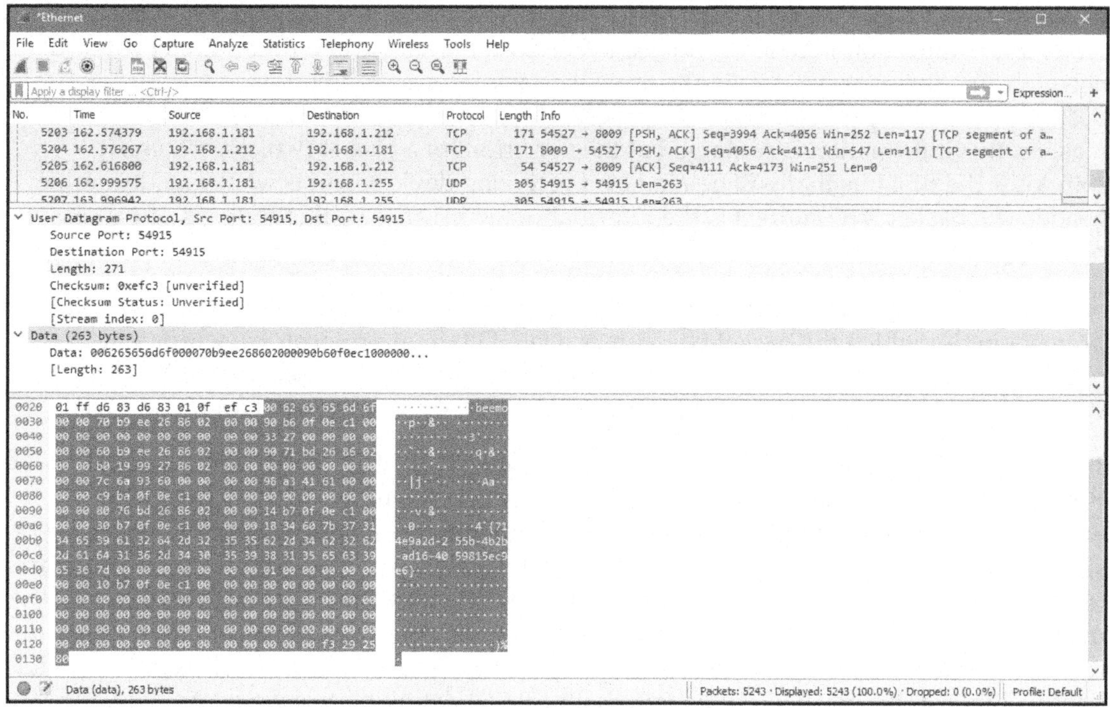

However, since TCP provides reliable delivery, guaranteed ordering, and leverages a handshake-protocol that UDP forgoes, the specification of a TCP packet header is much longer. Where sufficient context for UDP could be encapsulated in a mere 8 bytes, sufficient context for TCP demands a header of up to 20 bytes. This is including a number of flag-bits indicating the state of the individual packets in the context of the larger session, and a sequence number to provide the protocol-specified ordering of packets. A brief examination of the **Packet Details** view of a simple TCP packet within Wireshark should illuminate the disparity in the expected context provided by a TCP packet header, as follows:

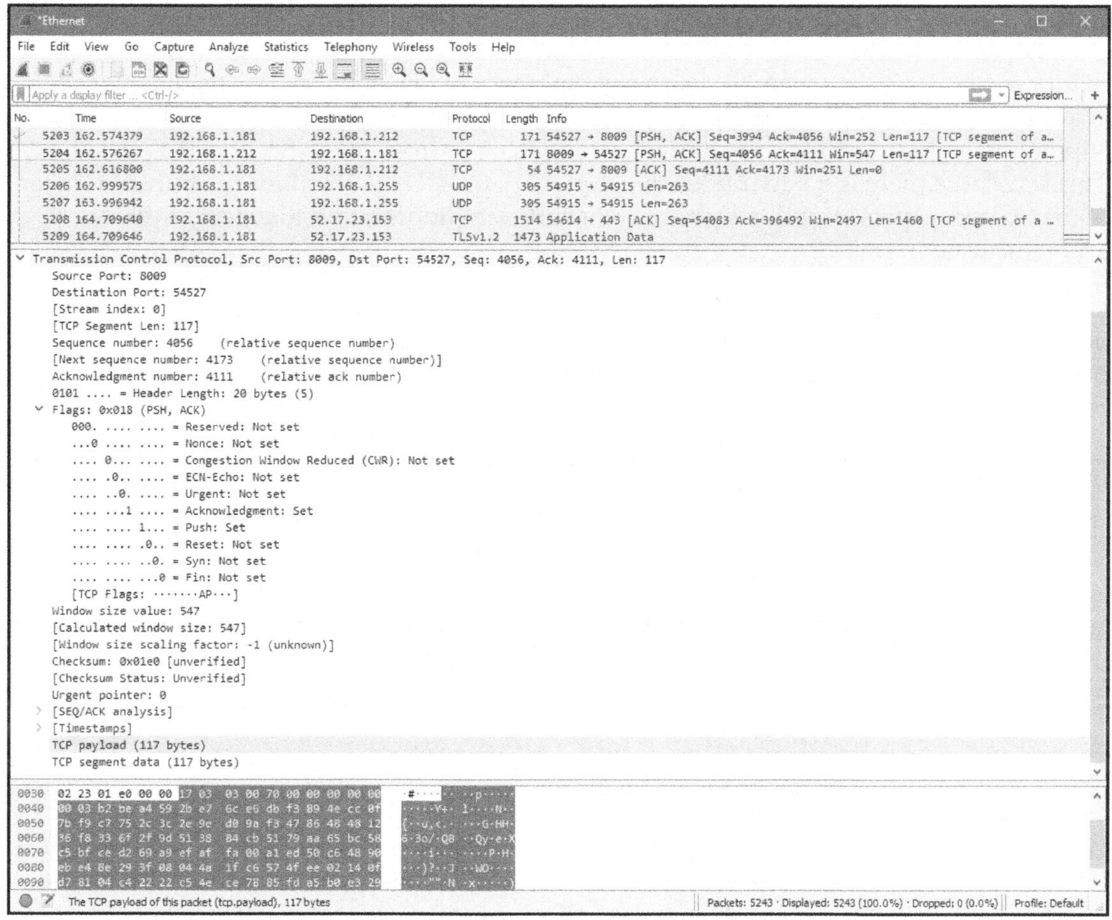

As you can see here, even though the actual length of the TCP packet in bytes is shorter than the UDP packet that we looked at previously, the header provides substantially more information than was necessary for a valid UDP connection. There was obviously overlap (of the source and destination ports, and a checksum), but there was a wider gap between the two headers than there was common ground.

So, hopefully, it's now clear why what constitutes sufficient context is driven by the protocol under which a packet was constructed. The specifics of what is sufficient can change, but for every protocol, there will always be a minimum amount of context that is sufficient to be forwarded or processed.

Error detection and correction

Before we move on, I do want to take a brief moment to talk about the distinction between error detection and error correction. You might have wondered why I left out any stipulation regarding error correction or error detection from my definition of a packet. This is because there is no guarantee that, for every protocol defined for the transport layer of the OSI stack, packets will always contain sufficient information to detect or correct errors incurred in transit.

I will say, however, that it is extremely common to have at least some kind of error detection in a given protocol specification. TCP, and even the unreliable UDP transport protocol, provide a checksum for simple error detection, as seen in the following two packets on Wireshark:

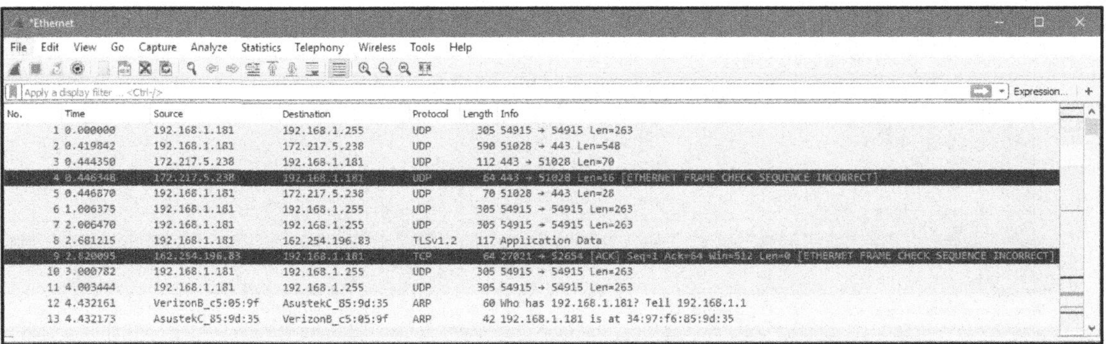

What those protocols don't provide, however, is any mechanism for error correction, which is actually much more difficult to implement, and for anything other than trivial correction capabilities, will require the packet size to balloon upwards. For example, while a checksum can tell you whether the payload has altered in transit somehow, it cannot tell you specifically where, or to what extent, the payload may have been altered. To do so would require enough additional data to reconstruct the packet from scratch. Since packet transmission is generally reliable over time (which is to say, even if one transmission failed, retrying the transmission is likely to succeed), and generally exceptionally fast at the transport layer, it's always a much better idea to simply detect an error, discard the erroneous packet, and request retransmission.

With this in place, we have a solid idea of everything that a packet defined under a given protocol must have, and of how we can examine or use individual pieces of network data. But our software won't be using tiny little pieces of individual data. Our software will be expecting JSON objects, XML payloads, or serialized byte-streams of C# objects. So, how does software that consumes network traffic make heads or tails of those random flows of bite-sized packets? By using them as streams.

Streams and serialization – understanding sequential data transmission

So with our fat, chunky JSON requests being broken up into tiny, sub-kilobyte packets, and sent over as an array of seemingly random, disjointed pieces of data, how can we possibly expect our recipients to process this data? Well, in C#, that's where the concept of a data stream comes in. Within the context of our application code, we can reliably assume that the transport layer will recompose our packets into a sequence of bits for us to consume as soon as it becomes available to us. So once we get that sequence of bits back, how do we consume it? As an IO stream!

The Stream class

If you've done any reading or writing of files on your local file system in C# on older .NET Framework versions, you'll already be familiar with this concept. In .NET Core, we can import the `System.IO` namespace to our application to start working directly with the data returned by a TCP/IP socket by simply opening up a new `StreamReader` object, initialized with a `NetworkStream` instance connected to the target socket. So, what is a stream and how should you use it?

Streams are a powerful concept in processing serialized data. They provide one-way access to a sequential data source and allow you to handle the processing of that data explicitly. Executing the `Read()` or `ReadAsAsync()` methods, or other associated methods, will trigger this one-way traversal; starting at the beginning and reading, on demand, byte by byte through the entire sequence, until a Terminal character has been reached. The .NET implementation of this concept is extremely flexible, such that, regardless of the specific instance of the `Stream` abstract class you're using, the `StreamReader` class will be equipped to accept the data, traverse it accordingly, and allow you to build out a non-serialized instance of a C# data structure as needed.

We'll examine streams more thoroughly in later chapters, but for now, I wanted to highlight how, in the context of network communication, streams are composed of the sequence of packets received by a specific port or socket, and returned to your application through a normalized implementation of the `Stream` class.

This is just one example of the power suite of abstractions provided by .NET Core. So, even though you now have the understanding necessary to explicitly handle individual packets returned from your transport layer to rebuild the response of a network request from scratch, you thankfully never have to do that. The Core framework handles that headache for you. And with this added perspective of what's happening under the hood, I hope you feel better equipped to address potential performance issues or subtle network bugs in your network-dependent applications going forward.

Summary

Looking back, this chapter covered the lowest-level details of network communication. First, we learned about the three most common constraints of a physical network infrastructure that demand the decomposition of a network request into packets. We looked at how different aspects of the hosting context of our application can contribute some measure of latency to our requests, how bandwidth can change the way requests move from one node to another, and how signal strength can compromise the integrity of a packet.

Next, we explored how those factors necessitate small, contextually-complete, atomic packets as our transport format for network requests. We unpacked how some common protocols provide that complete context with each packet through standardized formats. This gave us a clearer idea of how a larger network request is decomposed and sent over our network pipes.

Finally, we looked at how a set of packets, delivered at inconsistent intervals, can be consumed as a sequential stream. With all of this, the lowest level of our foundation is set, and we have the complete context of network infrastructure and communication standards necessary to fully explore how C# provides that functionality in our .NET Core applications. And that's exactly what we'll be looking at in the next chapter, as we finally generate a network request in a user-facing application, and fully unpack every step of that process as implemented by the .NET Core hosting platform.

Questions

1. What are the three constraints of a network that necessitates the decomposition of a network request into packets?
2. List each of the types of latency discussed in this chapter.
3. Why does unreliable signal strength warrant smaller packet sizes?
4. What is the definition of a datagram?
5. What are the two components of a datagram?
6. What is sufficient context in terms of a datagram or packet?
7. Which feature of .NET Core facilitates the processing of unreliable data streams?

Further reading

For a better understanding of how packets and data streams operate over a distributed system, check out *Packet Analysis with Wireshark, Anish Nath, Packt Publishing,* here: `https://www.packtpub.com/networking-and-servers/packet-analysis-wireshark`.

For a closer look at data streams in practice, consider *Stream Analytics with Microsoft Azure, Anindita Basak, Krishna Venkataraman, Ryan Murphy, and Manpreet Singh, Packt Publishing,* here: `https://www.packtpub.com/big-data-and-business-intelligence/stream-analytics-microsoft-azure`.

2

Section 2: Communicating Over Networks

Part two of the book will begin to dive deeper into the specific implementation details of writing software for networks in C#. It will begin by explaining the most accessible and basic abstractions the .NET framework exposes for generating and handling network requests. Finally, it will explore the details of how that data transfer impacts software design and complexity.

The following chapters will be covered in this section:

`Chapter 5`, *Generating Network Requests in C#*

`Chapter 6`, *Streams, Threads, and Asynchronous Data*

`Chapter 7`, *Error Handling Over the Wire*

5
Generating Network Requests in C#

So, now we've got a deep and complete understanding of the nature of networks. We understand the demands that networks place on the design and implementation of the software and hardware that is meant to be deployed on those networks. But what are we supposed to do with this knowledge? In this chapter, we'll finally explore the most common paradigms for leveraging network resources in .NET Core. We'll be looking at the common interface for implementing the request/response transaction model on the internet (the most ubiquitous network with which you'll work), and examine some of the specific implementations of it. Along the way, we'll take a look at what happens under the hood by taking apart some of the source code for the .NET classes that we'll be using.

The following topics will be covered in this chapter:

- The basic structure of the `WebRequest` class, and what functionality each of its sub-classes is assured to expose through their methods
- How to leverage different sub-classes of the `WebRequest` class, based on different use cases you may encounter, and understanding the distinct operations that they provide
- The internal phases of request execution as implemented by C#

Technical requirements

All of the code for this chapter is available at the GitHub repository for this book at `https://github.com/PacktPublishing/Hands-On-Network-Programming-with-CSharp-and-.NET-Core/tree/master/Chapter 5`.

As mentioned before, all of the code in this chapter can be read, manipulated, built, and deployed with Visual Studio Code or Visual Studio Community Edition (or Visual Studio for macOS, for those of you on a macOS system). The specific source control editor you use is typically a matter of opinion, but I assure you that whatever you use to work with the code in this chapter will be sufficient for all of the code throughout the rest of this book. I'd encourage you to stick with that decision and take some time to familiarize yourself with it. I expect most of the readers of this book will already have some deeply entrenched opinions about the best environment for .NET Core development. If you don't, however, I encourage you to pick whichever one feels most comfortable for you (either the feature-richness of Visual Studio Community Edition, or the lightweight, multiplatform friendliness of Visual Studio Code). Once you do, make sure you take a significant amount of time to familiarize yourself with the tools of that environment. Learn the keyboard shortcuts and set your auto-formatting options. Make it yours; once you do, you'll be ready to begin.

One class to rule them all – the WebRequest abstract class

As any software craftsman will tell you, if you want to understand how to leverage a library or toolset provided to you by another developer, just look at the public interface. If the interface is designed well enough, it will be obvious as to how that tool should be used. A good interface design communicates a lot about the limits and original intentions for the use of a piece of library software, and that's what we'll be looking at in this section.
The `WebRequest` abstract class of the `System.Net` namespace is the public interface for creating and working with general-purpose network requests that are meant to be sent over the internet.

The interface or abstract class

I've been describing the abstract `WebRequest` base class as providing an interface for how Microsoft intends developers to interact with network operations. However, I must admit that this isn't entirely accurate; `WebRequest` is, technically, an abstract class. For those readers who are unfamiliar with the distinction, it's actually quite trivial for our purposes.

Abstract classes do, in fact, define an interface for working with their implementations. The relevant distinction between the two is that, with an abstract class, any given method provided as part of the interface will typically have a default implementation defined within the abstract base class itself. So, the methods provided by an abstract class still define the interface through which you, as a consumer of the concrete classes, will interact with the implementations of the class. It's really just a distinction of where the obligation falls to define the expected behavior for that interface. Since you can't instantiate an abstract class any more than you can instantiate an interface definition, the difference is entirely trivial. Unless, of course, you choose to inherit from the `WebRequest` class yourself (which we will do at the end of this chapter). For now, though, let's just review the specification provided by `WebRequest`.

The interface

With any type of abstract class or interface definition, their proper use can best be understood through two distinct lenses. The shape of the abstraction is made clear by the properties of the interface. This gives users a concrete idea of the proper context in which instances of the interface should be used. It should clearly convey the domain around which the abstraction should operate. Meanwhile, the scope of the abstraction is conveyed by the classes' method signatures. This is what tells users how the class operates over the domain, as defined by its shape or properties.

An interface of well-named methods should give clear boundaries to the limits of the usefulness of the class. If an interface is well defined, as with the `WebRequest` base class, its properties and method signatures should make it clear exactly when it should, and should not be used. What's more, if it should be used, well-named and well-scoped method signatures will tell users exactly how to use the method.

So, with that perspective in mind, let's take a look at what is in the base definition of the `WebRequest` class. This specification will tell us how it is meant to be used and how to extend or implement it for ourselves. And what better place to start than with the constructors?

The constructors

`WebRequest` defines only two base constructors for its sub-classes. The first is the default parameter-less constructor. The second allows developers to specify an instance of the `SerializationInfo` and `StreamingContext` classes to more narrowly define the scope of valid use cases for the newly-created instance of the class. So, our constructor signatures will look like the following code block:

```
public WebRequest() {
    ...
}

public WebRequest(SerializationInfo si, StreamingContext sc) {
    ...
}
```

So far this is pretty straightforward, but why use the second constructor at all? What is so common about using `SerializationInfo` and `StreamingContext` in `WebRequest` instances that the base class defines a constructor which accepts instances of those classes?

We'll look more closely at streaming contexts in later chapters, but we did briefly discuss the need for reliably serialized data in the previous chapter, and this is a good place to consider the concept more fully. Every request or response payload will need to be serialized prior to transport, and deserialized upon arrival at the destination machine. As we discussed before, this is the process of taking unordered, locally-addressed chunks of data and converting it into ordered strings of zeros and ones. Specifically, it must be ordered in such a way that the same strings can be traversed in order and used to compose locally-addressed in-memory objects by the recipient machine.

So, while our software might store an ordered list of integers as an array of contiguous memory addresses, this is an implementation detail that is fundamentally independent of the data structure it represents. The only key details are that the list is ordered, and that it is a list of integers. It could just as easily be represented as a linked list under the hood, with each node in the list containing the integer stored at that node, as well as the address of the next node in the list, which may or may not be contiguous. In memory, these two data structures are significantly different:

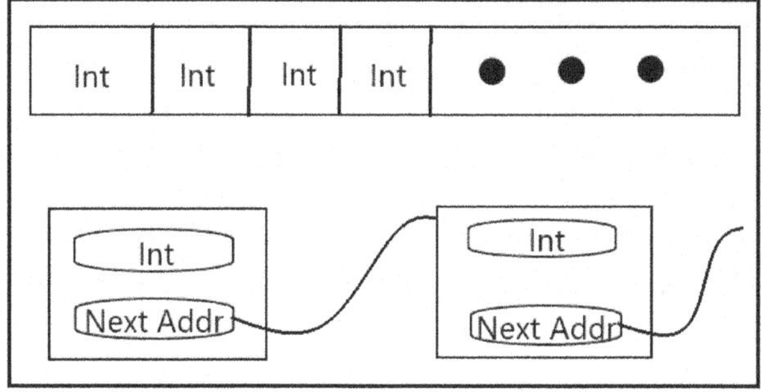

However, as long as the proper serialization information is given for how those two lists should be represented, they should look the same to any recipient receiving those lists as the payload to a request or response over the network. They should be nothing more than a well-delimited list of the integers. If your serialization mechanism is in the typical **Javascript Object-Notation** (**JSON**) format, both of those implementations would serialize the same output:

```
[
    int,
    int,
    int,
    ...
]
```

Often, you'll find that `WebRequest` and `WebResponse` instances are instantiated and leveraged over and over again for the same kinds of messages, and their payloads should be serialized in the same way each and every time. Being able to provide `SerializationInfo` as a constructor input gives you the flexibility to define your serialization rules and details once, and then leverage them for a theoretically infinite number of requests.

The same goes for the `StreamingContext` parameter. As most network software is written to facilitate the same sorts of operations that are being executed in the same way over the lifespan of the software, it's unlikely that in a given application, your requests will need to leverage different kinds of I/O streams. Later on, we'll look more closely at the different kinds of streams available to you. It's a dense topic; however, for now, just know that this input parameter gives you the same flexibility as the `SerializationInfo` parameter. It allows you to define your streaming context once, and use it over and over again.

And with only those two signatures, we've covered the only constructors explicitly defined by the `WebRequest` base class. This should give you a pretty clear idea of how the writers of this library anticipated it would likely be used. Of course, if you wanted to, you could write a sub-class that accepted HTTP verbs and default header values, and all sorts of other aspects of a given request that you will likely need to define before you can send the request. But at its most basic, these constructor signatures tell you that this is a class that is meant to provide **reliable serialization** of data over a **reliable data stream**.

Class properties

So, your constructors give you a clear idea of the context in which the classes are expected to be used, and your properties define the overall shape of a request. They define the clearest and most unambiguous description of what the class actually is. What can we learn about `WebRequest`, based on its properties? Well, let's take a closer look.

According to the base class specification, the public properties of the class are in alphabetical order (as they're listed in the Microsoft documentation, here: `https://docs.microsoft.com/en-us/dotnet/api/system.net.webrequest?view=netcore-3.0`), as follows:

- `AuthenticationLevel`
- `CachePolicy`
- `ConnectionGroupName`
- `ContentLength`
- `ContentType`
- `Credentials`
- `DefaultCachePolicy`
- `DefaultWebProxy`
- `Headers`
- `ImpersonationLevel`
- `Method`
- `PreAuthenticate`
- `Proxy`
- `RequestUri`
- `Timeout`
- `UseDefaultCredentials`

So, what does this tell us about instances derived from this abstract class? Well, the obvious information is that it encapsulates common aspects of requests made over any protocol leveraged on the internet. `Headers`, `Method` (that is, the specific protocol method, such as a `GET`, `POST`, or `PUT` HTTP method), and `RequestUri` are all that you would expect from a utility class. Others, though, such as `ImpersonationLevel`, `AuthenticationLevel`, and `CachePolicy` indicate that more than simply encapsulating a request payload, the `WebRequest` class is truly meant to encapsulate an operation.

The actions of authenticating and caching responses fall outside of the responsibility of the simple-request payload and fall more into the segment of your software responsible for brokering requests and responses between your application and external resources. The presence of these methods indicates to us that this class (and its sub-classes) is intended to be the broker of requests and responses network resources. Its definition makes clear that it can handle the nitty-gritty details of connecting to remote hosts, authenticating itself, and, by extension, your application, serializing payloads, deserializing responses, and providing all of this through a clean and simple interface.

With the `ContentType` and `ContentLength` properties, it provides a clean way to access and set the values for the most commonly required headers for any request with a payload. The specification is telling you to just give me that package, tell me where you want to send it, and let me handle the rest. It even gives you an interface for lumping similar operations together in a connection group through the `ConnectionGroupName` property.

Imagine that you have multiple requests to the same external RESTful API living at `https://financial-details.com/market/api`, and there are a dozen different endpoints that your application accesses over the course of its runtime. Meanwhile, you also have a handful of requests that need to be routed to `https://real-estate-details.com/market/api`. You can simply associate all of the requests made to the financial details API under one connection group name, and the real estate details API requests under another. Doing so allows .NET to more reliably manage connections to a single `ServicePoint` instance. This allows multiple requests to a single endpoint to be routed over the same active connection, improving performance and reducing the risk of what's known as connection pool starvation.

Whenever possible, make sure you're using `ConnectionGroupName` to associate requests to a single endpoint through a single connection. There is a finite number of active connections that you can hold at a given time in any .NET Core application, and without `ConnectionGroupName` tying requests to a single connection, each request will be given its own connection from the .NET Core runtime's pool of available connections. In applications with high network traffic or frequent external requests, this can lead to thread-starvation and unreliable performance.

Implementing this feature is quite trivial, but it can save you a mountain of time in performance tuning and chasing bugs. Simply define a static constant name for each connection group that you want to leverage, as follows:

```
namespace WebRequest_Samples
{
    // Service class to encapsulate all external requests.
    public class RequestService {
        private static readonly string FINANCE_CONN_GROUP =
"financial_connection";
        private static readonly string REAL_ESTATE_CONN_GROUP =
"real_estate_connection";

...
```

Then, whenever you need to instantiate a new request for the target endpoint, you can simply specify the connection group name through the assignment, and under the hood, the `ServicePoint` instance that is associated with the `WebRequest` instance will check for any connections that share the group name, and, if one is discovered, leverage the connection for your new request:

```
public static Task SubmitRealEstateRequest()
{
    WebRequest req =
WebRequest.Create("https://real-estate-detail.com/market/api");
    req.ConnectionGroupName = REAL_ESTATE_CONN_GROUP;
    ...
}
```

And just like that, your request will take advantage of any established connections to that same external resource. If there are no other requests associated with the specified `ConnectionGroupName` property, then .NET Core will create a connection in its connection pool, and associate your request as the first in the connection group. This is especially useful if a set of requests are targeting a resource that requires access credentials, as the connection is established with those access credentials once, and then shared with the subsequent requests!

Once the connection is established, we'll need to know what to do with the responses for that request. For that, we have the `CachePolicy` property. This specifies how your requests should handle the availability of a cached response from your remote resource. This property gives us granular control over exactly how and when we should rely on a cached response, if at all. So, for example, if we have a dataset that is updated almost constantly, and we always want the most up-to-date response, we could avoid the cache entirely, by setting the policy accordingly:

```
using System.Net.Cache;
...

public static Task SubmitRealEstateRequest()
{
    WebRequest req =
WebRequest.Create("https://real-estate-detail.com/market/api");
    req.ConnectionGroupName = REAL_ESTATE_CONN_GROUP;
    var noCachePolicy = new
RequestCachePolicy(RequestCacheLevel.NoCacheNoStore);
    req.CachePolicy = noCachePolicy;
    ...
}
```

And just like that, the request will ignore any available cached responses, and likewise, it won't cache whatever response it receives from the external resource itself. As you can see, the property expects an instance of a `RequestCachePolicy` object, which is typically initialized with a value from the `RequestCacheLevel` enum definition found in the `System.Net.Cache` namespace (as indicated by its inclusion at the top of the code block).

This is another instance where familiarizing yourself with the IntelliSense tools of Visual Studio can give you a clear idea of what values are available in that enum. Of course, if you're using something such as Visual Studio Code or another source code editor, you can always look up the source code or the documentation for it on the manufacture's website. No matter which editor you use, in the case of properties or methods whose use is not easy to infer, make a habit of looking up implementation details and notes on Microsoft's documentation. But with something as obvious and straightforward as an enum defining cache policies, Visual Studio's autocomplete and IntelliSense functionality can save you the time and mental energy of context-switching away from your IDE to look up valid values.

In the same way that you define the behavior around cached or cache-able responses, you can use the public properties of the `WebRequest` instance to define and specify the expected behavior for authentication of your application and any expectations you have of the remote resource to authenticate. This is exposed through the `AuthenticationLevel` property and behaves much the same way as the `CachePolicy` property that we just looked at.

Suppose, for instance, that your software depends on a remote resource that is explicitly configured to work with only your software. The remote server would need to authenticate requests to ensure that they are generated from valid instances of your software. Likewise, you will want to make sure that you are communicating directly with the properly configured server, and not some man-in-the-middle agent looking to swipe your valuable financial and real-estate details. In that case, you would likely want to ensure that every request is mutually authenticated, and I'm sure you can already see where I'm about to go with this.

Since the `WebRequest` class is designed to encapsulate the entire operation of interacting with remote resources, we should expect that we can configure our instance of that class with the appropriate authentication policies, and not have to manage it ourselves. And that's exactly what we can do. Building on our earlier example, we can define the `AuthenticationLevel` property to enforce the policy we want to use once, and then let the `WebRequest` instance take it from there:

```
using System.Net.Security;
...
public static Task SubmitRealEstateRequest()
{
    WebRequest req =
WebRequest.Create("https://real-estate-detail.com/market/api");
    req.ConnectionGroupName = REAL_ESTATE_CONN_GROUP;
    var noCachePolicy = new
RequestCachePolicy(RequestCacheLevel.NoCacheNoStore);
    req.CachePolicy = noCachePolicy;
    req.AuthenticationLevel = AuthenticationLevel.MutualAuthRequired;
    ...
}
```

Note the inclusion of the `System.Net.Security` namespace in our `using` directives. This is where the `AuthenticationLevel` enum is defined. This makes sense, as authentication is one-half of the authentication and authorization security components of most network software. But we'll get more into that later.

As you can guess, getting your own software authenticated will likely require some credentials.

Assigning credentials is as easy to do as defining your authentication or caching policies. In the `WebRequest` class definition, the `Credentials` property is an instance of the `ICredentials` interface from the `System.Net` namespace, typically implemented as an instance of the `NetworkCredential` class. Again, the full scope of implementing reliable security for network requests will be covered later in this book, but for now, let's take look at how we might add some credentials to our mutually- authenticated web requests. It uses the `System.Net` namespace, so no additional `using` statements are required. Instead, we can simply set the property to a new instance of `NetworkCredential` and move on, as follows:

```
req.Credentials = new NetworkCredential("test_user",
"secure_and_safe_password");
```

We should actually be storing the password as `SecureString`, but this constructor is valid, and as I said, we'll look closer at security in later chapters.

With this short, straightforward example, we can clearly see how the class properties of `WebRequest` define the expected use case for instances of the concrete sub-classes that implement and extend it. Now that we understand the shape and scope of the operations `WebRequest` intends to abstract away for us, let's take a look at the actual execution of those operations through the public methods exposed by the class.

The class methods

Now that we have a sufficiently complete picture of the shape of the `WebRequest` class, let's explore its scope, or proper use. Let's take a look at its public methods. Understanding what's available through the base class will give you everything you need to leverage any concrete implementation in the vast majority of your use cases, with perhaps only minor modifications. So, just as we did with the class properties, let's take look at the following list of public methods and see what we can infer about how the class is meant to be used:

- `Abort()`
- `BeginGetRequestStream(AsyncCallback, Object)`
- `BeginGetResponse(AsyncCallback, Object)`
- `Create(string)`
- `Create(Uri)`
- `CreateDefault(Uri)`
- `CreateHttp(string)`
- `EndGetRequestStream(IAsyncResult)`

- `EndGetResponse(IAsyncResult)`
- `GetObjectData(SerializationInfo, StreamingContext)`
- `GetRequestStream()`
- `GetRequestStreamAsync()`
- `GetResponse()`
- `GetResponseAsync()`
- `GetSystemWebProxy()`
- `RegisterPrefix(string, IWebRequestCreate)`

I only included the methods specific to the `WebRequest` class, and left out the public methods inherited from parent classes, such as `MarshalByRefObject` and `Object`, since those aren't relevant to our purpose. However, with this basic list of operations, the utility of the class should be pretty obvious.

The first thing that likely stands out is that the class should be used asynchronously. All of the `Begin` and `End` methods, as well as the `Async` suffix on a number of other methods, tell you that the class supports fine-grained control of the lifetime of your requests through the asynchronous features of .NET Core. Now, if you've never done async programming (as I often find to be the case with newer programmers just starting out of school, or programmers new to web development) we'll be covering that mental leap in much greater detail in the next chapter. It's not always intuitively obvious how best to leverage the features of async, or what's going on behind the scenes; so, for now, just think of it as deferring the actual execution of the method until later. Just like all those methods suggest, you `Begin` doing a task, and whenever you're ready to, you `End` it and look at your result.

The methods in this class can be broken up into two conceptual groups. There are methods for state management and methods for request execution. The state management methods allow you to modify or further define the state of your instance of the `WebRequest` utility class. Leveraging them to further configure and define the behavior of your instance is similar to setting any of the public properties on the class as we did in the last section on *Class properties*. The reason there are methods to do this, instead of simply having more settable properties, is because doing so involves at least some non-trivial logic or circumstance-specific details that are applied with each invocation of the methods. Meanwhile, the request execution functions allow you to define, invoke, and resolve web requests using the behavior of your instance. They're the workhorse methods that make all of the earlier configuration worthwhile. So, let's take a look at each of these sets of methods in turn and fully crystalize our understanding of this class.

State management methods

I'd encourage you to try to sort the methods I've listed into the two categories I'm about to describe for you. And in the future, I'd encourage you to try to categorize interfaces and public class definitions in this way. Doing so will improve your ability to read and internalize new software features quickly, and leverage them efficiently, instead of copying code snippets from `StackOverflow.com` until you find something that works. That said, let's take a look at the state management functions.

First, we have the `Create` methods. Each of these methods will return a usable instance of a concrete `WebRequest` sub-class. They're all static, and so can be invoked from the class definition without first needing to create an instance of it (for obvious reasons; why would you need to create an instance of a class to then create an instance of a class?). Depending on the specific method used, this sets up an instance of the default sub-class for the given scheme specified in the URI supplied to the method. So, if we wanted instances of `WebRequest` for accessing data from a RESTful HTTP service, collecting files from a designated FTP server, and reading data from a remote file system, we could do all of this with a simple call to `Create(uriString)`:

```
var httpRequest = WebRequest.Create("http://test-domain.com");
var ftpRequest = WebRequest.Create("ftp://ftp.test-domain.com");
var fileRequest = WebRequest.Create("file://files.test-domain.com");
```

You may recognize this code from the `SubmitRealEstateRequest` sample method we wrote in the *Class properties* section. I didn't explain it until now, but because the class is so clearly and simply defined, I expect you were able to infer its use just fine from my code without this explanation. But in case you were wondering why it seemed like I was creating an instance of an abstract class (a compile-time error in C#), that's why. I was actually requesting an instance of an appropriate sub-class from the abstract base-classes, static definition.

Those three use cases in the preceding code block cover just about everything you can do with `Create()` out of the box, but that certainly doesn't mean those are the only use cases `Create()` can apply to. The functionality uses common protocol prefixes for URIs to determine default sub-classes to instantiate. So, simply passing `http://test-domain.com` to the method is all the default implementation needs to then return an instance of the `HttpWebRequest` class. The same logic that allows the `Uri` class to parse the preceding string is used to tell `WebRequest` which protocol it should be creating a sub-class for.

As I said, though, the default behavior is only defined for a limited set of use cases out of the box. There are four specific protocols whose concrete sub-classes are preregistered with the `WebRequest` class at runtime; they are as follows:

- `http://`
- `https://`
- `ftp://`
- `file://`

So, any URI string given to the `Create` method with any of these four prefixes as the first characters in the string will be reliably handled by the `WebRequest` base class. And since the base class provides a sufficient interface for executing the core operations of its sub-classes, you don't even have to know specifically what sub-class was returned. Thanks to type inheritance, you can just declare your instance as being of type `WebRequest`, and use it accordingly, just like I did in the sample method from earlier.

But what if you don't want to work with one of these four preregistered types? What if you wrote your own custom `WebRequest` sub-class specifically for working with a **WebSocket** (**WS**) protocol, and you'd like to get the same support from `WebRequest` just by passing in a URI with the WebSocket prefix of `ws://`? Well, that exact use case leads us to another state management method: `RegisterPrefix(string, IWebRequestCreate)`.

`RegisterPrefix` is a powerful new tool that supports what's known as **pluggable protocols**. It's basically a way for you to incorporate custom implementations and sub-classes of the `WebRequest` and `WebResponse` base classes into the runtime of your application. When done properly, your custom code can be treated as a first-class citizen in the `System.Net` namespace, being appropriately delegated to by system types and methods, and having full access to the network stack, just like the native library classes you'll be learning about next.

The scope and depth of fully implementing a custom protocol handler are beyond this chapter, and will be explored in more detail later in this book. For now though, just know that once the work of writing a custom protocol handler is completed, wiring it in is as simple as calling `RegisterPrefix`. That's why this falls under the domain of state management methods; because it's about configuring the working conditions of `WebRequest` for the duration of your application's runtime.

The method returns a `bool` to indicate the success or failure of your attempt to register your custom protocol, and throw or process exceptions accordingly. So, while the process of setting up a pluggable protocol is outside the scope of this chapter, for now just trust that, once the work is done, configuring it as part of the valid state of the `WebRequest` class is a straightforward affair:

```
if(!WebRequest.RegisterPrefix("cpf://", new CustomRequestCreator())) {
    throw new WebException("Failure to register custom prefix protocol
handler.");
}
```

And with that, we have every tool we need to properly configure and initialize network requests. State management is complete, and all that's left is to begin submitting requests and processing responses.

Request execution methods

As I said before, most of these methods are designed to be leveraged asynchronously, but at least a few of them have synchronous, or blocking, counterparts. While we'll talk more about async programming later, what's important now is to note that there are two primary operations or tasks around which the `WebRequest` class is focused. The first is accessing the actual request data stream, and the second is accessing the response returned by the remote resource.

With a `WebRequest` instance, the `RequestStream` is .NET's representation of the open connection. Think of it as the wire over which you can transmit your signal. Anytime you want to pass data through a `WebRequest` instance, you'll first need to access that wire. Once you have it, you can start passing data through that stream, and trust that the `WebRequest` class is going to broker its transmission accordingly.

Bear in mind that writing to a stream typically requires the raw byte array for a given object (this is where serialization comes into play), so once we have our stream, writing to it isn't as simple as passing our objects or messages directly over the wire, although it's not prohibitively complicated either. In practice, however you choose to access the request stream for an active instance of `WebRequest`, writing to it will typically look similar to the following code block:

```
using System.Text;
...
// convert message to bytes
string message = "My request message";
byte[] messageBytes = Encoding.UTF8.GetBytes(message);
```

```
//write bytes to stream
Stream reqStream = req.GetRequestStream();
reqStream.Write(messageBytes, 0, messageBytes.length);
```

And that's all there is to it. There are some nuances with this method in some of the common sub-classes of `WebRequest`, but the basic principle will always apply.

That, right there, accounts for about half of the request execution methods. The `BeginGetRequestStream()/EndGetRequestStream()`, `GetRequestStream()`, and `GetRequestStreamAsync()` methods are three different ways of accessing the same logical component of your network transaction. They simply provide varying degrees of control over the synchronization of the operation. For example, the `BeginGetRequestStream()/EndGetRequestStream()` method provides an opportunity for the user to cancel the request before it has completed transmission by explicitly calling the `Abort()` method. Meanwhile, the `GetRequestStreamAsync()` method doesn't provide the opportunity to explicitly abort the operation, but it does perform the operation asynchronously. Circumstances will dictate what method or methods you should be using, but if handled correctly and resolved properly by the underlying connection, the result object is the same.

Finally, we can look at the response processing methods, and it should be no surprise to you that in the request/response pattern that is typical of most network transactions, the response handlers match, almost exactly, with the request handler method signatures. So, where the act of retrieving a request stream from the `WebRequest` instance was exposed through four different methods with various levels of granular control over the synchronization of the operations, so too is response processing. The methods we have available to us are `BeginGetResponse()/EndGetResponse()` (the processing for which cannot be interrupted by `Abort()`, however), `GetResponseAsync()`, and of course, `GetResponse()`.

Understanding the shape of a given response will depend on the specific protocol over which it was received. Just as the `WebRequest` class has protocol-specific sub-classes, so too does the `WebResponse` base class. We'll explore each of them in their respective chapters, and look at how their responses can be handled more concretely. But for now, it is sufficient to say that the `WebResponse` class provides us with a reliable enough interface to meaningfully interact with whatever we get back from our request.

So, by now, you should have an extremely clear understanding of exactly what problem the `WebRequest` class was written to solve. You should understand its scope and the limits of its use cases, and hopefully, you will know exactly how to tune it so that you can fully leverage it for any scenario in which it could save you time and effort. With this understanding in mind, let's take a look at some of the most common ways the base class is explicitly leveraged through some of the sub-classes provided as part of the .NET Standard.

The sub-classes of the WebRequest class

For a lot of typical use cases, you can rely on the basic functionality provided by the underlying `WebRequest` class. However, you'll never actually be using instances of it directly in your code (you can't... it's abstract, remember?), so now is the time to look at what other functionality or features exist when you're using common concrete instances of it. We'll look at each of the sub-classes for which `WebRequest` has a default, preregistered handler.

A note on obsolete sub-classes

Here, it's important to note that the `WebRequest` class is primarily a tool for creating lower-level, protocol agnostic request/response transactions with other resources on your network. The .NET Standard provided sub-classes that, while not explicitly deprecated, have been made mostly obsolete by slightly more robust client classes, such as the `HttpClient` or `WebClient` classes.

As a matter of fact, Microsoft recently released a recommendation for always using the newer client classes over any of the slightly older sub-classes that I'm about to discuss. That's precisely why so little of this chapter is dedicated to the concrete classes. The important aspects of the request/response model are still handled by .NET's `WebRequest` and `WebResponse` classes under the hood of the new `WebClient` class. More importantly, those base classes are the most basic building blocks from which you can build your own custom protocol handlers. That's why it's so important to understand, especially for readers new to any sort of web or network programming, how and why the `WebRequest` class is written the way it is. However, as is often the case with software, times are changing, and so the extent that this lesson will remain useful as a practical guide for specific implementation of common patterns will only diminish with time.

That being said, it is worth examining what is different about those classes and how they can be used to build up a network request from scratch, so let's take a brief look.

HttpWebRequest

The `HttpWebRequest` class is interesting in that until very recently, it was the workhorse class of network programming in .NET. This is evident in the huge explosion of the class specification when compared to the relative simplicity of the `WebRequest` class. There are properties for each standard HTTP header that could be defined for a given payload, as well as a headers property inherited from the base class for specifying custom or non-standard headers. There are properties to specify the transport details, such as the `TransferEncoding`, or whether or not to send data in chunked segments. There are properties to specify how to handle exceptional behaviors from the remote host, such as the `MaximumResponseHeadersLength` and `MaximumAutomaticRedirections` properties. All of these properties allowed you to build a complete and strong payload for an HTTP request from scratch. As you can imagine, though, it was often tedious, error-prone, and verbose to do this for every request to every HTTP resource. Often, developers would hand-roll custom HTTP client classes of their own to isolate that aspect of their application in a write once, use everywhere approach. This degree of granularity is why the engineers at Microsoft decided to write a more robust and easy-to-use client for brokering common HTTP requests.

It is interesting to note, however, that if you look at class specifications side by side, the method signatures exposed by `HttpWebRequest` are exactly the same as those exposed by `WebRequest`. The only meaningful distinction between the two is the context-specific configurations that `HttpWebRequest` provides as class properties. This further highlights the elegance of the design of `WebRequest`. By taking a straightforward, generic approach to the problem, it can serve all possible specific use cases using the same patterns.

FtpWebRequest

The `FtpWebRequest` class provides many of the same properties as the `HttpWebRequest` class. The distinction comes in the form of a few specific properties for configuring reliable behavior when processing potentially large files over a potentially unreliable or slow connection. To that end, it provides the `ReadWriteTimeout` property that specifies the maximum amount of time allowed for processing the file stream. There's also the FTP-specific `UsePassive` property that allows a user to specify the use of the passive transfer process, leaving an open listening connection on the server for clients to access files accordingly.

There's also the explicit `EnableSsl` parameter, which you might have noticed was not a property of `HttpWebRequest`. Interestingly, this is necessary for the `FtpWebRequest` class but not the `HttpWebRequest` class because the use of **Secure Sockets Layer** (**SSL**) in HTTP is actually specified in the protocol component of the URI (that is, HTTP versus HTTPS); whereas with FTP, that feature must be enabled explicitly.

Once again, the actual use of the `FtpWebRequest` class is exactly the same as with the `WebRequest` base class. Once the protocol-specific settings are properly configured through the class properties, FTP is ultimately just another request/response protocol for accessing remote resources.

FileWebRequest

The `FileWebRequest` is probably the least commonly used sub-class of them all. Its signature almost perfectly matches that of the `WebRequest` base class. Its purpose is to expose the same reliable request/response pattern for accessing resources on the local file system.

At this point, you may be wondering why on earth such a class would ever be useful. Well, like any good engineer, we'll eventually want to be able to do a unit and integration test on our network software. However, that won't always be feasible, since remote resources that we can expect to be available to our production environment might not always be available to our development environment. In that case, you'd want to be able to access your mock resources on your local system. Thanks to the shared parent class of the `WebRequest` class, it's a trivial matter to swap out an instance of `FileWebRequest` and `HttpWebRequest` in your development and production environments, respectively. Since each of these sub-classes is only ever instantiated through the `Create()` method on the `WebRequest` class, doing so is as easy as changing the URI of the remote resource stored in your application's configuration files.

The power of the `FileWebRequest` class comes from the consistency of its interface. So, while there are no special properties or methods associated with this instance of the class, extending the behavior of `WebRequest` to local file access is really what makes this class valuable.

And with that, our crash-course on the building blocks of network interactions is complete.

Summary

In this chapter, we took a thorough look at the `WebRequest` utility class, and how it can be used to handle a wide variety of common network operations within the context of a .NET application. We used the public interface of the class definition to infer the proper use and use cases for the class, as well as identifying the limits of its scope and operations. We considered the proper use and invocation of each of the public properties and methods defined on the base class, and wrote out some broadly applicable examples to demonstrate the simplicity and utility of the class and its children. Then, we considered the three most common concrete sub-classes of `WebRequest`. We examined some of the nuances between each of them and looked at how they facilitate the specific details of the protocols they were designed to operate over. Now we're ready to look at how to process the results of those requests in the most optimal way for the .NET runtime. It's time we looked at data stream processing, multi-threading, and asynchronous programming, which we'll explore in the next chapter.

Questions

1. What are the valid values for the `CachePolicy` property of the `WebRequest` class, and where can they be found?
2. What is the method used to associate the custom sub-classes of the `WebRequest` class with requests to the associated protocol for that custom sub-class?
3. What property is used to associate multiple requests to the same connection in the .NET connection pool?
4. What are the four preregistered protocols for which the `WebRequest` class is configured to return a valid sub-class from the `Create(uri)` method?
5. What is the difference between `BeginGetRequestStream()`, `GetRequestStreamAsync()`, and `GetRequestStream()`?
6. Name some of the ways the `HttpWebRequest` class differs from the default behavior of the `WebRequest` class?
7. Why is it important to always leverage `ConnectionGroupName` whenever possible?

Further reading

For additional reading on this subject, or to expand your horizons once you've conquered the realm of network programming, check out *Building Microservices with .NET Core, Gaurav Aroraa, Lalit Kale, and Kanwar Manish,* available through Packt Publishing at `https://www.packtpub.com/web-development/building-microservices-net-core`.

Additionally, I'd recommend checking out *C# 7 and .NET: Designing Modern Cross-platform Applications, Mark J. Price and Ovais Mehboob Ahmed Khan, Packt Publishing,* for some solid advice for practical applications of the concepts discussed here. You can find this book at `https://www.packtpub.com/application-development/learning-path-c-7-and-net-designing-modern-cross-platform-applications`.

6
Streams, Threads, and Asynchronous Data

With the resources available to us to start working with sending network requests, we need to look at how we can best incorporate those requests into our applications. We'll need to work with those resources in a way that won't impact the performance of our application's business logic or our user's experience. So, in this chapter, we'll look at how we can process data streams in such a way as to be resilient and non-blocking to the rest of our application's performance.

The following topics will be covered in this chapter:

- Understanding the nature of I/O streams in C#, and how to write to, read from, and manage open streams
- How different I/O streams expose access to different types of data, and how the parent `Stream` class simplifies the use of those distinct stream types
- The potential performance cost of processing large, or poorly performing data streams and how to mitigate that cost
- Leveraging C#'s asynchronous programming feature set to maximize the performance and reliability of your software

Technical requirements

This chapter will have a number of samples and driver programs to demonstrate the concepts discussed, all of which are available at `https://github.com/PacktPublishing/Hands-On-Network-Programming-with-CSharp-and-.NET-Core/tree/master/Chapter 6`.

As always, you're encouraged to clone this repository locally and begin playing with the source code, or writing your own in order to get comfortable with some of the topics in this chapter.

Check out the following video to see the code in action: `http://bit.ly/2HYmhf7`

Going with the flow – data streams in C#

We looked briefly at accessing data streams in the last chapter when we talked about the request stream property of the `WebRequest` class. I glossed over that subject then, but now we should really understand how our data is prepared for transmission as a request payload. We'll look at the common interface for data streams in C#, and give special consideration for some of the trickier or less obvious aspects of streams that can introduce some difficult-to-find bugs into your code. So, let's start with the `Stream` class and go from there.

Initializing a data stream

Just like with network requests, writing to and reading from data streams is a common and straightforward task in software engineering. So much so, in fact, that Microsoft provided an extremely well-designed common specification for doing this in C#. The methods defined by the base class are the same ones you'll use for any kind of data transmission that you would reasonably have to execute, so with that as our starting point, let's take a look at what the class provides.

The objective of the `Stream` class is, quite simply, to provide direct access to an ordered sequence of bytes. There is no additional context around this information, so the sequence of bytes could be anything from a file on your local disk storage, to the bytes of a packet from an incoming request stream, or to an open communication pipe between two co-located application processes and existing entirely in memory.

What this simple definition provides is an easy way to define generic environment and context-agnostic methods for working with the ordered list of zeros and ones. What it doesn't provide, however, is any useful way to parse, process, and convert those bytes to and from meaningful in-memory objects that make sense to the rest of your application. As a programming task, this can be a bit tedious, but thankfully, some of the specific implementations provide some reliable utility methods for more common parsing situations. This is especially nice because that's where most of the work of streams lie.

Once you've got your information ready to pass over a binary data stream, or ingest bytes from a data stream, there are only three primary operations that you'll care about. The first two are obvious: reading and writing, collecting bytes, in order, from the data stream, or pushing your own bytes onto it. The third is less obvious but just as important. Because the data stream is an ordered array of arbitrary bytes, reading from and writing to it are unidirectional operations. They are always processed in order. However, we don't always need or want the information from a data stream in order, so the ability to seek out a specific index in the stream is key, and will be the primary mechanism for traversing your data stream out of order.

So, with that in mind, let's take a look at it in action. First, create a basic application to take advantage of a data stream. To do so, you can use the .NET Core CLI, and create a new console app, as shown in the following screenshot:

```
Administrator: Command Prompt
C:\Users\shurns\Desktop\streams_and_async>dotnet new console
The template "Console Application" was created successfully.

Processing post-creation actions...
Running 'dotnet restore' on C:\Users\shurns\Desktop\streams_and_async\streams_and_async.csproj...
  Restoring packages for C:\Users\shurns\Desktop\streams_and_async\streams_and_async.csproj...
  Generating MSBuild file C:\Users\shurns\Desktop\streams_and_async\obj\streams_and_async.csproj.nuget.g.props.
  Generating MSBuild file C:\Users\shurns\Desktop\streams_and_async\obj\streams_and_async.csproj.nuget.g.targets.
  Restore completed in 109.99 ms for C:\Users\shurns\Desktop\streams_and_async\streams_and_async.csproj.

Restore succeeded.


C:\Users\shurns\Desktop\streams_and_async>dir
 Volume in drive C has no label.
 Volume Serial Number is 68EA-D78F

 Directory of C:\Users\shurns\Desktop\streams_and_async

01/01/2019  10:32 PM    <DIR>          .
01/01/2019  10:32 PM    <DIR>          ..
01/01/2019  10:32 PM    <DIR>          obj
01/01/2019  10:32 PM               199 Program.cs
01/01/2019  10:32 PM               178 streams_and_async.csproj
               2 File(s)            377 bytes
               3 Dir(s)  340,495,458,304 bytes free

C:\Users\shurns\Desktop\streams_and_async>
```

Similarly to how we created our sample project in `Chapter 2`, *DNS and Resource Location,* in the, *The DNS in C#* section, we used the `dotnet new` command to stand up a basic console application as our test bed. This time the difference is that we'll specifically create a new console app with the `dotnet new console` command. I'll keep making a note of this as we work with new projects to highlight the speed and value of the .NET Core CLI; its speed and utility really cannot be overstated.

Now, we want to establish a stream to work with, so we'll start by adding a using directive to include the `System.IO` namespace since I/O streams live in the I/O namespace. Then, for the sake of demonstration, we'll read from the file, and write to a file on disk with `FileStream`. We'll declare our variable to be of type `Stream`, so that the compiler's type checking doesn't allow us to use the `FileStream` specific methods or properties. The point is to understand how to use the abstraction that's provided by the `Stream` class. It doesn't actually matter what we're reading from; by the time it gets to our application code, it's all just incoming bytes, anyway. Using the local filesystem just gives us more direct access to the results of our actions without having to go through the process of setting up a local API and posting data to it.

To the extent that you can, it's usually wise to use as generic a type as possible when declaring your variables. This allows you a lot more flexibility if you need to change your implementation strategy down the line. What might be a locally stored filesystem access today could become a remote API call tomorrow. If your code is only concerned with the generic concept of a `Stream` class, it's a lot easier to change it later for different sources later.

To write this demo, the first thing you'll want to understand is that a Stream is an active connection to a data source. That means it needs to be opened before it can be used, and it should be closed, and then disposed of before you're done with it. Failing to do so can result in memory leaks, thread starvation, and other performance or reliability issues with your code. Thankfully, .NET Core provides a built-in pattern for each of these life cycle tasks. The constructors for most `Stream` classes will return an already-opened instance of the class you're creating, so you can start reading from and writing to your streams right away. As for guaranteeing the disposal of your streams, we have the eternally useful `using` statement.

If you haven't seen it before, a `using` statement is different from the `using` directives at the top of your file that allows you to reference classes and data structures outside of your current namespace. In the context of a method, in C#, the `using` statement is used to instantiate a disposable class (which is to say, any class that implements the `IDisposable` interface), and define the scope within which the instance should be kept alive. The syntax for using this is as follows:

```
using (variable assignment to disposable instance) {
    scope in which the disposable instance is alive.
}
```

We'll see this in action momentarily. But just like declaring variables within the scope of a `for` loop or an `if` statement, the variable you create inside the signature of the `using` statement ceases to exist outside of the scope of the open and close curly brackets of the code block.

Alternatively, with C# 8, you can avoid the deep nesting created by the `using` statement by choosing instead to leverage the `using` declaration. This functions the exact same as the `using` statement, but it declares the variable to the scope of the encapsulating method instead of establishing an inner-scope for the lifetime of the instance. So, instead of defining the scope with the `using` statement and its opening and closing curly braces, you would simply create your variable and declare it with the `using` keyword, as seen here:

```
using var fileStream = new FileStream(someFileName);
```

The only major distinction between the two is the scope to which the instance is bound. With a `using` statement, the scope of the instance is defined by the curly braces of the statement block. Meanwhile, with the `using` declaration, the scope is defined by the code block in which the disposable instance was declared. In most cases, the `using` declaration should be sufficient, and will help reduce deep nesting within your methods. However, you should always take care to consider how the disposable instance will be used and bind it to the appropriate scope for its use case.

Once the flow of program control exits the scope to which your instance is bound, the .NET runtime will take all the necessary steps to call the `Dispose()` method, which is responsible for ensuring that the state of the object is valid for disposal. In doing so, the `using` statement implicitly assumes the responsibility of cleaning up any unmanaged resources and any connection pools set up for the object it created. This well-defined scope means that anytime you step out of the scope of the `using` directive, you lose your resource handle and will have to instantiate a new one.

This well-defined scope means that any time you close your `using` statement, you lose your resource handle. This means that accessing the resource later will require you to create a new handle for it and then dispose of it accordingly. This can incur a performance cost over the lifetime of the application, and so you should take care to dispose of a resource handle when you are certain you no longer need it.

Interestingly, while the object declared within the scope of the `using` statement will always be properly disposed of, the `using` statement does not guarantee the disposal of any disposable instances that the object creates. The assumption is that if any `A` class creates an instance of a disposable `B` class as a member of itself, the owning instance of the `A` class should also be responsible for cleaning up the member instance of the `B` class whenever the owning instance of the `A` class is, itself, disposed of. The rule is, if you create it, you dispose of it.

Now that we know how to create an instance of `Stream`, let's get our hands dirty and start working with one.

Writing to and reading from a data stream

Now that we know how the life cycle of the `Stream` class is managed, let's use it to write a message to a local file. First, we'll write a string to the stream, and then inspect the destination of the stream to confirm that it was written properly:

```
using System;
using System.Text;
using System.IO;
using System.Threading;

namespace StreamsAndAsync {
  public class Program {
    static void Main(string[] args) {
      string testMessage = "Testing writing some arbitrary string to a
stream";
```

```
        byte[] messageBytes = Encoding.UTF8.GetBytes(testMessage);
        using (Stream ioStream = new FileStream(@"stream_demo_file.txt",
FileMode.OpenOrCreate)) {
          if (ioStream.CanWrite) {
            ioStream.Write(messageBytes, 0, messageBytes.Length);
          } else {
            Console.WriteLine("Couldn't write to our data stream.");
          }
        }
        Console.WriteLine("Done!");
        Thread.Sleep(10000);
    }
  }
}
```

Just like in `Chapter 5`, *Generating Web Requests in C#,* we couldn't write our string directly to the stream. It's not the job of a stream of bytes to figure out how more complicated objects should be represented as bytes. It's just the road over which they travel. So, we're responsible for first getting the byte representation of the string that we want to send. For this, we use the `System.Text.Encoding` class to get the byte representation for the specific string encoding that we want to use.

Once we have this, we can write it to the stream. Or, at least, we assume we can. It's always wise to check first, though. That's why the `Write` operation is wrapped in the conditional block that checks the `CanWrite` property of our stream. This is a wonderful convenience provided by the `Stream` class that allows you to confirm a valid state in your stream for the operation you're about to perform before you try to perform it. This puts error handling and correction in our control without having to use clunky `try/catch` blocks around everything.

So, we declared our `Stream` object in our `using` block and initialized it to open or create a file called `stream_demo_file.txt` in the root of the application executable's directory. Then, once we checked on it, we passed it our byte array and instructed the stream to write that array to its destination resource. But what were those two additional parameters in the `Write` method? Well, in the same way that a stream wouldn't reasonably have any knowledge of what is passing over it, it doesn't know what bytes should be read from the byte array when. It needs the array of bytes, then instructions on where to start reading from, and precisely how many of those bytes it should write. The second parameter in the `Write` method signature is your starting index. It starts at zero, just like the array does. The third parameter is the total number of bytes you want to send in this `Write` operation. There is a runtime error checking on this and if you try to send more bytes than there are left in the array (starting from whatever index you designate), you'll get an index out-of-bounds error.

So, if you navigate to the folder from which the application was run, you should find a new text file. Opening it, you should discover our message; it's as easy as that. But what happens if we run the file again? Will the message be concatenated to the first message that we wrote? Will it overwrite the existing message?

The seek operation

Run your application again, and then reload the file in a text editor. Whatever you were expecting to happen, you should see no change to the file. However, assuming your application ran successfully, and you saw the **Done!** message on your console for 10 seconds instead of our error message, you should have confidence that the write operation was executed a second time. So, this should tell you that the operation was successful and it did, in fact, overwrite the value of the original message. It might not be initially obvious, because we used the same message the second time around, but if you want to confirm this behavior, just change the `testMessage` variable in your program to read *Testing writing a different string to a stream* and run it again. You should see the new message and, hopefully, it's a little more obvious what's happening.

Every time we open a stream connected to a data source, we're getting the complete ordered list of bytes stored at that source, along with a pointer to the start of that array. Every operation we execute on the stream moves our pointer in one direction. If we write 10 bytes, we find ourselves 10 positions further down the array than when we started. The same happens if we read 10 bytes. So, each of our primary operators can only ever move in one direction from whatever point along the stream we happen to be at when we start executing them. How, then, do we set those operations up to read or write what we want, where we want? The answer is, with the `Seek()` method.

The `Seek` method gives us arbitrary access to any index in our byte array through the specification of a few simple parameters. Simply specify where you want to start relative to a designated starting position, and then designate the starting position with one of the three values of the `SeekOrigin` enum.

So, if I wanted to start on the last byte of the current array, and append my current message onto the end of my last message, that would look like the following code block:

```
using (Stream ioStream = new FileStream(@"../stream_demo_file.txt",
FileMode.OpenOrCreate)) {
  if (ioStream.CanWrite) {
    ioStream.Seek(0, SeekOrigin.End);
    ioStream.Write(messageBytes, 0, messageBytes.Length);
  } else {
    Console.WriteLine("Couldn't write to our data stream.");
```

```
    }
}
```

Modify your using statement accordingly, and run the program again. Looking into your output file, you should see the following message:

```
Testing writing a different string to a streamTesting writing a different
string to a stream
```

We started with our original byte array, navigated to the end of the stream of written bytes, and then wrote our message from there; easy as that.

This might seem like a trivial thing, but imagine that you're unpacking a message payload whose data is of a variable size. Typically, you'd have a series of headers or a map of your byte array designating the starting index and the total length of the different components of the payload. Using only those two pieces of information, you can navigate directly to the relevant components of the message and read only and exactly as much as you need to. Reducing this kind of data manipulation in the way that the Stream class does is incredibly powerful in its simplicity.

But maybe you don't want to write your data to a request stream. Maybe you've written the server code to read from requests and respond to them accordingly. Let's take a brief moment to look at how that's done.

Reading from streams

As I said, reading is a one-way operation. Whatever your current index, you will always read from the stream one byte at a time, and in doing so, move your cursor forward by one in the index. So, your next Read operation always starts one byte after wherever you last read. The trick here is that every time you want to read anything more than a single byte (which you can simply assign to a variable of the byte type), you have to read it into a destination array. So, you'll need to declare and assign a target destination array before you can read it. Let's see this in action; first, though, remove the Seek operation so that every time you run your app, you don't grow your text file:

```
using (Stream ioStream = new FileStream(@"../stream_demo_file.txt",
FileMode.OpenOrCreate)) {
  if (ioStream.CanWrite) {
    ioStream.Write(messageBytes, 0, messageBytes.Length);
  } else {
    Console.WriteLine("Couldn't write to our data stream.");
  }

  if (ioStream.CanRead) {
```

```
        byte[] destArray = new byte[10];
        ioStream.Read(destArray, 0, 10);
        string result = Encoding.UTF8.GetString(destArray);
        Console.WriteLine(result);
      }
    }
```

So, like we did before, we check whether it's even valid to try to read from our stream. Then, we designate a new byte array into which we'll be reading our bytes, and then `Read`, starting at index zero, and reading for 10 bytes.

I'm sure at this point you're seeing a lot of the issues that this approach poses for developers. Even just the use of old-style square-bracket arrays instead of the more flexible and easy-to-work with List classes introduces a number of pain points for developers. In order to use an old-style array as the target of a `Read` operation, you must know the exact size of the array beforehand. This means that you'll either need to explicitly set a predetermined length for your array (and the subsequent `Read` operation), or you'll need to have an assigned variable from which you can determine the initial length of the array (since you can't initialize square-bracket arrays without specifying their length).

This is rigid and tedious to use. It makes your deserialization code brittle. The alternative is to designate a reasonable maximum length and use that value to initialize any byte arrays that will be read to from your data stream. Of course, this approach fixes your software to currently known limitations and makes it inflexible and difficult to extend in the future. All of these are challenges posed by the otherwise elegant simplicity of the `Stream` class definition. Thankfully, though, along with the power of the `Stream` class, comes the simplicity of a number of utility classes .NET Core provides out of the box.

The right stream for the job

Working with the lowest-level data streams representing your network connections does give you a lot of power and control over exactly how incoming messages are parsed and handled. When performance or security is an issue, that byte-level control is invaluable in providing a skilled developer the tools they need to produce the most optimal solution for the task at hand.

However, most of us won't be writing network code with such high demands for performance or security. In fact, most of the code we write will all follow the same series of simple and straightforward patterns of serialization and message generation. That's where the additional `Stream` classes really come in handy.

Stream readers and writers

While it is immeasurably useful to understand how to work directly with data streams and bend their use to your specific purposes when you need to, the simple fact is that most of the time, you won't need to. In fact, over my many years as a software engineer, I can count on two hands the total number of times I've needed to devise my own serialization strategies and implement them with lower-level classes for the sake of performance or security. In my professional career, it's much more common to use simpler, well-established serialization strategies that leverage the utility classes provided by the .NET core library.

On the modern web, the common language for communication is, irrefutably, **Javascript Object Notation (JSON)**. This simple specification for composing and parsing hierarchical data translates so elegantly to almost every data structure you could possibly devise in almost any language that, at this point, it is the transport format of choice for almost every API or web service being written today.

Like everything we've talked about so far, its power comes from its simplicity. It's a string representation of data with simple rules for delimiting and nesting different objects and their respective properties. And while the hierarchy of a JSON object is rigidly defined, the order of properties within that object is entirely arbitrary, giving users a high degree of flexibility and reliability.

With such a ubiquitous standard for serialization, it should come as no surprise that there are widely supported and easy-to-use tools for working with objects in JSON notation. Not only that, but since simple strings account for so much of what we read and write between data sources on a network, there are `System.IO` classes designed explicitly for working with them over streams.

Newtonsoft.Json

Let's familiarize ourselves with a non-Microsoft library that was so reliably popular it was ultimately adopted by Microsoft as the official library for parsing JSON in C# and .NET. The more you work with network transactions, the more you will come to appreciate the powerful simplicity of the `Newtonsoft.Json` library. There's not a whole lot to it, so let's take a moment now to take a peek under the hood, since we'll be relying on it quite a bit going forward.

It's important to know that while Newtonsoft.Json remains the library of choice for JSON parsing in C#, Microsoft has actually developed an alternative approach for .NET Core 3.0. The new library has been added as the System.Text.Json namespace. However, where Netwonsoft.Json is written for user-friendliness, providing a rich set of easy to leverage features, the focus of this new JSON library is on performance and fine-grained control over the serialization process. As a result, the feature set of the System.Text.Json library is severely limited when compared to Newtonsoft.Json. Since we're more concerned with the fundamental concepts behind JSON serialization than with performance, we'll be using Newtonsoft.Json as our library of choice throughout this book.

To get started with it, you'll need to include the library into your project. If you're using Visual Studio Code, it's as simple as entering the following command into the Terminal window of the editor:

```
dotnet add package Newtonsoft.Json
```

If you're using Visual Studio, you can simply right click on your project's **Dependencies** in your **Solution Explorer**, and select **Manage NuGet Packages**. From there, search for Newtonsoft.Json and install the package.

Once you have it available, we'll want an object with a little bit of complexity to it to really show off what Newtonsoft can do. So, let's add a model definition to our project by adding a new file named ComplexModels.cs and define a few classes inside:

```
using System;
using System.Collections.Generic;

namespace StreamsAndAsync {
    public class ComplexModel {
        public string ComplexModelId { get; set; } =
Guid.NewGuid().ToString();
        public int NumberDemonstration { get; set; } = 12354;
        public InnerModel smallInnerModel { get; set; }
        public List<InnerModel> listOfInnerModels { get; set; } = new
List<InnerModel>() {
            new InnerModel(),
            new InnerModel()
        };
    }

    public class InnerModel {
        public string randomId { get; set; } = Guid.NewGuid().ToString();
        public string nonRandomString { get; set; } = "I wrote this here.";
    }
}
```

Here, we have one type with properties that are instances of another type and lists of instances of another type. Notice that I'm using the inline property initialization feature that was added with C# 6. This allows us to ensure the initialization of each member of our class without having to define the default constructor to do so. So, just by adding up an instance of our `ComplexModel`, we will have one fully initialized.

Now, I'm sure you can imagine the pain of trying to traverse that nested structure on your own and then parsing it into a well-formed serialized string. And that's for an object that we got to define ourselves! Consider the added complexity of writing a generic serialization code for any object that you might need to travel over your own network stream classes. It would be a mess of recursion or reflection and a whole bunch of other tedious and time-consuming tasks that few developers enjoy doing.

Thankfully, we often won't have to. If we wanted to take an instance of the class we just defined and write it to our data stream, it's as simple as a single line of code to generate the output string. Let's re-work our sample program to start with an instance of our new `ComplexModel` class, and then use `Newtonsoft.Json` to serialize it into something more stream-friendly:

```
using System;
using System.Text;
using System.IO;
using System.Threading;
using Newtonsoft.Json;

namespace StreamsAndAsync
{
    public class Program
    {
        static void Main(string[] args)
        {
            ComplexModel testModel = new ComplexModel();
            string testMessage = JsonConvert.SerializeObject(testModel);
            byte[] messageBytes = Encoding.UTF8.GetBytes(testMessage);

            using (Stream ioStream = new
FileStream(@"../stream_demo_file.txt", FileMode.OpenOrCreate)) {
                if (ioStream.CanWrite) {
                    ioStream.Write(messageBytes, 0, messageBytes.Length);
                } else {
                    Console.WriteLine("Couldn't write to our data
stream.");
                }
            }

            Console.WriteLine("Done!");
```

```
                Thread.Sleep(10000);
            }
        }
    }
```

In that simple declaration in the second line of our method, we convert our model into a complete string representation fit for serialized transport. Run the program and then inspect your destination file once again. You should find yourself with a nest of double-quote-delimited property names and their values, and curly and square braces galore. Going the other direction is as simple as passing in your JSON string to the `Deserialize<T>()` method, as follows:

```
ComplexModel model = JsonConvert.Deserialize<ComplexModel>(testMessage);
```

And just like that, you can cleanly and reliably serialize and deserialize your data into a well-understood and widely-used format for network messaging.

The specification of the JSON notation isn't outside the scope of this book, but it should look pretty familiar to you if you have any experience programming JavaScript. Otherwise, I'd recommend checking out the MDN article on the subject here: `https://developer.mozilla.org/en-US/docs/Web/JavaScript/Reference/Global_Objects/JSON`.

And if you ever need help organizing a JSON string into something a little more well-structured, you can paste it into `http://jsonlint.com` to validate that the structure is well-formed, and get a prettified version of the string.

The StreamReader and StreamWriter classes

So, if we can easily and efficiently serialize almost any object we can conceive of to a string, surely (you must be thinking) there is an easier way to write to and read from streams, directly with strings.

Of course, there is; you knew it when you started this section. Enter the ever-versatile `StreamReader` and `StreamWriter` classes. Each of these classes is explicitly designed to read/write strings specifically. In fact, they both sub-class the `TextReader` class from the `System.IO` namespace, and extend its functionality to interface directly with byte streams. They are tailor-made to work with strings, and each of them, combined with the simplicity of `Newtonsoft.Json`, can make short work of transporting even the most complex data structures over the wire. So, let's see how to use them for the purposes of our network streams.

First, we want to get our stream, just as before, with the `using` statement, as follows:

```
using (Stream s = new FileStream(@"../stream_demo_file.txt",
FileMode.OpenOrCreate)) {
```

However, before we do anything else, we also want to initialize our `StreamWriter` instance, providing our stream as its initialization parameter:

```
using (StreamWriter sw = new StreamWriter(s)) {
```

There are a number of constructors for `StreamReader/StreamWriter` that accept encoding specifications, byte order mark detection, and buffer size for buffered streams. However, for network programming, we'll always be using the constructors that accept a `Stream` as their first parameter. The constructors that accept strings only ever create `FileStream` instances pointing to a local file path. Even though we're using a `FileStream` here for demonstration purposes, for real network programming, we'll want to connect directly to a data stream to a remote resource. To do so, we'll have to initialize the stream (likely an instance of the `NetworkStream` class) first, and then provide that to our writer/reader instances.

Once the `StreamWriter` is initialized, writing is as simple as calling `Write(string)` or `WriteLine(string)`. Since the class assumes it will be working with strings, our example method is simplified as follows:

```
static void Main(string[] args) {
  ComplexModel testModel = new ComplexModel();
  string testMessage = JsonConvert.SerializeObject(testModel);

  using (Stream ioStream = new FileStream(@"../stream_demo_file.txt",
FileMode.OpenOrCreate)) {
    using (StreamWriter sw = new StreamWriter(ioStream)) {
      sw.Write(testMessage);
    }
  }

  Console.WriteLine("Done!");
  Thread.Sleep(10000);
}
```

And in only five lines of code, we're successfully serializing a complex, nested object instance, and writing it to our output stream.

When working with strings from remote resources, knowing the specific encoding with which to translate the incoming bytes is key. If a character is encoded as UTF32, and decoded using ASCII, the result wouldn't match the input, rendering your output string a garbled mess. If you ever find a message that you've parsed to be indecipherable, make sure you're using the right encoding.

Since these classes are designed to work exclusively with string content, they even provide useful extensions, such as a `WriteLine(string)` method that will terminate the string you've passed in with a line terminator character (in C#, this defaults to a carriage-return followed by a line feed, or `\r\n`, though you can override this value based on your environment). Meanwhile, the `ReadLine()` method will return characters from your current index up to and including the next line terminator in the buffer. This isn't terribly useful with a serialized object, since you don't want to read a line of a JSON string. However, if you're working with a plain-text response, it can make reading and writing that response a breeze.

Seek versus Peek

One caveat that may not be obvious, however, is the difference in changing your current index with a `StreamWriter` or `StreamReader` instance. With the `Stream` class and its sub-classes, we simply applied the `Seek` operation to move through our byte array by a given number of positions forward from a given starting point. However, when you're working with the writer/reader utility classes, you'll notice that you don't have that option. The wrapper classes can only move forward with their base operations using the current index on the stream. If you want to change that index, though, you can do so simply by accessing the underlying stream directly. It's exposed by the wrapper classes through the `BaseStream` property. So, if you want to change your position in the stream without performing the operations of the wrapper, you'd use the `BaseStream`'s `Seek` operation, as follows:

```
using (Stream ioStream = new FileStream(@"../stream_demo_file.txt",
FileMode.OpenOrCreate)) {
    using (StreamWriter sw = new StreamWriter(ioStream)) {
        sw.Write(testMessage);
        sw.BaseStream.Seek(10, SeekOrigin.Begin);
        sw.Write(testMessage);
    }
}
```

Modifying the `Stream` class that is underlying the wrapper class will directly change the position to which the wrapper class can write. After running this code, our output file should look like the following screenshot:

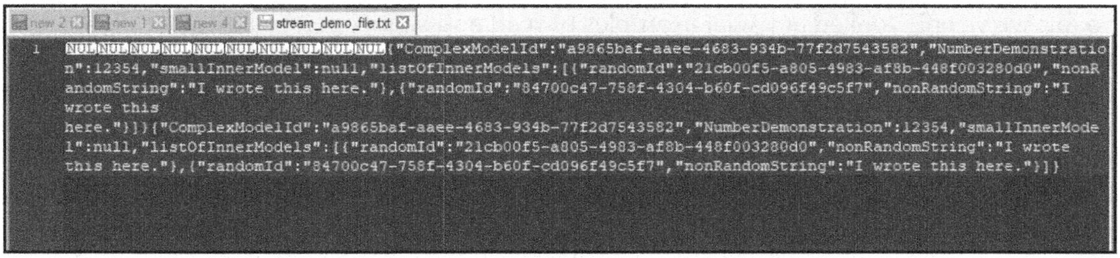

The first 10 characters of our output are `null` because the underlying `Stream` class had its write index shifted forward by 10 characters!

It's not uncommon to forward search through a string until arriving at a terminating character or flag value. Doing so with the `StreamReader.Read()` operation will result in moving the index past the terminating character and popping the terminating character off the array. If you want to simply read the last character before the terminating character, though, you have the `Peek()` operation. `Peek()` will return the next character in the array without advancing the current index of the `StreamReader`. This little tidbit can provide a fair bit of flexibility when you're determining when to stop reading a segment from a string whose length is indeterminable.

The NetworkStream class

While we're looking at the right streams for the right job, we should take a moment to look at the `NetworkStream` class. Operating much the same as the `FileStream` class that we've been using in our sample code thus far, its underlying data source is an instance of the `Socket` class connected to an external resource. Other than designating the underlying `Socket` connection for the stream to read from and write to, however, it functions almost entirely the same as the `FileStream` class. The various `Read`, `Write`, and `Seek` methods behave exactly as you've seen with our local file samples. And, just as importantly, an instance of `NetworkStream` can be used as `BaseStream` of an instance of the `StreamReader` and `StreamWriter` classes, so sending raw text messages over the wire is as easy as it is to write to a local text file. We'll use this class heavily when we start implementing our own socket connections in later chapters, but those will only build on the foundations that we've laid out in this chapter.

Picking up the pace – multithreading data processing

So far, we've only looked at trivial examples of read and write operations on our data streams, and we've only done so with the synchronous `Read()` and `Write()` methods. This hasn't been an issue for our 50 or 500 character-long messages and single-purpose test applications. However, it isn't hard to imagine scenarios where the data stream is large enough to take a considerable amount of time just to be read through from start to finish. Imagine requesting a file over FTP that is 200 MB large, or imagine requesting 2 million records from a database table hosted on a remote server. If the process that had to perform those operations was also responsible for responding to user behavior through a graphical interface, the long-running data processing task would render the GUI completely unresponsive. Such behavior would be absolutely unacceptable. To that end, .NET Core provides programmers with the concept of **threads**.

With threads, certain operations can be relegated to background tasks that are executed as soon as is feasible for the host process to do so, but won't block the operations of the main thread of your application. So, with this simple, powerful concept, we can assign our potentially long-running, or processor-intensive operations to a background thread, and mitigates the impact of that operation on the performance of the rest of our application. This performance improvement is the single biggest benefit of working with threads.

This aspect of .NET Core applications is accessed through the `System.Threading` namespace, which provides everything from `ThreadPool` classes to **semaphores** for protecting resources from concurrent access or mutation, to `Timer` classes and `WaitHandles` classes for more granular control over when and how your background threads are provisioned.

Because of the volatile nature of network connections and the unreliable availability of remote resources, any attempt to access data or services from a remote resource should be handled on a background thread. Fortunately, assigning those tasks to a background thread for parallel processing is actually fairly simple to do. All we have to do is start leveraging those asynchronous methods that we've been glossing over until now.

Asynchronous programming for asynchronous data sources

If you're not familiar with asynchronous programming then what we're about to talk about may seem a little confusing at first, but I promise that in practice, it's actually quite simple. All it means is performing individual computational tasks out of order, or out of sync. It allows engineers to defer blocking the execution of their program to wait for a long-running task until they absolutely have to. To make this clear, let's look at an example.

Let's imagine we have a method that must have step **A** send a request for a massive amount of data, with step **B** performing long-running calculations locally, and finally, **C** returns the two results as a single response. If we were to read the response from our network request synchronously, then the time it takes to complete our method would be the total of the time for each step, **A** + **B** + **C**. The processing time would look like the following diagram:

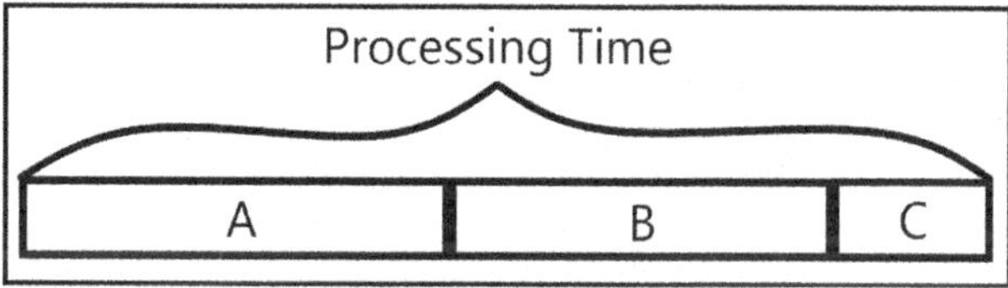

But if we run our web request asynchronously, we can let this run in a background task simultaneously with our long-running local process. In doing so, we reduce the processing time down to only the longer of the two tasks between **A** and **B**, plus **C**. Our processing time now looks like the following diagram:

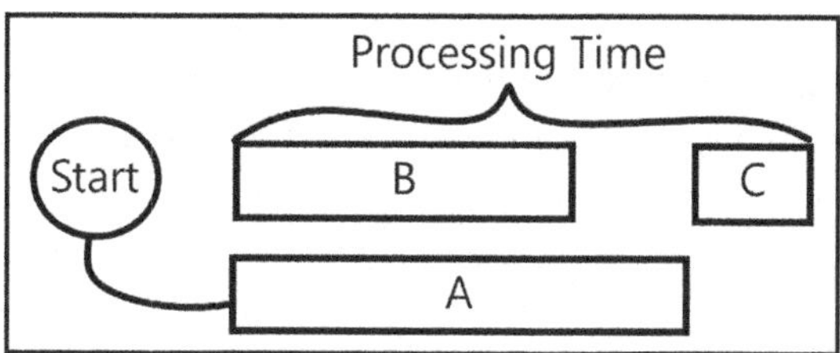

Since **C** is the only step that is dependent on **A** to complete processing, we can defer blocking our application code on the completion of **A** until we're ready to execute **C**. To see what that looks like in code, let's first say that we have a `ResultObject` class that holds the local and remote information that we want to return to our users. Next, let's assume that the long-running work being done in part **B** of this method is done in the private local method named (appropriately) `LongRunningSlowMethod()`. So, with those simple assumptions, let's look at an asynchronous method for processing long-running network requests, as follows:

```
public async Task<ResultObject> AsyncMethodDemo() {
  ResultObject result = new ResultObject();
  WebRequest request = WebRequest.Create("http://test-domain.com");
  request.Method = "POST";
  Stream reqStream = request.GetRequestStream();

  using (StreamWriter sw = new StreamWriter(reqStream)) {
    sw.Write("Our test data query");
  }
  var responseTask = request.GetResponseAsync();

  result.LocalResult = LongRunningSlowMethod();

  var webResponse = await responseTask;

  using (StreamReader sr = new
StreamReader(webResponse.GetResponseStream())) {
    result.RequestResult = await sr.ReadToEndAsync();
  }
  return result;
}
```

There's quite a lot going on here, but hopefully, now it's obvious why we approached these last couple chapters the way we did. Let's look at this a little at a time; first, notice the method signature, as follows:

```
public async Task<ResultObject> AsyncMethodDemo() {
```

Any method you write that takes advantage of asynchronous operations must be flagged with the `async` keyword in its signature. This tells users of the method that the operations in this method may take a while, and will run on background threads. And you might have noticed, the return type isn't simply `ResultObject`, even though our return value, `result`, is declared as such at the start of the method. This is because there are only three valid return types for an asynchronous method: `void`, `Task`, and `Task<T>`.

If your method returns a result, you must wrap that result's type in `Task<>` in your method signature. You do not, however, have to wrap the actual returned value in a `Task<>` object. This is done for you by the compiler when you have an asynchronous method signature. That's how we're able to declare a return type in our method signature that seems to mismatch the declared type of our returned value in the body of our method.

Moving on in our method, we create a `WebRequest` class pointing to our test domain, and then use `StreamWriter` to write our data query directly onto the `WebRequest`'s request stream. What happens next is where it gets interesting, though, that is, we get to call this following line in our code:

```
var responseTask = request.GetResponseAsync();
```

The result of the `GetResponseAsync()` method that is assigned to our `responseTask` variable is actually not the `WebResponse` class. Instead, it's a handle to the task that is started in a background thread by the `GetResponseAsync()` method. So, instead of waiting around for the response to come back from our server, `GetResponseAsync` just gives us a handle to the thread that is fetching that response, and then immediately returns the flow of control to the next operation in our method. This allows us to start our `LongRunningSlowMethod()` almost immediately.

Now, since our `LongRunningSlowMethod()` is not asynchronous, the flow of control blocks until it completes executing, and its output is assigned to `result.LocalResult`. Once that's complete, we can't actually proceed with the function until we've finished getting the result from our web request. Thus, the next line in our program is as follows:

```
var webResponse = await responseTask;
```

By calling the `await` keyword, we're telling our program that we cannot meaningfully proceed until the awaited operation is complete. So, if the task isn't done yet, the program should now block further execution until it is. This is what I meant by defer blocking the execution of their program. We were able to proceed with executing other, unrelated code while this task was finishing up. It's only when there is no more work that can be done without the result of the asynchronous task that you must block, and await the result. That's what we're doing here with the `await` call.

The result of awaiting this `async` task is whatever was wrapped by the `Task<T>` return type in the `async` method. So in this case, what gets assigned to the `webResponse` variable is the instance of the `WebResponse` class we were expecting earlier.

Now that we have our response, we can read from it. In our next few lines, we instantiate `StreamReader`, and provided it the response stream from the `WebResponse` instance we got back. Finally, we read from the response stream and assign it to our result object:

```
result.RequestResult = await sr.ReadToEndAsync();
```

Note that even though we have no additional code to execute in this function, we still use the `ReadToEndAsync()` method and await the result. The reason for this is because while we don't have anything further to execute in our method, someone invoking our method may be able to defer processing the result we pass back. Using the `await` operator tells the compiler that this is another opportunity for deferred execution, and so when this point is reached in our method, control may well return to the calling method until the result of our method is awaited again. For this reason, it's important to always use async methods wherever available, and use them all the way up the call chain. The performance gains will add up substantially over time.

A final note on blocking code

You might notice that there is a `Result` property on the task instance returned whenever you call an asynchronous method. While it may seem tempting to simply use `GetResponseAsync().Result` to avoid having to await your asynchronous operations, as well as avoid having to apply asynchronous patterns all the way up the stack, this is a terrible practice.

Never use `.Result` to access the result of an asynchronous task.

It not only blocks your code by forcing synchronous execution, but it also prevents anyone who is calling your methods from being able to defer execution either. Unfortunately, this is one of the most common mistakes that new developers make when they first start working with asynchronous programming. However, you should almost never mix async and blocking code together. As a very simple rule, if any of your code requires async processing, all of it does.

Summary

In this chapter, we further built on the foundations from which all network programming in C# is supported. We learned about how .NET encapsulates the basic physical concept of a physical stream of incoming or outgoing bits into an elegantly simple and broadly useful `Stream` class. Then we looked at the best patterns for working with `Stream` through the `StreamWriter` and `StreamReader` wrapper classes. To facilitate the ease with which we could transmit data through those classes, we got our first look at the incredible power of JSON, and the `Newtonsoft.Json` library.

Once we got data streams firmly under our belt, we looked at how to optimize working with them. We talked about the power of multithreading, and what that can mean for performance improvements with long-running tasks and operations. Finally, we took a crash course in asynchronous programming. Learning about how to leverage background tasks and the power of asynchronous method definitions, we saw how we could fully leverage multithreading and background tasks to mitigate the operation latency of potentially long-running operations. Now that we're more comfortably positioned to be working with remote data sources, we'll take the next chapter to learn how to respond to errors from remote data sources.

Questions

1. What does JSON stand for and why is it useful?
2. What are the three primary operations available to you through the `Stream` class?
3. What is the purpose of a `using` statement?
4. What is the most important factor in working with strings through the `StreamReader` and `StreamWriter` classes?
5. What is the biggest single benefit of leveraging background threads in your programs?
6. What is the most common mistake programmers make when using asynchronous methods?
7. What are the only three valid return types of an asynchronous method?

Further reading

For more information about these subjects, I'd recommend taking a look at *Multithreading with C# Cookbook, Eugene Agafonov, Packt Publishing,* at `https://www.packtpub.com/application-development/multithreading-c-cookbook-second-edition`.

For a deeper dive into modern asynchronous programming practices, you should check out *C# 7.1 and .NET Core 2.0 - Modern Cross-Platform Development, Mark J. Price, Packt Publishing*. You can find this at `https://www.packtpub.com/application-development/c-71-and-net-core-20-modern-cross-platform-development-third-edition`.

7
Error Handling over the Wire

This chapter will explore the many possible failure points of a distributed application, and how the impact of a failure can be felt by downstream consumers of your application. We'll examine how different errors are reported or detected depending on the severity, context, and stage of the life cycle of network traffic. We'll explore a variety of error-handling strategies as they are implemented in C#, and demonstrate how conventions and standards can be leveraged to ensure that your application behaves as expected for any potential downstream consumers. Finally, we'll look at how to generate meaningful errors for your application's consumers when their requests cannot be reasonably serviced.

The following topics will be covered in this chapter:

- How different points of failure should generate different error messages, and how to recover from them
- Common error codes and messages returned by services that have correctly implemented their respective communication protocols
- Strategies for handling different kinds of errors depending on the needs your application must meet
- Using status codes, errors, logs, and messages to generate and report your own errors for downstream consumers

Technical requirements

We'll be writing a substantial amount of sample code, which can be found on GitHub here: `https://github.com/PacktPublishing/Hands-On-Network-Programming-with-CSharp-and-.NET-Core/tree/master/Chapter 7`.

Check out the following video to see the code in action: `http://bit.ly/2HT1l9z`

This chapter will introduce a resilient network client called **Polly** to demonstrate common error-recovery strategies. I'd recommend reading up on some of the features of that particular library here: `https://github.com/App-vNext/Polly`.

Multiple devices, multiple points of failure

There is an inexhaustible number of problems that can occur on even simple software when you introduce the unpredictability of network interactions. A single off-by-one error in an upstream service could mean a missing the closing curly-brace in a JSON string, rendering an entire payload impossible to parse. **Internet service provider** (**ISP**) service interruptions or weak wireless signals can result in timeouts and incomplete payload delivery. Meanwhile, the stability of the remote system you're requesting a resource from is entirely out of your control. With all these factors introducing the potential for errors, we can't simply hope to avoid errors or exceptions in our software. We must assume they will occur, and design around that eventuality.

External dependencies

In our time as professional engineers, we can count on one hand the number of application we wrote that neither served as a network dependency for a downstream consumer, nor had a dependency on an upstream network resource. Every time your software must make a network hop to access a necessary resource, you're introducing the risk of failure.

As a rule, any time you are reading data from an external dependency, you must implement proper exception handling. Always assume that something could go wrong. We didn't do this in the last chapter because we didn't want to introduce unnecessary complexity while I was still trying to fully elucidate the concepts and uses of data streams. However, in this chapter, we'll be looking exclusively at error-handling strategies. And the first strategy is to *always* assume accessing external dependencies will eventually fail.

This is fairly straightforward when you are handling the response from another external dependency, but what if your own software is a dependency for another application? The next strategy for resilient application behavior is to always assume that your own software will eventually fail. This will encourage you to account for that fact and provide fault tolerance and useful error messaging for anyone who may be using your software at the moment of failure. With that in mind, let's start with our network access code from the last chapter and modify it for better resiliency.

Looking back at our method, we had the following:

```
public async Task<ResultObject> AsyncMethodDemo() {
  ResultObject result = new ResultObject();
  WebRequest request = WebRequest.Create("http://test-domain.com");
  request.Method = "POST";
  Stream reqStream = request.GetRequestStream();

  using (StreamWriter sw = new StreamWriter(reqStream)) {
    sw.Write("Our test data query");
  }
  var responseTask = request.GetResponseAsync();

  result.LocalResult = LongRunningSlowMethod();

  var webResponse = await responseTask;

  using (StreamReader sr = new
StreamReader(webResponse.GetResponseStream())) {
    result.RequestResult = await sr.ReadToEndAsync();
  }
  return result;
}
```

Within this method, we have one external dependency. We could encounter a failure when we attempt to access and process the response we receive from the server. Any number of issues could arise here for any number of reasons, so we'll want to wrap that code in a `try/catch` block, or apply an exception filter in our code (more on that shortly). We'll start with a simple `try/catch` block, looking at an incredibly useful built-in `Exception` class for our purposes, the `WebException` class. So let's catch that, and see what kind of utility we can get from it:

```
try {
  var webResponse = await responseTask;
  using (StreamReader sr = new
StreamReader(webResponse.GetResponseStream())) {
    result.RequestResult = await sr.ReadToEndAsync();
  }
```

```
} catch (WebException ex) {
  Console.WriteLine(ex.Status);
  Console.WriteLine(ex.Message);
}
```

Here, you'll note that we don't have to look for exceptions until we block our code and wait for the response to return. If we kick off an asychronous task and, while executing, that task throws an error, it doesn't reach our code until we `await` the result of that task. When we catch the error that we know we'll get (since the `test-domain.com` resource doesn't actually exist), we catch it as `WebException`. This class is the base exception class you will receive from any network-specific exceptions your code encounters. What makes this especially useful, as opposed to the `catchall Exception` class, is the availability of the network error-specific `Status` property.

In this sample, we're merely logging the status and the exception message to our console. If the code existed in an API that we wrote, however, and was exposed exposed to downstream entities over a network, we would be responsible for returning a meaningful status code of our own. Doing so ensures that if our specific application code is the primary point of failure in a process pipeline, we are providing as much information as possible to reliably respond to, and recover from, our exceptions.

Parsing the exception status for context

When there is an error status returned in `WebException`, the value of that property can tell us a lot about what failed and why. The `Status` property is an instance of the `WebExceptionStatus` enum, and the values returned can tell us a lot about the conditions that caused our external dependency to fail. It may have been a routing issue, or an inability to resolve a cache lookup or to maintain an active connection.

The information you can discern simply from checking the value of the status code can tell you a lot about what specifically failed and what recovery strategy is most likely to yield positive results. For example, if your exception has a `Status` of `NameResolutionFailure`, you can safely assume that retrying the request won't be an effective strategy. If the DNS failed to identify the host based on the provided name at your first attempt, subsequent attempts with the same hostname are unlikely to prove fruitful. However, if you receive an error status of the `Timeout` type, you could potentially increase your timeout threshold on your request client and submit a series of retries, up to a predetermined maximum timeout length.

The documentation for the `WebException` status is freely available, and it's up to you to identify which possible exception statuses you can encounter. Furthermore, once you know where or what in the request chain failed, you can determine the best recovery strategy for your application code. The main takeaway here, though, is that you should check for and attempt to recover from the `WebException` occurrences at any point in your application in which a request is transmitted.

Status codes and error messages

Now that we know where we should be checking for potential exceptions (or providing them for our consumers), it's important to understand what those exceptions could ultimately look like. Identifying the full scope of possible exceptions and writing recovery solutions for each possibility will make our code nearly bulletproof against the unreliability of distributed resource acquisitions. While we've already seen that we can access hugely useful information just by inspecting the `WebException` exception that is thrown by any failed network requests we could make, there's still a lot to understand about the standards of Internet status code specifications and exceptional response handling.

Status messages and status codes

First, let's look at a reliable approach to handling different status responses in the case of an error from an upstream dependency. Let's use the same snippet of code from our earlier example, but respond more robustly to the variety of possible statuses we could receive. To keep our request code short, we'll delegate the exception handling code to a different method named `ProcessException(WebException ex)`. The two parameters of this method will be the exception that was generated, as well as the original request that triggered the exceptional state in our code. This will give the exception-processing method sufficient context about the original request to attempt to recover gracefully from the error. So, inside the `catch` block of our earlier example, we'll replace our two `Console.WriteLine()` statements accordingly:

```
} catch (WebException ex) {
    ProcessException(ex);
}
```

Then, from within our `ProcessException(WebException ex)` method, we'll switch on the possible value of the exception `Status` property, performing useful recovery logic based on the status or messages received:

```
public void ProcessException(WebException ex) {
    switch(ex.Status) {
      case WebExceptionStatus.ConnectFailure:
      case WebExceptionStatus.ConnectionClosed:
      case WebExceptionStatus.RequestCanceled:
      case WebExceptionStatus.PipelineFailure:
      case WebExceptionStatus.SendFailure:
      case WebExceptionStatus.KeepAliveFailure:
      case WebExceptionStatus.Timeout:
        Console.WriteLine("We should retry connection attempts");
        break;
      case WebExceptionStatus.NameResolutionFailure:
      case WebExceptionStatus.ProxyNameResolutionFailure:
      case WebExceptionStatus.ServerProtocolViolation:
      case WebExceptionStatus.ProtocolError:
        Console.WriteLine("Prevent further attempts and notify consumers to
check URL configurations");
        break;
      case WebExceptionStatus.SecureChannelFailure:
      case WebExceptionStatus.TrustFailure:
        Console.WriteLine("Authentication or security issue. Prompt for
credentials and perhaps try again");
        break;
      default:
        Console.WriteLine("We don't know how to handle this. We should post
the error message and terminate our current workflow.");
        break;
    }
}
```

By using the descriptive and reliable status codes returned by `WebException`, we can group similar errors together, and respond to them with resolutions that will likely resolve the common issue for each of them. If there were issues with connectivity or timeouts, there may simply have been an issue with your ISP, or the remote host simply didn't have the resources loaded from the cache, and so took too long to process the request. In that case, simply trying again may well prove to be a consistently reliable solution. However, if the exception was due to an inability to resolve the target hostname, then subsequent requests will likely fail in the same way. They'd all be processed by the same DNS, so unless the request URI is updated to a valid host name, there's no benefit in retrying the request. Meanwhile, security issues can likely be resolved by refreshing authentication or authorization credentials.

You'll note that the default simply recommends publishing the inner message returned with the `WebException` class. This is because, in cases where there is no common status code returned by the server, the class itself will have some default messaging about what has probably gone wrong. So even if we get back an instance of `WebExceptionStatus.UnknownError`, there will likely still be useful information returned as part of the error message.

Useful error messages

If we find ourselves in a scenario where we cannot gracefully recover from a failed attempt to request resources from an upstream dependency, and we cannot proceed with the service our application provides, it's time to send an error message of our own. It is our responsibility to provide as much information about the failure state as we can for the user to understand what went wrong while avoiding sending back any potentially compromising details that could open our application up to vulnerabilities.

This is where status codes become your best friend. When you're handling HTTP requests against your application, you should be as specific as you possibly can with which status codes you return. It may seem extremely simple to return a **500** status code every time something goes wrong, with your own software, since 5XX is the blanket code designation for a server error. If you want people to be happy to use your services, though, I would recommend you don't. The more specific you can be with your status codes, the less work any of your consumers have to put in to understanding and recovering from issues on their own side of the equation.

Using the most specific status codes possible also gives us a risk-free way of communicating enough information about what went wrong, while not communicating anything that could put our software at risk. If you respond to a bad authentication request with a **401** status code (the status code for "unauthorized"), users will know that they have to adjust their authentication mechanism. However, if you simply returned a blanket **400** status code, along with a message indicating that the minimum character requirements for a password is eight, then you've just given potential malicious actors more information about your authentication scheme than they had before their failed attempt. And with malicious software, *any* information about the specifics of your system is dangerous.

Understanding how much information is enough, versus too much, can be a delicate balancing act. Much of knowing what others will want to see from your software will come from experience. The more external services you see sending useless **Something went wrong. Oops!** error messages, the more you'll have an idea of what you would have wanted to know, and how you can do better in your own code in the future. A good rule of thumb when you're starting out, though, is that status codes should be as specific as possible, and error messages should be as vague as you can get away with. In HTTP, error status codes are all isolated to the 4XX and 5XX values. These two groupings designate request servicing errors and server errors, respectively.

A request-servicing error relates to anything about the structure, origin, or nature of the request that caused the failure to occur. So, anything from requesting a resource that doesn't actually exist at the requested location (**404 - Not Found**), to requesting a resource with an HTTP verb that isn't supported by the listening server (**405 - Method Not Allow**) to requesting access to resources for which the client isn't authorized (**401 - Unauthorized**).

Server errors, on the other hand, relate to issues that have occurred after a correct and well-formed address has been received. There are far fewer of these since most well-formed requests are considered well formed specifically because there is a server configured to process it. The reasons for a 5XX response range from failure of an upstream server to process some aspect of the client request (**502 - Bad Gateway/504 - Gateway Timeout**), to the target server simply being out of commission or unavailable at the time of the request (**503 - Service Unavailable**).

If you're sending correct error codes, it is incredibly unlikely that you will ever find yourself returning a 5XX error code explicitly from within your own code. If your software is written well, issues that cause it to throw an error will almost always be ultimately traceable to some aspect of an incoming request. When that happens, though, it is absolutely your responsibility to do your best to find out what, specifically, about the request caused the error, and report it back promptly.

Error-handling strategies

Now that we've seen the tools available to you when encountering error messages from network resources (and when sending error messages of your own), let's take a look at what to do with them.

How should we best respond to a `RequestCancelled` exception status? Which failure states are likely to have a common root cause, and thus a common shared solution? How should our software respond to our own users when we can't recover from errors further upstream? In this section, we'll take a look at each of these questions, and leave with some concrete approaches that can be adapted and scaled to almost any circumstance.

Resilient requests with Polly

As we already saw in our previous code sample, it's not uncommon to respond to a number of similar error statuses with the same general recovery solution. This is a great practice for simplifying your code base, and can provide durable exception handling in a wide variety of common situations.

This act of associating common network issues into groups that can be resolved with similar strategies is exactly the idea behind the Polly library for resilient HTTP clients. While we're not looking specifically at HTTP now, it is one of the most robust libraries out there for one of the most common network protocols, so I think it bears examination as we continue to look at error-recovery strategies.

The first order of business is to include the package in our project either through an explicit inclusion in the NuGet package manager, or with the following command-line input:

```
dotnet add package Polly
```

Once it's installed, we can declare a `Policy` class for how we plan to handle various network exceptions using Polly's declarative handler and recovery methods. The `Policy` class is a robust, transient container for a given task. We define a delegate, and then we provide that delegate to a `Policy` for execution. The `Policy` class then uses the actively-defined error handlers and their recovery definitions to execute the task, and then listen for and respond to exceptional states accordingly.

Exceptions that we want Polly to respond to are set with the generic `Handle<T>()` method, where `T` is some subclass of the `Exception` type. The `Handle<T>()` method also takes optional conditional parameters specifying the state of the `Exception` type we want to respond to with the corresponding recovery specification. This gives us the ability to define specific recovery strategies for different states. Let's look at this in action to see what I mean.

First, we're going to define a method for requesting some remote resource. This will only be used for demonstration purposes, so we'll want it to occasionally fail and occasionally succeed. For that, we'll just generate a random number, and if the number is even, we'll throw an exception; otherwise, we'll return a valid response. Importantly, though, we'll want to log our failed attempts onscreen so we can see the retry in action:

```
public static HttpResponseMessage ExecuteRemoteLookup() {
    if (new Random().Next() % 2 == 0) {
        Console.WriteLine("Retrying connections...");
        throw new WebException("Connection Failure",
WebExceptionStatus.ConnectFailure);
    }
    return new HttpResponseMessage();
}
```

This will be the delegate that we pass to our `Policy` object once we've defined our recovery strategy and want to try to execute it. Next, we'll define behaviors for a couple of the error states we defined in our naive error-handling code from earlier. For the sake of readability, we'll define some private class variables to hold the groups of the `WebExceptionStatus` values that we had logically lumped together:

```
private List<WebExceptionStatus> connectionFailure = new
List<WebExceptionStatus>() {
 WebExceptionStatus.ConnectFailure,
 WebExceptionStatus.ConnectionClosed,
 WebExceptionStatus.RequestCanceled,
 WebExceptionStatus.PipelineFailure,
 WebExceptionStatus.SendFailure,
 WebExceptionStatus.KeepAliveFailure,
 WebExceptionStatus.Timeout
};

private List<WebExceptionStatus> resourceAccessFailure = new
List<WebExceptionStatus>() {
 WebExceptionStatus.NameResolutionFailure,
 WebExceptionStatus.ProxyNameResolutionFailure,
 WebExceptionStatus.ServerProtocolViolation
};

private List<WebExceptionStatus> securityFailure = new
List<WebExceptionStatus>() {
 WebExceptionStatus.SecureChannelFailure,
 WebExceptionStatus.TrustFailure
};
```

With that, we can easily define a `Policy` object that responds to `WebException` with a status in one of our groupings, as follows:

```
public static void ExecuteRemoteLookupWithPolly() {
    Policy connFailurePolicy = Policy
        .Handle<WebException>(x => connectionFailure.Contains(x.Status))
        .RetryForever();

    HttpResponseMessage resp = connFailurePolicy.Execute(() =>
ExecuteRemoteLookup());
    if (resp.IsSuccessStatusCode) {
        Console.WriteLine("Success!");
    }
}
```

Note that when we execute `Policy`, we specify that as long as we get `WebExceptionStatus` defined in our `connectionFailure` grouping, we want to retry the request. So, let's now call this from a driver program a few times and see what our console looks like after each run. The assumption is due to the sufficient randomness of the pseudo-random number generator, there should be at least a few runs that fail multiple times before returning a valid response. (Note that, for the purposes of this demo, all of the Polly code exists in a `static PollyDemo` class). Let's have a look at the following code:

```
using System.Threading;

namespace ErrorHandling {
    public class Program {
        static void Main(string[] args) {
            PollyDemo.ExecuteRemoteLookupWithPolly();
            Thread.Sleep(10000);
        }
    }
}
```

If you have your IDE configured to break on errors, you'll get a pause in execution every time your code fails. Just running this code myself, though, I saw an instant success, and then five consecutive retries before my code successfully executed. The fact that I was able to define that in fewer than 10 lines of code is incredible, and speaks to the value of Polly in providing resiliency to an application.

However, if we want to truly mirror the behavior we established in our naive error-handling code from earlier, we want to respond to a variety of exceptional states with specific recovery codes based on which state was reached. For that, Polly allows you to define multiple state handlers and then wrap them together in a `PolicyWrap` class, which does precisely. It will allow you to define the recovery policies for as many conditional states as you need, and then wrap them up in a single common policy to be respected when your `PolicyWrap` instance's `Execute(delegate)` method is called.

To demonstrate this, we'll define a few additional exceptional states for our delegate, such that if the random number generated is divisible by `3`, we'll throw a name resolution error, and if the number is divisible by `4`, we'll throw a security error:

```
public static HttpResponseMessage ExecuteRemoteLookup() {
    var num = new Random().Next();
    if (num % 3 == 0) {
        Console.WriteLine("Breaking the circuit");
        throw new WebException("Name Resolution Failure",
WebExceptionStatus.NameResolutionFailure);
    } else if (num % 4 == 0) {
        Console.WriteLine("Falling Back");
        throw new WebException("Security Failure",
WebExceptionStatus.TrustFailure);
    } else if (num % 2 == 0) {
        Console.WriteLine("Retrying connections...");
        throw new WebException("Connection Failure",
WebExceptionStatus.ConnectFailure);
    }
    return new HttpResponseMessage();
}
```

Now that we have a random chance that at least one of our exceptional conditions is met, let's define the behavior for each circumstance. As you might have noticed from my console messages, we'll use a different strategy for each specific error case. Polly defines a small number of policies out of the box, and you can invoke each one in the case for which it is most useful. I won't go into all of them now, but I will take a moment to encourage you to read up on Polly's documentation (`https://github.com/App-vNext/Polly`). It's longer than this whole chapter, but well written and immeasurably useful for anyone looking to provide more reliable stability to a production application. For now though, we'll just be looking at the `Circuit-breaker` policy and the `Fallback` policy. These two seem most useful for our use cases since they most closely match the strategy we identified in our naive approach.

The `Fallback` policy is by far the simpler of the two. It simply allows you to designate an alternative response to return in the event of the specified exception being handled. In our example, since we'll be using `Fallback` for our security exceptions, we'll simply return a new instance of `HttpResponseMessage` with a **401** status code set to notify our downstream consumers that there is an issue with authorization that needs to be resolved.

The Circuit-breaker policy designates that multiple failed attempts to resolve a request should open the circuit to the requested resource, and stop subsequent requests before they start. This is useful in scenarios like the one we've defined for name resolution failures, where, based on the error message subsequent attempts are no more likely to be successful than the original request. Opening the circuit (and thus stopping the flow of requests over that circuit) gives the upstream system a chance to recover without being bombarded by a series of retry attempts. You can configure the circuit to open after a designated number of failed attempts or after a designated timeout, and you can set it to stay open for as long as you determine would probably be necessary to allow the upstream system to recover.

Unlike the retry policy and its variants, though, the Circuit-breaker doesn't actually do anything in response to errors being thrown. In fact, it will always re-throw any caught errors; even if the circuit has already been broken. If you want to retry requests after the designated reset period for an open circuit, you are free to implement that behavior yourself, but by default, the Polly `spec` doesn't do so with its Circuit-breaker implementation. So in our example, we're going to break the circuit after only one failed attempt, and we'll still need to look for the appropriate error messages in `try/catch` from our calling code.

With that in mind, let's update our previous example. The first thing we'll do is add a method to return the **401** status code in `HttpResponseMessage` for our `Fallback` policy:

```
private static HttpResponseMessage GetAuthorizationErrorResponse() {
    return new HttpResponseMessage(HttpStatusCode.Unauthorized);
}
```

Then we'll set policies for each of our two alternative error states, and wrap them accordingly:

```
public static void ExecuteRemoteLookupWithPolly() {
    Policy connFailurePolicy = Policy
        .Handle<WebException>(x => connectionFailure.Contains(x.Status))
        .RetryForever();

    Policy<HttpResponseMessage> authFailurePolicy =
Policy<HttpResponseMessage>
        .Handle<WebException>(x => securityFailure.Contains(x.Status))
        .Fallback(() => GetAuthorizationErrorResponse());
```

```
        Policy nameResolutionPolicy = Policy
            .Handle<WebException>(x =>
    resourceAccessFailure.Contains(x.Status))
            .CircuitBreaker(1, TimeSpan.FromMinutes(2));

        Policy intermediatePolicy = Policy
            .Wrap(connFailurePolicy, nameResolutionPolicy);

        Policy<HttpResponseMessage> combinedPolicies = intermediatePolicy
            .Wrap(authFailurePolicy);

        try {
            HttpResponseMessage resp = combinedPolicies.Execute(() =>
    ExecuteRemoteLookup());
            if (resp.IsSuccessStatusCode) {
                Console.WriteLine("Success!");
            } else if (resp.StatusCode.Equals(HttpStatusCode.Unauthorized)) {
                Console.WriteLine("We have fallen back!");
            }
        } catch (WebException ex) {
            if (resourceAccessFailure.Contains(ex.Status)) {
                Console.WriteLine("We should expect to see a broken circuit.");
            }
        }
    }
```

So, in our revised method, we define a policy for each possible scenario we want to respond to, including the specific state of the exception that should be handled and the recovery process we want to implement. Of note, though, are the two different calls to the `Policy.Wrap()` method. The reason for this is that using the `Fallback()` method on a strongly-typed instance of `Policy<HttpResponseMessage>` is the only way we can designate the type of the return object from the delegate method we passed into `Fallback()`. However, by strongly typing the policy, we can't `Wrap()` it with the other weakly-typed policies in a single call. The `Wrap()` method of strongly-typed policies can take at most one argument. So the workaround for this is to first wrap all of the weakly-typed policies we've defined, and then use that wrapped `Policy` instance as the input to the `Wrap()` call on our strongly-typed `Policy`. This is confusing, initially, I realize, but will become clearer as you work with Polly, read their excellent documentation, and most importantly, implement these error-handling strategies in any networked software you write.

To make our driver program a little simpler to use for test purposes (instead of having to run the program by hand two dozen times to see all possible outcomes), we'll update that as well. Let's have a look at the following code:

```
public static void Main(string[] args) {
    for (var i = 0; i < 24; i++) {
        Console.WriteLine($"Polly Demo Attempt {i}");
        Console.WriteLine("-------------");
        PollyDemo.ExecuteRemoteLookupWithPolly();
        Console.WriteLine("-------------");
        Thread.Sleep(5000);
    }
}
```

Run that program once (maybe twice, since randomness is random, after all) and you should see the appropriate log statements for each of our possible scenarios. I'm counting on you to understand the nature of the flow of control through our program to understand why the results onscreen demonstrate the promised functionality of the `Policy` objects we defined.

As we move forward and look at specific implementations of different network protocols, we'll be leaning heavily on Polly to define our recovery strategies. There's a lot of depth to the library, and you'll get out of it whatever you choose to put in to learning it. With this foundation, though, you'll be well equipped to move forward through the rest of this book.

Summary

In this chapter, we took a close look at how the .NET Core `WebException` class provides engineers with a stable, reliable, and informative interface for understanding network errors as they arise. We looked at where and when we should expect and account for network exceptions, and how we could inspect the `Status` property of those exceptions to determine their root cause. We also considered our responsibility in providing meaningful exception messaging, as well as the value of providing as specific a status code as possible for any consumers of our software. Finally, we looked at some common strategies, and an extremely useful library in the form of Polly, for consistently recovering from network exceptions to maximize our application's up time and increase our consumers' trust in our software. It will be important to keep these ideas of resilience and optimization in mind going forward.

In our next chapter, we'll be stepping into the world of low-level data transmission and host-to-host communication.

Questions

1. What is one thing we should always assume about external dependencies?
2. What are the two categories of error status codes in HTTP?
3. Which property of the `WebException` class can we use to determine the nature of the exception we received?
4. What does Polly's fallback policy provide for an exception state?
5. How does a Circuit-breaker policy specification differ from a `retry` policy specification?
6. Write a sample method that combines `fallback` and `retry` policies based on the `StatusCode` of the response from a sample request.
7. In which circumstances would you not want to retry a web request after an initial failure?

Further reading

For more information about specific error-handling strategies with various network software architectures, check out the book *Learning ASP.NET Core 2.0*, by *Jason De Oliveira* and *Michel Bruchet*. This will provide more in-depth guidance on error handling in ASP.NET Core-based HTTP application scenarios. The book is available electronically or in print, here: `https://www.packtpub.com/application-development/learning-aspnet-core-20`.

Alternatively, I would once again recommend *C# 7 and .NET: Designing Modern Cross-platform Applications*, by *Mark J. Price* and *Ovais Mehboob Ahmed Khan*. The content on exception handling is useful and well focused for many common use cases. Once again, the link to purchase as an e-book or printed copy is here: `https://www.packtpub.com/application-development/learning-path-c-7-and-net-designing-modern-cross-platform-applications`.

3

Section 3: Application Protocols and Connection Handling

In this part, the reader will take a deep dive into the different components of network applications, with extensive examples of code, exploring each layer of the network stack.

The following chapters will be covered in this section:

8
Sockets and Ports

At this point, we understand how to handle data streams from remote hosts, process those streams asynchronously on background threads, and handle the errors that arise from processing that data. Now we're going to look at the most primitive connections you can make with a remote host. In this chapter, we'll be looking at the physical ports through which your machine is going to do this, and we'll be looking at the concept of a socket: the software structure that exposes access to a port for network interaction. We'll examine the WinSocks library for instantiating and working with those ports, and we'll consider the various ways sockets can be leveraged by your application code for efficient, low-level communication with a target host.

The following topics will be covered in this chapter:

- How the `System.Net.Sockets` classes serve as the C# interface to your hardware-level network APIs for communication with external machines
- How to establish a connection to a socket exposed by another machine on your network
- How to program server applications that expose sockets to accept external connection requests
- The nature of communicating over serial ports and exposing serial ports to accept serial data for processing, and how this can open you up to interesting use cases for C# and .NET Core

Technical requirements

This chapter will have a number of samples and driver programs to demonstrate the concepts discussed, each of which will be available here: `https://github.com/PacktPublishing/Hands-On-Network-Programming-with-CSharp-and-.NET-Core/tree/master/Chapter 8`.

As always, clone the repository locally and begin playing with the source code, or writing your own along with the topics in the chapter to get comfortable with it.

We'll also start using external tools to test and inspect the behavior of a sample API. For this, you'll need to download and install either Postman, which can be found here: `https://www.getpostman.com/apps/` ,Or you'll need the Insomnia REST client, which can be found here: `https://insomnia.rest/`.

The feature set of each of these applications is almost identical, and each will allow you to send arbitrary requests to a local API through an intuitive UI. We'll be using them to test out our web software going forward, and I'd recommend spending at least a little time getting familiar with some of the basic functionality of whichever tool you choose to use. Throughout this chapter I'll be presenting screenshots captured from Postman, but that's not an endorsement of Postman over Insomnia, and the steps and UI when following along should be virtually identical in both.

Finally, we'll be using Docker to demonstrate port mapping. While you could manage an understanding of the specific concepts of this chapter without this tool, I'd strongly recommend downloading and familiarizing yourself with it. It is core to the modern web application development experience, and you will only benefit from practicing with it. This chapter provides one of the best opportunities to do so, and I'd certainly encourage you to try. Docker can be downloaded here: `https://hub.docker.com/editions/community/docker-ce-desktop-windows`.

Check out the following video to see the code in action: `http://bit.ly/2HYmX49`

Sockets versus ports

The first thing we should do as we look at these connection mechanisms is to distinguish between the two. While they are two words identifying a common hardware interaction, the software or abstract concepts each term identifies are actually mutually exclusive. These terms aren't as interchangeable as abstract class and interface were in previous chapters, so when we use each term, it will be for a specific purpose, and you'll need to know what it is.

Ports – a hardware interface

As we already know, machines are identified by their IP address, or the hostname mapped to that IP address in the DNS registry. So for any given connection between machines to be resolved, the initiating host will ultimately need the underlying IP address of the target host. However, simply specifying the target IP address is insufficient to target a service or application running on the host. It only gives us the location of the host itself. That's where ports come in. A port is a two byte unsigned integer that identifies a running process on a target machine.

Each application on your host that will interact with remote processes must do so on a designated port. Furthermore, no two applications can listen on the same port. Every time you want to start up your application and designate it as listening for network requests, you must assign it to an unsigned port on your machine. If you've ever tried to run multiple instances of an API project on the `8099` or `8080` port (or any other common listening port) on your local machine, you'll have seen the startup failure message indicating that the target port is already in use. That port is occupied, so you'll have to find a different one to process transactions targeting your new application.

The reason for this should be fairly obvious. If you want to host multiple services on a single device, you will need some way of distinguishing between incoming requests for service *A* and incoming requests for service B. By designating mutually-exclusive listening ports for each hosted application, you move the burden of proper routing back to the client. This is perfectly acceptable, since the client already has to keep track of the remote hosts URI, and if you remember from our earlier chapter, the port number is simply another component of that API. The alternative would require an application to serve as an intermediary between your hosted listening applications and all incoming network requests. Such an application would have to have reasonable knowledge of the state or expectations of each listening application, then it will parse every incoming request to identify which expectation the following requests meets. It would be just a whole mess of state management that would become infeasible incredibly quickly. So instead, we simply add 2-byte address suffixes to specify the target listening application built directly into our URI specification.

Reserved ports

If you know the valid integer values of an unsigned 2-byte `int`, you already know the full range of possible exposed ports for a machine. Using this data type, a port specification could have a value from `0` to `65535`. However, just because a port designation falls within the range for the data-type of a port, it doesn't mean you should attempt to listen on it. There are in fact a number of port ranges that your user-application code should never attempt to listen on. These are designated as reserved ports and typically handle very specific functions.

The first set of ports that are reserved, and thus unavailable for you to register your application to, are called the **well-known ports**. These ports fall between `0` and `1023`, and are used for anything from DNS address resolution (the port `53` used to make sure there is still a machine listening at the address listed in the registry) to FTP data and control ports (the ports `20` and `21` , respectively). If you've done any sort of network programming prior to reading this book, you're already likely to be familiar with the fact that the `80` port is the designated port for incoming HTTP requests and the `443` port is reserved for HTTPS.

The other list of ports that you won't be able to register your application to is what's known as the **dynamic port range**. Dynamic ports, or private ports, are used to establish connections for private or customized services or interactions, or used for temporary **Transmission Control Protocol** (**TCP**) or **User Datagram Protocol** (**UDP**) interactions between two hosts. When used in a temporary context to service a brief need from either machine, the designated port is known as an **ephemeral port**. These ports cannot be registered with the **Internet Assigned Numbers Authority** (**IANA**) for use in general-purpose network interactions on a given host. The range for these ports begins at port number `49152` and ends at `65535`.

The IANA is a non-profit organization responsible for managing the allocation of IP addresses, among other things. As I mentioned in `Chapter 1`, *Networks in a Nutshell*, a centralized system for standards (and names) is important to guarantee that every device routes requests for one IP address to the same device.

With that specification, that appears to leave everything between and including `1024` and `49151` as available for use by your applications. These are what's known as **registered ports**. They are available for assignment by user applications or system services as needed, and won't interfere with default behavior from your hardware or other connected hosts.

It probably seems like configuring your application to listen within the registered port range will be sufficient for use. However, that's still not *quite* the case. If you've ever run a JBoss application server (back in the bad old days of bloated application servers like JBoss, you probably remember accessing your locally-hosted development environment by accessing `http://localhost:8080/my-java-application`, or at least that's what I used to have to do. The reason JBoss always configured that port specifically is because it actually serves as an alias for the `80` port, the HTTP port. The same is true for `8008`. So, even though the ports fall within the registered port range, there are specific expectations around their behavior. It really just provides a value within the registered ports range for users to define default HTTP handlers, since you can't really assign an application directly to the `80` port.

There are other ports within the registered port range that will likely be occupied by common services and applications on your local machine. Since .NET Core will stop if it can't register itself with the designated port, though, you'll notice immediately if you need to update your configuration with a different port number.

Exposing multiple applications on a single port

If you have been working in web development for a substantial amount of time, you may already be familiar with wrangling the various configurations and settings in **Internet Information Services** (**IIS**) or the aforementioned JBoss whenever you wanted to deploy a web application on a Windows host. This is what's called an **application server**, and it essentially serves as a shared hosting environment for any network-exposed applications on your system. When working with IIS, you can register any number of applications to respond to requests against a single port (`80` for HTTP, or `443` for HTTPS) and distinguish between them with application paths in the URI, or sub-domain specifications.

So if you had two applications named, for instance, `TestApp` and `SampleApp`, and you wanted to host both on a single machine, but expose both over the HTTP port, you would do so by registering them and deploying them within IIS. In doing so, you would specify an application directory within IIS, such as `/sample` and `/test`. This would tell IIS that any requests to your hostname over the `80` port, the request paths had as their first component the `/sample` directory, should be routed to your `SampleApp` as though the request went directly to that application. This essentially moved the problem of mapping specific ports to mapping specific application directories.

While IIS still supports deployment of .NET Core applications, it's much less common in modern web-hosting contexts. IIS specifically is known for its convoluted configuration schemes and the immense memory and CPU usage footprint it imposes on your host machine. That's not to mention the fact that IIS is exclusive to Windows operating systems, making portability of IIS hosted applications non-existent.

More typically, engineers are embracing a more lightweight approach to hosting concerns. With the cross-platform support of the .NET Core runtime, engineers that have the benefit of working in greenfield applications are encouraged to pursue more cutting- edge solutions. Typically, .NET Core developers deploy your application to a remote host by way of a Docker container. Docker provides an isolated hosting context for your application, and exposes the ports your application is listening on to the outside world by mapping the container's internal listening ports to an available port on the machine that's actually running your Docker container. You can specify the port you'd like your application to listen on within what's called a **Dockerfile**, which specifies the build and deployment steps for a Docker-hosted application. It's not unlike a PowerShell script or bash script for automating common OS-level operations. Once you specify your desired port, you can map it to a port on the host machine within the `run` command like so:

```
docker run -p 80:5000 -p 443:5001 SampleApp
```

This command will map from the port `5000` inside our **Docker Container** to the `80` port on the host machine, and the `5001` port to the `443` port. So from our hosting context, we'll get a request against the `80` port, and that will be listened to by our Docker instance, which will forward the request into our running **.NET Core App**, which will be listening on the `5000` port:

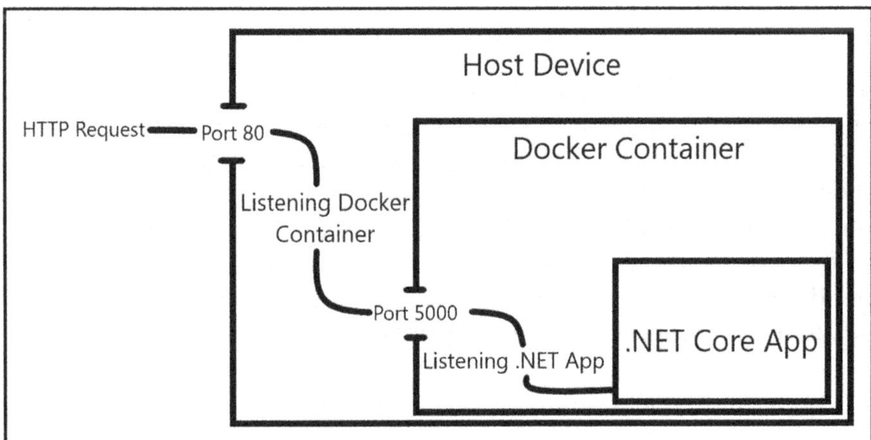

From here, the problem of hosting multiple applications behind a single port that was solved by IIS or JBoss is often simply a matter of configuration. If your application is cloud-hosted, you can typically do the same sort of route-prefix mapping that was provided by IIS. In other contexts, you can host your suite of applications behind what's called a **reverse-proxy**.

We'll take the time to look at, and in some cases even build, each of these approaches in later chapters. For now though, it is sufficient that you understand the nature of ports as a mechanism by which external requests can access specific services or applications hosted on a target device. When exposing your application to network resources, the specific port over which you do so is typically a matter of simple configuration and convention; for now, we'll take a look at how to interact with those specific ports in our software through sockets.

Sockets – a software interface to a port

So now that we understand how ports are used to route requests to specific processes on a host device, how do we set up our applications to actually *accept* requests over those ports? This is where a socket comes in.

A socket provides a software interface to a specific port on a specific remote host. It's an open connection stream between your application and any remote application exposed at the server and port address you specify. Once this connection is established, you're free to write (or read) any data to the open stream of that connection that you need. Sockets are a versatile concept, implemented in almost any server-side programming language, and .NET Core is no different.

One key distinction between a socket and its underlying port is that the port represents access to a single process on a remote device. Therefore, a port can only be registered for a single application. Sockets, however, represent active connections to that single resource. Therefore, there can be as many active sockets connected to a resource as can be supported by the network and the remote host:

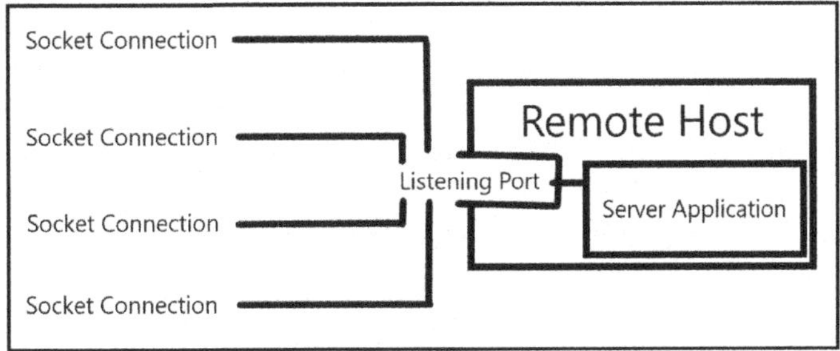

So, a port represents a single process running on a remote machine, while a socket represents a connection to a process on a remote machine, designated by a port number. When we run our applications and intend to expose them to remote resources, we must register them to a specific port. If we want to connect to our application to an exposed port, we do so with a socket. A port is merely a configuration concern, whereas leveraging sockets is an implementation detail, so let's take a look now at how to instantiate and leverage sockets for network communication.

While I brush aside port registration as *merely* a configuration concern, that doesn't mean it's not your responsibility to understand and configure. Full-stack network engineering requires you to understand not only how to write your applications, but how to properly configure and deploy them to your various preproduction and production environments so that others can use them. We'll take a look at application deployment in the next chapter.

Leveraging sockets in C#

Sockets in C# are an extremely versatile and flexible concept. As their definition indicates, they only expose a connection to a remote resource, and how that connection is used is almost entirely up to the developer who establishes it. An instance of the `Socket` class in C# provides synchronous and asynchronous data transfer of packets of arbitrary collections of bytes. The contents, structure, and even protocol used to transmit those packets is up to you (though I do strongly recommend that you always leverage asynchronous communication over synchronous communication). So, let's look at how we'll use it.

The socket specification

The first thing to know about a socket is how to initialize it. The most basic information necessary to initialize a socket is understanding what kind of socket we'll be working with, and what protocol it will be operating on.

The first aspect of that specification, the socket type, tells our code how we'll be interacting with the connection once it's established. This is defined in a `SocketType` array, located in the `System.Net.Sockets` namespace, which defines the full set of valid interaction mechanisms. The values of `enum` include `Dgram`, which indicates that we'll be working directly with unordered, connectionless datagrams between our software and the connected host; the `Seqpacket` type, which operates with ordered, boundary-protected bytes transmitted back and forth over a stream; and the `Stream` type, which provides the asynchronous flow of bytes over a `Stream` instance that we've become familiar with so far. There are a handful of other `SocketType` values, and you can find them and descriptions of what they mean, and how they're used on the Microsoft documentation page. For this chapter, we'll just be working with a `Stream` type, since that most closely resembles the `Stream` classes from the `System.IO` namespace that we're already so familiar with.

A `Socket` can connect and communicate over a wide array of protocols from the transmission layer of the OSI network stack. This means that when you're constructing a socket, you'll need to specify specifically what protocol you'll be using to communicate once the connection is established. This informs the remote host of how it should be parsing the primitive datagrams or packets it will be receiving once the connection is established (provided the host supports the requested protocol in the first place). To define the protocol your `Socket` instance will be using, you'll be looking to values of the `ProtocolType` enum found in the `System.Net.Sockets` namespace. There are a number of defined values that correspond to well-established transmission protocols, including IPv4, IPv6, TCP, UDP, IDP, Raw, and others. For the purposes of our code, we'll be connecting to a local application listening for HTTP requests, which is handled by the TCP protocol, so we'll specify the TCP protocol when we initialize `Socket`.

And those two pieces of information are the minimum details we're required to specify for a socket, the public constructor signature being as follows:

```
public Socket (System.Net.Sockets.SocketType socketType,
System.Net.Sockets.ProtocolType protocolType);
```

There is also an option to specify what's known as the `AddressFamily` of your connection. This can actually be derived from your connection endpoint and provided to the constructor for your socket. Typically, for an HTTP resource transmitted over TCP, your specification will be `AddressFamily.Osi`, indicating that you're using OSI addressing schemes. So now that we know how to initialize a socket, let's look at what it takes to connect a socket to a remote endpoint.

Establishing a socket connection

The first thing we'll want to do is set up a simple listening server to which we can connect our socket driver program. To do this, we'll spin up a simple, `WebAPI` project and run it. Start by opening up Command Prompt and navigating to the directory where you want to create your sample API. Next, create a new `WebAPI` with the following command from the .NET Core CLI:

```
dotnet new webapi -n SampleApp
```

This will spin up a new application from scratch that will be ready-made to receive and respond to HTTP and HTTPS requests made to your local machine and a pre-configured port.

For the purposes of this demonstration, we'll actually want to disable some default functionality in this application. The template for a WebAPI will redirect all calls made to the HTTP port to the HTTPS port instead. We want to prevent this from happening so the HTTP port, can service requests directly. You'll see why later, but for now you can disable this functionality by opening up your `SampleApp` project and navigating to the `Startup.cs` file. Within this file, you'll find a method with the following signature:

```
public void Configure(IApplicationBuilder app, IHostingEnvironment env)
```

At the bottom of this method, delete or comment out the line of code that reads:

```
app.UseHttpsRedirection();
```

Once that's done, you can close that folder and ignore its contents for the rest of this sample project. Now, let's run it and test it, first by navigating into the folder that was just created, and then calling the CLI `dotnet run` command. Once you've done that, you should see the following output from your running application:

```
Administrator: Command Prompt - dotnet run
C:\Users\shurns\Desktop\Code\Book Code\Chapter 8>cd SampleApp

C:\Users\shurns\Desktop\Code\Book Code\Chapter 8\SampleApp>dotnet run
info: Microsoft.AspNetCore.DataProtection.KeyManagement.XmlKeyManager[0]
      User profile is available. Using 'C:\Users\shurns\AppData\Local\ASP.NET\DataProtection-Keys' as key repository and
 Windows DPAPI to encrypt keys at rest.
Hosting environment: Development
Content root path: C:\Users\shurns\Desktop\Code\Book Code\Chapter 8\SampleApp
Now listening on: https://localhost:5001
Now listening on: http://localhost:5000
Application started. Press Ctrl+C to shut down.
```

You can take your time investigating the project template created by the `dotnet new` command if you're curious, but we'll be covering WebAPI applications, among many others, in much greater detail in the next chapter. For now, it's just important that we have an application that's listening for requests and returning responses. You can simply take my word on its expected functionality going forward, if you'd rather defer learning that until later.

The last three lines of your console output give you some valuable information; they tell you the exact host and port through which your application is exposed to outside connections. As you can see, the default from new WebAPIs created by .NET is going to be port `5000` for incoming HTTP requests, and `5001` for HTTPS.

To confirm that the application is responding to requests, open up Postman (or Insomniac, if that was your REST client of choice), and send a GET request to `http://localhost:5000/api/values`. You should see the following response in your output:

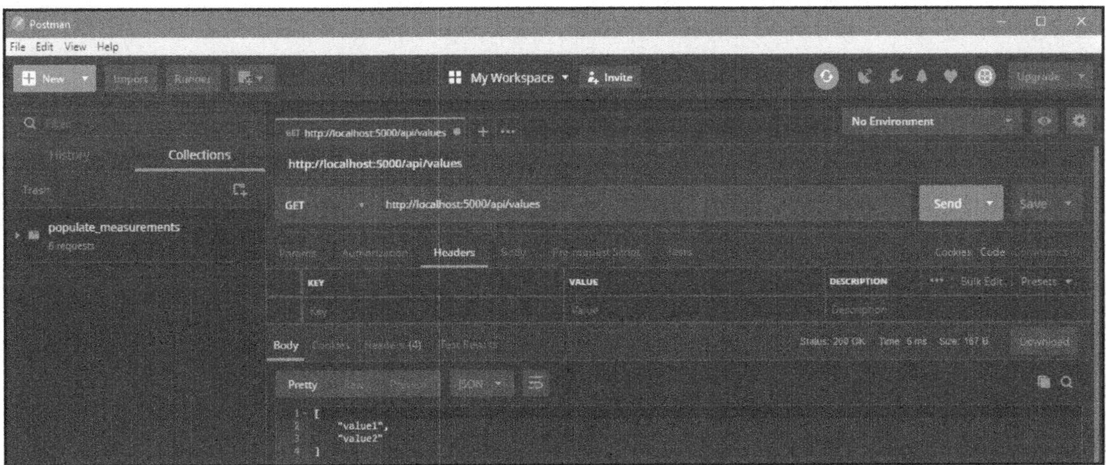

We can see a valid response with two strings in a `JSON` array. Once you have this, we're ready to connect with `Socket`.

Create a new console application in the parent directory of `SampleApp`, using the `dotnet new console -n SocketTest` command in the CLI. This will be our driver application for working with the `Socket` class. The objective of this sample project is to connect to our `SampleApp`, which is listening on the `5000` port, submit a request to the `/api/values` endpoint, and then parse and print the response.

So, the first thing we'll have to do is define an `IPEndPoint` instance for `Socket` to connect to. `IPEndPoint` is a specific implementation of the `EndPoint` abstract class required by the `Socket.ConnectAsync()` method we'll be using. It defines the specific location of the remote resource we intend to connect to, and exposes metadata about that endpoint. It also provides the `AddressFamily` value for our `Socket` constructor signature. So let's first define that with the host address and port, and use it to construct `Socket`.

To do so, we need an `IPAddress` instance, which we could build ourselves based on the 4 bytes stored in our localhost address of `127.0.0.1`, or we could simply request it explicitly from our DNS using the `Dns.GetHostEntry()` method from `Chapter 2`, *DNS and Resource Location*. You can do as you please when following along, but since it involves less math, I'll be using the DNS. However, since `AddressList` returned by a host entry can have an arbitrarily large list of IP Addresses to which the name could resolve, we'll want to connect to the first address that allows us to, and proceed from there. This means looping through `AddressList` until a connection is established. So the initial setup to attempt to establish our connection will look like this:

```
static async Task Main(string[] args) {
  string server = "localhost";
  int port = 5000;
  string path = "/api/values";

  Socket socket = null;
  IPEndPoint endpoint = null;
  var host = Dns.GetHostEntry(server);

  foreach (var address in host.AddressList) {
    socket = new Socket(address.AddressFamily, SocketType.Stream,
ProtocolType.Tcp);
    endpoint = new IPEndPoint(address, port);
    await socket.ConnectAsync(endpoint);
    if (socket.Connected) {
      break;
    }
  }
  ...
}
```

One thing that might jump out to you about this code is that we're using the `async` version of the `Main()` method. This is a feature that was only added in version 7.2 of C#, and if your project isn't configured to target at least that version, you'll encounter build errors. To resolve them, simply modify the `PropertyGroup` tag of your `.csproj` file to include the `LangVersion` tag with its version set to `latest`, as seen here:

```
<PropertyGroup>
    <OutputType>Exe</OutputType>
    <TargetFramework>netcoreapp2.2</TargetFramework>
    <LangVersion>latest</LangVersion>
</PropertyGroup>
```

Once you've made this change, your source code will always target the latest minor version of C#. With that in place, you should have no problems running your `Main()` method asynchronously.

If you want to make sure things are behaving as expected, you can go ahead and run your application, placing a breakpoint on the `break;` operator, and you should see that the breakpoint is hit, and so a connection was established between your two applications. You'll notice, though, that simply establishing the connection didn't trigger any log messages in your running WebAPI application. This is because, while a connection was established, no request was made of the resource to which we connected. Requests must be sent as a well-formed message over an established connection. So now, let's build our request and send it over the connected socket.

Sending requests is as simple as calling the `SendAsync()` method on our socket with a byte array representing our data buffer to be sent over the connection. So for an HTTP request, we have to build our message from scratch. That means specifying the method or HTTP verb we'll be using, the specific URL of our requested resource, the size of any content we intend to send over, and any request headers we need to attach. I'm sure by now you can already see how tedious it is to work directly with sockets. For such a simple request, however, we can easily construct our message with a simple utility function:

```
private static string GetRequestMessage(string server, int port, string
path) {
  var message = $"GET {path} HTTP/1.1\r\n";
  message += $"Host: {server}:{port}\r\n";
  message += "cache-control: no-cache\r\n";
  message += "\r\n";
  return message;
}
```

Then using this, we can build our byte array just as we did when writing to streams. So back in our main method, we'll get our request message, convert it to a byte array, and then send the request to our remote host (*SampleApp*, running at `http://localhost:5000`). Add the following lines into the main method after the connection has been established by the `Socket` instance:

```
var message = GetRequestMessage(server, port, path);
var messageBytes = Encoding.ASCII.GetBytes(message);
var segment = new ArraySegment<byte>(messageBytes);

await socket.SendAsync(segment, SocketFlags.None);
```

If you add this code and then run your application, you'll know you've succeeded when you begin to see logging information in the console displayed by your WebAPI project, as seen here:

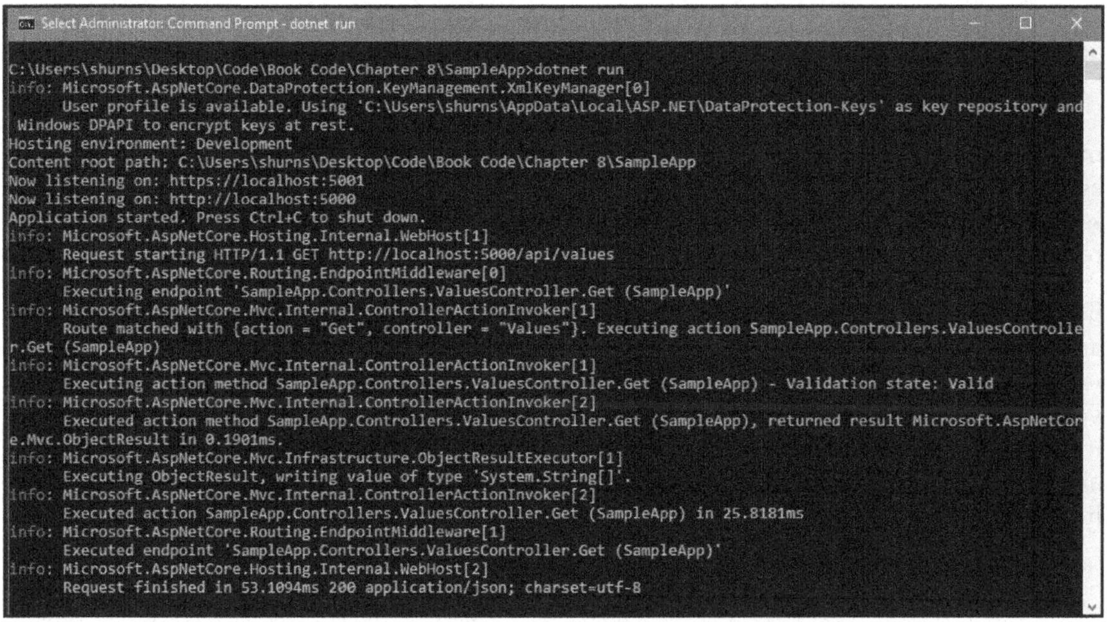

```
Select Administrator: Command Prompt - dotnet run

C:\Users\shurns\Desktop\Code\Book Code\Chapter 8\SampleApp>dotnet run
info: Microsoft.AspNetCore.DataProtection.KeyManagement.XmlKeyManager[0]
      User profile is available. Using 'C:\Users\shurns\AppData\Local\ASP.NET\DataProtection-Keys' as key repository and
 Windows DPAPI to encrypt keys at rest.
Hosting environment: Development
Content root path: C:\Users\shurns\Desktop\Code\Book Code\Chapter 8\SampleApp
Now listening on: https://localhost:5001
Now listening on: http://localhost:5000
Application started. Press Ctrl+C to shut down.
info: Microsoft.AspNetCore.Hosting.Internal.WebHost[1]
      Request starting HTTP/1.1 GET http://localhost:5000/api/values
info: Microsoft.AspNetCore.Routing.EndpointMiddleware[0]
      Executing endpoint 'SampleApp.Controllers.ValuesController.Get (SampleApp)'
info: Microsoft.AspNetCore.Mvc.Internal.ControllerActionInvoker[1]
      Route matched with {action = "Get", controller = "Values"}. Executing action SampleApp.Controllers.ValuesControlle
r.Get (SampleApp)
info: Microsoft.AspNetCore.Mvc.Internal.ControllerActionInvoker[1]
      Executing action method SampleApp.Controllers.ValuesController.Get (SampleApp) - Validation state: Valid
info: Microsoft.AspNetCore.Mvc.Internal.ControllerActionInvoker[2]
      Executed action method SampleApp.Controllers.ValuesController.Get (SampleApp), returned result Microsoft.AspNetCor
e.Mvc.ObjectResult in 0.1901ms.
info: Microsoft.AspNetCore.Mvc.Infrastructure.ObjectResultExecutor[1]
      Executing ObjectResult, writing value of type 'System.String[]'.
info: Microsoft.AspNetCore.Mvc.Internal.ControllerActionInvoker[2]
      Executed action SampleApp.Controllers.ValuesController.Get (SampleApp) in 25.8181ms
info: Microsoft.AspNetCore.Routing.EndpointMiddleware[1]
      Executed endpoint 'SampleApp.Controllers.ValuesController.Get (SampleApp)'
info: Microsoft.AspNetCore.Hosting.Internal.WebHost[2]
      Request finished in 53.1094ms 200 application/json; charset=utf-8
```

And just like that, you've managed to send your first transport-level message over a socket connection.

Now, to confirm that we're receiving the responses from the server properly, we'll try to write to our `SocketTest` application's console the same message that we saw earlier in the responses from our Postman (or Insomnia) requests. In order to do that, we'll have to use the `ReceiveAsync()` method to accept whatever byte arrays were returned by the server in response to our request.

Just like with the instances of the `Stream` class we used in earlier chapters, the `ReceiveAsync()` method accepts a byte array into which it will write. For this, we'll provide it with an empty array, 512 bytes long. Once we define that, we can receive the response from the remote resource, and simply write it to our console, one line at a time. Just add the following lines of code to the bottom of your `Main()` method:

```
var receiveSeg = new ArraySegment<byte>(new byte[512], 0, 512);

await socket.ReceiveAsync(receiveSeg, SocketFlags.None);

string receivedMessage = Encoding.ASCII.GetString(receiveSeg);

foreach(var line in receivedMessage.Split("\r\n")) {
    Console.WriteLine(line);
}
Thread.Sleep(10000);
```

When you run the application now, you should see the message headers, along with the body containing the string array we saw earlier in Postman, printed to your console:

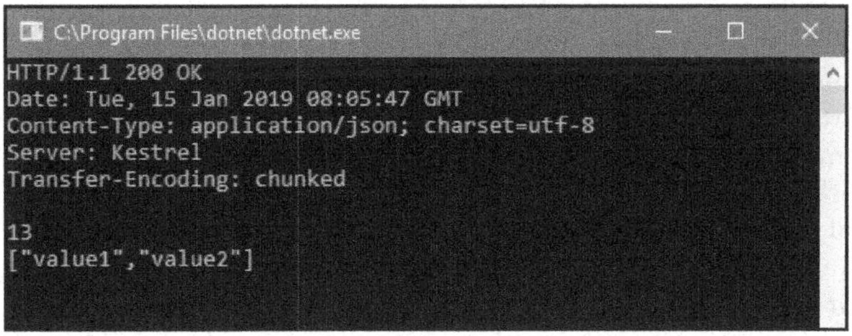

```
C:\Program Files\dotnet\dotnet.exe
HTTP/1.1 200 OK
Date: Tue, 15 Jan 2019 08:05:47 GMT
Content-Type: application/json; charset=utf-8
Server: Kestrel
Transfer-Encoding: chunked

13
["value1","value2"]
```

And just like that, you've successfully executed an HTTP request over TCP from scratch.

The last order of business is to disconnect from your host, and dispose of your socket. Let the last two lines of your application `Main()` method read as follows:

```
        ...
        socket.Disconnect(false);
        socket.Dispose();
    }
```

This is a major courtesy on your part. Even though a port can handle multiple connections simultaneously, there is an upper limit to how many connection requests it can service at a given point in time. Disconnecting your own Socket frees up resources on the remote host for others to take advantage of. While there is a maximum time limit for an inactive connection, after which the remote host will forcibly cancel the connection, you shouldn't ever let an inactive connection remain alive for that long. If you're done with the host, disconnect from the host.

Parsing responses

As I'm sure you already figured out, the simple string of ASCII characters that encapsulated the entirety of a response from your remote host is not exactly a computer-friendly format. Receiving a response is one thing, but leveraging its contents in your application is a whole different kinds of beast. Doing this kind of work from scratch every time you needed to access something on a different machine would slow the software development life cycle down to a crawl.

This is why .NET Core provides so many functional flexible wrapper and utility classes for the specific protocols and interactions you're most likely to deal with day to day. So, while I think it's important that you understand exactly how to establish and then leverage a direct connection from your application to any other application running on any other machine on your network, it's also not exactly so common that you'll find yourself needing to do so. As we move into the next few chapters, we'll see how the templates and libraries provided by .NET Core (and ASP.NET Core, in the case of HTTP) do all the heavy lifting so that we don't have to. If you're curious to learn more about low-level network interactions in C#, there's an entire ocean of knowledge and use cases that I simply didn't have time to cover in this chapter, and I would encourage you to spend some time digging in. If this content seemed a bit boring or tedious, though, don't worry. It's about to get a lot more fun.

Summary

In this chapter, we began to leverage and finally build from the foundation we've laid in previous chapters, opening up our applications to the full spectrum of network functionality available in C#. We learned that any application we write that we expect to be used by resources on our network must first be exposed to those resources through a port on our host machine. We looked at how ports are specified and registered, and learned about some restrictions that exist on how we can register our own, looking at the reason for, and the range, of well-known port addresses and the range of dynamic or ephemeral ports to which we cannot (or at least should not) register our applications.

Once we cemented that concept, we looked at the other side of the connection, and started working with sockets. We learned that sockets are a generic in-code representation of an active connection to an open port on a remote machine. We saw how the simplicity of that concept opened up a wide array of applications for socket-based network code and the low-level control it gives over packet-level communication.

With the concepts we've covered in this book so far, you have the resources necessary to write any network software you could ever need. Understanding the nature of asynchronous streams, packet construction and parsing, and socket connections to remote resources would be sufficient to implement any piece of networking functionality possible. It would be far from ideal, though, using such primitive building blocks. That's why the .NET Standard provides so many useful templates, patterns, and libraries for the myriad of applications you might have to write, and that's what we'll start looking at in the next chapter, starting with HTTP-based applications.

Questions

1. What is the definition of a port?
2. What is the range of well-known ports?
3. What is the dynamic port range?
4. What is one of the primary functions of an application server?
5. What is the definition of a socket?
6. What are some of the primary distinctions between a socket and a port?
7. Which construct provides the range of protocols over which a socket can connect?
8. What are some of the protocols that sockets support?

Further reading

For further reading on this subject, many of the books I've recommended in previous chapters still apply.

For additional insight, though, you can look at *ASP.NET Core 1.0 High Performance, James Singleton*, Packt Publishing. While the subject of that book is specifically application-layer network programming, he addresses the performance benefits of managing direct connection I/O, and the subject may be of interest. You can find it through *Packt Publishing*, here: `https://www.packtpub.com/application-development/aspnet-core-10-high-performance`.

9
HTTP in .NET

In each of the previous chapters, we explored the fundamental building blocks with which network software is built. In this chapter, we'll use those building blocks to construct an application that leverages the most common network protocol, **Hypertext Transfer Protocol** (**HTTP**). We'll re-examine where in the **Open Systems Interconnection** (**OSI**) network stack HTTP falls, and why it is categorized as such. We'll more deeply consider the conventions around HTTP requests and responses, and spend some time exploring request, response, and content headers. We'll demonstrate how to use standard headers for specifying the content you want from an external HTTP resource, and how custom headers can be used to toggle specific features and functions of your application. Lastly, we'll explore how to serve content over the protocol to service HTTP requests made to your application.

The following topics will be covered in this chapter:

- The background for the HTTP protocol, and the strengths and limitations of its specification
- The HTTP request methods, including how to generate, and respond to, those requests out of the box with C#
- How to construct `HttpRequestMessage`, or use `HttpClient` to send requests, and the various classes available for responding to requests with a valid HTTP response
- How HTTPS is implemented in C#
- New features supported by HTTP/2 and how to leverage those features in .NET Core

Technical requirements

In this chapter, we'll be using sample applications available in the GitHub repository for the book here: `https://github.com/PacktPublishing/Hands-On-Network-Programming-with-CSharp-and-.NET-Core/tree/master/Chapter 9`.

We'll also be using each of the tools we leveraged in `Chapter 8`, *Sockets and Ports*. So, if you didn't take the time to install and start working with them before, I suggest you do so now. Specifically, I recommend installing Postman from here: `https://www.getpostman.com/apps`.

Alternatively, you can use the Insomnia REST client, which can be found here: `https://insomnia.rest/`.

And, while it's not going to be featured heavily in this chapter, since deployment options will fall outside the scope of this chapter, I would encourage you to use this opportunity to begin working with Docker. I'll point out opportunities to modify and extend your Dockerfile and deploy your changes locally.

Check out the following video to see the code in action: `http://bit.ly/2HY5WaA`

Cracking open HTTP

In `Chapter 3`, *Communication Protocols*, we had a section, *The application layer*, where we looked at why certain protocols fell at that layer. With a little bit more exposure to the nitty-gritty details of network transactions under our belt, I'm hoping it will be easier to distinguish between the transport layer and the application layer. With HTTP, we have the best opportunity to explore that distinction. As a protocol, it has by far the broadest, and most robust, support from out-of-the-box C# libraries. That depth of in-language resources will give us a sharp lens through which to view the distinction between the application layer and its underlying transport layer. So, before we learn how to use HTTP, let's learn just exactly what it is.

The nature of HTTP

When we worked with low-level streams in `Chapter 8`, *Ports and Sockets*, we saw the responsibility that falls on a developer when you have to work directly with byte streams, serializing and deserializing data, and manually parsing your input headers. There's a mountain of boilerplate code just to get a simple string from one machine to another. Obviously, writing the same boilerplate code every time you need to make an external resource request is tedious and error-prone. This is where protocols come in.

We discussed the topic briefly in `Chapter 3`, *Communication Protocols*, where we looked at the protocols defined for each layer in the network stack. However, in the intervening chapters, we've established a better understanding of how different protocols are separated across the OSI stack. So, hopefully, some of the distinctions that may have been hazy back in `Chapter 3`, *Communication Protocols*, will be a bit more clear now.

When writing networked software in .NET, there are two primary tiers in the OSI stack on which we'll be working. The first, and most obvious, is the application layer. That's where HTTP lives, where FTP and SMTP live, and where any web application software that you likely have interacted with in the past would have lived. The other layer that's commonly written for in .NET, though, is the transport layer. Handling TCP and UDP calls directly within a listening server is easily done (and we'll see how in later chapters) using some of the versatile and easy-to-use utility classes you've likely come to expect from .NET Core. But what's the difference between those two layers, from the perspective of the programmer? When we're writing HTTP software, we're still very much concerned with the format and structure of our serialized data. So, why is that concern different when writing HTTP than when handling streams directly with a TCP client?

The application layer and the transport layer

The most important thing to internalize when you're trying to understand this distinction is the smallest piece of data with which each layer is concerned. The application layer is predominantly concerned with application objects. So, as long as the language you're working with provides a fully-realized abstraction of the rest of the network stack (as is the case with C#), you can write code that communicates with external resources exclusively through business and application models. You'll never have to worry about composing those models from their serialized datagrams, or wondering about the character encoding, or the endianness of integers.

Instead, you'll be speaking and thinking in terms of the end result of the network transaction—for example, *"I'm requesting a database record,"* instead of *"I'm requesting a series of bytes for the database record."* If you find yourself falling into the anti-pattern of making your application layer software over-generalized and abstract, you'll quickly find that it doesn't provide any meaningful value. Application layer software should describe and rely on at least some concrete business models; otherwise, it's just an unnecessary additional layer in between the transport layer and the segment of your code that does use those business models.

Meanwhile, on the other side of this conceptual coin, we have the transport layer. And as you've likely figured out, software written at this level needs no business context to be implemented properly and provide its expected value. In fact, any representation of non-primitive `Objects` beyond simple generics, such as `Serialize<T>()`, would render your transport layer software pretty much useless outside the context of a specific business application. Any architecture for transport-layered software built around concrete business objects would be like a house made out of toothpicks and held together with bubblegum: unstable and short-lived.

I highlight the distinction between application- and transport-layer software now to make the content of the rest of this chapter more intuitive. Going forward, some of the classes we'll be working with and thinking about in .NET, and some of the advice I'll be giving you around this, will rely on your understanding of this distinction. Moreover, though, it's good to understand how HTTP came to be, and how it transformed into what it is today.

The history of HTTP

As I mentioned in `Chapter 3`, *Communication Protocols*, while, today, HTTP is the de-facto protocol of web-based software, its original design and intent is actually much simpler and more limited. Even its namesake, **hypertext**, has grown well beyond its original conception.

First described in 1965, hypertext was defined as a specification for rendering text on a computer, or other electronic device, with references to other hypertext documents, which could be immediately accessed through a system of references, known as **hyperlinks**. At its most basic, this describes little more than a primitive web page. In fact, you've undoubtedly already realized the link between *hypertext* as a concept and the hypertext markup language, or HTML, file format, which is used to render web pages. These basic specifications served as the precursor to the modern internet.

Like much of our modern world, the origins for hypertext, HTML, and HTTP can be traced back to an influential work of science fiction! A 1941 short story titled *The Garden of Forking Paths*, by Jorge Luis Borges, is often credited with being the inspiration for the first definition of hypertext.

Decades later, in 1989, researchers at the **European Organization for Nuclear Research (CERN)** began to formalize their efforts to define the standards for a global computer network, now known as the **World Wide Web (WWW)**. This work included defining a standard for document representation, as well as a protocol for transmitting those documents between machines. In 1991, the first ever formal definition for HTTP was drafted, and dubbed **v0.9**.

This original definition was extremely limited in its scope, intended only to define the process of requesting hypertext pages from a given server; the specification defined a single method, which is `GET`. As the early internet began to reach consumers, however, the needs of the wider audience forced the evolution of the standards for the network. By the time HTTP v1.0 was formalized and broadly recognized in 1996, the standard grew to include message headers, security, and a wider array of operations.

Still, though, it was almost exclusively used to transmit web pages from servers to clients. Each request had to negotiate its own connection with the server, and once that request was serviced, the connection was closed. This kind of behavior makes sense if you're only requesting a static web page, but what if you wanted to incorporate user interaction? That connection negotiation comes at a cost.

The engineers at CERN recognized this, and in only one year, in 1997, they released an updated HTTP v1.1 (often written as HTTP/1.1) specification that provided an even richer feature set. This included headers to specify response-caching behavior, persistent connections, authentication and authorization, message syntax, and routing or redirection behavior. In fact, HTTP/1.1 remains largely unchanged and widely used today. However, while the protocol has remained largely unchanged until the recent advent of HTTP/2, introduced in 2015, the ways in which engineers *use* the protocol have grown exponentially.

Web services and HTTP

As the internet began to grow from a niche utility for business and engineering professionals to share resources and information in the early-to-mid 1990s to the wide-spread platform it is today, the software written for the internet had to grow along with it. The simplicity and extensibility of HTTP provided such a reliable, broadly understood, and broadly supported protocol that it rapidly outgrew its original stated intent. Engineers began to leverage it for almost every instance of networked services and resource access. Now HTTP is the protocol of choice for almost any open API available on the internet.

Early on, Microsoft recognized this, and when it released the first version of the .NET framework back in 2001, it did so with full support for HTTP as the de-facto application layer protocol for general-purpose network-resource access. Later, with the advent of the **Windows Communication Foundation** (**WCF**), along with the **Windows Presentation Foundation** (**WPF**), Microsoft continued to lean heavily on HTTP for application-layer network services.

For those who may not know, WCF was Microsoft's suite of libraries and frameworks for network-specific, service-oriented application development. Meanwhile, WPF was Microsoft's framework for asynchronous user-interface code paradigms. It sought to provide the same rich set of features and controls for any desktop or web applications with a UI, with a consistent look and feel.

The advent of SOAP

Much of WCF was tailored specifically to the implementation of **Simple Object Access Protocol** (**SOAP**) services. At first glance, SOAP seems to be an application-layer protocol in itself. However, in practice, it's actually a protocol that exists one layer above the actual OSI network stack. So, while an application that implements the SOAP protocol ensures reliable behavior for any consumers, it doesn't do so in any way that is necessary for interaction between network-available resources, as we discussed in `Chapter 3`, *Communication Protocols*. Instead, it sits comfortably on top of the OSI stack, interacting directly with application-layer protocols to service the actual network interactions required by SOAP applications and their consumers. So, while SOAP-based applications rigidly defined their interactions through a protocol, those interactions were still most often initiated over an HTTP network transaction.

This had an interesting side effect, however. While SOAP services were leaning heavily on HTTP as their transport protocol of choice, it carried with it several drawbacks for the emerging web ecosystem of consumer-facing applications and services. SOAP was notoriously verbose in both its request and response message structure. It had slow transfer and message-parsing performance due to its heavy reliance on XML for serialization. Lastly, as a protocol, its implementations were heavily fragmented, leading to no reliable SOAP request pattern for use across the vast array of services that were, ostensibly, SOAP-based.

Beginning in the year 2007, with the release of the first iPhone, and continuing into the next decade, smartphones rapidly became a viable platform for dedicated, consumer-facing applications. While access to broadband internet connections was exploding across the globe, cellular networks, which served most of the internet-connected devices entering the market, were still several years behind in terms of performance and reliability. Meanwhile, all of the disadvantages of SOAP led to poor performance and longer development cycles for engineers writing applications to consume one or more SOAP-based web services. Across the industry, engineers were realizing that they needed an alternative. Millions of dollars were there to be made, but with the change needing to be made seemingly overnight for the mobile app market, there was almost no time for SOAP to adapt, or even for an alternative version to materialize.

The rise of REST

So, how did engineers and leaders in the market space adapt? They went back to the basics and looked to leverage the underlying protocol more robustly—less bloat, fewer intermediary interactions, and less serializing and parsing and negotiating connections. Instead, they would use HTTP as the interaction protocol and leverage its features to allow for more dynamic and robust interaction while minimizing time spent writing custom, service-specific access protocols. To satisfy these goals, engineers across the world would leverage REST.

Short for **Representational State Transfer**, REST was designed as an architectural pattern, as opposed to an access protocol. It is convention-based, instead of contract-based. This means that anyone familiar with the conventions can use any RESTful web service simply by following those conventions. This reduces development time for engineers, because it means they can learn the architectural patterns once, and then use them everywhere that REST is used. This is obviously much more preferable than having to consume and develop for a given contract for a single SOAP service, and then having to do the same for each new contract for each new service they might have to consume.

By refusing to implement a custom protocol on top of the application layer of the OSI stack, REST reduces overhead in terms of message negotiation and parsing. And since HTTP is, far and away, the most common application-layer protocol used for REST services, those services are free to serve up their responses in whatever format HTTP can deliver. This means no more strict reliance on XML as your serialization language of choice. Instead, JSON has risen as the quick-to-serialize and quick-to-parse format of choice for RESTful web services.

The improved performance and increased flexibility of pure HTTP meant that any APIs or services that were intended for consumption by mobile applications were, almost universally, REST services. So, in effect, REST rose to replace SOAP as the web service paradigm of choice for modern network interactions, and it did so on the back of HTTP.

HTTP web services in .NET core

With the broad applicability of the convention-based REST paradigm, Microsoft's WCF has fallen, somewhat quickly, by the wayside. In its place has risen the web API template from ASP.NET, and now ASP.NET Core. Leveraging the patterns first formally described in the book *Design Patterns: Elements of Reusable Object-Oriented Software*, by Gang of Four, ASP.NET released the **Model-View-Controller** (**MVC**) application template and libraries to enable the use of clean, convention-based software patterns right out of the box.

For those not familiar with it, the MVC design pattern describes a strategy for isolating the logical responsibilities of complex, user-interactive software into logical groupings and organizational structures. The view tier was exactly what it sounds like: any UI code or markup that would be sent to the client (typically, a user's web browser of choice). The model tier described your data models, and how you access them from whatever persistence mechanism the application is using. It typically includes your data-access code as well as any data models that are sent to or from your application. Finally, the controller tier describes the business application logic that ties your models into a useful context for your users, and ultimately returns that context to your user as a view. It serves as an intermediary between the other two tiers.

When the ASP.NET team wanted to define a newer, REST-based pattern for full-featured web applications that would leave the bloat of SOAP behind, its members looked to MVC. The MVC project template associates every available public resource (in the case of early MVC, this was almost always a web page, or a fragment of a web page) with a specific HTTP verb at a specific URI. This simplified access to resources, as developers only ever needed to know what the target address was and how to make a generic HTTP request against that address. It also communicated a lot about the nature of the resource based on the HTTP verb required to access it. We'll see more of this later in the chapter, but that correlation of semantic structure to operational use is a massive shortcut when working with new web services.

From MVC to web API

Originally, MVC was designed for full-featured web applications serving a UI with which users could interact with their backend services. However, the extent to which the project template so closely matched the REST paradigm made it a popular choice for backend web services that provided no UI whatsoever. In the early 2010s, it was common for .NET developers to start from an MVC template, only to scrap any semblance of frontend UI code, instead allowing their controller components to return raw JSON responses. Needless to say, it didn't take very long for Microsoft to recognize the trend and release the Web API project template with an update to Visual Studio's project template library.

With the Web API template, developers can have a basic, RESTful web service up and running with only two simple commands in the .NET Core CLI. Controller endpoints listen for designated HTTP request methods and return arbitrary responses, with no assumptions made about any corresponding UI components. Almost every modern REST API implemented in .NET will have been created with this project template as its starting point. To that end, we'll spend the rest of this chapter exploring HTTP from the context of a Web API project, which will both listen for, and respond to, incoming HTTP requests, as well as sending outgoing requests to external APIs. This pattern of writing an intermediary aggregator API is extremely common in modern enterprise web development, especially in the growing trend of microservices and cloud-hosted applications. With that in mind, let's stand up our application and start exploring how .NET makes HTTP programming enjoyable.

The many methods of HTTP

While we took some time to explore the concept all the way back in `Chapter 3`, *Communication Protocols*, in this section, we'll take a much closer look at the modus operandi of HTTP: the methods. We'll look at each one in the context of our Web API app, and discuss their intended use case, limitations, and the conventions of those methods that you would do well to follow. To do that, though, we'll need our app up and running. So, let's first take a look at how that happens with the Web API project created by the .NET CLI.

Creating a web API project

Just as we did for our sample application in `Chapter 8`, *Sockets and Ports*, we'll be creating an instance of a Web API project with the following command:

```
dotnet new webapi -n FitnessApp
```

That name might seem odd, so let's describe our application's basic expected functionality, and then hopefully it will make more sense. We'll be writing an API that will allow users to track fitness activity over time, along with an almost identical API that will serve as our data source. This will give us an opportunity to see how to listen for different HTTP requests made of our own app, while also giving us just enough context to work with generating HTTP requests to an outbound service. The actual shape and functionality of our data store app will be almost identical to the user-facing API. The only difference is that when our `FitnessApp` needs to persist data, it will do so by making HTTP calls to our `FitnessDataStore` app. Meanwhile, when our `FitnessDataStore` app needs to store data, it will do so by writing to a file on disk.

The only code we'll be working with in this chapter will be the `FitnessApp` code, since that will encapsulate all of the interactions we'll want to learn about. The backend data service is available in the sample code for this chapter, though, so feel free to browse it, extend it, and modify it if you're curious. Also, since our focus will be on the HTTP interactions of this application, and it's for demonstration purposes only, we'll be making a lot of naive assumptions about data modeling, persistence, and error handling. Instead, I'll leave those considerations as an exercise for you to consider and re-evaluate in your own time.

Our application will allow consumers to create new workouts with titles; workout types and comments; look up previous workouts by their title, workout type, or the contents of their comments; retrieve a list of all previous workouts; edit an existing workout's comments; and, finally, it will allow users to delete previous workouts from their history. As I said before, each of these operations is specifically designed to highlight some aspect of HTTP, as implemented by a .NET Core Web API, so the implementation details of these operations will be somewhat simplistic and naive, or even overlooked entirely. What's important here is to understand the expected I/O and how to model these operations to their appropriate HTTP methods. With that in mind, let's look at the project we've just created for ourselves.

The web server

Looking at our Solution Explorer, you'll notice that there's not a whole lot to this project template:

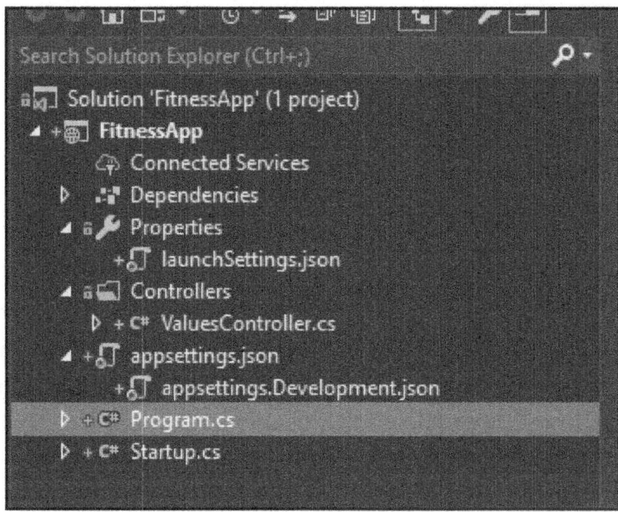

There's just two configuration `.json` files, a single controller class, and then the initialization and program files. At this point, those new to web development in .NET Core might be wondering why we have both a `Program.cs` file and a `Startup.cs` file. This is because, like all .NET Core applications, our Web API project is actually a console application executed in the context of the `dotnet` host application running on the target machine. So, our `Program.cs` provides the conventional `Main()` method as the entry point for our `dotnet` execution context to start our application.

However, since we're running an active web application, we'll want to stand up a listening web server and provide it the context of our application so that it responds to requests appropriately. That's where the `Startup.cs` file comes in. This provides all of the configuration, including registering our concrete types for dependency injection, and defining the active features and services we intend to leverage. Once we've defined all of that, the `Startup` class is provided to our web server instance and used to configure the server.

IWebHostBuilder

Looking at our `Program.cs` file, you can see that's exactly what happens: the `Main()` method only builds our web host, and starts it running with no terminating condition:

```
public class Program
{
    public static void Main(string[] args)
    {
        CreateWebHostBuilder(args).Build().Run();
    }

    public static IWebHostBuilder CreateWebHostBuilder(string[] args) =>
        WebHost.CreateDefaultBuilder(args)
            .UseStartup<Startup>();
}
```

The `WebHost` class is part of the `Microsoft.AspNetCore` namespace, and its default implementation provides a running Kestrel web server that interacts with your application code using the `Startup.cs` file provided to the `UseStartup<T>()` method on the `IWebHostBuilder` instance you return to your `Main()` method to be run by your program.

By default, the web server created by the call to `CreateDefaultBuilder()` is going to be an instance of a **Kestrel** web server. Kestrel is a cross-platform server that will acquire a designated port so it can listen for inbound requests against that port, passing all received requests through to your application code. It supports HTTP/HTTPS, WebSockets, Unix sockets, and HTTP/2, all out of the box. In modern .NET Core apps, there's rarely an occasion to use anything other than the default Kestrel server anymore. It can run as an edge server, which means it is the first point of contact for any incoming requests made of your application (listening at the edge or boundary of your host machine). Likewise, it can be run behind a reverse proxy, such as **Internet Information Services** (**IIS**) or Nginx, as discussed in `Chapter 8`, *Sockets and Ports*.

There are a number of advantages to running Kestrel behind a reverse proxy. For example, a reverse proxy allows your Kestrel instance to listen for requests targeting the same port registered for other listening applications, while running it as an edge server blocks the port it is registered to from being used by other applications. This leaves your Kestrel instance to handle every inbound request made to its registered port, regardless of the targeted URI path or host name specified in the requests headers. If the IP is resolved to your application's host machine, and the port is the one Kestrel is registered on, Kestrel will service it.

This port-blocking behavior might make perfect sense if your application is the only software deployed and running inside a Docker container published to a cloud-hosting platform. However, if it's deployed to an on-premises server hosting dozens or even hundreds of other web services, then managing the port registration, traffic load, and other resourcing or configuration would likely be unwise, or at the very least unpleasant. In that case, a reverse proxy would be the most reliable deployment solution. It's up to you to determine the pros and cons of using a reverse proxy or running Kestrel as an edge server, but whatever you choose, you'll have the tools you need to enable your decision.

So, when you want to define the behavior of your application code, you do so in the `Startup.cs` file, whereas when you want to define the behavior of the Kestrel web server that exposes your application code, you do so with your `IWebHostBuilder`. Let's look at how to configure our server for now, and then dive into our application code's configuration.

First, let's set the URLs we want our application to listen on. For our purposes, we'll have direct control over the entire hosting context of any software on our machine, so we'll be running Kestrel as an edge server for simplicity's sake. Now, to register our server to listen at a specific port, we'll be using the extension methods made available on our `IWebHostBuilder` instance that are returned when we call `WebHost.CreateDefaultBuilder(args)`.

It might not be obvious when you look at it, but the `UseStartup<T>()` method is actually one of those extension methods. It just happens to be so common that the Web API project template pre-configures that for you whenever you create a new project. And this is a good thing. The methods in `Startup.cs` provide users with the opportunity to centralize a lot of boilerplate code and dynamically register their concrete classes for dependency injection at runtime. If you haven't used dependency injection before, you'll quickly see why this is a huge quality of life improvement, and why this little snippet of code is included by the default template.

The first extension method we'll use is the `UseUrls(string[])` method to register the IP addresses and ports on which our Kestrel instance will be actively listening for incoming requests. To do so, change the `CreateWebHostBuilder(string[] args)` method to the following:

```
public static IWebHostBuilder CreateWebHostBuilder(string[] args) =>
    WebHost.CreateDefaultBuilder(args)
        .UseUrls(new string[] { "http://[::]:80", "https://[::]:443",
"http://[::]:65432", "https://[::]:65431" })
        .UseStartup<Startup>();
```

You'll note that I've registered our server to listen on multiple ports for both HTTP and HTTPS requests. I mostly did this for demonstration purposes. It's rare that you'll want to actively listen on multiple ports with a single application, but this highlights that the `UseUrls()` method will allow you to register and listen on an arbitrary number of available ports.

This code won't work if you plan to ping your API using a mock host name by adding entries into your `hosts` file, as we did in `Chapter 2`, *DNS and Resource Location*. Because any host entries you create will be explicitly mapped to the IP address `127.0.0.1`, you'll have to explicitly configure Kestrel to listen for that exact IP address. You can look at the `FitnessDataStore` sample code for an example.

Using launchSettings.json

Alternately, you can define your application's listening URLs using the `launchSettings.json` file. This file allows you to specify behavior based on the specific environment your application is deployed under. Launch profiles can be customized based on the web server hosting your application (IIS Express, or Kestrel, which is defined as a profile under your project's name when you first create a project using the CLI).

When you launch your application with the `dotnet run` command, .NET will look for a `launchSettings.json` file, then search for the first profile whose `commandName` parameter has a value of `"Project"`, which will use the Kestrel web server. From within this profile, you can set environment variables that you intend to be leveraged by your application. Any environment variables you define in your launch profile will override the values of environment variables that exist on your host system. This allows you to define different values for environment variables for different circumstances, simply by setting them in their corresponding launch profile.

You can also set various configurations for your web server inside your launch profile. If you look in the `launchSettings.json` file that was created when we stood up our `FitnessApp`, you'll see that it has a profile named `FitnessApp`, with a `commandName` value of `Property` as seen here:

```
"FitnessApp": {
    "commandName": "Project",
    "launchBrowser": true,
    "launchUrl": "api/values",
    "applicationUrl": "https://localhost:5001;http://localhost:5000",
    "environmentVariables": {
        "ASPNETCORE_ENVIRONMENT": "Development"
    }
}
```

Pay special attention to the `applicationUrl` property there, as it will come up in just a moment, as we're running our app for the first time.

Now, for the sake of simplicity when using Postman, we'll change our server settings to not use HTTPS redirection for inbound requests to `http://` URLs. This just prevents us from having to configure Postman to follow re-directs, and gives us a more direct correlation between the code we're writing and the behavior we observe when we test it. To disable the behavior, simply navigate to your `Startup.cs` file and, near the bottom of the file, find and remove the line that reads as follows:

```
app.UseHttpsRedirection();
```

Once that's done, it's time to run our application. Simply navigate to the folder you created the project in with your command prompt and then execute `dotnet run`. Once you have, you should see the following in your terminal:

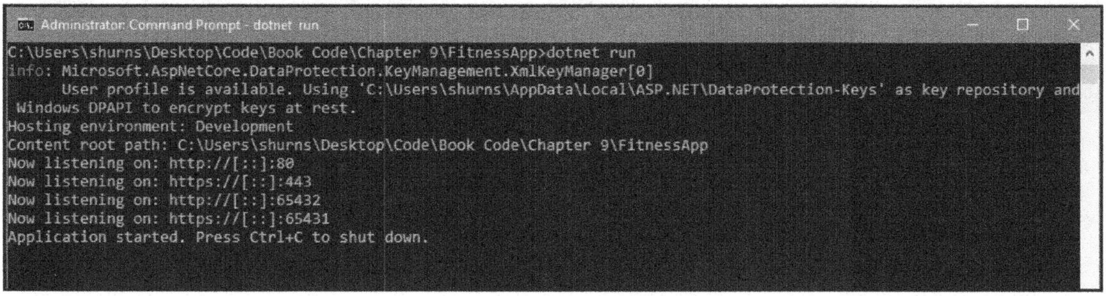

```
Administrator: Command Prompt - dotnet run
C:\Users\shurns\Desktop\Code\Book Code\Chapter 9\FitnessApp>dotnet run
info: Microsoft.AspNetCore.DataProtection.KeyManagement.XmlKeyManager[0]
      User profile is available. Using 'C:\Users\shurns\AppData\Local\ASP.NET\DataProtection-Keys' as key repository and
 Windows DPAPI to encrypt keys at rest.
Hosting environment: Development
Content root path: C:\Users\shurns\Desktop\Code\Book Code\Chapter 9\FitnessApp
Now listening on: http://[::]:80
Now listening on: https://[::]:443
Now listening on: http://[::]:65432
Now listening on: https://[::]:65431
Application started. Press Ctrl+C to shut down.
```

You probably noticed that the application is currently listening on each of the ports we specified in the array we passed to the `UseUrls()` method, but on none of the ports that were specified by the `launchSettings.json` profile.

In order to test this code, you'll first need to prevent Postman from checking for the SSL certificates it's expecting whenever you navigate to an `https:// url`. To do so, simply open your **SETTINGS** and disable **SSL certificate verification**, as seen here:

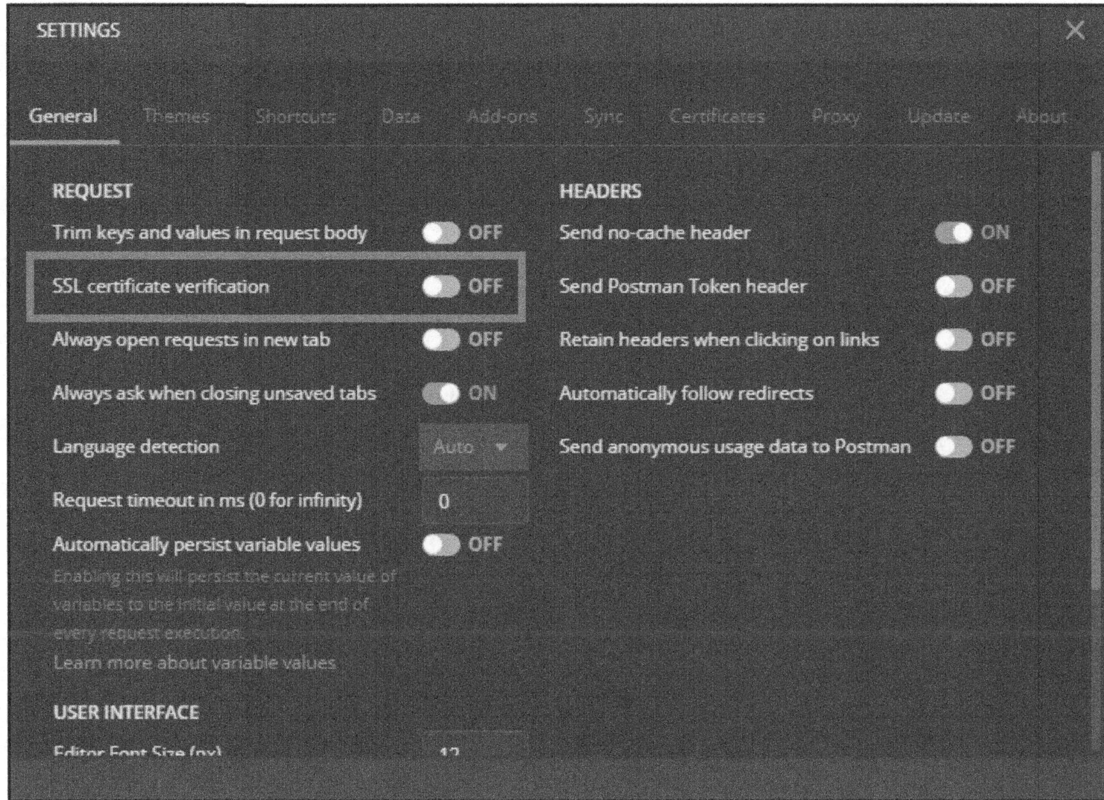

We'll look closer at SSL certificates and what this particular Postman setting means in `Chapter 13`, *Transport Layer Security*. For now, though, it's sufficient to simply disable that setting and proceed accordingly. Once that's done, open Postman and send `GET` requests to each of the following URLs:

```
http://localhost/api/values
https://localhost/api/values
http://localhost:65432/api/values
https://localhost:65431/api/values
```

You should see the following JSON get returned by all four:

```
[
    "value1",
    "value2"
]
```

You might have noticed we didn't have to specify ports 80 or 443 in that list. This is because, as discussed in `Chapter 8`, *Sockets and Ports*, each of those ports is reserved for HTTP and HTTPS, respectively. So, no port specification on an `http://` or `https://` request is the same as specifying 80 or 443.

Meanwhile, if you try to navigate to either of the URLs configured in the `launchSettings.json` file, you'll get no response at all. This is because, while settings configured in a launch profile in your `launchSettings.json` file will always override any system settings that have already been defined, settings configured inside your application code when you launch and run your Kestrel server will always override any launch profiles. Settings lower down in your scope will always override settings configured higher up in your scope.

Since configuring your web server in your application's code will always override any other configuration values, you should only use that for the most important settings that you always want to behave in a single, specific way. Otherwise, the `ASPNETCORE_*` environment variables and launch profiles should be used. They provide a high degree of flexibility with a low maintenance cost.

Now that our web server is configured to listen for requests to our designated ports, let's use our `Startup.cs` file to set up our application to make HTTP requests of its own.

Registering dependencies in startup.cs

We'll be using the `ConfigureServices(IServiceCollection services)` method in our `Startup.cs` class to register our specific classes for dependency injection, starting with our `IHttpClientFactory` class instances. If you've never used it before, dependency injection is a great tool for creating loose coupling between different aspects of your software that are likely to change over time. Essentially, whenever one class (`ClassA`) leverages the properties or methods of another (`ClassB`) in order to perform its own functions, a dependency is created. We can say that `ClassA` depends on `ClassB`. There are a number of ways to resolve that dependency. The naive approach would have us creating instances of `ClassB` directly inside of `ClassA` wherever its methods are used, as seen here:

```
public class ClassA {
    public string CreateStringWithoutClassB() { ... }
    public string CreateStringWithClassB() {
        var bInstance = new ClassB();
        var builder = new StringBuilder();
        builder.Append(CreateStringWithoutClassB());
        builder.Append(bInstance.GetSpecialString());
        return builder.ToString();
    }
}
```

But this brings with it a whole host of problems over the course of development. If `ClassB` ever needs to be changed, then we'll have to change it everywhere it's referenced. The more explicit dependencies we have, the more places we have to change it.

Instead, we can inject the dependency. To do so, we define an interface for the useful functionality that `ClassB` provides for `ClassA` and then define `ClassB` as an implementer of that interface. In our example, this `IClassB` interface would need to define a method with the signature `string GetSpecialString();` and that's it. Next, we can simply say that `ClassA` needs something that implements the `IClassB` interface. To make this dependency clear, without demanding an instance of the concrete `ClassB`, we define a constructor that accepts any implementer of `IClassB`. This changes our naive approach into the following definition for `ClassA`:

```
public class ClassA {
    private IClassB _classB;
    public ClassA(IClassB classBInstance) {
        _classB = classBInstance;
    }
    public string CreateStringWithoutClassB() { ... }
    public string CreateStringWithClassB() {
        var builder = new StringBuilder();
```

```
            builder.Append(CreateStringWithoutClassB());
            builder.Append(_classB.GetSpecialString());
            return builder.ToString();
        }
    }
```

So, now, the `ClassA` class doesn't depend on the `ClassB` class; instead, we can say it depends on some functionality that the `ClassB` class happens to provide. But it doesn't concern itself with how it gets that functionality. Instead, determining what the best concrete class to use is falls on the calling code that instantiates `ClassA`. Whatever uses `ClassA` has to determine the best concrete instance of `IClassB`, create an instance of it, and then inject it into the newly created instance of `ClassA`. If the `IClassB` implementer will ever change based on context, or new project requirements, we can make those functional changes without having to modify `ClassA` at all. And that is dependency injection in a nutshell!

There's actually a whole lot more to dependency injection when you find yourself using it in a professional context. Entire books have been written about the subject. And, as with any design pattern, you'll find as many opinions about it as engineers you ask for those opinions, and it can be a subject of heated debate in some circles. It is way beyond the scope of this chapter (and even this book) to go into detail about the many nuances of dependency injection. However, my hope is that this explanation will serve as enough of a primer for any readers who have never used it before to understand the concept enough to understand how to register dependencies in our `Startup.cs` file.

The IHttpClientFactory class

The first service we'll want to register will be our `HttpClientFactory`. This class is an incredibly useful factory class that will provide managed instances of the `HttpClient` class. Prior to this wrapper class managing instances of `HttpClient` for us, there was actually a very painful and difficult-to-track-down bug that would arise when using common patterns for creating and disposing of instances of `HttpClient` by hand. Since the `HttpClient` class implements the `IDisposable` interface, many developers would instantiate it within the context of a `using(var client = new HttpClient())` statement. While this is the recommended pattern for almost every other class that implements `IDisposable`, in the specific case of `HttpClient`, there was an issue with instances of the client failing to release their listening threads. This bug lead to infrequent and inconsistent thread starvation in applications with high volumes of outbound HTTP requests. It was a painful problem, and the solution we have for it is the `HttpClientFactory` class.

With this class, we can request instances of `HttpClient` and trust that they will be allocated resources on the thread pool properly, and reused wherever possible to reduce memory overhead and performance concerns. Given that, it only seems appropriate that this is where we take our first steps with registering our dependencies in the `Startup.cs` folder.

First, though, we'll need to create a class that has a dependency on the `HttpClientFactory` class. In the root of your project folder, create a new folder named `Services`, and inside that folder, create a new class file named `FitnessDataStoreClient.cs`. This is the class we'll eventually use to write our data back to our `FitnessDataStore` API, which means this is the class that will need an `HttpClient` class to send those requests.

Once you have the file created, add a `private readonly` instance of the `IHttpClientFactory` interface. Then create a single constructor for your new class that accepts an instance of `IHttpClientFactory` as its only argument. Finally, assign the argument instance to your private member variable. After doing so, your file should look like this:

```
namespace FitnessApp {
  public class FitnessDataStoreClient {
    private readonly IHttpClientFactory _httpFactory;

    public FitnessDataStoreClient(IHttpClientFactory factoryInstance) {
      _httpFactory = factoryInstance;
    }
  }
}
```

You might be wondering why you can assign to a variable that's marked as `readonly`. Any class property or member variable that is marked as `readonly` can be written to only in the constructors for the class, or when they are explicitly declared. This little feature of the language is especially nice in the case of dependency injection, as it gives developers the opportunity to inject dependencies that might otherwise need to remain immutable.

And now that we've established our dependency, we'll need to register a concrete instance of it for use in our `Startup.cs` file. With this particular class, since the need for an `HttpClient` class is so common in so many web applications, there's actually an extension method on the `IServiceCollection` to register an `IHttpClientFactory` instance for injection. To use it in its most basic form, we'll only need to add a single line to our file. In the `ConfigureServices(IServiceCollection services)` method, simply insert the following line:

```
services.AddHttpClient();
```

And just like that, when you run your application, your `FitnessDataStoreClient` will have access to a valid instance of `HttpClientFactory`.

Unfortunately, though, this implementation is fairly basic. With what we've written, we'll have to configure our `HttpClient` instance every time we request it from the factory class. That means defining the base URL, any default headers we may want to apply, and other minutia. Instead, we can use the overload method of `AddHttpClient()` to create a named client. By doing this, we can centralize some of the boilerplate client configuration into our `Startup.cs` file, and then when we invoke the named client in our application code, we can skip straight ahead to sending requests with it. Using named clients also gives us a simple way to manage the need to connect to multiple distinct data sources. Doing so not only makes our code easier by eliminating some of the boilerplate of establishing a connection for HTTP requests, but can also improve performance by sharing connections between various references to the same named `HttpClient` instance.

To demonstrate this, I'll actually be creating two distinct aliases in my hosts file for the `FitnessDataStore` API. So, even though, behind the scenes, all requests to that API will be going to the same IP address, from the perspective of our `FitnessApp` API, it will look as though we're leveraging two distinct APIs with two distinct URLs, and two distinct named `HttpClient` instances. To test out this code for yourself, add the following lines to your hosts file, similar to how we did it in `Chapter 2`, *DNS and Resource Location*:

```
127.0.0.1 fitness.write.data.com
127.0.0.1 fitness.read.data.com
```

Now we can configure our `HttpClient` instances for each of these host names. With named instances of `HttpClientFactory`, we can specify the name by which we'll identify the specific instance we want to create, as well as define some default behavior for the client we're naming. We'll just call our different clients `WRITER` and `READER` for now. So, modify our `ConfigureServices(IServiceCollection services)` method as follows:

```
public void ConfigureServices(IServiceCollection services)
{
services.AddMvc().SetCompatibilityVersion(CompatibilityVersion.Version_2_2)
;

    services.AddHttpClient("WRITER", c => {
        c.BaseAddress = new Uri("http://fitness.write.data.com:56789");
        c.DefaultRequestHeaders.Add("Accept", "application/json");
    });

    services.AddHttpClient("READER", c => {
        c.BaseAddress = new Uri("http://fitness.read.data.com:56789");
        c.DefaultRequestHeaders.Add("Accept", "application/json");
    });
}
```

While the `Accept` header isn't usually the most important thing to concern ourselves with, this should be sufficient to demonstrate how you might configure the common properties for all requests bound generated by the named client. If you have a common authorization scheme, you can simply define those values once, in your `Startup.cs` class, and not have to concern yourself with updating authentication or authorization keys everywhere in your code that makes requests using those keys.

Since named `HttpClient` instances must be created using the same name they were registered with, it's usually best to keep the names in a central configuration file, and then reference the value out of that file in both the `Startup.cs` code that registers the named client, as well as the application code that requests it. Always avoid magic strings wherever possible.

Now that we have our named clients registered, let's get our data-access client set up to register with the dependency injection framework so we can start working with our controller class.

Registering services in Startup.cs

In the sample code, you'll find a simple model representing a record in our fitness activity database. I placed it in a `Models` folder, which is located in the root of the `project` directory. This is a common convention in MVC/Web API applications, but you can organize your code however makes the most sense for you. This class itself is relatively straightforward, and represents all the fields described in the project requirements I set out at the start of this section:

```
namespace FitnessApp {
    public class FitnessRecord {
        public string title { get; set; }
        public string workoutType { get; set; }
        public string comments { get; set; }
        public DateTime workoutDate { get; set; }
    }
}
```

So, now, inside our `FitnessDataStoreClient` class, we'll want to define the operations we expect to be able to perform on our data store. According to our specs, we'll want to be able to look up all current records, look up individual records by their unique `title` property, look up records by `workoutType`, modify the `comments` field, and delete a record with a given `title`. For now, let's define those methods to return either a mock response, or just throw `NotImplementedException()` to satisfy our build system. We'll come back to fill out the implementation later in the chapter when we look at formatting and generating our requests using `HttpClient`:

```
public class FitnessDataStoreClient : IDataStoreClient{
  private readonly IHttpClientFactory _httpFactory;

  public FitnessDataStoreClient(IHttpClientFactory httpFactoryInstance) {
    _httpFactory = httpFactoryInstance;
  }

  public async Task<bool> WriteRecord(FitnessRecord newRecord) {
    return false;
  }

  public async Task<List<FitnessRecord>> GetAllRecords() {
    return new List<FitnessRecord>();
  }

  public async Task<List<FitnessRecord>> GetRecordsByWorkoutType(string
workoutType) {
    return new List<FitnessRecord>();
  }
```

```
  public async Task<FitnessRecord> GetRecordByTitle(string title) {
    return new FitnessRecord();
  }

  public async Task<bool> UpdateRecord(string title, string newComment) {
    return true;
  }

  public async Task<bool> DeleteRecord(string title) {
    return true;
  }
}
```

While we have our implementation defined, we still need to define the interface that we'll use to register the class for dependency injection into our controller. We've already declared our `FitnessDataStoreClient` class to implement `IDataStoreClient`, so that's the name of the interface we'll create for dependency injection. So, either at the top of the current file, or in a new file located in the same folder, add the following interface definition:

```
public interface IDataStoreClient {
  Task<bool> WriteRecord(FitnessRecord newRecord);
  Task<List<FitnessRecord>> GetAllRecords();
  Task<List<FitnessRecord>> GetRecordsByWorkoutType(string workoutType);
  Task<FitnessRecord> GetRecordByTitle(string title);
  Task<bool> UpdateRecord(string title, string newComment);
  Task<bool> DeleteRecord(string title);
}
```

And since our data store client is going to be entirely stateless (that is to say, having no instance properties that might vary between instances of the class), we can safely register it as a singleton instance in our `Startup.cs` file. So, from inside the `ConfigureServices(...)` method, add the following line:

```
services.AddSingleton<IDataStoreClient, FitnessDataStoreClient>();
```

This particular helper method will allow our dependency injection container to create a single instance of the concrete class the first time the class is created. The dependency injection container will then provide a reference to that single created instance for all subsequent requests for an instance. WebHost will then inject a reference to that single instance into each other class that requests an implementer of the IDataStoreClient interface for dependency injection. If you need multiple instances created for requesting your API handles, you can use the services.AddScoped<Interface, Implementation>() variant of this method, as this allows new instances to be created with a state that lives only as long as it takes to return a response for a given request. Alternatively, if you need a new instance every time an instance is injected anywhere in your application, regardless of scope, you can use the services.AddTransient<Interface, Implementation>() variant. Each of these alternatives will provide the same inversion of control that is necessary for dependency injection without holding a single managed instance of the implementation class over the lifetime of the application, as is the case with AddSingleton().

Handling incoming HTTP methods

Now that we have our service class defined and registered for use in our Startup.cs file, it's time to leverage it in our controller and start responding to incoming HTTP requests. First, though, we'll want to modify our controller class so it's a bit more useful for our purposes. Start by changing the name of the class to FitnessController and removing all of the method stubs provided by the initial project template. At the top of the class definition, you'll see two DataAttributes defined, like so:

```
[Route("api/[controller]")]
[ApiController]
```

These provide context for your WebServer about the nature of this class file. The first one specifies that your WebServer should respond to all requests to the URI path api/[controller] by looking for valid methods inside this particular class. Now, here, [controller] is a special placeholder that is replaced with the name of your controller class (the segment of your class name that prefixes controller), so when we change the name of our class file to FitnessController and run the application, we should begin seeing valid responses by navigating to http://localhost/api/fitness.

The second DataAttribute, `[ApiController]` method, is actually very important if we want our controller to behave as expected. Using that attribute at the top of a type definition tells our `WebHostBuilder` to use this particular class as a controller and explore its method signatures to discover endpoints that should be exposed by the server. It also notifies our `WebServer` to perform automatic model-binding validation. What that means is that whenever a request comes in targeting one of the controller's endpoints, the inputs specified in the signature of the endpoint should match the shape of the request message. By specifying our controller as an `ApiController`, `WebServer` will make sure that requests messages match our expected inputs before it invokes our controller's methods.

With the name changed, and the methods removed, we need to set up our controller to use the registered instance of the `IDataStoreClient` implementation. So, let's create a private member variable and inject our instance with a constructor for our controller:

```
public class FitnessController : ControllerBase {
    private readonly IDataStoreClient _dataStore;

    public FitnessController(IDataStoreClient data) {
        _dataStore = data;
    }
    ...
}
```

Now, with the `IDataStoreClient` operations as our guide, we can start implementing our controller endpoints. Each of our endpoints will demonstrate a different HTTP method, so let's consider how those methods are used and how that impacts the implementation of our endpoints.

The GET method

The first and most basic method we'll implement a listener for is the `GET` method. This method is used to access a resource at a specific endpoint, and, conventionally, `GET` requests carry no content, as specific constraints on the lookup are typically passed along as either segments of the URL path, or as key-value specifications sent as part of the URL's query parameters. It's up to you (or your project's specifications) to enforce those conventions, if you choose to. It's worth noting, though, that for most engineers, and for the `HttpClient` methods implemented by C#, the assumption is that those conventions will be followed by active HTTP services.

One other important note about the `GET` method is that it is generally considered both *safe* and *idempotent*. For an HTTP method to be considered *safe*, then a request of that method must not have any impact on the state of the resource on which the request was made. So, if I request a list of names from a server using a simple `GET` request, the server should still have those names stored in its database. The server should be exactly the same after it services my request as it was before it serviced my request. Meanwhile, if an operation is not safe, that means that the state of information stored on the server will be different after it processes a request of that unsafe method. The only HTTP methods that are always considered safe are `OPTIONS`, `HEAD`, and `GET`.

If you've never seen the word idempotent before, don't worry; it's nothing complicated. For a method or operation to be considered idempotent, you should be able to execute that operation any number of times without ever getting a different outcome from the first time you executed it. So, if I request a record with its ID, it doesn't matter how many times I request that record, I should always get the same response back that I got the first time I requested it. So, naturally, `GET` is considered an idempotent HTTP method.

So, now that we understand how a `GET` method should be handled (that is to say, safely, and in such a way to render `GET` requests idempotent), how do we configure our controller to respond to a `GET` request? Well, if you read the source code I told you to delete before you deleted it, you already know the answer to this. But for those who don't know, we specify our methods as handlers for `GET` requests using the `[HttpGet]` method attribute. So, let's look at all of our `read` operations and implement their methods in our controller using `IDataStoreClient`:

```
[HttpGet]
public async Task<ActionResult<IEnumerable<FitnessRecord>>> Get() {
  return await _dataStore.GetAllRecords();
}
[HttpGet("{title}")]
public async Task<ActionResult<FitnessRecord>> GetRecord(string title) {
  return await _dataStore.GetRecordByTitle(title);
}
[HttpGet("type/{type}")]
public async Task<ActionResult<IEnumerable<FitnessRecord>>>
GetRecordsByType(string type) {
  return await _dataStore.GetRecordsByWorkoutType(type);
}
```

Note that the attribute takes an optional string argument specifying a more specific URL path that the annotated method is meant to respond to. When the attribute is used without the optional parameter, though, the method annotated by the `[HttpGet]` attribute will simply respond to any `[HttpGet]` requests made to whatever URL path is handled by the parent `Controller` class. So, in this case, our `Get()` method will respond to any `GET` requests made against the `api/fitness` path. Meanwhile, requests made to `api/fitness/type/{type}` will return all records whose `workoutType` field contains the value of the `{type}` parameter.

I should also note here that (as you probably already guessed) the curly-brace syntax in the route specification is used as a placeholder for dynamic path variables. What's more, you can always safely reference any variable used inside curly braces in a route as an argument to your implementing method, and the web server will properly map whatever value was used in the request URL's path to its invocation of your method.

You may have also noticed that each of our methods has a return type of `ActionResult<T>` (ignoring the `Task<T>` outer type that's required for asynchronous methods). This is a custom wrapper around our return object that is applied to our methods' return values by `ControllerBase`. It will provide the appropriate HTTP status code and response headers for whatever result we return within our methods, and it does so entirely behind the scenes.

The POST method

So, with our `GET` requests serviced, let's look at what a `POST` request is, and how to handle it with our application. The `POST` method is typically used when a client needs to send a payload of content to the listening server, usually for storage or as an input to some calculation or processing that the server is responsible for. While, in some cases, some specific `POST` endpoints might be both safe and idempotent (because, again, it's up to each developer to adhere to the conventions of HTTP and RESTful API development), in the general case, `POST` as a method should be assumed to be neither safe nor idempotent.

The primary distinction between a `POST` request and a `GET` request is the payload associated with the `POST` request. So, let's look at how we can access and parse that payload for processing by our Web API:

```
[HttpPost]
public async Task<IActionResult> NewRecord([FromBody] FitnessRecord
newRecord) {
    if (await _dataStore.WriteRecord(newRecord)) {
        return Ok("new record successfully written");
    }
```

```
        return StatusCode(400);
    }
```

Here, we're using the `[FromBody]` parameter attribute on our method's only argument, and we're specifying that we expect to receive an instance of the `FitnessRecord` class from our request's content body. This attribute will use the `Content-Type` header of the request to determine how to parse the incoming message's content body and attempt to de-serialize the message into the type specified as the parameter. So, here, it would expect the message to be in the format of the `FitnessRecord` type. If the message body cannot be deserialized to the expected type, Web API will throw an appropriate 4XX status code response indicating some form of a bad request was sent.

I've used the `[FromBody]` attribute here primarily for demonstration purposes, as a way to illustrate the various `[From*]` attributes. Interestingly, though, because of our use of the `[ApiController]` attribute at the top of our class definition, we actually already reap the benefits of this input validation without needing to specify the `[FromBody]` attribute when we only have a single class specified as the input for a `POST` method.

There are a number of `[From*]` attributes you can apply to incoming messages to map your formal argument variable to some part of the incoming request. These include the following:

- `[FromBody]`
- `[FromForm]`
- `[FromQuery]`
- `[FromRoute]`
- `[FromHeader]`

Each of these parameter bindings will attempt to retrieve your the value of your formal parameter from the target location, and, if possible, will attempt to de-serialize the specific message component into the simple type you've declared for your formal parameter.

Additionally, there is a `[FromServices]` attribute. This is unique from the others in that it doesn't actually attempt to parse the designated argument from any part of your incoming message. Instead, this allows you to retrieve an instance of a dependency-injected interface from your registered services and assign it to a variable scoped to that single method, instead of having a class member variable whose value is assigned in the constructor.

The other interesting concept we've introduced with this method is sending generalized HTTP responses using the built-in methods of the `BaseController` class. Our two possible return values are determined by the `Ok()` and `StatusCode()` methods. Each of these will do the work of formatting an `HttpResponse` object for the desired `StatusCode`, with `Ok()` obviously returning a `200` code, and the `StatusCode()` method returning a response with whichever status code you specify as your argument.

The PUT and PATCH methods

Next let's look at the HTTP methods that will allow us to apply updates to records that already exist on the server. This can be done with either of the `PUT` or `PATCH` methods. Now, since I've just described them as updating the state of the server, it should be obvious that neither of these methods are considered safe. However, a `PUT` method should be idempotent (when properly implemented). We'll see why momentarily, but `PATCH` is not considered generally idempotent. The difference between the two is subtle, and often they are implemented in a way as to be interchangeable, so let's learn how they work and think about which is the most appropriate for our update operation.

When a `PUT` method has been implemented to the HTTP standard, the client is expected to provide a full instance of a minimum payload and a target destination for that payload. If there is a record at that target destination, then the payload is considered an update to that record, and the entire existing record is overwritten with the payload. Meanwhile, if there is no record at that target destination, then the payload is inserted, just as with `POST`, at the target URI. So, now, hopefully, you can see why this operation is idempotent. Using a single given payload, it doesn't matter how many times we execute the `PUT` method; it will always set the record at the target location to the value of that same payload. Subsequent executions have no effect after the first operation succeeds.

Some of the more astute readers may have identified a risk inherent to the `PUT` operation. Specifically, unless you have the most up-to-date version of the record you intend to update, you run the risk of overwriting recent changes to the record that you were unaware of with your `PUT`. Thus, it's usually wise to do a `GET` operation on the target record prior to applying any `PUT` updates to it to ensure that no recent updates are accidentally reverted. This introduces a performance hit in the form of additional round trips to your server, and, likely, a resource-locking mechanism to ensure that no one updates your target record in the time between your `GET` and your `PUT`.

The `PATCH` method, on the other hand, only requires that a *set of changes, as described in the request payload,* be applied to an entity identified by the request URI. This means that our payload could describe a change be made to only a specific property on the target resource, without having to send the new, wholly updated state of the record with each `PATCH` request. For example, a properly formatted `PATCH` request could have a payload that describes your changes as follows:

```
{ "operation": "update", "property": "comments", "new_value": "new comments
to use for record" }
```

Thus, when the operation is called, your API would have the information necessary to update only the relevant field you hope to update. You'll note, though, that the definition of a patch is vague enough that you could describe a set of changes that apply new content and change the state of the server with each subsequent request. For example, imagine the following description:

```
{ "operation": "append", "property": "comments", "suffix": "... and a
longer string" }
```

If this operation appended the value of a suffix to the target property, then each subsequent `PATCH` with the same payload would result in a longer and longer `comments` field. Because of this broad spectrum of a possible *set of changes, as described by the payload,* the `PATCH` operation is not assumed to be idempotent.

Now, technically, the standard produced by the **Internet Engineering Task Force (IETF)** that describes the `PATCH` operation (RFC 5789) specifies that the payload of a `PATCH` request contains a set of instructions describing how a resource currently residing on the origin server should be modified to produce the new version. This seems to indicate that the payload actually explicitly describes a sequence of operations to perform on the target resource, as opposed to representing a partial object state with only the fields that are meant to be updated. Under this interpretation, the following `PATCH` payload might be considered non-standard, or incorrect:

```
{ "comments": "New comment to update the record with" }
```

In fact, there are a number of purists who insist that using `PATCH` to send only partial object structures is an explicitly incorrect use of the method as defined in the standard. However, I would argue that a payload containing a partial object structure is itself a highly streamlined description of a set of changes to apply to the resource. I would actually make the case that such an implementation does not violate the spirit or letter of the standard. To wit, the stated intent of RFC 5789 is to provide the partial-update functionality that is not provided by the `PUT` operation, and a partial object structure does exactly that. In fact, there is even a new standard out for comment that specifies that exact payload structure: RFC 7936.

As you decide how to implement `PATCH`, I would encourage you to read the opinions of others on how it should be written so as to meet the standard, and then decide for yourself whether you should take a more pure approach, or allow the partial object structure. I've already explained my reasoning for accepting the partial object approach, and so that's how we'll implement our comment-update method in our API:

```
[HttpPatch("{title}/comments")]
public async Task<IActionResult> UpdateComments(string title, [FromBody]
string newComments) {
  if (await _dataStore.UpdateRecord(title, newComments)) {
    return Ok("record successfully updated");
  }
  return StatusCode(400);
}
```

Here, since we're only allowing our users to update their comments, we'll use the REST paradigm of using our path to describe the most specific part of our system that we want to interact with. Thus, our path and method specify that we want to `PATCH` the value of the comments at the record with the given title. This, semantically, communicates everything we need to know about this operation, and I would assert accomplishes all of the goals of RESTful design, within the standards of the HTTP operation.

The DELETE method

Finally, we'll look at perhaps the most intuitive method described for HTTP, the `DELETE` method. Sending a `DELETE` request to a target resource will do exactly that: it will delete the resource from the server, replacing it with nothing. Since this updates the state on the server, the method is not safe. However, since you can't delete a record that's already been deleted, the operation is considered idempotent.

A `DELETE` request may receive a response with a body describing the object that was deleted, or the success or failure of the operation, but, typically, just a 2XX status code message is delivered on a successful deletion. This method is as simple as it sounds, so let's implement it in our controller:

```
[HttpDelete("{title}")]
public async Task<IActionResult> Delete(string title) {
    if (await _dataStore.DeleteRecord(title)) {
        return Ok("record successfully deleted");
    }
    return StatusCode(400);
}
```

Exactly as you would expect, the method is defined as a valid handler for `DELETE` requests using the `[HttpDelete("{title}")]` attribute, and merely returns a status code of either `200` or `400`, with a success message.

And just like that, we've written a service that will listen for and properly respond to the full suite of valid HTTP methods for which you'll be expected to write custom software. So, now that we can handle incoming HTTP requests, let's look at how to build and send outbound requests of our own.

HTTP request formatting

With it being such a common aspect of most modern software projects, it should come as no surprise that generating HTTP requests has been so thoroughly streamlined by the .NET Core standard that it's an absolute breeze to use. We'll be using the `HttpClient` class to send outbound requests that perfectly mirror the `FitnessApp` API we just defined in our controller class, so understanding the expected paths and inputs should be a straightforward endeavor. So, with that in mind, let's crack open our `FitnessDataStoreClient` class and start generating requests.

Creating HttpClient instances

We'll start with the simple read operations in our API, but in order to do that, we'll need to spin up an instance of the `HttpClient` class for use to use to generate our requests. To do this, we'll want to request the instance of the class that we registered for read operations. This is as simple as calling `CreateClient()` with the same key we used to register the `READER` instance in the first place. So, inside our `GetAllRecords()` method, simply add the following line to the start of the method:

```
var client = _httpFactory.CreateClient("READER");
```

And now, our client variable contains an instance of `HttpClient` that's already configured with the `BaseAddress` and `DefaultHeaders` properties we set in our `Startup.cs` file.

If you ever need to create an `HttpClient` class without pre-registering it (suppose you needed it to access a URL that you don't know the value of until runtime), you can do so by simply leaving the arguments of the `CreateClient()` call empty. You'll then be responsible for setting the `BaseAddress` property for your requests and any necessary headers on your newly created client, but that's done in exactly the same way as we did it in our `Startup.cs` file.

Building a request message

Now that we have our client, creating an outbound `GET` request is as simple as defining an `HttpRequestMessage` instance and specifying the method and target path we intend to send our request with. And since `GET` requests conventionally have no content body, that initial `HttpRequestMessage` definition is sufficient to give to our `HttpClient` for transmission. If you need to apply headers, you can do so with the `Headers` property of the `HttpRequestMessage` class, but since we don't, let's just create our message, and send it with our client:

```
HttpRequestMessage message = new HttpRequestMessage(HttpMethod.Get,
"/api/fitness-data");

var response = await client.SendAsync(message);
```

And just like that, we have the response from our server in a variable for us to work with. Before we proceed with parsing the response message, though, we'll want to make sure that our operation completed successfully. A common pattern is to wrap any error-handling code (which we won't be implementing here, for brevity's sake) in a conditional clause checking the success of the request. Once we've confirmed that behavior, though, we can safely attempt to parse our `response` object:

```
if (!response.IsSuccessStatusCode) {
  return new List<FitnessRecord>();
}

var json = await response.Content.ReadAsStringAsync();
var result = JsonConvert.DeserializeObject<List<FitnessRecord>>(json);
return result;
```

The `response` object we get back represents the entirety of the HTTP response from the server, including any headers the server sent back, and the status code, and even the content of the original request message. Typically, though, you'll only be concerned with the `StatusCode` property, and the `Content` property. The `StatusCode` property is actually an enum type that enumerates all valid HTTP response status codes, and is what's used to determine the result of the derived `IsSuccessStatusCode` property. Meanwhile, the `Content` property is an instance of the `HttpContent` class, which contains an array of headers specific to the content, as well as a number of utility methods for reading and parsing the body of the content.

Since we know that the output of our request will be the JSON representation of a list of fitness records, we can use the `JsonConvert` static class to de-serialize and return the response content. And with that simple pattern, we can proceed to define the rest of our `GET` operations. First, we have the `GetAllRecords()` method, which will simply return the list of any records stored in our data source:

```
public async Task<List<FitnessRecord>> GetAllRecords() {
    var client = _httpFactory.CreateClient("READER");

    HttpRequestMessage message = new HttpRequestMessage(HttpMethod.Get,
"/api/fitness-data");

    var response = await client.SendAsync(message);

    if (!response.IsSuccessStatusCode) {
        return new List<FitnessRecord>();
    }

    var json = await response.Content.ReadAsStringAsync();
    var result = JsonConvert.DeserializeObject<List<FitnessRecord>>(json);
```

```
        return result;
    }
```

Next, we have our `GetRecordsByWorkoutType()` method, which allows the user to filter based on the `workoutType` field of the fitness record:

```
public async Task<List<FitnessRecord>> GetRecordsByWorkoutType(string
workoutType) {
    var client = _httpFactory.CreateClient("READER");

    HttpRequestMessage message = new HttpRequestMessage(HttpMethod.Get,
$"/api/fitness-data/type/{workoutType}");

    var response = await client.SendAsync(message);

    if (!response.IsSuccessStatusCode) {
        return new List<FitnessRecord>();
    }

    var json = await response.Content.ReadAsStringAsync();
    var result = JsonConvert.DeserializeObject<List<FitnessRecord>>(json);
    return result;
}
```

Finally, we'll implement our `GetRecordByTitle()` method, which allows us to search our fitness records by the (presumably) unique `title` assigned to them:

```
public async Task<FitnessRecord> GetRecordByTitle(string title) {
    var client = _httpFactory.CreateClient("READER");

    HttpRequestMessage message = new HttpRequestMessage(HttpMethod.Get,
$"/api/fitness-data/{title}");

    var response = await client.SendAsync(message);

    if (!response.IsSuccessStatusCode) {
        return new FitnessRecord();
    }

    var json = await response.Content.ReadAsStringAsync();
    var result = JsonConvert.DeserializeObject<FitnessRecord>(json);
    return result;
}
```

With each of these methods, you'll notice that we're not actually implementing any additional filtering logic inside our data service class. Instead, we're relying on that work to be done by the server. The abstraction we're introducing is over the direct interaction with the server, and not on the logic of filtering the records. So, now that we have our GET operations in place, we can look at what additional steps we need to take to POST data.

Posting request content

Since the main difference between a GET request and a POST request is the content attached to the POST request, let's take a look at how to apply our content to our request message. First, we'll change the method specified when we create our HttpRequestMessage instance:

```
public async Task<bool> WriteRecord(FitnessRecord newRecord) {
  var client = _httpFactory.CreateClient("WRITER");

  HttpRequestMessage message = new HttpRequestMessage(HttpMethod.Post,
"/api/fitness-data");
```

Then, we'll need to create our Content. The HttpContent class is an abstract class instantiated by a variety of sub-classes that each implement different valid formats for POST content. You can define FormContent for an x-www-form-urlencoded request; MultiPartFormContent for large messages, file transfer, or binary data transmitted in several discrete chunks; StreamContent to represent an open and active stream connection; and many more. For our purposes, though, since we'll be serializing to and from JSON, we'll just define the payload as an instance of StringContent.

When you're using StringContent, there are several override implementations that allow you to specify the specific character encoding and the media type for the message. This is used by the HttpClient class to apply the appropriate content-type header to the request, which means that in most cases, you'll never have to concern yourself with that specific value. Since our string will be well-formed JSON, the HttpClient class will be able to infer our media type from the string alone, so applying the POST body is a fairly straightforward task:

```
var requestJson = JsonConvert.SerializeObject(newRecord);
message.Content = new StringContent(requestJson);
```

With our message body in place, the rest of our code proceeds exactly as it did with our GET requests, leaving us with a final implementation:

```
public async Task<bool> WriteRecord(FitnessRecord newRecord) {
```

```
    var client = _httpFactory.CreateClient("WRITER");

    HttpRequestMessage message = new HttpRequestMessage(HttpMethod.Post,
"/api/fitness-data");
    var requestJson = JsonConvert.SerializeObject(newRecord);
    message.Content = new StringContent(requestJson, Encoding.UTF8,
"application/json");

    var response = await client.SendAsync(message);
    return response.IsSuccessStatusCode;
}
```

So, with this pattern in place, we can complete our implementation by adding the code to update and delete records:

```
public async Task<bool> UpdateRecord(string title, string newComment) {
    var client = _httpFactory.CreateClient("WRITER");

    HttpRequestMessage message = new HttpRequestMessage(HttpMethod.Patch,
$"/api/fitness-data/{title}/comments");
    message.Content = new StringContent($"\"{newComment}\"", Encoding.UTF8,
"application/json");

    var response = await client.SendAsync(message);
    return response.IsSuccessStatusCode;
}

public async Task<bool> DeleteRecord(string title) {
    var client = _httpFactory.CreateClient("WRITER");

    HttpRequestMessage message = new HttpRequestMessage(HttpMethod.Delete,
$"/api/fitness-data/{title}");

    var response = await client.SendAsync(message);
    return response.IsSuccessStatusCode;
}
```

Running this application side by side with the `FitnessDataStore` app, you should see all of the expected behavior described in our initial project description. Fire them up, bring up your REST client of choice, and start hitting every endpoint. Set breakpoints in your code, and see what happens every step of the way. And with that, we've covered the essentials of HTTP in .NET Core.

HTTPS – security over HTTP

While we'll discuss it more in `Chapter 13`, *Transport Layer Security*, we should take a moment to consider how to establish secure connections at the application layer. In the HTTP protocol, security is achieved through **Hypertext Transfer Protocol Secure** (**HTTPS**). This provides a mechanism for authenticating the source of a remote resource, such as a web page or an API response. HTTPS also provides protection of the data in transit that is passed between client and server with each request/response interaction. This is done by leveraging the **Secure Sockets Layer** (**SSL**) or, more recently, the **Transport Layer Security** (**TLS**) on the underlying transport-layer interactions.

Establishing outbound HTTPS connections

With outbound connections, using HTTPS is as simple as defining the schema in your request URL to be of type `https://....` While this may seem trivial, the value in HTTPS connections comes from a trusted and validated server certificate, usually signed by a third party, which gives consumers confidence that the site they are trying to access is, in fact, the site they intended to access.

In many cases, you'll want to test out your application on a development server using production-ready configurations. Typically, in these scenarios, you won't have the requested **Certificate Authority** (**CA**) provide you with a trusted, signed SSL certificate for that development server. When that happens, your calling code will throw an error warning users that the HTTPS connection couldn't be validated with an SSL certificate signed by a trusted CA. This happens because, behind the scenes of the `HttpClient` class, there is an `HttpClientHandler` function that validates any outbound HTTPS connections before checking for an SSL certificate signed by a trusted CA. This means that, in a case where you're connecting to a trusted and certified resource over HTTPS, you don't have to do any additional work to ensure that security. A successful connection with your `HttpClient` ensures that security.

There is a way to override that behavior with a custom server certificate validator, which we'll look at in later chapters focusing on security. In general, though, if you're getting that error from any remote resource that you don't directly control, *listen to it*. It's a fantastic warning system that you get for free from .NET Core, and you'd be wise to leverage it.

Supporting HTTPS on your server

This should come as no surprise to any of you, but we've already seen exactly how we can support HTTPS for incoming HTTP requests being made of our application. It's that tricky little line of code we keep removing:

```
app.UseHttpsRedirection();
```

Provided we have this line of code, and our web server is configured to listen over at least an HTTPS URL, our application will support HTTPS. With this value set, the web server will respond to all incoming HTTP connection attempts with a `302`, which is a redirection status code notifying the client that their request should be redirected to the HTTPS URI for processing.

The reason I've been removing this particular piece of code and using HTTP in all of our examples so far is because of what I mentioned in the previous section titled *Establishing outbound HTTPS connections.* Trying to connect to a server over HTTPS will cause our software (and most REST clients such as Postman or Insomnia) to attempt to validate an SSL certificate. However, while we're in development, our local machines typically won't have a signed certificate to return with HTTPS responses. So, by removing the `UseHttpsRedirection()` method, we simply remove that variable from the equation while we're still in development. However, once you're ready to deploy your code to a production environment, you'll want to enforce HTTPS wherever possible, and I would even go so far as to recommend you configure your server to only listen on HTTPS URLs.

HTTP/2

In 2015, the **Internet Engineering Task Force (IETF)** introduced the first major revision of the HTTP standard since HTTP 1.1 was codified in 1997. This new protocol, now named HTTP/2, introduces a number of extension features on top of the existing HTTP 1.1 protocol definition, while leaving the expected behavior of the previous standard almost entirely unchanged.

New features of HTTP/2

Originally developed by Google under the moniker **SPDY** (short for *speedy*), HTTP/2 was designed to provide major speed improvements over HTTP 1.1. Its objectives were to reduce latency to improve the performance of web browsers loading content. This latency reduction is accomplished by the following:

- **Header compression:** All transmission headers are compressed with either gzip or DEFLATE compression mechanisms by default. The reduced packet size and volume for basic protocol/request negotiation has a noticeable impact on high-latency network connections, such as cellular networks (thus improving page-load performance on mobile devices, such as Google's Android phones).
- **Request multiplexing:** Sends multiple queued outbound requests over a single active connection. This can prevent bottlenecks of outbound requests for web resources on pages with a lot of content, and head-of-line blocking, which occurs when the first request in a queue hangs, preventing the processing of subsequent, potentially smaller and faster requests, from resolving.
- **Server push:** This allows a server to send content directly with a client over a previously established connection. This is useful if, for instance, you know that every request for a web page will be shortly followed by requests for additional resources referenced by the web page. Instead of forcing the client to initiate an additional HTTP request cycle for those additional resources, the server can simply push out the data directly and, if configured properly, the client can handle the incoming data without the overhead of processing the full HTTP message structure.
- **Request prioritization:** This enables the developer to determine which requests will most likely need to be resolved first and provide priorities to ensure they are. Similar to multiplexing, it seeks to reduce the impact of head-of-line blocking, but can do so without needing to fully support a multiplexing transport mechanism.

HTTP/2 in .NET core

Configuring your application to start leveraging these features happens at with your `WebHostBuilder`, since the web server negotiates all of the incoming HTTP requests and determines support for various protocols. Once that's done, though, your clients will begin seeing the benefits of the protocol extensions without any additional change in your code to support it.

Unfortunately, at the time of writing, Kestrel doesn't support some features, such as server push and stream prioritization. So, while the client can send a prioritization tag with its requests, Kestrel simply won't act on that request. And one other caveat to HTTP/2 support is that your hosting environment's native cryptography library must support **Application Layer Protocol Negotiation** (**ALPN**) to establish the secure connection necessary for HTTP/2. That means HTTP2 is supported only for .NET Core apps deployed to either Windows environments or Linux hosts with OpenSSL 1.0.2 or higher. Thankfully, though, if your environment doesn't support HTTP/2, Kestrel will silently fall back to using standard HTTP 1.1 request processing. That means you can configure the protocol and deploy it to any environment without worrying about environment specific Kestrel configurations.

If you want to support HTTP/2, simply leverage the `ConfigureKestrel()` method on your `WebHostBuilder`, like so:

```
WebHost.CreateDefaultBuilder(args)
  .ConfigureKestrel(options => {
    options.Listen(IPAddress.Any, 8080, listenOptions => {
      listenOptions.Protocols = HttpProtocols.Http1AndHttp2;
      listenOptions.UseHttps("testcert.pfx", "testPassword")
    });
  })
  .UseStartup<Startup>();
```

And just like that, you've got support for multiplexing, header compression, and request streaming, out of the box, with no change to your application code. And I'll note that further support for HTTP/2 is on the horizon for Kestrel, so as the protocol matures (it's only been a standard for about three years at the time of writing), expect to see wider adoption, and the improved performance that goes with it.

Summary

We covered a lot in this chapter, and for good reason. HTTP is, as I suggest in the title of this chapter, integral to programming software being able to function on the web. We learned about the distinctions between application-layer protocols and transport-layer protocols with a bit more clarity and context. We explored the history of HTTP, and saw how its design lent itself for use far beyond its original intended purpose.

Once we had that background, we looked at the Web API project template, and learned how .NET Core leverages the cross-platform Kestrel web server to expose network-aware applications to incoming requests. We looked at how to configure our web server using the `WebHostBuilder` extension classes. We learned how to configure our application code for use on our web server, in our given hosting environment, using the `Startup.cs` class. Then we took the time to set up our application to leverage ASP.NET Core's dependency injection framework for our service and utility classes.

With our application wired up and ready to go, we looked at how to expose the controller endpoints to listen for each specific HTTP method at specific routes, and the various ways we could respond to those requests. Then we looked at how to format outbound HTTP messages of our own, including building a content body, formatting and applying request headers, and finally sending our requests using the `HttpClient`. Finally, we took some time to consider how to allow secure connections with HTTPS, and what the future holds with the HTTP/2 specification. With this perspective, we're well positioned to explore how some of the other application-layer protocols are tuned to their specific use cases in the next chapter, where we'll dive into the **File Transfer Protocol** (**FTP**) and the **Simple Mail Transfer Protocol** (**SMTP**).

Questions

1. What is the definition of HTTP?
2. What does SOAP mean? What does REST mean?
3. What are some of the primary differences between SOAP services and REST services?
4. What does MVC stand for, and how does it apply to the Web API project template?
5. What is Kestrel and how is it used in ASP.NET Core?
6. What are the various methods of HTTP? Which are safe? Why are they safe?

7. What does HTTPS stand for? How does it provide security?
8. What new features are supported in HTTP/2? What requirements must be met to leverage it?

Further reading

For more information about HTTP in .NET Core, or using ASP.NET Core, you have a wealth of resources at your disposal. Particularly, I'd recommend *Hands-On Full-Stack Web Development with ASP.NET Core*, by Tamir Dresher, Amir Zuker, and Shay Friedman, available through Packt Publishing here: `https://www.packtpub.com/web-development/hands-full-stack-web-development-aspnet-core`.

If you want to take a deeper dive into the patterns and principles that informed the developers of ASP.NET Core, I'd recommend reading *ASP.NET Core 2 Fundamentals*, by Onur Gumus and Mugilan T S Ragupathi. It's also available from Packt, and you can find it here: `https://www.packtpub.com/web-development/aspnet-core-2-fundamentals`.

If you're more interested in the fundamentals of the MVC design pattern, and how ASP.NET Core uses it to provide clean architectural templates for web applications, check out *ASP.NET Core MVC 2.0 Cookbook*, by Engin Polat and Stephane Belkheraz. That book can be found through Packt Publishing here: `https://www.packtpub.com/application-development/aspnet-core-mvc-20-cookbook`.

10
FTP and SMTP

Having explored the heavy-hitter of application-layer protocols with a chapter on HTTP, it will serve us well to look at some of the other less common protocols. That's what we'll be looking at in this chapter. While HTTP is a general-purpose, workhorse protocol, there are a number of reasons why you might consider using **File Transfer Protocol** (**FTP**) or **Simple Mail Transfer Protocol** (**SMTP**) for specific tasks in your own software, or why those protocols might be leveraged by .NET Core under the hood of some of their more common abstractions. So, in this chapter, we'll see what those reasons might be and learn how to implement those protocols when the situation arises.

The following topics will be covered in this chapter:

- How the FTP standard is defined and how C# implements the protocol in .NET Core
- Understanding the processes for securing file transport
- Understanding the nature of SMTP and the role it fulfills

Technical requirements

In this chapter, we'll be using sample applications available in the GitHub repository for the book here: `https://github.com/PacktPublishing/Hands-On-Network-Programming-with-CSharp-and-.NET-Core/tree/master/Chapter 10`.

We'll be working mostly with console applications, so you won't need any sort of REST or web client specifically for this chapter.

Also, in this chapter, we'll be writing a client to engage with an FTP server. To that end, we'll need an FTP server we can administer ourselves. I will be using FileZilla for this and recommend you do the same. It's lightweight, stable, and open source. It can be found here: `https://filezilla-project.org/download.php?type=server`. If your development environment doesn't support FileZilla, don't worry. The goal is simply to have a server available and listening for our application to interact with. The demonstrations should be easy enough to follow along with using any FTP server with support for your OS.

Check out the following video to see the code in action: `http://bit.ly/2HYmsHj`

File transfer over the web

The first thing to note about FTP and file transfer is that, as an application-layer protocol on the **Open Systems Interconnection** (**OSI**) stack, the primary concern of its design is in optimizing a specific common business task for execution over a network. However, just because a task is optimally done over a given protocol, it doesn't mean it *must* be done over that protocol. Indeed, almost anything done at the application-layer could, in theory, be accomplished by any application-layer protocol. So, what is it that makes FTP useful for us as engineers?

The intent of FTP

While FTP is optimized for a file transfer between hosts, I'd wager every dollar I have that there isn't a single reader of this book who hasn't transferred files over a network as an attachment of their email. The same task is accomplished, namely, a file was transferred from one host on a network to another, over that network, but it was accomplished using a different application-layer protocol (SMTP instead of FTP). Indeed, the versatility of the specification for HTTP has allowed it to grow well beyond the task for which it was optimized (transferring hypertext documents) and into a general-purpose workhorse of web communication.

In fact, there are countless applications that transfer files directly over HTTP. There's even a well-known and broadly supported media type for precisely that kind of interaction with `multipart/form-data`. So, what advantages are there to be gained by using FTP for file transfer instead of other more general-purpose application-layer protocols?

Built on a client-server model architecture, FTP is designed and implemented to leverage two separate connections for establishing the state of the target filesystem and transferring files. The first of these connections is what's called a control connection, and it is used to hold various details about the state of the remote host, such as the current working directory exposed to the FTP client. Meanwhile, for each transfer of data, a second data connection is established using information maintained by the control connection. When the data connection is engaged and transferring data, the control connection is idled.

In most implementations, establishing a control connection can be a bit of a pain, and often slow-performing. This is because each connection requires multiple round trips, sending various commands to the remote host establishing the target directory, negotiating any authentication, and determining and storing the remote state for use by the data connection. This high performance cost, as well as the statefulness of the control connection, is what made FTP ill-suited for use in transferring simple, brief hypertext web pages, thus necessitating HTTP. However, that stateful connection and the information it provides a client regarding the current state of the directory is essential to some operations FTP is used to support (such as detecting the presence of a file on a remote host or bulk downloads of all files in a directory).

Active and passive connections

Once a control connection is established, the data connection can be made using one of two possible modes. The server can establish an active connection, which is the default state for most FTP servers, or a passive connection. These different types of connection refer specifically to how the data connection is established and handled. In either case, the client initiates a control connection with a message using the underlying transport protocol (usually **Transmission Control Protocol** (**TCP**)).

In an active connection, once the control connection is established and the data transfer can begin, it's the server that establishes a data connection to transmit the file over the wire. The client transmits information during the command connection phase, notifying the server about which port is actively listening for the data connection. Then the server attempts to establish a connection with the client on the designated port, which is used for the server to push out the file data. The server is said to be *actively transmitting* the data to the client.

In a passive connection, the client uses the control connection to notify the server that the connection should be passive. The server then responds with an IP address and port designation for the client to establish a connection with. At that point, it's the client that establishes the data connection to the server's designated IP address and port. Once this connection is established, the client can transmit the file data.

Transfer modes and data representations

Once the actual data connection has been established as either active or passive, and the file transfer is ready, there are a number of ways to transmit the file in such a way as to have it readable on the target machine. Keep in mind that a text file written on a Unix system will have different character encodings or line terminals from a text file written on a Windows machine. If you've ever opened up a text editor or source control interface and been prompted to normalize the line endings of your files, this is why. It's a way of accounting for the subtle discrepancies between different native environments.

Since FTP is a platform-agnostic network transmission protocol, it must account for the possible disparities between binary representations of a file's content on different systems. To that end, FTP provides three different common data representation mechanisms for files being transferred over a connection:

- **ASCII mode:** This should only ever be used for text files. The character and bytes are converted from the source machine's native character representation to an 8-bit ASCII encoding prior to transmission, and then converted, again, to the target machine's native character representation from that 8-bit ASCII encoding. Of course, if either machine's native character encoding already is 8-bit ASCII, no conversion happens between that machine and the data connection.
- **Image (or binary) mode:** In this mode, the underlying binary data of the file on the source machine is sent over, unchanged, in a sequential byte stream. The target machine then stores that stream at the target file location on its local system, byte by byte, as it receives packets from the source.
- **Local mode:** This is for two computers with a shared local configuration to transfer data in any proprietary representation without a need to convert it to ASCII. It's not entirely dissimilar to the image mode, except that, where the proprietary format allows, data could be transferred non-sequentially.

Once you've determined the best way to represent your data for transmission, though, FTP will also provide three mechanisms for actually executing that transmission. They are as follows:

- **Stream mode:** Datagrams are sent as a continuous stream. This has a number of performance advantages, as there's no need to encapsulate discrete packets in any headers or metadata to enable the parsing. Bytes are simply sent out as they are read until the end of the file is reached on the source system.
- **Block mode:** This mechanism will chunk the file data into discrete application-layer packets and transfer them one block at a time to the source system, which is then responsible for reconstructing the original file structure based on the information in the packet metadata.
- **Compressed mode:** This mode simply enables a simple data compression algorithm to minimize the total volume of data sent between hosts.

Exposing directories for FTP

All of the features I've described in this section serve the specific purpose of negotiating the efficient transfer of files between two remote hosts. While the protocol obviously would not be well suited for a task such as transferring web pages to be rendered by a remote web browser, it does leverage a number of advantages over other application protocols such as HTTP. This includes giving engineers the flexibility to determine precisely how, and in what format, they can transfer large files.

So, now that we understand how and why FTP is used, let's look at how we can use it in our own programs. We'll be writing a simple client using the .NET library classes. The end state will be a client that can upload and download files, as well as request directory information from the remote host.

Our application will be a console application this time, so navigate via your terminal of choice to your working directory and create a new project:

```
dotnet new console -n FtpClientSample
```

Next, you'll want to make sure your fileserver is up and running locally. When you install the software, you should have see a window prompting you to choose a port that the server will be listening on for administration connections.

Configuring your FTP server

If you read that prompt carefully, you will have noticed that it was very explicit that the port you were choosing was for administrative connections to your FTP server, and not active FTP connections. This is because (if you remember back to the *Reserved ports* section in `Chapter 8`, *Sockets and Ports*) there is already a default port configured to listen for incoming FTP command connections. Just like how the `80` port is the default listening port for HTTP, the `21` port is the default port for FTP command connections. That means that, in general, connections sent to a URI with a schema of `ftp://...` and no port specification will automatically connect to the `21` port.

This is why the port you configure on FileZilla is explicitly designated as being for administration only. You're not connecting to the FTP command connection. You're connecting to the FileZilla server that is managing that FTP command connection. So, with that in mind, start the server and configure it to point to the localhost and the port you specified at the time of installation.

Once the application starts running, you'll see a notification that FTP over **Transport Layer Security** (**TLS**) is not enabled. Even though this message is written in alarming red text, you can ignore it for now. We'll look at it further when we explore TLS in a later chapter. For now, the lack of security keys will just make our lives a bit easier as we try to understand FTP, specifically. The fewer variables we introduce at once, the easier it is to understand new information as we receive it.

Finally, we need to register a user for our application in the FTP Administration UI, and set a working directory for the user. To do so, click on **Edit** | **Users** in the menu on the FileZilla administrator console. Then navigate to the **Shared folders** configuration page to set which specific directory you want to allow for which specific user:

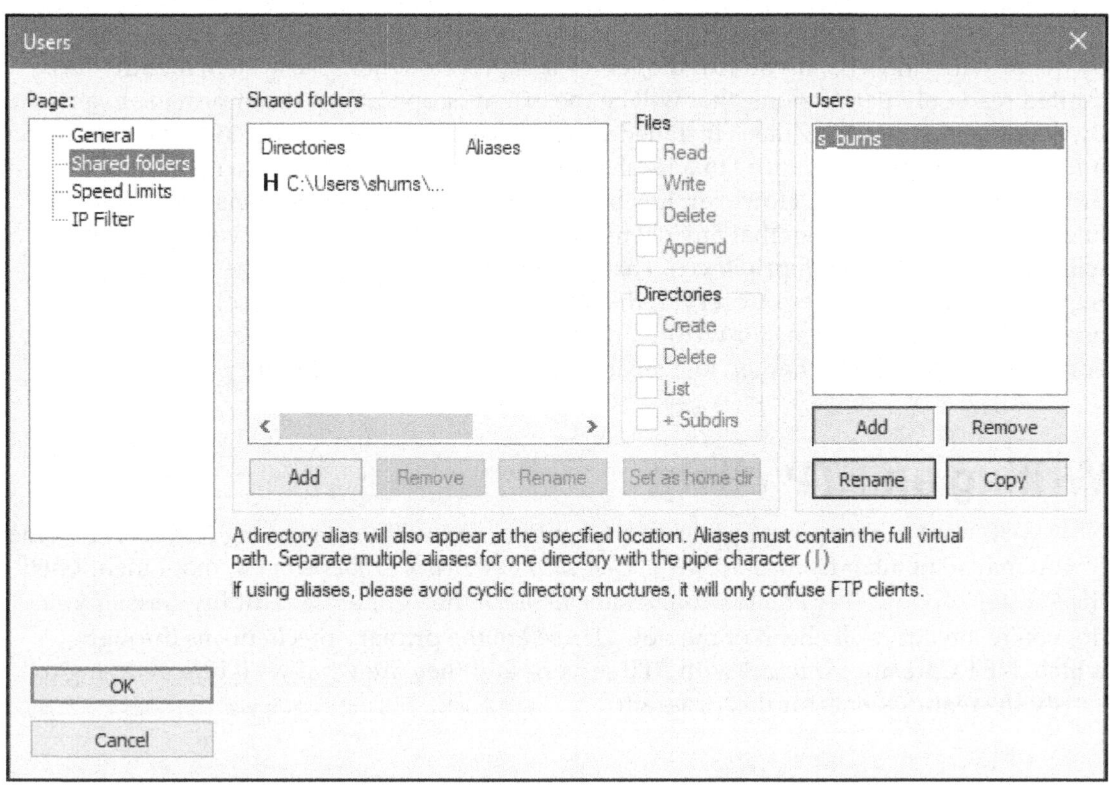

For the purposes of this demo, I'm going to create a new user named `s_burns`, and we'll give that user permissions to access the source code directory of `Chapter 9`, *HTTP in .NET*. Note that the user I created for the FTP server is distinct from my local machine username. When you're writing an FTP client to log in and access a remote directory, you need the credentials for a user that is registered with the FTP server software, not with the host machine. If I were to try to download a file from my local server using my operating system username, I would get an unauthorized exception in response, even with the correct password. The user credentials should always for a user as registered with the server itself, and in general, unless you've written an FTP server to allow open and anonymous connection, you should always be connecting with credentials.

The FTP server itself will have whatever permissions for a given directory are granted to it by the host machine. So, if you run the server in a process where the system identity has limited read-only permissions, that will be the extent of operations it can provide to a client. By default, however, FileZilla is installed with the same privileges granted to the user who initiated the installation. Since I'm a local admin, FileZilla was installed with local admin privileges for my system. However, just because those are the permissions granted to the FileZilla, that doesn't mean that any client connecting to the server with valid credentials will also have local admin privileges. That would be a huge security hole! Instead, when registering a new user for your server, the administrator (you, in this case) grants that new user individual permissions for writing, reading, and deleting files in the shared directory. For the purposes of this chapter, just create yourself a new user with full permissions.

Writing an FTP client

Now we'll want to set up our application for interacting with our running FTP server. Some of you may remember from `Chapter 5`, *Generating Network Requests in C#*, that I mentioned the `FtpWebRequest`/`FtpWebResponse` subclasses of the `WebRequest` utility class. If you do, you're already well ahead of me now. These are the primary mechanisms through which .NET Core apps interact with FTP servers, and they are what we'll be leveraging to satisfy the requirements for this program.

Fetching a directory listing

We'll request an instance of the `FtpWebRequest` class and then use its methods to view directory information about our listening FTP server. The instance will be pointing to `ftp://localhost`, which, as I mentioned, defaults to port `21` without actually specifying it, thanks to the `ftp://` schema. Just as HTTP has methods for interacting with the server, FTP has its own methods for determining how it intends to interact with the server. In code, that is set with a series of static constant properties that are used by the `FtpWebRequest` class to determine how to initiate the desired behavior:

```
static async Task<string> GetDirectoryListing() {
  StringBuilder strBuilder = new StringBuilder();
  FtpWebRequest req = (FtpWebRequest)WebRequest.Create("ftp://localhost");
  req.Method = WebRequestMethods.Ftp.ListDirectoryDetails;
  ...
}
```

The difference between HTTP methods or verbs and the `.Method` property you can set for `FtpWebRequest` is how they operate under the hood. As we saw in `Chapter 9`, *HTTP in .NET*, an HTTP method is specified as a header on the request itself. If the method is permitted for the address specified, then the rest of the request is simply parsed and processed right away, and a response generated. In an FTP connection, however, the `Method` property you set on the `FtpWebRequest` instance is actually an abstraction for a sequence of commands sent to the server over the FTP command connection. The `FtpWebRequest` client will actually send the appropriate commands over its underlying TCP connection, and only proceed if it gets the expected responses from the server throughout the entire exchange.

Now, before we can request the information we asked for with the server, we need to authenticate our application as acting on behave of a registered user of the server. For that, we'll use the helpful utility class, `NetworkCredential`. This class encapsulates the basic concept of a username and password, and maps it to the underlying representation necessary for an authenticated network request. So, instead of having to worry about whether your authentication mechanism is a basic authentication or digest authentication, this class just lets you think of it in terms of your login information. Simply instantiate a new instance of it with the login credentials of the FTP user you created in FileZilla's administration application, and apply those credentials to your request:

```
req.Credentials = new NetworkCredential("s_burns", "test_password");
```

And once we're logged in, we can interact with the request object the same as we did back in `Chapter 5`, *Generating Network Requests in C#*. We'll request the response for our request, and then read the response data stream with `StreamReader`, writing the results to our output to confirm our expected results:

```
using (FtpWebResponse resp = (FtpWebResponse)await req.GetResponseAsync())
{

  using (var respStream = resp.GetResponseStream()) {
    using (var reader = new StreamReader(respStream)) {
      strBuilder.Append(reader.ReadToEnd());

      strBuilder.Append($"Request returned status:
{resp.StatusDescription}");
    }
  }
}
return strBuilder.ToString();
```

Now simply await a call to this method in your `Main` method, and observe the results. Since the user I registered in my FTP server only has permissions for the root of the source code directory of `Chapter 9`, *HTTP in .NET*, I see the following output in my console when I run my application:

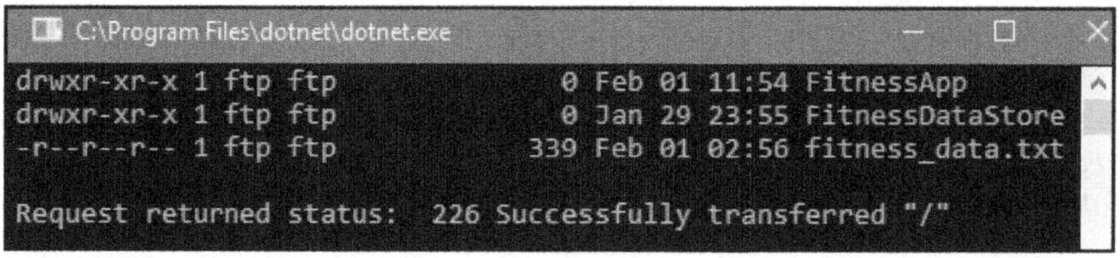

```
C:\Program Files\dotnet\dotnet.exe
drwxr-xr-x 1 ftp ftp              0 Feb 01 11:54 FitnessApp
drwxr-xr-x 1 ftp ftp              0 Jan 29 23:55 FitnessDataStore
-r--r--r-- 1 ftp ftp            339 Feb 01 02:56 fitness_data.txt

Request returned status:  226 Successfully transferred "/"
```

If you've never seen the string of characters at the start of each of those lines before, those are codes that define the permissions you have for each file in the directory listing. If there is a letter present, it means the permission or status is true for that folder. The structure is as follows:

```
[directoryFlag][owner-set][group-set][other-set]
```

The directory flag indicates whether the entry listed is, itself, a directory that can be navigated to and have files pulled from it. If `d` is present at the start of the entry, it's a folder containing files, not a file itself. Next is the permission sets for each kind of user that might want to interact with it. These are groupings of three characters indicating which permissions members of the set have for the file listed. In the order they are displayed, those characters are as follows:

- `r`: read
- `w`: write
- `x`: execute

So, for each set, there are three characters that are either set or null (represented here as a - character) indicating whether that set has the permission.

Using this, we can see that, for the files in our directory, `FitnessApp` and `FitnessDataStore` are both directories (they have `d` at the start of their permissions record), and both of them have the following permissions for each group:

- Owner: Read, write, and execute permissions
- Group: Read and execute permissions
- Other: Read and execute permissions

Meanwhile, we can see that the `fitness_data.txt` file is not a directory, and the permissions for each group for that listing are as follows:

- Owner: Read and write permissions
- Group: Read-only access
- Other: Read-only access

After the permissions, you see the current owner and group for the file (in this case, FTP) then the file size in bytes (0 for a directory), the last modified date, and the name of the file or sub-directory. So, here we can see that our FTP server is listed as the owner of our files and thus the permissions `rwx` are available for it to grant to users.

Now that we're successfully connected to our FTP server and able to access the directory information for the directory we have access to with our credentials, let's look back at how the server responded to that request. If you have your FileZilla server administration console open, you would have seen all of the interactions between our running application and the server show up in the server console:

```
Retrieving account settings, please wait...
Done retrieving account settings
Retrieving account settings, please wait...
Done retrieving account settings
(000010)2/3/2019 18:56:44 PM - (not logged in) (127.0.0.1)> Connected on port 21, sending welcome message...
(000010)2/3/2019 18:56:44 PM - (not logged in) (127.0.0.1)> 220-FileZilla Server 0.9.60 beta
(000010)2/3/2019 18:56:44 PM - (not logged in) (127.0.0.1)> 220-written by Tim Kosse (tim.kosse@filezilla-project.org)
(000010)2/3/2019 18:56:44 PM - (not logged in) (127.0.0.1)> 220 Please visit https://filezilla-project.org/
(000010)2/3/2019 18:56:44 PM - (not logged in) (127.0.0.1)> USER s_burns
(000010)2/3/2019 18:56:44 PM - (not logged in) (127.0.0.1)> 331 Password required for s_burns
(000010)2/3/2019 18:56:44 PM - (not logged in) (127.0.0.1)> PASS **************
(000010)2/3/2019 18:56:44 PM - s_burns (127.0.0.1)> 230 Logged on
(000010)2/3/2019 18:56:44 PM - s_burns (127.0.0.1)> OPTS utf8 on
(000010)2/3/2019 18:56:44 PM - s_burns (127.0.0.1)> 202 UTF8 mode is always enabled. No need to send this command.
(000010)2/3/2019 18:56:44 PM - s_burns (127.0.0.1)> PWD
(000010)2/3/2019 18:56:44 PM - s_burns (127.0.0.1)> 257 "/" is current directory.
(000010)2/3/2019 18:56:44 PM - s_burns (127.0.0.1)> TYPE I
(000010)2/3/2019 18:56:44 PM - s_burns (127.0.0.1)> 200 Type set to I
(000010)2/3/2019 18:56:44 PM - s_burns (127.0.0.1)> PASV
(000010)2/3/2019 18:56:44 PM - s_burns (127.0.0.1)> 227 Entering Passive Mode (127,0,0,1,194,43)
(000010)2/3/2019 18:56:44 PM - s_burns (127.0.0.1)> LIST
(000010)2/3/2019 18:56:44 PM - s_burns (127.0.0.1)> 150 Opening data channel for directory listing of "/"
(000010)2/3/2019 18:56:44 PM - s_burns (127.0.0.1)> 226 Successfully transferred "/"
(000010)2/3/2019 18:56:44 PM - s_burns (127.0.0.1)> QUIT
(000010)2/3/2019 18:56:44 PM - s_burns (127.0.0.1)> 221 Goodbye
(000010)2/3/2019 18:56:44 PM - s_burns (127.0.0.1)> disconnected.
ID   Account   IP   Transfer
```

Note that the first line indicates that the TCP connection was initiated on `21`, even though we never specified the port in our URI. That first line beginning with a timestamp is the initiation of the command connection. From there, every blue line in the console indicates a signal sent from our application to the server, and each green line represents the response from the server. The upper-case four-letter words and abbreviations sent from our application are all FTP commands from the FTP standard for interactions, and they were all sent by our application code without us even realizing it. This all happened under the hood of our application software just because we set our request method to `WebRequestMethods.Ftp.ListDirectoryDetails`.

Transferring a file

So, now that we understand how the command connection to an FTP server is initiated under the hood, and how that allows us to open a data connection, let's use that to actually request a file. We'll use the same request processing structure we saw for building a request and then fetching the response back in `Chapter 5`, *Generating Network Requests in C#*. This should all feel pretty familiar at this point, but I will take advantage of a few of the `FtpWebRequest` class's specific properties to highlight some of the options at your disposal. So, let's write the method to download a file.

The first thing we'll do differently will be specifying the sub-directory path for the file we want to look up. We'll just use the `Startup.cs` file from FitnessApp, so it's easy enough to confirm that we transferred it correctly. Then, we want to set the request `Method` property to the value of `WebRequestMethods.Ftp.DownloadFile`. Finally, we'll explicitly notify our server to operate in passive mode, which means our application will, behind the scenes, establish its own connection to the remote server on `20` (the default connection port for data connections to an FTP server) and then request the file once the connection is open. So, the initialization code for our download method will look like this:

```
public static async Task<string> RequestFile() {
  StringBuilder strBuilder = new StringBuilder();
  FtpWebRequest req =
(FtpWebRequest)WebRequest.Create("ftp://localhost/FitnessApp/Startup.cs");
  req.Method = WebRequestMethods.Ftp.DownloadFile;

  req.Credentials = new NetworkCredential("s_burns", "test_password");
  req.UsePassive = true;
  ...
  using(FtpWebResponse resp = (FtpWebResponse) await
req.GetResponseAsync()) {
    ...
  }
}
```

Now, to copy the file, we'll be reading directly out of the response stream, and writing it into `StreamWriter` for our destination file. This will look complicated because of the nested scope, but all those tabs are only there to handle contexts for each disposable `Stream` object and its respective `Reader` or `Writer` helper class:

```
using (var respStream = resp.GetResponseStream()) {
  strBuilder.Append(resp.StatusDescription);
  if(!File.Exists(@"../Copy_Startup.cs")) {
    using (var file = File.Create(@"../Copy_Startup.cs")) {
      //We only use this to create the file in the path if it doesn't
exist.
    }
  }
  using (var respReader = new StreamReader(respStream)) {
    using (var fileWriter = File.OpenWrite(@"../Copy_Startup.cs")) {
      using (var strWriter = new StreamWriter(fileWriter)) {
        await strWriter.WriteAsync(respReader.ReadToEnd());
      }
    }
  }
}

return strBuilder.ToString();
```

Now let's add a call to this method to our `Main` method, which should look like this:

```
static async Task Main(string[] args) {
  Console.WriteLine(await GetDirectoryListing());
  Console.WriteLine(await RequestFile());
}
```

If you run this project from your terminal, your output should list the directory structure, and when navigating to the root of the project, we should find our `Copy_Startup.cs` file, looking exactly as we expect it to!

Uploading a file via FTP

To complete this sample client, let's look at uploading to the server. Remember, it's the FTP, not the file download protocol. File transmission can go both ways. For this method, we'll be converting our file to a byte stream to upload to pass along with our request once the connection is established.

We'll also be pointing our `WebRequest` URI to the new yet-to-be-created file. We'll just be copying the `Program.cs` file from our current project to the root of the remote directory. So, let's see how the initialization code looks:

```
public static async Task<string> PushFile() {
    StringBuilder strBuilder = new StringBuilder();
    FtpWebRequest req =
(FtpWebRequest)WebRequest.Create("ftp://localhost/Program.cs");
    req.Method = WebRequestMethods.Ftp.UploadFile;

    req.Credentials = new NetworkCredential("s_burns", "test_password");
    req.UsePassive = true;
```

So far, so good. Now we'll need to create a byte array and write our `Program.cs` file to it. Then, write that byte array to the request stream. This should be pretty familiar territory for you after `Chapter 6`, *Streams, Threads, and Asynchronous Data Transfer*:

```
byte[] fileBytes;

using (var reader = new StreamReader(@"Program.cs")) {
    fileBytes = Encoding.ASCII.GetBytes(reader.ReadToEnd());
}

req.ContentLength = fileBytes.Length;

using (var reqStream = await req.GetRequestStreamAsync()) {
    await reqStream.WriteAsync(fileBytes, 0, fileBytes.Length);
}
```

Finally, to actually transmit the request to upload our file and the data stream with that file's contents, we just have to request a response from the server.

```
  using (FtpWebResponse resp = (FtpWebResponse)req.GetResponse()) {
        strBuilder.Append(resp.StatusDescription);
  }

  return strBuilder.ToString();
}
```

And with that, we're uploading a file to our remote FTP server. Simply add a line to our `Main` method, and run the application. If you've configured your server the same way I did, you should now see a copy of the program we just wrote sitting in the root directory for the `Chapter 9`, *HTTP in .NET,* source code, right next to the `FitnessApp` and the `FitnessDataStore` project folders.

Securing FTP requests

While you may suspect that the act of providing user credentials to our server meant there was some measure of security involved in our file access, we were actually interacting with our server in an entirely unsecure manner. Those credentials were only of value the moment they were received by the server and our command connection was established. After that though, they provided no more security of the data we were transmitting than if we had allowed entirely anonymous access to our directory. So, let's look at why that is, and how to fix it.

The risks of FTP

With our example software, there isn't any real concern for security because our data is never transmitted over an actual network connection. Our requests are never making it past our `hosts` file, because we are always pointing to `localhost`. However, if that wasn't the case, and we needed to authenticate with a remote server, and we did so using the standard FTP connection we set up for this demo, we'd be in trouble. Those credentials we used to log in to the server were sent entirely in plain text. Furthermore, the data connection that was eventually established was also sent over the wire in an entirely unsecured fashion.

If we attempted to communicate with a remote server using only the server credentials we provided, we would have been at risk of falling prey to a variety of different malicious attacks. Imagine a simple man-in-the-middle attacker reading the byte stream for a file containing **Personally Identifiable Information** (**PII**), such as a social security number, medical information, or bank account details. The FTP standard isn't actually designed to account for that kind of risk. What's more, since the file transfer mechanisms are negotiated ahead of time via the command connection, the actual file data is usually sent as an uninterrupted stream of bytes, easily re-assembled and read by a malicious party. Simply accept the underlying packet stream in order, remove the standard transport layer headers, and concatenate the bytes as they are received. For this reason, it's generally pretty risky to use standard FTP connections outside of the context of a well-protected private network.

Securing FTP with SFTP and FTPS

While there are security concerns inherent to FTP, there are, fortunately, a couple of approaches that you can take to mitigate your exposure to those risks. The two we'll be looking at both seek to make it substantially more difficult for a malicious actor to interfere with or read the content of your files in transit. So what are they?

SFTP

Our old friends the **Internet Engineering Task Force** (**IETF**) designed a new standard for file transfer interactions that leveraged the **Secure Shell** (**SSH**) protocol for authentication and secure tunneling. Dubbed **SSH File Transfer Protocol**, or **Secure File Transfer Protocol** (**SFTP**), it was built as an extension to SSH that provisioned file transfer capabilities where they didn't previously exist.

This application protocol provides security by establishing a secure tunnel between the two host machines. All data is sent that via tunnel once the client host has been authenticated by the server host machine (as opposed to the simple server-user authentication of our example in the previous section). This is not entirely dissimilar to simply transferring files over a VPN. It simply uses a different security protocol. This mechanism is less an implementation of FTP with security, though, and more an extension to SSH to also provide FTP functionality. As such, the out-of-the-box support for it in .NET Core is almost non-existent.

FTPS

While SFTP exists as a file transfer subsystem added as an extension to SSH, the alternative approach for encrypting traffic sent over an open connection (one that hasn't established a secure tunnel between hosts) is to use what's called FTPS. An abbreviation of FTP over SSL, or FTP Secure, FTPS leverages the encryption mechanisms of the underlying transport layer to provide encryption for data transferred between hosts. This is almost exactly the same mechanism that underlies the HTTPS protocol we looked at in `Chapter 9`, *HTTP in .NET*.

In modern implementations, this will use the secure transport mechanism of whatever underlying transport-layer protocol is being used by the FTP client. Today, that means that it's often leveraging TLS, but historically the encryption mechanism of choice has been SSL. Thus, when you want to configure your FTP clients to leverage FTPS, you simply set the `EnableSsl` property on your `FtpWebRequest` object to true. Then, provided your server supports FTP over TLS (or SSL), you'll be taking advantage of it every time you connect.

While there is a fair bit more to say on the subject of SSL and TLS and the security they provide, that's the subject of a later chapter. So, for now, just follow the simple rule of always using FTPS in your code where possible. The risks are just not worth it.

SMTP and MIME

Finally, we'll round out our exploration of the application-layer protocols with what is probably the second most common protocol (behind HTTP). And yet, as commonplace as it is, I would guess that a staggering number of people who benefit from SMTP don't even know it exists. So, what is it? How would we use it, and why would we use it?

The email protocol

First defined all the way back in 1982, the **Simple Mail Transfer Protocol** (**SMTP**) is the de-facto protocol for transmitting electronic messages. It's a connection-oriented protocol using the client-server architecture we've become so familiar with over the course of this book. Similar to FTP, SMTP transactions happen over a sequence of commands and responses transmitted over a dedicated SMTP session. Those commands notify the server of what the addressing information is for a message (the To: and From: components of an email), transmit the message itself, and finally confirm receipt of the message.

Unlike FTP, though, these interactions all happen over the same single connection to the server. Once a connection is established to the server (usually on the default SMTP port, `25`, for those who were curious), that connection constitutes a session. Once that session has begun, the commands sent by the server are received and responded to until all of the components of the message have been transmitted and the session is terminated.

The important thing to note about SMTP is that it is entirely about the *outbound* transmission of a new message. There is no mechanism in the protocol itself to request messages back from a server. Applications that maintain a mailbox for users to access are doing so by leveraging entirely different messaging protocols, such as the **Internet Message Access Protocol** (**IMAP**) or the **Post Office Protocol** (**POP**). However, while those protocols are useful to update your phone's mail app, the application will still depend on SMTP to transmit any new messages you want to send to a remote address.

This outbound-only property and the need for software implementing various distinct protocols to meet the expectations of users of an email app means that the full process of managing the receipt and delivery of email can be a painful one. It typically involves multiple subsystems working in tandem to process every step of the transaction reliably.

Extending SMTP with MIME

Having been defined in 1982, there are a number of limitations to SMTP when implemented strictly according to the standard. This includes the range of valid character encodings and alternative representations of certain content, such as images or sounds, directly in the message body of an email. To that end, IETF extended the protocol with the **Multipurpose Internet Mail Extensions** (**MIME**).

MIME provides users with the following: non-ASCII character representation; audio, image, video, and application attachments; multipart message bodies; and additional context and metadata in the message headers. Interestingly, this is where SMTP overlaps the most with HTTP. Even though MIME was originally designed and implemented as an SMTP extension, the ability to specify the character encoding and data structure of an incoming message was quickly identified as a useful feature for other application protocols transmitting text content. Naturally, it was adopted into use by HTTP in no time. `MIME-type` is the name of the value of the `ContentType` header sent with HTTP messages that contain a message body, and this is exactly how the extension is used by SMTP.

Hopefully, these commonalities between SMTP, FTP, and HTTP highlight for you just how much of the core application-layer protocol implementations are similar to one another.

SMTP in .NET Core

There are a lot of reasons why you might want to incorporate SMTP into your software. Maybe you want to give users a feedback mechanism for emailing the development team directly, and you want to do that with an SMTP client behind the scenes. Or maybe you want to wire up your error-handling infrastructure to send out emails to the support staff whenever exceptions of an unacceptable nature start getting thrown by your application. Whatever the case, you'll likely need a client for building those mail messages and sending them out to the target recipient.

While there are solutions for just such a problem available to you, they are not currently provided by Microsoft or the .NET Core framework. While the .NET Framework contained a `SmtpClient` class which, along with a `MailMessage` class, and could be used to generate and send automated emails to a valid SMTP server, those classes didn't make it into the spec for the .NET Core 1.0 release. They did make it into the initial .NET Core 2.0 release, but almost as soon as they arrived, they were deprecated by Microsoft for insufficient support for modern features of the protocol. What's more, in their deprecation notes, they explicitly state that they deprecated the libraries because they were "poorly designed." I took this to mean "not designed well enough to grow with the protocol."

So, now, instead of their internal libraries, Microsoft recommends using a third party called MailKit, the source control and documentation for which can be found here: `https://github.com/jstedfast/MailKit`.

So, while there is support for robust message generation for SMTP, the nature of the interactions is such that we won't be covering them here. Instead, I'll just allow this to serve as an example as to why you should always check on the status of any libraries you've used in the past before you incorporate them into a new project. Even if they were excellent when you last used them, the march of progress might have rendered them obsolete and deprecated before you managed to use them in a new project. And with that, we can move on from the application-layer protocols and start looking at the lower-level transport layer that makes it all possible.

Summary

In this chapter, we covered a lot of ground on some of the most common application-layer protocols still in use today. We looked at how different protocols were designed and optimized to perform different distinct tasks. Then we looked at exactly how FTP is optimized to perform its task of remote file transfer and directory lookup.

We learned how FTP uses two separate connections to communicate between clients. We saw how the command connection is set up to initialize the transfer of files, negotiate authentication, and determine the mechanism for the subsequent data connection. We looked at the variety of ways FTP can format the file for data transmission, and the various transmission techniques an FTP connection can be configured for. We also leveraged our FTP server admin console to observe the under-the-hood interactions going on between our application and the remote server when we were leveraging the high-level abstractions of the .NET `FtpWebRequest` and `FtpWebResponse` classes.

Once we were able to programmatically interact with our server, we looked at what sort of security considerations need to be made for FTP and got a general sense for how that was accomplished.

We wrapped up this chapter by looking at another common application-layer protocol with SMTP. We compared and contrasted its implementation with that of FTP and HTTP to understand what it does well, and then looked at its future on the .NET Core platform with the deprecation of the .NET libraries and the endorsement of third-party open source solutions. With that topic rounding out our exploration of the application layer of the OSI stack, we're well positioned to finally take a deep dive into the lower-level software components that enable all of this. In the next chapter, we'll finally be looking at the transport-layer protocols that make HTTP, FTP, and SMTP possible in the first place.

Questions

1. What are the primary differences between FTP and HTTP?
2. What are the two phases of FTP connections? How do they work?
3. What are the two modes for data transfer in FTP and how are they different from one another? When should you use one over the other?
4. What are the three modes of FTP data transfer?
5. What are the three ways to encode data in transit in FTP? When should they be used?
6. What are the definitions of SMTP and MIME? How do they relate to one another?
7. How is SMTP distinct from HTTP or FTP?

Further reading

If you're interested in some of the ways others have used FTP and SMTP libraries, you can check out *.NET Standard 2.0 Cookbook,* by *Fiqri Ismail*. There's a chapter dedicated to networking applications that includes an SMTP implementation. You can find it here: `https://www.packtpub.com/application-development/net-standard-20-cookbook`.

11
The Transport Layer - TCP and UDP

In previous chapters, we've looked at the interactions of different application layer protocols and how to program those interactions in .NET Core. In this chapter, we'll go one step closer to the hardware and start looking at transport layer protocols with **Transmission Control Protocol** (**TCP**) and **User Datagram Protocol** (**UDP**). We'll look at the connection-based and connectionless communication patterns that each implements, and we'll look at the strengths and weaknesses inherent to each approach. In addition, we'll examine how to write and interact with a software client that implements each protocol and use that to extend the functionality of our networked applications with custom behavior. Finally, we'll look at some of the advanced features of transport layer protocols, such as multicasting, for interacting with several hosts simultaneously to improve the performance of our network software.

The following topics will be covered in this chapter:

- Which responsibilities are delegated to the transport layer and how this layer meaningfully differs from the application layer and HTTP/SMTP/FTP
- The distinction between connection-based and connectionless protocols and the challenges they seek to solve
- How to initiate a TCP connection and send and receive TCP requests
- How to establish and leverage UDP communication in C#
- How to leverage multi-casting to improve performance in our TCP client

Technical requirements

We'll be using sample applications available in the GitHub repo for the book here: `https://github.com/PacktPublishing/Hands-On-Network-Programming-with-CSharp-and-.NET-Core/tree/master/Chapter 11`.

Check out the following video to see the code in action: `http://bit.ly/2HY61eo`

We'll also be continuing to leverage the tools we used in `Chapter 8`, *Sockets and Ports*. Specifically, if you haven't already done so, I recommend installing Postman, from here: `https://www.getpostman.com/apps` Or you can install the Insomnia REST client, which can be found here: `https://insomnia.rest/`

The transport layer

As we start to examine the intricacies of the transport layer, it's important to remember one of the most fundamental distinctions between the protocols of the transport layer and the protocols of the application layer; specifically, the distinction between what kinds of interactions each layer is concerned with. The protocols of the application layer are concerned with the communication between business objects. They should only deal with the high-level representations of your application's domain entities, and how those entities move through your system.

Meanwhile, with transport layer protocols, the concern is around **atomic network packets**, which are used to transmit context-agnostic data packets as well as to establish and negotiate connections.

The objectives of the transport layer

In all of the application layer protocols we've examined thus far, we've been able to make some generous assumptions about the network requests we were transmitting. We just assumed that provided our **Uniform Resource Identifier** (**URI**) was correct and the remote host was active, we could establish a **connection** to our target system. Additionally, we could assume that the connection we established was a **reliable** one and that any requests we transmitted would be delivered, in their entirety, in such a way as to be readable by the remote host's listening application. We could comfortably assume that if an error occurred in transit, we would get sufficient information to identify the nature of the error and attempt to **correct** it.

Let's review if any of these assumptions can also be applied to the transport layer.

Establishing a connection

In the transport layer, we can't make assumptions about an existing connection, because that's the layer at which the connections are established in the first place. Transport layer protocols are what expose specific ports on the local machine and negotiate the delivery of a packet to the designated port of a remote machine. If that connection requires a session to be maintained for the duration of the interaction, it's the transport layer protocol that's responsible for maintaining the state of that session (we'll see more about this when we explore connection-based communication).

Ensuring reliability

When it comes to reliability, the stable and consistent delivery of network packets, and the acceptance of response packets, this the job of the transport layer. If a session is broken due to a break in the chain of communication between two hosts, transport layer protocols are responsible for attempting to re-establish a connection and resume the network session based on its previous state. Transport protocols that guarantee successful delivery of packets must accept the responsibility of communicating with the transport layer of the remote host to validate that the application layer data was received successfully.

This is especially important for application layer software that treats an open connection like a serial data stream. The notion of incoming data being processed in order requires that it can be read in order. That means the transport layer must have some mechanism for ensuring reliable, same-order delivery of network packets.

Error correction

This reliability is also key to another responsibility of the transport layer: error correction. This includes being able to fix discrepancies in data received due to complications or interruptions at the network layer of the interaction. And, make no mistake, there are a lot of opportunities for potential interference, manipulation, or loss of the content of a network packet. The transport layer is responsible for mitigating these eventualities and re-requesting a fresh packet in the event of corruption. This data correction is usually accomplished with a simple `checksum` value, which can give a reliable indicator of any change being made to the data in transit.

Error handling should also be present to ensure the reliable ordering of packets. Because physical network infrastructure can, and often does, route multiple requests from one single host to another over multiple available network connections, and through multiple different switches, it's not uncommon for a packet that was sent later in the stream to arrive before packets that were sent earlier. The transport layer must have some way of identifying when that has happened, and be able to re-request the missing packet or re-arrange the received packets into their proper ordering.

Managing traffic

It might not be obvious initially, but when we talk about thousands of ports being available to listen on a given machine, those thousands of ports exist only virtually. Obviously, there aren't 65, 536 wires plugged into the motherboard of your PC. Those ports are just a way for your (usually only one) network adapter to route traffic to the appropriate process currently running on your operating system. All incoming and outgoing network traffic has to pass through that single network adapter.

While it's the network layer software that manages direct traffic control, it typically does so by only provisioning access to the physical connection in short segments of uptime for the transport layer. It's the job of the transport layer software to manage a queue of incoming, unprocessed data, as well as one for outbound requests, and provision their delivery to the network layer when the resources are made available to do so. This use of resources with limited, intermittent availability can be a major boost to performance when done well, and a major bottleneck when implemented poorly.

Segmentation of data

As I mentioned when I discussed this topic in `Chapter 3`, *Communication Protocols*, the large, contiguous objects that are used to encapsulate data at the application layer are unsuitable for transport over a network. If you tried to block your network adapter for the duration of the transport of a 20 MB file, or a 13 GB file for that matter, the impact on the performance of any other network-dependent software on your machine would be absolutely unacceptable. Attempting to do so would block operations for any outgoing or incoming requests for far too long.

While application layer protocols can send massive payloads with all of their requests and just assume they'll be delivered correctly, the same cannot be said of transport layer packets. There is no other intermediary between the transport layer and the network adapter, so it's the responsibility of the transport layer to decompose large request payloads into smaller, discrete network packets that are suitable for transport over the network layer. This means that transport layer protocols have the added responsibility of applying sufficient context for the decomposed packets of an application layer payload to be reconstructed by the recipient machine, regardless of delivery order, typically accomplished with packet headers.

This isn't typically something you'll be implementing yourself with a language as high-level as C#, but understanding that it is going on behind the scenes will make concepts such as packet-sniffing and network-tracing much easier to grasp down the line.

The classes of transport layer protocols

While we just discussed a number of responsibilities that transport layer protocols might assume, not every protocol at the transport layer implements every one of these features. Since it's important to understand what optional features will be available in a given implementation, standards organizations have defined a classification system for connection mode protocols based on the features they implement. According to this classification scheme, there are five different classes of connection mode (or transport layer) protocols, with each implementing different combinations of the list of services that a transport protocol might implement.

Defining the classification scheme for different implementation classes of transport protocols was actually a joint effort between standards organizations. The **International Organization for Standardization** (**ISO**), along with the **International Telecommunication Union** (**ITU**), issued recommendation X.224 for this exact purpose.

The list of classifications is zero-indexed, from class `0` to class `4`, and they are described as follows.

Class 0 – Simple class

This is described as providing the simplest type of transport connection, with sufficient data segmentation. It is explicitly described in the standard as being suitable only for network connections with acceptable residual error rate and an acceptable rate of signaled errors. Basically, given the simplicity of the protocol, it is only suitable for use on highly reliable local networks with nearly guaranteed error-free connections between hosts.

Class 1 – Basic recovery class

Protocols that fall under class `1` are specified to provide basic transport connection with minimal overhead. However, what distinguishes class `1` from class `0` is that class `1` protocols are expected to recover from signaled errors, or errors that are immediately detectable, such as a network disconnection or a network reset. Protocols of this class are sufficient for use on networks with an acceptable residual error rate, but an unacceptable rate of signaled errors.

Class 2 – Multiplexing class

The defining characteristic of class `2` protocols is their ability to multiplex several transport connections on to a single network connection. It's designed to work on the same exceptionally reliable networks as class `0` protocols. Because of the potential for multiple network connections to be leveraged over a single transport layer protocol, protocols within this classification may end up leveraging explicit flow control for the optimized use of the network layer resources. However, that explicit flow control is not a guaranteed property of class `2` protocols. In fact, it may be avoided in cases where multiplexing isn't necessary, as not managing flow control explicitly can reduce the overhead applied to packets in transit.

Class 3 – Error recovery and the multiplexing class

The multiplexing class is, essentially, a combination of classes `1` and `2`. Protocols in class `3` introduce the performance benefits (or packet overhead) of the class `2` multiplexing functionality into a protocol with sufficient error recovery for a network with less-reliable signaled error rates, where class `1` would otherwise be preferred.

Class 4 – Detecting errors and recovery class

Class 4 protocols are by far the most robust of any protocol. They are explicitly stated to be suitable for networks with an unacceptable residual error rate and an unacceptable signal error rate, which is to say, basically, any large-scale distributed network with a high probability of interference of interruption of service. Given the suitability of a class 4 protocol for use on such an unreliable network, it should come as no surprise that class 4 protocols are expected to both detect, and recover from, errors on the network. The errors for which a class 4 protocol should provide recovery include, but are not limited to, the following:

- Data packet loss
- Delivery of a data packet out of sequence in a data stream
- Data packet duplication
- Data packet corruption

Protocols in class 4 are also expected to provide the highest degree of resiliency against network failure, as well as increased throughput by way of improved multiplexing and packet segmentation. Needless to say, this is also the class of transport layer protocols with the highest amount of per-packet overhead introduced with each transaction over the network.

Interestingly, the classification of a protocol only determines the minimum set of services you should expect the protocol to implement. That doesn't preclude that protocol from implementing a broader set of services than specified by its classification. Such is the case with TCP, which actually provides a handful of additional services that might be provisioned by software higher up in the network stack under more rigid implementations.

Class 4 captures both TCP/IP, which is broadly considered the most robust (or at least the most complex/complicated) transport layer protocol in wide use today, as well as UDP, which is its connectionless peer in terms of broad support and adoption. These are the classes of transport layer protocols you'll be interacting with directly when working in C#. To that end, let's look at perhaps the biggest distinction between TCP and UDP: their connection-based and connectionless communication patterns. In doing so, we'll have a much better idea of when and how to leverage each protocol.

Connection-based and connectionless communication

There are two primary transport layer protocols we'll be working with in C#. The first is the TCP. Commonly called TCP/IP due to its prevalent use on the internet-based network software and tight coupling with the **Internet Protocol** (**IP**), TCP is the transport layer protocol underlying all of the application layer protocols we've looked at so far. The second protocol we'll be looking at is the UDP. It stands as an alternative approach to TCP with respect to transport layer implementations, aiming to provide better performance in more tightly constrained use cases.

The primary distinction between these two protocols, however, is that TCP operates in what's known as a **connection-based communication mode**, whereas UDP operates in what's called a **connectionless communication mode**. So, what exactly are these communication modes?

Connection-based communication

It may seem obvious what connection-based communication is at first glance. By its name, you might conclude it's just any communication that leverages a connection between two hosts. But what exactly do we mean when we say *connection*? It can't simply be some physical route between two hosts. After all, under that definition, how could two hosts communicate without connecting in some way? How would data travel between two machines if not over a connection?

The shortcomings of such a definition become even more obvious when you consider that connectionless communication is a valid mode of communication. With that point in mind, it's apparent that a connection, in this context, must refer to more than a simple channel between two hosts for data to travel across. So, then, what exactly is a connection? How do connection-based modes of communication leverage it?

Connections to establish sessions

For the purposes of clarity and understanding, I think we would benefit from thinking of a connection as a session. In connection-oriented protocols, a session must first be established between the two hosts prior to any meaningful work being done. That session must be negotiated with a handshake between the two hosts, and it should coordinate the nature of the pending data transfer. The session allows the two hosts to determine what, if any, orchestration must happen between the two machines over the lifetime of the request to fulfill the request reliably.

Once the session is established, the benefits of a connection-based communication mechanism can be realized. This includes a guarantee of the ordered delivery of data, as well as the reliable re-transmission of lost data packets. This can happen because the session context gives both machines an interaction mechanism that will allow them to communicate when a message has been delivered and received. This shared, active context is important for our understanding of connection-based protocols, so let's look at how that session context is provisioned by the underlying network layer.

Circuit-switched versus packet-switched connections

There are two ways that a session is provided for two hosts wanting to establish a connection. The first is to establish the session by way of a direct, hardware circuit link between hosts. This is what's known as a **circuit-switched connection**. The data needs no routing information applied to the header because it travels over a closed circuit between the two devices. This physical circuit connection is how public telephone networks were set up to establish connections. If you've ever seen old photographs of telephone operators using quarter-inch cables to connect two different ports in a gigantic circuit board, you've seen this exact routing mechanism in action (albeit in a very primitive implementation).

Establishing exclusive, direct, physical connections between two hosts has a lot of benefits. It guarantees that all packets will arrive in constant time since there's no downtime for intermediary routers and switches to parse the addressing information of the packet, or to wait for an opening in the data channel. It also guarantees the ordering of packets, since each one will travel across the same channel exactly ahead of the next packet transmitted.

The downside to this kind of connection-based communication, of course, is that it is incredibly costly to implement. There must be a mechanism at every possible intersection on the network to establish a dedicated circuit between any two other connections without interfering with other possible connections that may pass through that same intersection. Separately, it is incredibly costly to manage the mechanical switching necessary to engage and disengage a specific circuit as connections are established and closed. Thus, these kinds of physical networks haven't been in wide use for computational networks in decades.

The alternative approach is what's known as a **packet-switched connection**. These connections are established through the use of hardware switches and software deployed on routing devices that virtualize the behavior or a circuit-switched connection. With connection mode, routers and switches set up an in-memory circuit that manages a queue of all inbound requests for a target location. Those devices parse the addressing information of each incoming packet and pass it into the queue for the appropriate circuit accordingly, and then forward along messages from those queues, in order, as soon as the physical resources become available. In doing so, the expectations for the behavior of a physical circuit-switched connection are maintained. So, for any software that is written to leverage a connection-based communication scheme, there's no functional difference between a circuit-switched connection or a packet-switched connection.

With this virtualization, the costs of implementing circuit-switched connection functionality at a physical level are mitigated. Of course, by mitigating the physical costs of a circuit-switch setup, we pay for it in performance costs. With packet-switched connections, there's added overhead with each connection because each packet must be parsed by each switch in the network path between the two hosts. Moreover, unless there is no other traffic on a given network switch, there is undoubtedly going to be downtime for a packet-switched connection every time the packets associated with that connection are put into a queue to wait for physical resources to be made available. However, as most of these operations are implemented at a firmware level, the total time cost for any given connection is actually reasonably small. This model of a packet-switched network describes almost all modern **Wide-area networks** (**WAN**), including the internet.

TCP as a connection-oriented protocol

Establishing a connection is one of the most important functions a TCP implementation provides for application-layer software that is leveraging it. When the TCP layer breaks up a request into packets and applies its headers, it does so on the assumption that the packets will be sent over a packet-switched network.

That means it must be certain that switches and routers along the network path have provisioned a virtual circuit for each payload between the two hosts. This certainty is provided by a multi-step handshake between the two hosts. The specific details of the handshake are a bit more complicated, but it can be boiled down to three fundamental transactions for each step in the process:

1. **SYN**: This stands for **synchronization** and is a request sent from the client to the server indicating a desire to establish a connection. The synchronization happens because the client generates a random integer, *n,* and transmits it along in the SYN request as a sequence number, which the server uses to establish that the appropriate message was received.
2. **SYN-ACK**: This stands for **synchronization and acknowledgment** and is the response a server sends to an initial SYN request. To acknowledge that the request was received in the same state it was sent, the server increments and then returns the random synchronization integer it received from the client, *n+1,* as the acknowledgment message. It also sends a random integer of its own, *m,* as the sequence number.
3. **ACK**: At this point, the client acknowledges that its own synchronization request was sent and received correctly, and confirms the same for the server by sending a payload setting the sequence number to the acknowledgment value it received from the server, *n+1,* and then incrementing and returning the sequence number from the server as its own acknowledgment value, *m+1.*

Once these three signals have been sent and received accordingly, the connection has been established and data transfer can proceed accordingly.

Having this agreement between two hosts prior to data transmission is what allows TCP to achieve the resiliency that sets it apart from UDP. Since the host knows to expect an ordered sequence of packets, it can re-arrange packets that were received out of order once they arrive to ensure they are delivered in the appropriate order to the higher-level protocols that are expecting them. Moreover, if it doesn't receive all of the packets it's expecting, it can identify the missing packets based on the missing sequence numbers, and request re-transmission of exactly what was lost. Finally, this initialization of a connection gives the server an opportunity to communicate information about its processing capability and maximum throughput. By telling the client how much data can be processed at any given time, the client can throttle its own output to minimize data loss and network congestion.

The obvious downside, of course, is that all of these steps to establishing and leveraging a connection-parsing sequence of numbers and re-ordering data streams accordingly, and re-transmitting data, incurs a major time cost for the interactions. When such reliability is necessary (and in most enterprise network software, it is), you have no other choice but to leverage TCP or similarly resilient protocols. However, when the nature of your software, or the network infrastructure supporting it, can support less reliability, you have many high-performing alternatives for transport-layer protocols.

Connectionless communication

As we previously established, a connection in transport-layer communication can be thought of instead as a session for communication. Thus, **connectionless communication** is a mode of communication in which data is transmitted without first establishing a mutual session between hosts. Instead, packets are sent out with their appropriate addressing information, and the responsibility of ensuring delivery falls entirely to the lower layers of the network stack. This obviously introduces the risk of a failed delivery being undetected: since, without any acknowledgment expected from the server, the client wouldn't know the packet delivery failed and required re-transmission, whereas without synchronizing a session first, the server wouldn't know to expect an inbound message. So, why is this mechanism used, and when is this sort of risk acceptable?

Stateless protocols

Without any session to manage, connectionless protocols are typically described as being stateless. Without a state to manage, each transaction happens without any broader context telling the recipient how an individual packet fits into the wider stream of incoming packets. As such, there is almost no ability to determine and ensure the proper sequencing of packets for re-construction by the recipient. Without that ability, connectionless protocols are typically leveraged in cases where packets can be wholly self-contained, or where the information lost in a dropped packet can be reconstructed by the recipient application based on the next packet received.

In the latter case, we can account for the statelessness of the protocol with state management in our applications. For example, imagine your server hosting an application that keeps track of a deterministic state. Now let's say that state is updated by a remote client, and those updates are sent in real time, with minimum latency, over a connectionless protocol, such as UDP. Because the state of the application is deterministic, if a single packet is lost, the server may still be able to determine which update was made based on the next packet received if its own update could only be reached from a specific state set in the lost packet.

Using this architecture, there would be a time cost incurred by the application, as every time a packet was lost, some processing would need to happen to deduce the value of the lost packet and update its internal state accordingly. However, in cases where the network is reliable enough that packet loss is an infrequent occurrence, the reduced latency of a connectionless communication mode can more than make up for the occasional processing cost of a dropped packet over the lifetime of the application. So, on a reliable enough connection, the trade-off could prove extremely worthwhile. While less common in business applications, these protocols are frequently leveraged in high-throughput, low-latency interactive applications such as networked multiplayer video games.

Broadcasting over connectionless communication

One of the benefits of this lack of shared state being managed between two hosts is the ability of connectionless communication to multicast. In this way, a single host can transmit the same packet out to multiple recipients simultaneously, as the outbound port isn't bound by a single active connection with a single other host. This multicasting, or broadcasting, is especially useful for services such as a live video stream or feed, where a single source server is transmitting to an arbitrary number of potential consumers simultaneously. With the already-low overhead of connectionless packet transmission, this can allow high throughput of data to a broad spectrum of consumers.

Establishing connections over connectionless communication

If you're anything like me, you probably noticed a bit of a chicken-and-egg problem with connection-based communication modes as I initially described them. Specifically, how can you establish a session between two hosts that rely on connection-based communication without first having a session between those two hosts?

Of course, the obvious answer is that connections are established by way of an initial, connectionless communication request. The initial SYN message of a TCP connection request is sent over the connectionless communication IP. In this way, you could say that connection-based communication is built on the back of connectionless communication. In fact, in the case of TCP, the connection-based interactions are so dependent on the connectionless interactions of IP that the two are typically lumped together and identified as the TCP/IP suite.

UDP as a connectionless communication protocol

Just as TCP is the connection-based communication protocol of choice on the internet, UDP often serves as the connectionless communication protocol of choice. UDP exhibits all of the expected traits of a connectionless protocol, including the lack of any handshake or session negotiation prior to data transfer, and minimal error-checking and error correction techniques. So, what are the contexts in which UDP is useful?

The need for such speed and the acceptability of intermittent packet loss is perfectly suited to low-level network operations to send out notifications or basic queries of other devices on the network. It's for that reason that UDP is the protocol of choice for **Domain Name System** (**DNS**) lookups and the **Dynamic Host Configuration Protocol** (**DHCP**). In both of these contexts, the requesting host needs an immediate response to a single, simple query. In the case of DNS lookup, the request is for each IP address registered for a given domain name. The UDP packet can simply address the DNS server directly, and can contain only the domain name of the resource being looked up. Once that information is received, the DNS server can respond with addressing information on its own time, trusting that whichever application requested the IP addresses will likely be listening for the response. Once the DNS lookup request is initially sent out by the client, if there's been no response after a given timeout period, an identical packet will be transmitted from the client. This way, in the off-chance of a lost packet, there's a mechanism for error recovery (the timeout period); meanwhile, in the far-more-likely scenario that the packet is successfully transmitted, the query result will be returned substantially faster than if a connection were established first.

This same behavior is what enables a DHCP request to be satisfied in near-real time. When a new network device requests an IP address from the DHCP server, it has no specific information about the other devices on its own network. Therefore, it must broadcast out a DHCP request and hope that an adjacent node is available to act as the DHCP server and provision an IP address for the device. These needs, for low-latency and the need to broadcast packets, mean that DHCP requests are the ideal use case for a connectionless protocol such as UDP.

Detecting errors in connectionless protocols

I have discussed at length that connectionless transport layer protocols are far more susceptible to errors, as there is no mechanism inherent to the protocol for detecting errors. I've already discussed how we can detect and even correct for errors in a connectionless transport layer protocol from the application layer that's leveraging it. However, at least within UDP, there is at least one simple error-detection mechanism transmitted with each packet, and that is a **checksum**.

If you've never heard the term before, a checksum is similar to a hash function where each input will provide a drastically different output. In UDP packets, the checksum input is essentially the entirety of the headers and body of the packet. Those bytes are sent through a standard algorithm for generating the checksum. Then, once the packet is received, the recipient puts the content of the packet through the same checksum algorithm as the client, and validates that it received the same response as was delivered. If there is even a minor discrepancy, the recipient can be certain that some data was modified in transit and an error has occurred.

Responding to, or correcting, this error is outside the scope of the error-handling mechanisms of UDP. Typically, if the value of the packet was critical for continued operation of the recipient system, that system may request re-transmission of the packet. However, in most cases, a mismatched checksum simply indicates to the recipient that the packet is invalid and can be discarded from the processing queue.

TCP in C#

So, now that we've explored in-depth the objectives, functions, and limitations of various transport layer protocols, let's take a look at how we can interact with those protocols in C#. We'll start by taking a close look at the classes and features exposed by .NET Core for implementing TCP requests directly from our application code. We'll see how stepping down in the network stack gives us a degree of flexibility and control over our network operations that wasn't previously available in the application layer protocols we've explored in previous chapters. To do this, we'll be creating two applications, as we did in `Chapter 9`, *HTTP in .NET*. One of the applications will be our TCP client, and one will be the listening TCP server. We'll see the results from each request and response, confirming the expected behavior of our software, by writing to the standard output for each of our two applications.

Initializing a TCP server

Let's first create our `TCP` client, the same as we have with every application before, by creating a directory for it, and then using the CLI to create a console app:

```
dotnet new console -n SampleTcpClient
```

Then, within the same directory, we'll create our `TCP` server application with the same command:

```
dotnet new console -n SampleTcpServer
```

Now we're ready to start setting up our interactions. When we were last interacting directly with sockets exposing a port back in `Chapter 8`, *Sockets and Ports*, we were using Postman to generate HTTP requests against a given endpoint. Now, however, since we'll be writing our own TCP messages directly in code, we won't be constrained to processing the standardized HTTP headers generated by Postman. We can define our own mechanism for interactions between hosts. For ease of processing, we'll just let our client and server work with simple string messages.

To start these interactions, we'll set up a listening server. We need to do this to know what port our client will be connecting to. So, navigating to the `Main()` method of your `SampleTcpServer` application, we'll start by defining our listening ports, and then starting up an instance of the `TcpListener` class, like so:

```
public static void Main(string[] args) {
    int port = 54321;
    IPAddress address = IPAddress.Any;
    TcpListener server = new TcpListener(address, port);
    ...
}
```

The `TcpListener` class is a custom wrapper around a bare `Socket` instance. With the constructor, we designate the port and IP we want to listen on for incoming requests. If we had used a bare socket, we'd have to process and either respond to or discard every single incoming network request that ran against our designated port. With the `TcpListener` instance, though, we won't have to respond to any requests that aren't sent via TCP. We'll take a look at this once we set up our client class, but this is immensely useful when you're listening for such low-level network requests on an open port.

The constructor we used accepts an instance of the `IPAddress` class, and any `int` that designates a valid port (so nothing negative, and nothing above 65,535). So, for this project, we'll be using port `54321` to listen for incoming TCP requests. For our `IPAddress` instance, we're using the `Any` static `IPAddress` instance that is exposed by the class. By doing this, we'll see and be able to respond to any TCP request whose target host IP address or domain name would resolve to our host machine. If we didn't do this, and instead specified an individual IP address, we wouldn't respond to any requests whose IP address didn't match that exactly, even if the address resolved to the same machine. So, we would do this:

```
IPAddress address = IPAddress.Parse("127.0.0.1");
```

After doing so, we could send a TCP request to `tcp://0.0.0.0:54321`, and you wouldn't see any request register on our `TcpListener` instance. You might expect that our request would be detected, since the `0.0.0.0` IP addresses and `127.0.0.1` both resolve to the same local machine, but because, in this example, we designated our `TcpListener` to only listen for requests to the `127.0.0.1` IP address, that's exactly what it does. Meanwhile, our request to `0.0.0.0` goes unresolved. So, unless you're writing distinct listeners for distinct IP addresses held by your host machine, (or by a series of host machines your application might be deployed across), I would recommend using `IPAddress.Any` wherever possible.

Now we have to set up our server to run and listen for requests against that port. First, we'll start the server, and then we'll set up a context where we listen indefinitely for incoming requests. This is typically done with an intentionally infinite loop. Now, if you've ever accidentally found yourself stuck inside an infinite loop, you know it's something you should only ever start when you mean to. However, since we want our application to listen indefinitely, the simplest and most reliable way to do so is to prevent our `Main()` method from resolving by encapsulating our primary business logic in a simple infinite loop:

```
server.Start();

var loggedNoRequest = false;
var loggedPending = false;

while (true) {
  if (!server.Pending()) {
    if (!loggedNoRequest) {
      Console.WriteLine("No pending requests as of yet");
      Console.WriteLine("Server listening...");
      loggedNoRequest = true;
    }
  } else {
    if (!loggedPending) {
      Console.WriteLine("Pending TCP request...");
      loggedPending = true;
    }
  }
}
```

If you compile and build what we've written so far, you'll see the two console statements print to the screen, and then your application will look as if it's hanging for quite some time, and that's exactly what you would hope to see. What's happening behind the scenes is that you've initiated the `TcpListener` instance by calling `Start()` on it.

This will cause the instance to accept incoming requests on its designated port until either you explicitly call the `Stop()` method on the class, or it receives a total number of connections greater than the `MaxConnections` property of the `SocketOptionName` enum (which is set to over two billion, so it's unlikely that limit will be reached in our little local TCP server).

Once our server is listening, we start our listening loop and check to see whether our socket has received any pending requests. If it hasn't (and we haven't logged it since the last request), we indicate as much with a simple console log, and then move along, continuing with the `while` loop until we have something to process. For now, we shouldn't see anything in the pending state, so let's set up our client project to change that.

Initializing a TCP client

Now we'll need to initialize our TCP client application in much the same way as we did with our server. Instead of using the `TcpListener` class, though, we'll be using the `TcpClient` class to create connections with our server that we can write to and read from within our project. The difference between the two in our case is that, when we created a `TcpListener`, we needed to initialize it with the address and port on which it would be listening. There is no default constructor, because without a port on which to listen, the class can't perform its most basic functions.

With an instance of the `TcpClient`, however, we don't need to initialize it with an address or port specification. The client instance could feasibly be used to connect to multiple, distinct remote processes (ports on a single remote host) or hosts (different IP addresses altogether). As such, we only need to specify our connection target when we attempt to make a connection. For now, let's just establish the connection to confirm that our server responds to listening requests appropriately:

```
public static async Task Main(string[] args) {
  int port = 54321;
  IPAddress address = IPAddress.Parse("127.0.0.1");
  using (TcpClient client = new TcpClient()) {
    client.Connect(address, port);
    if (client.Connected) {
      Console.WriteLine("We've connected from the client");
    }
  }
  Thread.Sleep(10000);
}
```

Here, we specified IP address `127.0.0.1`, but, as I said before, we could have specified any alias IP address that would resolve to our local machine. Once we've created our client, we can use it to connect to the port we designated as listening on our server application. Then, just to confirm that the connection was established and that our client knows about it, we write a simple log statement, sleep the thread for `10` seconds to observe the message in our console, and then terminate the program.

In order to see this succeed, start your server application first, so that it's started and listening on the designated port. Then, once you see the messages show up in your console window indicating that the server is waiting for a pending request, start your client application. You should see the **We've connected...** message in your client window, and the **Pending TCP request...** message in your server window. Once you see both messages, you know your connections are being established, and you can terminate both applications.

And, here, let's consider why we use the `loggedPending` flag. It should be pretty obvious why we used the `loggedNoRequest` flag to prevent us from printing out the log messages every time we stepped through our loop until we received an incoming request. However, the reason we have to do the same thing when we have a pending request is the server will hold the `Pending` state until its inbound message queue has been read from and flushed. So, since our server doesn't yet read from and empty the incoming request stream if we didn't have that check, and we connected to our server, our console would quickly overflow with **Pending TCP request...** messages.

Connection information without data transfer

Before we get to the work of building and parsing TCP requests in our projects, I just want to take a moment to note the benefit of the connection-based approach, and how .NET Core leverages it to give engineers fine-tuned control over their network transactions. Note that once we send the connection request from our client, we get an immediate notification from the server that a connection was established. No message was actually sent, and no response was received by the server. In fact, the connection remains open even if the server is synchronously locked and prevented from actively transmitting anything. This is the handshake interaction of TCP at work, and gives us access to a lot of information about the state of the connection prior to actually sending a message.

What's especially nice for application developers, though, is that the connection is established and managed by the `TcpClient` class itself. With only a single call to the `Connect(IPAddress, int)` method, the TcpClient library notified our server that we wished to establish a connection, await the acknowledgment, and finally acknowledge the server's response to open the connection. This is one of the greatest strengths of .NET Core; the ease of use of a high-level application programming language, coupled with access to, and control over, low-level network interactions.

Transmitting data on an active connection

Now that we've established a connection, our server can decide what to do with that connection, and the requests transmitted across it. However, before we change gears back to our server, let's generate a message from our client for the server to process in the first place. We'll be using something of a mutation test to confirm that all of our data is being processed and returned by the server accordingly. So, at each step of the way, we'll be modifying our initial message and logging the results. Each step of the way, our message should look different than the last system that wrote it.

If you've never heard the term **mutation test**, it's a simple way of tracking that changes to your system are detected by the tests that validate your system. The idea is that you make a change or a mutation somewhere in your code, and confirm that somewhere downstream, usually in your unit tests, that change has an impact, typically by failing a previously passing unit test.

We'll start by writing a message with a header and a payload. This will just be a simple greeting for our server, and a message we expect our server to return to us, unchanged, as part of its response. We'll separate the two messages with a simple `|` delimiter. Then we'll convert it to a byte array that's suitable for transmission over our connection, and send the request. So, let's set that up before moving on to the server:

```
var message = "Hello server | Return this payload to sender!";
var bytes = Encoding.UTF8.GetBytes(message);
using (var requestStream = client.GetStream()) {
  requestStream.Write(bytes, 0, bytes.Length);
}
```

The requestStream variable we created is an instance of the NetworkStream class created to write and read data over an open socket. With this, we'll be able to send our initial message, and then, eventually, read the response from the server. But, first, let's take a look at how to use our TcpListener instance to accept and parse an incoming request.

Accepting an incoming TCP request on the server

Now that our client is actually sending a readable message, let's listen for the request on our pending connection. To do that, we'll actually get another instance of the TcpClient class directly from our listener. This is simply the class is used to interact with the open connection, so once we accept it, we'll be reading from and writing to that open connection in much the same way that our sample client program has been. First, though, we'll have to accept the pending connection, using the thread-blocking AcceptTcpClient() call. Since we're now responding to our pending request, we can get rid of our log message and replace it with our new code:

```
loggedNoRequest = false;
byte[] bytes = new byte[256];

using (var client = await server.AcceptTcpClientAsync()) {
  using (var tcpStream = client.GetStream()) {
    await tcpStream.ReadAsync(bytes, 0, bytes.Length);
    var requestMessage = Encoding.UTF8.GetString(bytes);
    Console.WriteLine(requestMessage);
  }
}
```

Starting our server, we should see in our server log that it's listening for pending connection requests. Then, once we run our client, we should see our request message from the client logged to the server's console, followed by another indicator that the server has started listening for incoming requests again. If we run the client again, we'll see the same sequence of events until we eventually shut down the server.

The request/response model on the server

To finish the request/response interaction, we'll generate a new message, using the payload of the original request, and return it to our client. As we complete these two applications, we'll have the client drive the interactions with the server from here on out. So, our server will be up and running, returning responses that echo the payload of the requests, until it receives a signal message indicating it should shut itself down. Meanwhile, our client will send intermittent requests with new payloads, until eventually sending the termination signal to our server. To serve that purpose, we'll add the following lines to our server application:

```
bool done = false;
string DELIMITER = "|";
string TERMINATE = "TERMINATE";
```

We'll use this as a signal that we should stop listening for requests and terminate the server. Next, we'll add the following conditional code to our server's listening loop:

```
  ...
  requestStream.Read(bytes, 0, bytes.Length);
  var requestMessage = Encoding.UTF8.GetString(bytes).Replace("\0",
string.Empty);

  if (requestMessage.Equals(TERMINATE)) {
    done = true;
  } else {
    Console.WriteLine(requestMessage);
  }
}
```

Our response transmission code will go inside the `else` statement in that conditional block, and so our loop will simply continue logging the request message, and then appending the payload to the response, until the terminating signal is received, at which point the loop is broken and we'll shut our server down. So, lastly, we'll modify our `while` loop to check for the value of our `done` condition instead of running in an infinite loop:

```
while (!done) {
    ...
```

Next, let's go ahead and parse the message for its payload, using our delimiter to separate the two components of our message, and then apply the result to our server's response:

```
} else {
  Console.WriteLine(requestMessage);
  var payload = requestMessage.Split(DELIMITER).Last();
  var responseMessage = $"Greetings from the server! | {payload}";
  var responseBytes = Encoding.UTF8.GetBytes(responseMessage);
  await tcpStream.WriteAsync(responseBytes, 0, responseBytes.Length);
}
```

Finally, on the line after the closing brace for our listening loop, let's shut down our server, and if you're running the application in Debug-mode from Visual Studio, allow our program to end after a brief delay to check the log results:

```
  }
  server.Stop();
  Thread.Sleep(10000);
}
```

And, with that, our `SampleTcpServer` application is complete. It will stay active and listen for requests until it's explicitly instructed to terminate itself. And the whole time, it will log each request it receives and return its own custom response. You can use the source code in the GitHub repository for this chapter to check your implementation against my own, but, as always, I'd encourage you to modify it on your own and start investigating what other methods are available. And, as you do so, always be thinking about how you could use this code in your own custom networking software.

Finalizing the TCP client

Our server is designed and written to remain active and listening for any potential incoming requests. A client, on the other hand, should only ever be set up for a single purpose, execute on that purpose, and then close its connection, freeing up the resources of the server for any other consumers that may need to access it. For this reason, we won't be writing any persistent listening loops. Instead, we will simply process each of a handful of request/response round trips before terminating the server and then shutting down our own application. However, to create a slightly more realistic simulation of multiple clients accessing our TCP server, we'll be dropping and recreating our `TcpClient` instance for each subsequent request, and injecting a random delay in between each request.

The first order of business, though, is accepting the response from our server. So, inside our `SampleTcpClient` application, we'll be adding a few lines to create a new byte array for use as a message buffer for the response and then reading our `requestStream` into our buffer for processing and logging. So, let's add that code and then we'll see how we can extend it to finish our simulation:

```
using (var requestStream = client.GetStream()) {
  await requestStream.WriteAsync(bytes, 0, bytes.Length);
  var responseBytes = new byte[256];
  await requestStream.ReadAsync(responseBytes, 0, responseBytes.Length);
  var responseMessage = Encoding.UTF8.GetString(responseBytes);
  Console.WriteLine(responseMessage);
}
```

I would think none of this is surprising at this point. We're essentially executing the exact same thing as the server, but in reverse order. Where as on the server, we were reading from the stream, and then writing *to* the stream, in the client code, we're first writing *to* the stream, and then reading from the stream. Mechanically though, this is the same sort of interaction we've seen since we first looked at how to interact with raw C# Stream objects back in `Chapter 4`, *Packets and Streams.* Hopefully, by now, you're starting to see the value in the incremental, brick-by-brick approach we've taken to building a foundation for network programming up to this point (assuming you haven't already).

At any rate, let's modify our client to transmit a handful of pre-defined messages before finally sending the termination signal. To do that, let's build out a short array of the messages we'll be sending to the server so that we can easily increment through them in our code, sending distinct messages with each outbound request:

```
var messages = new string[] {
  "Hello server | Return this payload to sender!",
  "To the server | Send this payload back to me!",
  "Server Header | Another returned message.",
  "Header Value | Payload to be returned",
  "TERMINATE"
};
```

Next, let's wrap the request/response transactions in a `while` loop (not an active listening loop as we saw with our server, but a simple incremental loop). We'll use an iterator variable, starting at zero, to move through the our messages, checking its value against the length of our messages array to determine when to break out of our loop and let our application terminate:

```
var i = 0;
while (i < messages.Length) {
  using (TcpClient client = new TcpClient()) {
    ...
```

Because our `TcpClient` instance is created by the `using` statement within our `while` loop, the variable goes out of scope with each iteration. We thus create a new connection every time we step back through the beginning of the loop. Next, we have to change the code that builds our request message byte-array to iterate through the `messages` string array:

```
var bytes = Encoding.UTF8.GetBytes(messages[i++]);
```

Finally, at the end of our `while` loop, we'll sleep our thread for a random amount of time between `2` and `10` seconds, logging the `sleepDuration` each time:

```
  ...
  var sleepDuration = new Random().Next(2000, 10000);
  Console.WriteLine($"Generating a new request in {sleepDuration/1000}
seconds");
  Thread.Sleep(sleepDuration);
}
```

Finally, if you're running in Debug-mode, you'll want to throw in one last `Thread.Sleep()` for good measure, after the `while` loop, to ensure we have enough time to examine the results of our requests before our application shuts down.

After completing the client and running both applications, my terminals logged exactly the messages that I hoped they would:

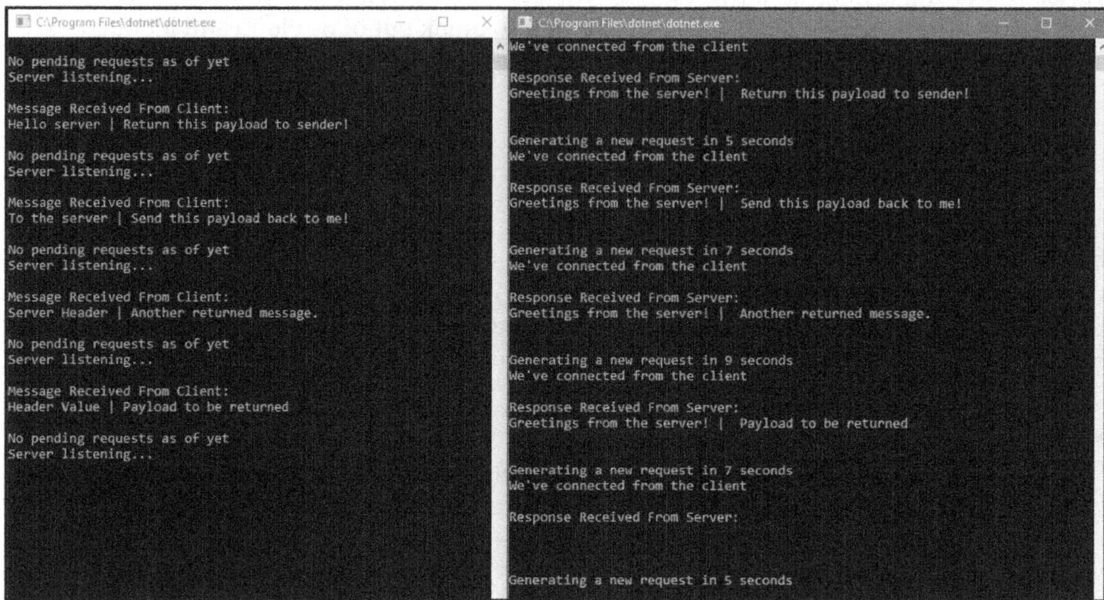

And, with this, we've written our own custom TCP server and clients. While this example was fairly trivial in its function, I hope you can see the high degree of flexibility these .NET classes open up for you with respect to custom TCP implementations. With these two sample applications, you have all the tools at your disposal necessary to write your own custom application layer protocol with a custom TCP server optimized to support it. Or you could write applications whose network interactions side-step the application layer protocol overhead altogether! The problems you encounter in your personal or professional projects will dictate how you choose to use this toolset, but now, hopefully, you'll be ready to leverage it when you need to.

UDP in C#

Now that we've looked at how to implement TCP in C#, let's take a look at its connectionless counterpart in the suite of transport layer protocols, UDP. By its very nature, the sample client and server we'll be writing will be a fair bit simpler than the TCP in terms of setup code, but we'll be using the same pattern we used in the previous section for defining the behavior of our sample application. So, we'll be transmitting requests and accepting and logging responses between a client and a server.

The difference here, however, is that both the client and the server will be implemented in the exact same way. This is because there is no `UdpListener` class, because UDP doesn't actively listen for connections. Instead, a UDP server simply accepts in bound packets whenever it is set up to look for a new one. For this reason, we'll only be looking at the client application's implementation, and I'll leave the server source code for you to pull down from GitHub and use to test and validate the behavior of the client.

Initializing a UDP client

We'll start by creating a new console app that will serve as our `UDP` client:

```
dotnet new console -n SampleUdpClient
```

Then inside our project, the first thing we'll want to do is define a well-known IP endpoint that our client will be interacting with. We'll be working against localhost once again, with an arbitrary port exposed, just as we did in the previous section about TCP. Once we have that defined, though, we're just about ready to start generating requests. The beauty of a connection-less protocol is that we don't have to first establish any sort of interaction with our remote host. Provided we know what the address of the host is, we can simply send out our datagrams.

```
public static async Task Main(string[] args) {
  using (var client = new UdpClient(34567)) {
    var remoteEndpoint = new IPEndPoint(IPAddress.Parse("127.0.0.1"),
45678);
    var message = "Testing UDP";
    byte[] messageBytes = Encoding.UTF8.GetBytes(message);
    await client.SendAsync(messageBytes, messageBytes.Length,
remoteEndpoint);
    ...
  }
}
```

And, just like that, if you run the server application and then run the client, you'll see your message logged to the server's console! So, what exactly is going on here, and what are we doing when we initialize our `UdpClient`?

The first thing we do is initialize our `UdpClient` with a port number. If we intend to use this client to receive incoming UDP datagrams (which we eventually will), it will be accepting them on the port it was initialized with. So, our client will be listening on port `34567`. Next, we take the time to define the explicit `IPEndPoint` that we would be sending our datagrams to.

This isn't technically necessary, as you can define your request target with their hostname and port as part of the `SendAsync()` method using an overloaded method signature. However, since we'll be extending this method to also accept responses, it's easier for our purposes to explicitly define the `IPEndPoint` instance once at the start of the method. Finally, we build our datagram as an array of bytes representing the characters of our message string, just as we did in the previous section, and send the message along with the help of our newly initialized `UdpClient`.

The send/receive paradigm

One thing you might have noticed about using a `UdpClient`, as opposed to the more robust `TcpClient` class, is that UDP doesn't leverage streams at all. With no underlying connection for a `Stream` to represent, and the potential for UDP data to be lost, or delivered out of order, there is no direct correlation between the behavior of a UDP request and the abstraction provided by a `Stream` instance. Because of this, the `UdpClient` class provided by .NET Core implements a simple call/response mechanism through its `Send` and `Receive` methods. Neither of these two methods requires a prior communication or interaction with the remote host to execute. Instead, they behave as more of a fire-and-forget trigger for some events to happen on the network.

Interestingly, though, when you want to leverage the `SendAsync()` method, which doesn't block your application's thread, you *can* choose to first establish a connection with your remote host. Keep in mind, though, that this isn't quite the same as establishing a connection in TCP. Instead, this simply configures your `UdpClient` so that it attempts to send all outgoing packets to the specific remote host to which it is connected.

The connection in this context is only a logical one and it only exists within the application it's established in. So, while an established TCP connection was detectable from both our client and server applications simultaneously, the same is not true in our UDP application. While running our UDP client and server simultaneously, the server application has no way of detecting the connection established by the client.

Once we've connected our `UdpClient` to a given `IPEndPoint`, every `SendAsync()` call is assumed to be configured for the connected endpoint. If you want to send a message to an arbitrary endpoint while your `UdpClient` instance is connected to a different endpoint, you'll have to disconnect your client first, or explicitly pass the new endpoint as a parameter for your `SendAsync()` call. In the context of our sample application, this won't come up as an issue, but it could come up fairly quickly in real-world contexts, so it's important you keep that in mind as you define your send/receive patterns for a given application.

With that understanding in mind, let's prepare to receive the response from our UDP server application. First, though, we'll modify our application to connect to our remote endpoint at the outset. Next, to demonstrate how to establish a connection with a `UdpClient` instance, we'll remove the endpoint parameter from our `SendAsync()` call. Finally, we'll listen for a message with `ReceiveAsync()`. At that point, we'll be handling the packet's buffer object just as we have with every byte-array buffer before:

```
public static async Task Main(string[] args) {
  using (var client = new UdpClient(34567)) {
    var remoteEndpoint = new IPEndPoint(IPAddress.Parse("127.0.0.1"),
45678);
    client.Connect(remoteEndpoint);

    var message = "Testing UDP";
    byte[] messageBytes = Encoding.UTF8.GetBytes(message);
    await client.SendAsync(messageBytes, messageBytes.Length);

    var response = await client.ReceiveAsync();
    var responseMessage = Encoding.UTF8.GetString(response.Buffer);
 Console.WriteLine(responseMessage);

 Thread.Sleep(10000);
 }
}
```

And, with that, we've got our UDP client wired up to send a packet and await a response from our server.

You may have deduced this from our discussions about connectionless communication throughout this chapter, but whenever you're sending a message using UDP (or any other connectionless protocol), it is an inherently non-blocking operation. This is due to the lack of any sort of acknowledgment from the server. So, from our application's perspective, once a UDP packet has reached our network card for transmission, its delivery is out of our hands.

Meanwhile, the `Receive()` operation in UDP is inherently blocking. Since there's no established connection or stream buffer to hold an incoming message until our server or client is ready to process the packet, any software we right that must accept and receive UDP packets will have to be very explicit about when and how long it is acceptable to block our execution while we wait for a packet that may never arrive. The asynchronous versions of the transmission methods provide some flexibility, but, ultimately, it's a limitation of the protocol that we can't escape. Given that, it's in your best interest to be mindful of that limitation and design your UDP software around it from the start.

Multicasting packets

Perhaps one of the single greatest advantages of using connectionless communication, such as UDP, is the ability to send out packets to a large number of recipients in a single transaction. This is commonly called **multicasting**, or **broadcasting**, and it enables everything from network device discovery and host registration to most live television or video streams broadcast over the internet. It's a somewhat niche feature that, if I had to guess, most of the people reading this will never have a good reason to leverage, but it is certainly worth understanding. With that said, let's look at how to enable this feature in our .NET Core apps.

Multicasting in .NET

With most of the packet transmissions we've looked at so far, we've been addressing a specific port on a specific machine, addressed via host name or IP address. However, this obviously won't suit our needs if our goal is to send the same packet to as many IP addresses as can listen for it. And it certainly won't work if we're trying to discover devices on our network and aren't even sure of their IP addresses in the first place. Instead, most network devices will listen for requests to their specific IP addresses as well as a special range of IP addresses designed specifically to catch broadcast packets from other devices on their network (typically, that multicast IP address is going to be `255.255.255.255`, but not necessarily).

If you want to multicast a number of packets out of a single port from your host, you can do so simply by configuring your `UdpClient` instance to allow multiple clients to access an open port with the `ExclusiveAddressUse` boolean property. By setting that property to `false`, you enable multiple `UdpClient` to leverage the same port at the same time, giving your application the ability to transmit messages to as many remote hosts as you have clients configured to interact with them.

Separately, if you want to listen for multicast packets, you can set up a `UdpClient` to be a part of a `MulticastGroup` by applying the appropriate `MulticastGroupOptions` settings to your client or socket. Doing so sets your client to listen along with any other registered listeners to packets being multicast by a single transmitting host.

As I said at the start of this section, multicasting and listening for multicast packets is an incredibly niche operation, and it's unlikely you'll find yourself needing to account for it in your daily work. As such, I won't be spending any more time on the subject. However, if you're curious, I would strongly encourage you to plumb the documentation for it online. For now, though, I just wanted to make sure you had at least some exposure to the concept and understood that there were features available to you in the `UdpClient` class that you could leverage to achieve or listen for multicast data transmission. For now, though, I think it's time we transition to a much more ubiquitously used transport layer protocol. And so, let's get our hands dirty with the internet protocol. It's time we explored IP.

Summary

This chapter served as a major paradigm shift for our understanding of network programming. We looked at how the responsibilities of the transport layer are wholly distinct from those of the application layer and we took an extremely close look at just what those transport layer responsibilities are. We learned that the **Internet Engineering Task Force** (**IETF**) has classified the various approaches to transport layer responsibilities based around the services and features a protocol might support, and how we can use those classifications to determine the best circumstances in which to employ a given transport layer protocol.

Next, we learned how connection-based protocols, such as TCP, use preliminary handshakes between clients and servers to establish an active connection, or session, between two hosts prior to the transmission of any data between the two. We saw how these sessions enable connection-based communication protocols to provide reliable interactions between the hosts, with substantial error-detection and error-correction support. Then we considered how connectionless protocols provide a number of advantages in their own right, including low-overhead and low-latency interactions between hosts over sufficiently reliable networks. Then we took a look at some of the strategies that can be employed by connectionless protocols, or the application layer protocols on top of them, to mitigate the unreliability of connectionless communication.

Finally, with this perspective in our minds, we were able to dive head-first into implementing both connection-based and connectionless clients and servers in C# and .NET using some incredibly simple libraries provided by the framework. We used a client and server designed to simulate interactions over TCP and UDP, and, in doing so, saw how the designers of .NET Core have conceptualized some of the characteristics of each protocol and implemented those characteristics in code. And now that we have such an in-depth understanding of both of these transport layer protocols, we're ready to fully examine the intricacies and nuances of the most ubiquitous transport layer protocol of all, the **Internet Protocol**. And that's exactly what we'll be doing in the next chapter.

Questions

1. What are the four classifications of transport layer protocols?
2. What are the primary functions and responsibilities of transport layer protocols?
3. What is meant by a connection in connection-based communication modes?
4. What does TCP stand for? Why is it typically referred to as TCP/IP?
5. Describe the handshake process used to establish a connection over TCP.
6. What does UDP stand for? What are some of the advantages of UDP?
7. What are the biggest drawbacks of connectionless communication?
8. What is multicasting? What is broadcasting, and how is it enabled in UDP?

Further reading

For additional information about TCP, UDP, and the transport layer generally, I recommend reading *Understanding TCP/IP* by Alena Kabelová and Libor Dostálek, available from Packt Publishing at the following link:

`https://www.packtpub.com/networking-and-servers/understanding-tcpip.`

4
Section 4: Security, Stability, and Scalability

In this part, the reader will closely explore how to make their software more reliable by writing more secure interactions between clients and servers. It will explain how to examine and profile the performance of your network software to improve and monitor performance. It will also examine strategies for scalability with caching.

The following chapters will be covered in this section:

12
The Internet Protocol

In the previous chapter, we got a comprehensive understanding of two of the most common and robust protocols in the transport layer of the **Open Systems Interconnection** (**OSI**) network stack, with the **Transmission Control Protocol** (**TCP**) and **User Datagram Protocol** (**UDP**). In this chapter, we'll look at the network layer protocol that enables each of those two transport layer services. In this chapter, we'll be learning about the **Internet Protocol** (**IP**). We'll look at how the IP standard has evolved to support a global network of billions of devices, allowing each of them to reliably communicate with one another. We'll consider the earlier, and more common IPv4, looking at what problems IPv4 was designed to solve, and discussing the limitations that it has reached. Next, we'll examine how IPv6 aims to solve those limitations. Finally, we'll take a closer look at the `IPAddress` class, and look closely at how the core libraries implement IPv4 and IPv6. We'll take the opportunity to discuss and consider how IP addresses map to domain names and learn how **Domain Name System** (**DNS**) servers will map an address to a resource, and we'll look at some code samples that will allow us to implement those mappings on our own.

The following topics will be covered in this chapter:

- What an IP address is composed of and how it is used, along with network masks, local addressing, and DNS servers, to identify physical devices
- How IP addresses are assigned using the IPv4 standard, identifying the limitations of IPv4
- The specifics of the IPv6 standard, enumerating the strengths of leveraging IPv6, and the costs of implementing it at the scale of the internet
- The hostname to IP address resolution at the DNS level

Technical requirements

In this chapter, we'll be writing sample software to resolve IP addresses configured from our hosts file to simulate a DNS server. You'll need your .NET Core **integrated development environment** (**IDE**) or a code editor. You can access the sample code at `https://github.com/PacktPublishing/Hands-On-Network-Programming-with-C-and-.NET-Core/tree/master/Chapter 12`. Check out the following video to see the code in action: `http://bit.ly/2HYmyi9`.

The IP standard

Before we start looking at how the IP standard has evolved from its inception to the widely adopted IPv4, and now on to IPv6, we first have to understand what the standard is and how it's distinct from the transport layer protocols that we've looked at. This is critical to cementing our understanding of the OSI network stack, as IP is fundamental to the operation of transport layer protocols that operate over the internet. So, let's figure out just what IP is designed for, how it accomplishes its design goals, and what sort of features it enables for network software and hardware.

The origins of IP

Originally implemented as a packet transmission mechanism in the earliest version of the TCP, IP was first formally described in 1974. Still early in the history of modern computing, computational networks were very much in their infancy. Those networks grew in scope, however, and began to encapsulate multiple sub-networks with various interaction mechanisms. And as those networks grew, the need for a standard across network-connected devices quickly became apparent.

To satisfy this need for a standard, the **Advanced Research Projects Agency** (**ARPA**) of the US government sponsored a series of experiments to define a protocol that could support a wide-scale interconnected network. With this sponsorship, the members of the **Institute of Electrical and Electronic Engineers** (**IEEE**) wrote a paper that described an inter-networking protocol that leveraged packet switching to share resources across and between hosts in a network. Beginning in 1977, the organization began experimenting with various drafts of the protocol described in this paper. Between 1977 and 1979, there were four experimental versions of IP described by **Internet Experiment Notes** (**IEN**), and labeled IPv0 through to IPv3. Each of these versions tackled some major deficiency in the previous iteration of the protocol until the team was certain their protocol was sufficiently robust for use by the wider public.

IPv0 – a network layer protocol for TCP

The first of these experiments, IEN 2, was written in August 1977. It explicitly states that engineers had been screwing up in their design of IPs by violating the principle of layering. In its initial draft, TCP was responsible for the abstraction of both the host-to-host transmission of application layer packets, and for negotiating the hops between network devices along the route between the two connected hosts. By over-engineering TCP in this way, engineers created a single protocol that spanned both the transport and network layers of the OSI network stack. This violation of boundaries between OSI layers was almost immediately recognized as a bad design, and a bad practice. So, with IEN 2, the authors proposed a new and distinct internetwork protocol, and that TCP be used strictly as a host level end-to-end protocol. And with this experiment, IP was born.

The protocols and interfaces described in IEN 2 described two primary operations that had previously both been performed by TCP. First, there was the **Internet Host-Hop Protocol**, which would become TCP. This was meant to describe the interface for complete end-to-end interactions between hosts, with no concern for how to navigate between those two hosts. It described a rudimentary process for payload fragmentation and many of the headers that are still used in TCP today.

The second protocol described was the **Internet Hop Interface**. It's this part of the IEN that described what would eventually become IP. The hops in this context are hops along a single edge in the network diagram between two nodes, or hosts. The goal of this section of the IEN was to define the minimum amount of information necessary to bundle with a packet to allow any step on the path to route it accordingly, without routing multiple instances of the same packet to the destination, and to allow fragmentation in such a way that the packet can be reassembled at the destination gateway.

IPv1 to IPv3 – formalizing a header format

Over the course of the two years that followed, several more IENs were written to describe an evolving IP interface. Each of these, in their own way, formalized some detail of IP that would eventually become the broadly-released and universally supported IPv4. Beginning with IPv1, as described by IEN 26, the first task engineers set to accomplish was defining the minimum necessary headers, along with their minimum necessary size specifications, to successfully route packets across an arbitrarily large and arbitrarily organized network.

Without universal acceptance of some sort of header, there could ultimately be no internet as we know it today. However, until there was universal acceptance of some interface, members of the **Internet Engineering Task Force** (**IETF**) knew that their work would be subject to feedback and changes. As such, one of the primary tasks of the first IP header description was to allow for the support of multiple versions and multiple kinds of services exposed over those networks. Thus, the header described in IEN 26 introduced fields such as the IP version header, and the **type of service** (**TOS**) header.

Shortly after, in IEN 28, the team defined IPv2, which further crystallized the interface's header, as well as the process of fragmentation of packets over a network. This was also the first IEN to posit a mechanism for detecting packet corruption, though it provided no guidance on how that could be accomplished. Finally, it described a rudimentary addressing component of a packet, and the addressing mechanism for hosts on a network. However, it's worth noting that the mechanism described was not quite what was ultimately released to the broader public.

IPv4 – establishing the IP

Over the course of several iterations on the protocol, the team worked through their design issues until, with IEN 54, they finalized the header definition that would be standardized by **Request for Comment** (**RFC**) 791, as IPv4. With RFC 791, the IETF finally established the details of the operation and implementation of the IP standard. This version of the protocol has been in use across the globe since 1981, and even today, this interface specification is used on almost 80% of all datagrams sent between hosts on the internet.

The functions of IP

As described in RCF 791, there are three primary functions that the IP is designed to provide for networks. In section 1.2 of that specification, the scope of the protocol is explicitly limited to just the functions necessary to deliver a package of bits (an internet datagram) from a source to a destination over an interconnected system of networks.

You'll note that nowhere in this definition do the authors mention reliability, ordered delivery, or connection negotiation. This is very much an intentional omission on their part. As they stated in IEN 2, attempting to account for those functions with a network layer protocol will be violating the boundaries of the OSI network stack. And that's not simply speculation on my part; in the definition of the scope of IP, the authors explicitly state that there are no mechanisms to augment end-to-end data reliability, flow control, sequencing, or other services found in host-to-host protocols. Here, by host-to-host protocols, the authors are referring to the responsibilities of transport layer protocols and interfaces.

So, if reliable delivery, flow control, and sequencing are all outside the scope of IP, you may well be wondering what functions it is responsible for, and how it implements them. Well, according to the standard, IP is responsible for precisely two functions: addressing and fragmentation. The protocol provides these functions for the transport layer protocol above it, and it does so by leveraging the local network protocols of the data link layer below it.

Addressing for IP

Addressing is used to uniquely identify a host (or set of hosts) that can service requests over a network. Any device that must be located by other hosts on a network to which it's connected must have an address associated with it. This is the only mechanism by which the IP can request routing information from the data link layer.

Here, it's worth distinguishing between an address and a name, hostname, or domain name. Names, or hostnames, are the human-readable **Uniform Resource Identifier** (**URI**) structures, while an address is a unique, semantically structured key that indicates where the owner of a hostname resides. According to the IP standard, transport layer protocols are responsible for resolving a hostname to its specific address before passing the addressing information to the network layer to be transmitted to the next device in the route.

And here, a further distinction should be made between addressing, or identifying the sub-network and specific location of the target host, and routing, or finding the complete path from the source host to the destination host. Once a datagram is received by a host's IP interface, the destination address is validated, and the packet is fragmented, with all IP headers applied. Then, the datagram is passed along, and it is the responsibility of the data link layer to actually perform the task of routing along links and nodes in the network to find a connected path between the two hosts.

So, addressing functions of an IP implementation revolves around assigning addresses to new nodes on a network, and parsing and interpreting addresses attached to packets. When assigning new addresses, they are done with a fixed-length, semantically significant data key. A semantically significant data key is simply one in which meaning can be inferred from the structure of the key.

In the case of IP addresses, different segments of the address contain details about the specific location of the host that the IP address identifies. For example, in an early specification for address resolution, the first 8 bits of a 32-bit addressing scheme were used to locate the specific subnet in which the target host resided. The next 24 bits in the address serve as the address of the host within the local network's addressing scheme.

The standards of the IP addressing scheme have grown and changed over the years to adapt to ever broadening networks and ever wider address spaces, but the principle of a well-formed, semantic key used as a host's address has remained unchanged since IPv4 was introduced in 1981.

The fragmentation of packets

The fact that IP is designed to facilitate hops between nodes in a network is why a specification for packet fragmentation (over the fragmentation that may already be performed at the transport layer) becomes necessary. Since each connected sub-network in the larger internet is free to specify its own constraints for packet size and delivery, there could be inconsistencies in the size and format requirements for a datagram as it moves across the network. It may well be the case that a datagram that is considered small enough by the sub-network of the originating host is actually too large for the sub-network of the target host. As such, it might be necessary for the IP implementation running on a router or bridge between two sub-networks to have to decompose or reassemble datagrams as they move between the two subnets.

The specification does provide a mechanism for indicating that a datagram should not be fragmented under any circumstances. However, if the specifications of the data link layer prevent a datagram from being delivered without being fragmented, and the datagram is marked as do not fragment, then it is simply discarded instead.

The actual process of fragmenting is defined by the standard as a general system for decomposing a longer datagram into some number, *n*, of smaller datagrams. The datagrams are broken up into smaller frames of binary data, with additional headers added incorporated to allow for the reconstruction of the smaller datagrams into an appropriate recreation of the original, larger datagram. Those additional fields added to the smaller datagrams are as follows:

- **Offset**: The position in the datagram that the new fragment came from. This allows for the proper reordering of datagram fragments that may have been delivered out of order.
- **Length**: This specifies the length of the content that was pulled out of the original datagram and stored in the payload of the current fragment.

- **Identification field**: The new, smaller fragments also use an identification number to specify which larger datagram they belong to. This helps ensure that smaller fragments from different parent datagrams are not mixed up during recomposition.
- **More-fragments flag**: Finally, there is a more-fragments flag field used to indicate whether or not there are additional smaller fragments that need to be added to the reconstructed parent datagram.

These fields taken together – offset, length, identification, and more-fragments – are sufficient to reconstruct a datagram from an arbitrary number of fragments on the destination host. The generalized nature of the description in the RFC that we've seen here allows for reliable fragmentation and recomposition in almost any use case across any network gateway, router, or subnet interface. Now that we understand what the protocol was designed to accomplish, let's look at how it has been implemented and deployed since its inception.

IPv4 and its limits

First defined in 1981, and widely deployed in 1983, IPv4 has been the standard for network layer interactions across the whole of the internet, and almost every local area network, for over three decades now. As I mentioned before, nearly 80% of all internet traffic is done using the IPv4 specification of the IP interface. Its stability, scalability, and reliability have been well-proven at this point. So, what is it about IPv4 that made its implementation of network layer responsibilities so successful? And what was it about the IPv4 specification that precipitated the need, after such a long and successful lifespan, to define and deploy a new protocol with IPv6?

The addressing standard of IPv4

As I mentioned in the previous section on the addressing functions of IP, the address of IPv4 is designed with a semantic structure, as opposed to simply having an arbitrary key allocated for each new device on a network. So, provided you understand how to parse the semantic meaning of an address, determining the specific location of a host can be done through a hierarchical analysis of each segment of an address.

The IPv4 address syntax

Addresses in IPv4 are 32-bits long, and are typically divided into four octets (bytes), separated by a decimal, with each byte expressed in its base-10 notation. However, the underlying structure of the address is flexible enough to be expressed as anything from the dot-decimal notation, to a raw base-10 integer representation of the 32-bit value, to hexadecimal, to a dotted hexadecimal format. Each of these representations is merely a different way of expressing the same binary value. In this way, the syntactical representation of a given IP address is unimportant, since the semantic meaning is preserved by the underlying 32-bit representation.

So, let's consider the following IPv4 address:

```
11000000101010000000000110110101
```

This probably doesn't seem familiar to you as an IP address, at least, not in that representation. So, let's look at how we can express this in a way we'd more easily recognize as an IP address. We'll start by separating the binary representation into four octets:

```
11000000.10101000.00000001.10110101
```

Next, we'll convert each of the dot-delimited bytes and convert their values to the corresponding base-10 representation:

```
192.168.1.181
```

And, just like that, we have an IP address format that we're more familiar with. However, we could have just as easily converted the string to its hexadecimal-dot notation, and gotten the following:

```
C0.A8.01.B5
```

As long as we preserve the ordering of the octets, the meaning remains true, and can provide us with useful information for routing requests to the given address.

Classful IP addressing

With IPv4, the value of each octet in an address can carry with it hierarchical routing information about the host at that address. When the protocol version was first defined, there was a specification that the first octet of an address value would designate the subnet to which the host belonged. This was dubbed the network field. The remaining three octets were then left to designate the address within that subnet at which the host could be found. These octets, together, were commonly called the **rest field**, short for the **rest of the address**.

Now, if you're on top of your binary math, you will have already recognized the issue with the structure that I just described. With only a single octet to designate a subnet, there could only be, at most, `255` subnets on the whole of the internet. Such a limitation was almost immediately recognized as infeasible, and so the standards document included a provision for different classes of addressing schemes. Described in RFC 791, there were three specific classes of IP addresses, each of which used a different number of bits to specify the subnet of a host, and with each having their own unique limits on the maximum number of hosts on a given subnet.

At the time that the RFC was drafted, there were only about `64` subnets in existence, meaning at most, that only the six least significant bits of the network field had been used to designate a known subnet, up to that point. Not wanting to reassign widely used subnet addresses, the most significant bits of the network field were set for use as the class flags for a given IP address. In the original RFC, there were three well-defined classes of IP structure, with a fourth left open for future specification as need demanded. These original three classes were defined as follows:

- **Class A**: In a **Class A** address, the most significant bit is zero, and the next seven bits are to be used for subnet identification. This leaves the remaining three octets as the rest field, allowing for up to `16,777,215` possible unique host addresses within a subnet identified by a **Class A** address.
- **Class B**: In a **Class B** address, the most significant bit of the address has a value of `1`, and the second most significant bit has a value of `0`. The next 14 bits of the address are used for subnet identification, leaving the two least significant octets available for unique host addresses within the subnet.
- **Class C**: Finally, in a **Class C** address, the first two most significant bits of the address have a value of `1`, while the third most significant bit has a value of `0`. With these values in the three most significant bits, the next 21 bits are to be used for subnet identification, allowing for `2,097,151` unique possible subnets. This leaves only the final octet for host addressing, leaving at most `255` host addresses available in a **Class C** IP address.

To further illustrate how these classes are semantically parsed, consider the following three IP addresses:

```
38.117.181.90
183.174.61.12
192.168.1.181
```

Now, by converting each address to their dot-binary representation, we can examine the most significant digits to determine the class of IP address under which each of them falls:

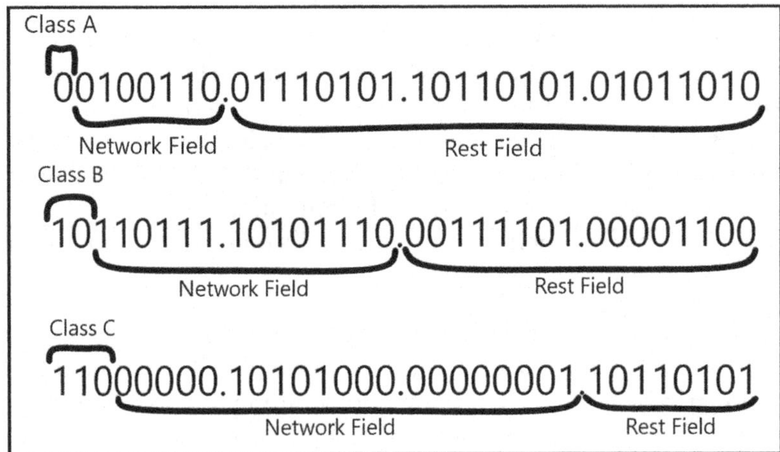

However, restricting use of the three most significant bits to indicate the class of a network was an untenable long-term solution. Soon enough, the IETF devised a new mechanism for determining the network field of an IP address.

Subnet masking

By 1993, the available pool of IP addresses under the classful address architecture was depleting at an untenable rate (a problem that we'll discuss more later). To mitigate this challenge, the IETF did away with the classful architecture described by RFC 791, and introduced the **Classless Inter-Domain Routing (CIDR)** address syntax. The CIDR syntax applies an additional, optional suffix to an IP address that is used to indicate precisely how many bits of the address are dedicated to the network field. The suffix is delimited with a leading / character, and then an integer that denotes how many leading 1s are in the subnet mask.

If the term **subnet mask** sounds familiar, you've likely seen it in the diagnostic output when you've run the `ipconfig` command in your terminal. The term **mask** in this context specifically refers to a bitwise mask. Basically, when you apply a mask to another binary number, the result is a `1` value in any position in which at least one of the two numbers has a `1` value. Consider the following IP address:

```
11000000.10101000.00000001.10110101
```

And then the following subnet mask:

```
11111111.11111111.11111111.00000000
```

The result of applying the mask to the IP address will be as follows:

```
11111111.11111111.11111111.10110101
```

So, in this example, if we convert our binary to its dot-decimal notation, we've got an IP address as follows:

```
192.168.1.181
```

And we also have the following subnet mask:

```
255.255.255.0
```

What this subnet mask does is indicate to a routing device what bits of the IP address are to be used for network identification. So, since the subnet mask we just looked at had all `1` values for the first 24 most significant bits, this means those first 24 bits should be used as the network identifier.

This specific subnet mask will likely look pretty familiar to you since it's the default local subnet and subnet mask for most modern routers. The sub-network identified by this IP address is the one created by your home router, which serves as a gateway between the wider internet and your home network. What this means, though, is that for any given household with a single router, there is a maximum number of devices that can be connected to the network.

Using the notation of CIDR, that same IP address and subnet mask combination is expressed as follows:

```
192.168.1.181/24
```

This gives us what's called **variable-length subnet masking** (**VLSM**). It allows us to use any arbitrary number of bits for network identification without having to reserve the most significant bits as flag values. This means that IP addresses could be used to identify a much larger set of unique sub-networks, and those networks could have a wider variety of maximum sizes.

Address space exhaustion

All of this work of adapting the standard to allow for a broader flexibility in the address syntax was done primarily to mitigate perhaps the greatest limitation of IPv4. I've alluded to it before, but the address specification for IPv4 allows for a maximum of 32 bits for an address. This means that the maximum number of unique IP addresses, no matter how you structure your network field and rest field, will always be at most `4,294,967,296` unique addresses.

In 1983, when IPv4 was standardized, the internet remained nothing more than an experiment. Certainly, the engineers working on the IETF had the foresight to expect their network experiment would eventually grow to the span the world. But the development of IPv4 was done on the assumption that their specific networking experiment wouldn't extend beyond the computer networks of ARPA. However, even as they saw the widespread adoption of their standard on hosts across the nascent internet, there was still an assumption that 4.3 billion unique addresses would provide ample time to devise a workable alternative before the address space was exhausted.

What they didn't predict though, was the rate at which computers would increase in power, and decrease in cost. This combination resulted in an explosion in the consumer computer market, and with it, an explosion in networked hosts in need of addresses. As the new millennium approached, so too did the assignment of the last available IPv4 address. And so, in 1998, a draft standard for the next IP version was released.

IPv6 – the future of the protocol

Designed to overcome an insufficient number of valid addresses for network hosts, IPv6 was first introduced in 1998, though it was only accepted as a formal standard in 2017 (which goes to show how diligent engineers can be about defining standards). The new specification was written to deal with a small number of issues presented by IPv4, including the limited address space. The standard also has native support for multicast transmission, as well as **IP security** (**IPSec**) security features.

The IPv6 addressing scheme

Where IPv4 had a 32-bit addressing mechanism, allowing for a maximum of about 4.3 billion unique addresses, the IPv6 standard provides a 128-bit addressing scheme, allowing for 3.4×10^{38} unique addresses. That's 340 billion addresses! For a bit of context, the scheme allows for more addresses than there are meters from the surface of the earth to the edge of the observable universe. With such a large addressing space, the IPv6 scheme allows for simpler address allocation, route aggregation, and unique addressing features that we'll look at later.

These 128 bits are organized into eight groups of 16 bits each. These groups are typically written as four hexadecimal digits (as opposed to the integral representation typical in IPv4), with each grouping separated by a colon. However, for the sake of minimizing the size of a packet header, there is a standard for abbreviating IPv6 addresses without the loss of meaningful information. The two steps to follow for address abbreviation are as follows:

1. Remove any leading zeros in any 16-bit (or four hexadecimal) segment of the route
2. Eliminate exactly one consecutive string of remaining zeros, and replace the removed segments with :

To see this in action, let's start with the following address:

```
fe08:0000:0000:0000:5584:7902:0028:6f0e
```

Now, after applying step 1, we have the following:

```
fe08:0:0:0:5584:7902:28:6f0e
```

Now, removing the longest string of consecutive zeros, we have the following:

```
fe08::5584:7902:28:6f0e
```

While this representation is substantially smaller, it's only really used as a convenience. The packet header for an IPv6 packet is configured to use the full 128-bit address for the source and destination of the packet, so, prior to transmission, the full address is applied to the packet regardless of how short it can be abbreviated.

Network fields and routing efficiency

With IPv4, a considerable amount of work was put into allocating sufficient space for a subnet identifier within the limited 32-bit addresses. However, since IPv6 is designed with such a vast address space, network identification is greatly simplified. All IPv6 addresses allocate the most significant 64 bits to subnet addressing, and the remaining 64 bits to host, or interface identification.

One of the simplest things this enables is more efficient processing by routers and network switches. Because the network identifier and host addresses are always of a fixed length, and those lengths are well-aligned with word length in 32- and 64-bit hardware, routers can parse the structure of the address with much greater efficiency.

Fragmentation in IPv6

Another major change between IPv4 and IPv6 comes in the delegation of responsibility to fragment packets appropriately for their route. With IPv4, this was explicitly a concern for the network layer, and one that IPv6 sought to solve. The guidance provided for the fragmentation of a data packet was a major part of the RFC that defined IPv4. Meanwhile, with IPv6, packet fragmentation is considered the joint responsibility of the transport layer and the data link layer.

The idea behind this change in responsibilities is the assertion that there should be a step in the end-to-end protocols of the transport layer. That step is nothing but determining the maximum packet size allowable along a route between two hosts. Meanwhile, the **Maximum Transmission Unit** (**MTU**) of every edge along a route between two hosts should be discoverable from the data link layer when the transmission is initiated. In cases of failure to discover the MTU of the specific route between two hosts, the transport layer should fall back to the default MTU of the internet, which is 1280 bytes of data. Thus, in an ideal case, the data link layer can provide the specific route MTU and the transport layer can fragment its packets accordingly. If the data link layer fails to provide the route's MTU, the transport layer uses a worst-case fragment size of the default MTU, that is, 1,280 bytes.

IPv6 to IPv4 interfaces

Because IPv6 so fundamentally alters the structure of the IPv4 packet header, the two versions are entirely incompatible. This obviously poses a problem when network engineers need to support the widely deployed IPv4 over the whole lifetime of the transition to IPv6. To facilitate that transition, a number of intermediary solutions have been devised to allow IPv6 traffic to function over IPv4 networks.

Side-by-side IP deployment

The simplest way to get IPv4 and IPv6 to coexist on a single network is to have each host on that network deploy a full protocol implementation of each version. This is commonly done at the operating system (OS) level and allows traffic travelling to and from a single hardware interface to interact with both IP versions once the physical data transmission is delivered to the OS. Devices that use this side-by-side deployment will acquire an address for IPv4 and IPv6 simultaneously, and if the host has a registered domain name, that domain name will be resolved for both address schemes by a DNS server. Of course, the obvious downside here is that a side-by-side deployment is only as good as the subnet to which it is deployed. If a host supports both protocols, but exists on a network that only supports IPv4, then there's no benefit to be gained. In a strictly controlled sub-network, however, side-by-side deployment is a viable and often simple option.

Tunneling interfaces

The other alternative for the cross-version support of IP traffic is known as **tunneling**. This is a mechanism by which IPv6 traffic is tunneled over an IPv4 network by wrapping the IPv6 packet in an IPv4 packet. This process is described in RFC 4213, and is widely used by servers leveraging strictly IPv6 packet schemes.

One of the most popular tunneling schemes, **Teredo**, is consistently used for integrating an IPv6 sub-network onto the wider IPv4 internet. The mechanism by which Teredo accomplishes this is by leveraging our old friend, UDP. The IPv6 packets are wrapped in a UDP packet header, which is itself wrapped in an IPv4 packet. The IPv4 packets are routed normally, until received by a Teredo client or server, which is configured specifically to decompose the IPv4 packets into their original IPv6 structure.

While this is useful information for any network engineer, though, as C# developers, we are lucky enough to not need to concern ourselves with the details of these interfaces. While we have access to the specific IP information from any network traffic in our software, the translation and parsing of IP packets is mostly abstracted away from us. So, let's look now at how we can investigate and understand the nature of IP traffic within our software.

Leveraging IP in C#

Since C# and the .NET Core runtime will abstract away most of the details of IP interactions from our application software, this demonstration will be relatively simple. What we're going to write is a simple web API that simulates a DNS name resolution. We'll use a simple JSON file to store domain names and their associated addresses and provide an instance of the `IPAddress` class (or a list of instances of it) as our response. This will demonstrate how the language provides a lot of parsing and negotiation behind the scenes for you, and how that can streamline your development process considerably. And since we've been working with IP addresses and ports throughout this book, much of this should seem familiar to you.

Setting up our server

We'll be using a simple web API project for this, so we'll create it with the **command-line interface** (CLI):

```
dotnet new webapi -n DNSSimulation
```

Once that's up, we'll go ahead and remove all of the scaffolded endpoints in our controller except for our POST endpoint. This will be the route by which users will look up hostnames from our DNS server. We'll also modify our route to more accurately express what our API provides. So, before we start coding, our controller should appear as follows:

```
[Route("dns/[controller]")]
[ApiController]
public class HostsController : ControllerBase {
    [HttpPost]
    public IEnumerable<string> Post([FromBody] string domainName) {
    }
}
```

Next, we'll need to add a simple host registry for our application to perform lookups on. So, create a JSON file that represents a list of key-value pairs. The keys will be the hostnames we're performing lookups on, and the values will be an array of string representations of arbitrary IP addresses. And for demo purposes, be sure to use both IPv4 and IPv6 addresses in our file. Mine looks like this, but yours can have whatever hostnames and addresses you feel like using:

```
{
    "test.com": [ "172.112.98.123" ],
    "fake.net": [
        "133.54.121.89",
```

```
        "fe80:0000:0000:0000:5584:7902:d228:6f0e"
    ],
    "not-real.org": [
        "123.12.13.134",
        "dc39::7354:23f3:c34e"
    ]
}
```

As a final setup step, we'll just add a simple static class to make our `hosts.json` file easier to work with from within our controller. To do that, we'll create a `Hosts` static class, give it a single public property called `Map`, and then use the static constructor feature of C# to initialize the `Map` property with the contents of our JSON file. Then, whenever we need to access our hosts file, we do so with a static reference to our `Hosts.Map` method and `query` its dictionary accordingly. This pattern is incredibly simple, and incredibly useful for providing straightforward and easily understandable access to static content files in your application code. Our example appears as follows:

```
public static class Hosts {
  public static IDictionary<string, IEnumerable<string>> Map;

  static Hosts() {
    try {
      using (var sr = new StreamReader("hosts.json")) {
        var json = sr.ReadToEnd();
        Map = JsonConvert.DeserializeObject<IDictionary<string,
IEnumerable<string>>>(json);
      }
    } catch (Exception e) {
      throw e;
    }
  }
}
```

And with that, we're ready to implement our IP lookup.

IP parsing in C#

Now that we're ready to read from our hosts file, we can start parsing incoming requests and returning IP information for our consumers as a JSON string. As with all of our demo code, we'll assume we're getting well-formed inputs and ignore error handling for the time being.

Our inputs will be a fully-qualified URI, and so we'll initialize a temporary URI variable to allow easier domain name acquisition:

```
public string Post([FromBody] string domainName) {
  var uri = new UriBuilder(domainName).Uri;
```

Next, we'll try to access the IP addresses for the hostname in our `Hosts.Map` method. If it fails, we'll defer to the outer DNS server, and return whatever addresses it can provide for our hostname. We'll do this using a utility method written to serialize `IPAddress` arrays into a string, called `GetSerializedIpAddresses()`, which we'll look at later. For now, though, the important thing to understand is that our fallback when we can't find the hostname in our own server registry is to look to an outer DNS server for our name resolution:

```
IEnumerable<string> ipAddressStrings;
if (!Hosts.Map.TryGetValue(uri.Host, out ipAddressStrings)) {
   return GetSerializedIPAddresses(Dns.GetHostAddresses(uri.Host));
}
```

Once we've made it past this point, we know that we hold the `IPAddress` entries for the requested host, and we can use C#'s `IPAddress` class to parse them accordingly. So, first, we'll create a container for our `IPAddress` instances. Then, we'll attempt to initialize each instance using the `IPAddress.TryParse()` method. Assuming that succeeds (which it does in my example, and provided you have well-formed IP addresses in your own file, it will with yours too), we add the new `IPAddress` instances to our list:

```
var addresses = new List<IPAddress>();
foreach (var addressString in ipAddressStrings) {
  if (!IPAddress.TryParse(addressString, out var newAddress)) {
    continue;
  }
  addresses.Add(newAddress);
}
```

If you've followed my example up to this point, you'll find that the `TryParse()` method of the `IPAddress` class will automatically detect and account for each of the addressing schemes that I've discussed so far. We could add everything from a human readable dot-decimal-formatted IPv4 address, to an abbreviated IPv6 address, to a raw 32-bit binary string, and the `TryParse()` method will build the address accordingly. This kind of utility is why the software demo for this chapter can be so light. Almost all the heavy lifting is done for you by the .NET Core runtime.

Using the IPAddress class in C#

Our last task for this service will be converting our list of IPAddress instances to their corresponding JSON. This is where you will likely hit a pretty substantial snag in your code. Unfortunately, the IPAddress class doesn't play very well with JsonConvert.SerializeObject(). In fact, if you tried to execute that method on an instance of IPAddress, you'll get an exception almost every time. That's because the IPAddress.Address property is actually deprecated. It's defined as a long type, which, in C#, is a 64-bit integer. However, as you now know, an IPv6 address is a 128-bit value. Unfortunately, though, the JsonConverter class isn't intelligent enough to determine at runtime which public properties are deprecated. That means it will attempt to access the Address property of your IPAddress instance for serialization, and that access will throw an error for any IPAddress instances containing an IPv6 address.

Now, if you're familiar with writing your own JsonConverter extension class, you can overwrite the JsonConverter class for IPAddress and use that to serialize your return object. However, as that's quite outside the scope of this book, instead, we'll take the less ideal shortcut of writing our own serialization with a GetSerializedIPAddresses() method. Since we know better than to use the IPAddress.Address property, we'll just use the ToString() method to get the value of our IPAddress instance. That method will simply build out the string representation of each of our IPAddress instances as JSON, using each public property that we know is not deprecated and safe to access. That method will read as follows:

```
private string GetSerializedIPAddresses(IEnumerable<IPAddress> addresses) {
  var str = new StringBuilder("[");
  var firstInstance = true;
  foreach (var address in addresses) {
    if (!firstInstance) {
      str.Append(",");
    } else {
      firstInstance = false;
    }
    str.Append("{");
    str.Append($"\"Address\": {address.ToString()},");
    str.Append($"\"AddressFamily\": {address.AddressFamily},");
    str.Append($"\"IsIPv4MappedToIPv6\": {address.IsIPv4MappedToIPv6}");
    str.Append($"\"IsIPv6LinkLocal\": {address.IsIPv6LinkLocal},");
    str.Append($"\"IsIPv6Multicast\": {address.IsIPv6Multicast},");
    str.Append($"\"IsIPv6SiteLocal\": {address.IsIPv6SiteLocal},");
    str.Append($"\"IsIPv6Teredo\": {address.IsIPv6Teredo}");
    str.Append("}");
  }
```

```
        str.Append("]");
        return str.ToString();
    }
```

And with that method, we see exactly what information the `IPAddress` class can provide for us regarding the nature of the IP version and its implementation just through its public properties. We can learn about the mappings or interfaces used to leverage IPv6 over IPv4, or simply learn about the feature support of an IPv6 host.

And with that last piece of the puzzle in place, our final controller method should read as follows:

```
    [HttpPost]
    public string Post([FromBody] string domainName) {
      var uri = new UriBuilder(domainName).Uri;
      IEnumerable<string> ipAddressStrings;
      if (!Hosts.Map.TryGetValue(uri.Host, out ipAddressStrings)) {
        return GetSerializedIPAddresses(Dns.GetHostAddresses(uri.Host));
      }

      var addresses = new List<IPAddress>();
      foreach (var addressString in ipAddressStrings) {
        IPAddress newAddress;
        if (!IPAddress.TryParse(addressString, out newAddress)) {
            continue;
        }
        addresses.Add(newAddress);
      }
      return GetSerializedIPAddresses(addresses);
    }
```

And if you run the application and `POST` hostnames to your endpoint, you'll notice that the IP addresses returned are always well-formed, and even the fully-qualified IPv6 addresses have been abbreviated. With this simple functionality, you can abstract away all of the mess of parsing and manipulating IP addresses within your application code. You can trust that the work is being properly handled for you by a robust implementation of both IPv4 and IPv6 under the hood.

Summary

In this chapter, we took an extremely close look at IP, first discerning precisely why IP, as a network layer protocol, was unique from the transport layer protocols that we've examined before it and then learning about the functions and use of IP through its origin. We looked at when the split was made between the transport layer responsibilities of TCP and the network layer responsibilities of what eventually became IP. In doing so, we established clear boundaries on the scope of IP and what functions it is meant to provide, and what functions fall outside its scope.

Once we established the scope and intent of IP, we looked closely at how it has evolved over the years. Starting with IPv4, we learned about the addressing scheme, how it came to be, and how it is used by network software to uniquely identify hosts on a network. We learned about the common mechanisms for distinguishing between a network address and a host address within the IPv4 addressing architecture. We also looked at how subnet masking can help with the distinction between those two fields in a single address. Once we covered the addressing architecture of IPv4, we looked at its limitations with regard to the total number of addressable hosts that IPv4 supports.

After exploring the full scope of IPv4, we looked at its current proposed replacement in IPv6, and saw how the updated addressing structure in the new standard can support an immense number of hosts in a single universal network. Then, briefly, we examined some of the interfaces that allow for IPv4 and IPv6 to coexist. Finally, we looked at the classes that C# provides for parsing and constructing IPv4 and IPv6 addresses in our software for the reliable routing of our network packets.

Now that we've seen how information is routed and delivered at the lowest level, it's time to consider perhaps the most important aspect of network interactions. So, in the next chapter, we'll be looking at how security is provided across networks.

Questions

1. What are the two primary functions of IP?
2. What is classful addressing? What are the classes of IPv4 addresses?
3. What is variable length subnet masking?
4. What is address exhaustion?
5. What is the upper limit of the IPv4 address space?

6. What is the structure of an IPv4 address? What about an IPv6 address?
7. What is Teredo tunneling?
8. What features does IPv6 enable?

Further reading

For your own reference, I strongly recommend reading the original RFC for IPv4. You'd be surprised how readable it is and how much information you can glean from just the underlying spec. It's also available for free, online, here: `https://tools.ietf.org/html/rfc791`.

I'd also recommend, simply for its brevity, that you read the original IEN 2 to understand exactly what motivated the development of IP in the first place. It's also free to read online, and surprisingly engaging: `https://www.rfc-editor.org/ien/ien2.txt`.

Additionally, if you'd like to understand other ways to program for IP, I once again recommend *Understanding TCP/IP*, by *Alena Kabelová* and *Libor Dostálek*, available from Packt Publishing here: `https://www.packtpub.com/networking-and-servers/understanding-tcpip`.

13
Transport Layer Security

Now that we've seen how network interactions are executed down to the lowest level, we need to understand how those interactions can be secured for users. One of the most fundamental aspects of the public Internet is the ability to secure certain interactions between two hosts. In this chapter, we'll explore how that's done. We'll start by looking at the underlying security mechanisms that supported the original **Secure Sockets Layer** (**SSL**), which was the standard for secured network interactions for decades. Then, we'll take a close look at its successor, **Transport Layer Security** (**TLS**), and consider some of the reasons for the transition. Finally, we'll see how both of these mechanisms are intended to provide secure interactions between network hosts by implementing our own simulation of the protocol. In doing so, we'll also see how we can leverage TLS and network security, right out of the box, with .NET Core.

The following topics will be covered in this chapter:

- The level of data integrity and session privacy users should expect when an application leverages TLS
- Why SSL is being deprecated, and what TLS does to support secure connections
- Understanding how to leverage the out-of-the-box capabilities of .NET Core to support TLS

Technical requirements

In this chapter, we'll be writing sample software that configures and leverages both SSL and TLS from a Web API application. You'll need your .NET Core IDE or code editor of choice, and you can access the sample code here: `https://github.com/PacktPublishing/Hands-On-Network-Programming-with-CSharp-and-.NET-Core/tree/master/Chapter 13`.

Check out the following video to see the code in action: `http://bit.ly/2HY63Ty`

Private connections and SSL

The moment the Internet began supporting something as simple as real-time chat, or even email, the need for a secure connection between two network hosts became apparent. Imagine sending a confidential message to a friend of yours without being able to make any reasonable assumption that your message would remain private. Certainly, you would restrict your online interactions to only the most mundane of tasks and messages. And that's only considering our intuitive desire for privacy in personal matters. That says nothing for the need to protect private, personally identifying information that could be used by a malicious actor to commit fraud.

Without some measure of security in our online interactions, no one would dream of doing anything as critical as banking, accessing medical information, or paying our taxes. Indeed, tasks that seem so basic and fundamental to a modern user of the Internet would be unthinkable without some measure of protection from malicious third parties. It's precisely these scenarios that secure connections are designed to facilitate. But have you ever wondered how they work? Have you ever considered what that lock icon in your Chrome address bar means?

That's what we'll be exploring in this section. We'll see what first prompted the need for a secure interaction mechanism between network hosts. Then, we'll look at how that secure interaction is secured. We'll find out how your browser knows how to warn you of potentially insecure connections, and how we can provide that level of security for our own users. Finally, we'll learn what SSL is and how to leverage it in our own software to provide peace of mind for our own consumers.

Establishing secure connections

If you've ever followed a link to a website and had your browser first warn you that you were about to enter an insecure connection, you may have wondered why and how that warning was generated. The answer is that your browser detected an attempt to establish a connection using the SSL standard. SSL is a universally agreed standard for establishing an encrypted link between a remote server and its client.

You might remember from `Chapter 9`, *HTTP in .NET*, that the `https://` schema designation is the schema for Hypertext Transfer Protocol Secure. That schema designation is a signal to your browser that the content sent back and forth between your machine, and the remote host should be encrypted first. When you navigate to a URL with a schema, your browser will first try to negotiate a secure connection with the server. Its ability to do so, or inability to do so in some cases, is what determines whether or not you are presented with a warning prompt prior to rendering the content that's received from the server.

When a user, or circumstance, dictates that a secure connection should be used (for instance, by specifying HTTPS as the schema in a URI) it's the responsibility of the software establishing that connection to ensure that it's secured. This means that if you were to write a web browser from scratch (in a lower-level language, like C++), your software would be responsible for authenticating the server on the receiving end for any https requests your users want to make. So, how is this connection established? The primary mechanisms for a well-established secure connection are cryptographic translation and third-party authority. Let's take a look at third-party authority first, as it's a bit more straightforward than the cryptography machinations at work with SSL.

Trusted certificate authorities

When a server claims to support a secure connection (historically, via SSL, and today, via TLS), the client must have some way of ensuring that the server is who it claims to be. Without this identity verification step, it would be very simple for malicious actors to invalidate the premise of a secure connection. You would simply need to set up a working dummy version of a targeted website as a trap. Then, by providing fraudulent links to their malicious site, disguised as a link to the legitimate site, they could trick vulnerable users into providing access credentials, user information, and more to a malicious dummy interface. The whole purpose of HTTPS is to provide users with an assurance that their information is being delivered to the entity they intend to deliver it to, in such a way that no one can see what they're sending while it's en route.

Establishing that a server on the other end of a secure connection is, in fact, the entity it is claiming to be is done with authentication certificates, issued by a **trusted certificate authority** (**CA**). A CA is an organization or entity that will generate, sign, and issue an authentication certificate to any server that wants to support interactions over HTTPS or TLS. Specifically, the certificates issued by a trusted authority are a cryptographically secure X.509 public key certificate.

This public-key encryption is something we'll see more of shortly, but it's basically a one-way security mechanism that allows the owner of a private key to validate a freely distributed public key. The public key is generated with a combination of the identity of the recipient and the private key, which must remain secret for the certificate to remain valid. Then, whenever a client wants to validate the identity of the **server**, they take the certificate, along with the identity of the server that presented it, directly back to the trusted authority. Using their private key, the trusted authority checks the identity and the certificate's public key to ensure that it hasn't been tampered with, or fraudulently generated.

The whole process can be broken down into two key steps. First, the server requests and is issued an X.509 certificate from a **trusted certificate authority**:

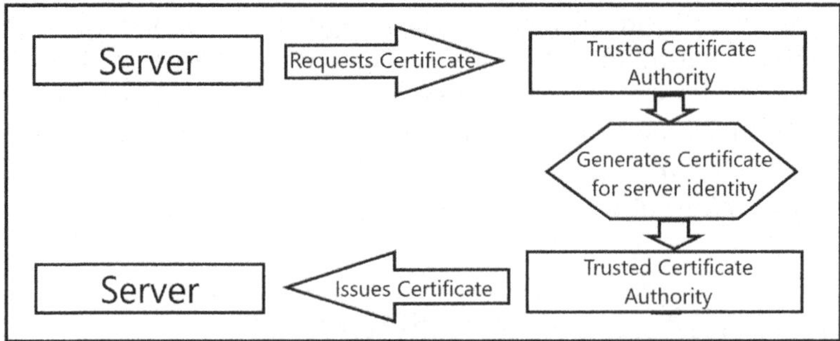

Then, whenever a client wants to establish a secure connection with the server, it must first establish the identity of the server by checking its X.509 certificate with the issuing CA:

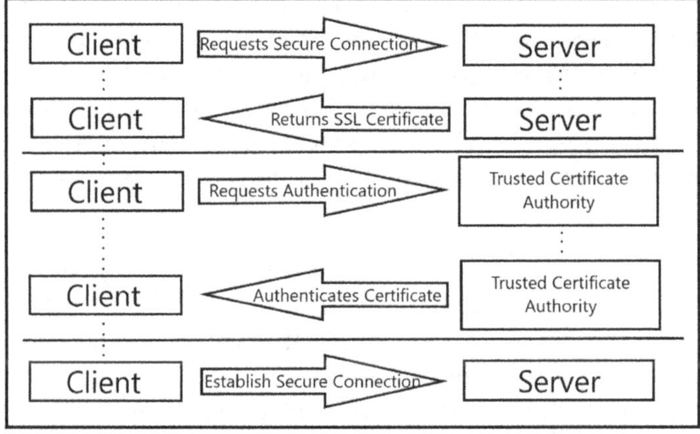

And through this series of round-trips, the server's identity can be assured, and the client can, to at least some degree, trust that the secured connection is with the intended entity.

The basis of trust in certificate authorities

As you've probably already guessed, though, this system of certificate authorities has a certain measure of trust baked in at various levels. First, the user must trust that their web browser has actually requested a certificate from the remote server, and requested authentication from the signing authority. Next, the user and the browser must trust that the CA is only authenticating valid certificates for valid certificate holders.

This may seem obvious, but it's entirely possible that a CA is not as trustworthy as you would hope. In 2013, we learned that there were serious violations of basic Internet security protocols by government intelligence agencies, including working with trusted certificate authorities to generate signed and authenticated certificates for invalid holders for the purposes of surveillance and counterintelligence operations. Regardless of your personal opinions about the ethical implications of such actions, it cannot be argued that by doing so, the agencies responsible severely undermined the trust of engineers and the broader public in the validity of a trusted third-party security measure.

So long as the CA can be (reasonably) trusted, though, the certificates that are issued and signed by that authority can also, generally, be considered trustworthy. And with those certificates and the validation of the trusted authority, the identity of the server can be established. Once that step is complete, it's time to secure the packets in transit.

Simple and mutual authentication

So far, we've only been concerned with validating the identity of the server when establishing a secure connection. This is what's called a **simple authentication** mechanism. The client is given a certificate from the server, and validates it with a certificate authority. Provided the certificate is valid, the client is permitted to proceed with a secure connection. There's no effort made by the server to authenticate the client.

However, this pattern could just as easily be applied to the client as well. This extension of certificate validation procedures is what's called **mutual authentication.** In a mutual authentication scheme, both parties are authenticated with their own certificates. This can allow the server to authenticate a user without having to request access credentials or authentication information directly from the client every time a connection is made.

With mutual authentication, the server is still required to deliver an X.509 certificate that's issued by a trusted authority to any client that wants to establish a secure connection. The client is also still responsible for validating that certificate with the authority. What's different is how the client's certificate is acquired and validated. While a server must allow a third-party authority to sign its certificate, the client need not bother. Instead, in most mutual authentication scenarios, the server itself signs and issues an X.509 certificate for the client.

The server will need its own private cryptographic key to generate the public key that was issued to the client, but as long as it has that key, it can validate any certificates it has issued. In this way, the server can reliably restrict access to only those clients it has issued a certificate too. The identity verification step is a matter of process, and the owner of the server is responsible for determining what constitutes sufficient identity verification prior to issuing a certificate. However, once that process is established, it should have every reason to trust certificates presented by a client, which it can validate.

Now, it might not be immediately apparent why a server would require a trusted authority to sign its identity certificate, while a client does not. This is because of the specific nature of client-server interactions on the internet. In almost all cases, a client is responsible for initiating a connection with the server. The server, by design, has no prior knowledge of when or from where a given request will be received from a given client.

For each request, the server must assert its own identity in such a way that the client can rely on the assertion. It must be able to do this for any client, regardless of whether a prior relationship has been established. There must be some way of validating the server's identity for any given client and any given request. So, the job of initially validating, and then subsequently verifying, the identity of the server is centralized to an entity all potential clients can trust, and use as a single shared resource: the trusted authority.

With a client certificate, however, the server can reasonably trust its own public key validation, and apply its private key to validate the certificate with the client's asserted identity. The encryption mechanism for generating an X.509 certificate is the same, regardless of whether it's being executed by a server or a trusted authority validating the certificate. The only difference is where trust is being placed and why.

A client uses third-party authority because, otherwise, how could a client trust a certificate signed by a server if the client doesn't know the server's assertions can be trusted in the first place? The server doesn't need to use a third-party authority, because there is no trust being placed in the client. The server is performing its own validation with its own private key. An invalid client certificate simply wouldn't pass validation. Thus, a server-issued certificate is sufficient to identify the client. So, once a client has installed the certificate on their host machine, they can use it to access the server, fully authenticated, and establish and leverage secure connections without any additional steps.

Encrypting transmitted data

Once the identity of the server has been established in such a way that the client can trust any interaction between the two hosts, the next step is to ensure no one else can observe those interactions. To do this, packets must be encrypted in transit. However, to leverage an encryption mechanism that both the client and the server can use, the specifics must be established beforehand.

Asymmetric and symmetric cryptography

When determining the identity of a server with a signed X.509 certificate, clients are using what's called **asymmetric cryptography**. All that means is that there is an imbalance between the parties with respect to the distribution of secret information that's necessary for the cryptography. Two parties are using the same cryptographic scheme, but only one party has access to the secret key. This system is necessary for something like a security certificate because some of that information must be made publicly available to anyone who asks for it. Remember, by the time the certificate is changing hands from a server to a client, a secure connection hasn't been established yet. Any malicious parties that want to read that information from the packets in transit can do so freely. Asymmetric cryptography schemes account for that inevitability and are designed to remain secure, even when the public keys are freely distributed.

Once a secure connection is finally established, however, hosts will leverage what's known as **symmetric cryptography**. This is where the secret information that's necessary to encrypt and decrypt a message is shared equally (or symmetrically) between all parties involved. Both parties in the exchange will have to agree upon a secure encryption algorithm for which both hosts have an implementation available to leverage. Next, they'll need to agree upon the cryptographic keys they will each use with that algorithm to decrypt messages that are encrypted by the other party. It's this symmetrical cryptography method that is used by two hosts to communicate over a secure transport protocol.

Negotiating cryptographic keys

Now, you might have noticed a bit of a chicken and egg problem with using symmetrical cryptography to avoid eavesdropping on packets that are transmitted between hosts. Specifically, how can you send shared private cryptographic keys that will be used to establish a secure connection without first establishing a secure connection? For that, we have to leverage the same asymmetric cryptography we looked at when we were considering how to validate client certificates in a mutual authentication setup.

The first step in establishing a secure connection after validating the identity of the server through a CA is to establish the algorithm both parties will use for the encryption of packets. There are a number of what are considered secure cryptographic algorithms (though there is a number which, for reasons outside the scope of this book, were previously considered secure but are not anymore), and each of them can be found in the `System.Security.Cryptography` namespace of C#. The reason for establishing the algorithm is that it's entirely possible that the two hosts don't have implementations of the same set of algorithms, so it's important that they identify a mutually implemented algorithm before they proceed.

Once the algorithm is selected, the hosts must exchange a set of unique private keys that they'll use for the lifetime of the session to encrypt and decrypt packets. To make this exchange, the server first sends a public key for which only it has the private key. Then, the client uses this public key to encrypt a random number, and returns the value to the server. At this point, it's perfectly acceptable if the packet is intercepted. The relevant information (the random number generated by the client) is encrypted, and the public key used for that encryption is useless without the private key, which hasn't been transmitted and thus cannot have been intercepted.

When the server receives the random number generated by the client, it can decrypt it using its private key, and then use the number as the initialization value for a cryptographic key that will be appropriate for the agreed upon an algorithm that will be used throughout the session. The client will have done the same, and with that both parties will have established a shared secret without ever having to transmit the details of that secret in an insecure way.

The SSL protocol

For years, the standard for implementing secure network connections was what's known as the **SSL**. Piggybacking on earlier efforts to develop a secure transport mechanism for network interactions, SSL was developed by a company called NetScape as a way of establishing a global standard for secure networking. The history of SSL as a standard actually serves as an illuminating warning about the nature of network security.

Security on a network will always be a cat-and-mouse game between hackers and security researchers. Every effort that's made to establish a secure algorithm for reliable encryption of data will almost always fall prey to an unforeseen exploit that renders the algorithm useless as a security measure. This has been true of everything, from network security protocols to digital rights management applications, to basic OS-level libraries and utilities.

While it's well outside the scope of this book, there's a very interesting bit of research being done in the computer science community that could have a major impact on the state of security software. It's around a theorem in algorithm analysis that, if it is eventually *dis*proved, could simultaneously invalidate every known security algorithm in use. If you're curious about it, I recommend researching the P=NP Problem. Be prepared for high-level math if you start reading it, but also be advised that there is still, at the time of this publishing, a million dollar reward for the first person to prove or disprove the theorem.

This constant leapfrogging of secure algorithms and exploits of those algorithms is especially true of early versions of SSL. In fact, SSL 1.0 was never even released to the public due to glaring security flaws discovered in the protocol during testing phases. Instead, SSL 2.0 was released to the public in early 1995. It was barely a year later, however, that the next version, a complete overhaul of the protocol, was released as SSL 3.0 in 1996. This was due to another series of major flaws that were quickly discovered by the hacker community that rendered SSL 2.0 insufficiently secure for many confidential transactions. Compared to its previous iterations, SSL 3.0 enjoyed a relatively long shelf life before a successor was finally designed for it again in 1999.

The somewhat jarring leaps from one version to the next in the SSL lifespan were precipitated by flaws in the hashing and encryption algorithms underlying each standard. With SSL 2.0, a combination of vulnerable processes in handling secure keys, along with flaws in the algorithms that were used to generate those keys, added up to a glaringly insecure protocol. It provided no protection for the initial handshake, leaving the interaction open to exactly the kind of man-in-the-middle attacks we described in the previous section. It used hash algorithms that had known collisions (when two different inputs can generate the same hashed output), rendering its keys functionally insecure. Finally, quirks in its implementation of the CA verification process rendered most consumer-facing websites unable to support the protocol in the first place. All of this combined illustrates why such a major redesign of the protocol was necessary so quickly for version 3.0.

The story of SSL 3.0 is a fair bit more successful than its predecessor. While some parts of its cryptographic key generation algorithm relied entirely on insecure hash functions, it also incorporated the new (at the time, at least) SHA-1 standard. This new algorithm had no known hash collisions and thus strengthened the secure claim of the new protocol. It also introduced the pattern for CA support that is still seen today, enabling wider adoption and support of the protocol by public-facing websites.

The 3.0 iteration was not without its flaws, though. Because it still relied, at least in part, on a hash algorithm with known collisions, it was not considered sufficiently secured for highly critical or classified applications by the US government's **Federal Information Processing Standard** (**FIPS**). Furthermore, while there were far fewer procedural vulnerabilities in the design of the protocol (as opposed to cryptographic vulnerabilities), it was found to be vulnerable to a rather sophisticated procedural attack in October 2014. This vulnerability cemented the need for the official deprecation of the standard in 2015. This opened the door for its successor, TLS.

TLS as the new standard

Currently, the global standard for secure network interactions, TLS, was originally developed as an improvement over the then standard SSL protocol back in 1999. While it was designed to be an upgrade to the existing SSL 3.0 protocol, there were sufficient differences in the design of each protocol to make interoperability between the two schemes infeasible. Instead, the authors released it as the first version of a newer, more secure protocol.

A minor evolution from SSL

When it was introduced, TLS certainly represented an improvement over SSL 3.0. However, the major distinctions were in the header design for the packets exchanged during the handshake phase of connection establishment. The underlying algorithms and principles remained mostly unchanged. In fact, were it not for the header incompatibility, TLS might just as well have been named SSL 4.0 at the time of its release.

Remember from `Chapter 12`, *The Internet Protocol*, that it was this same header-incompatibility issue that made IPv4 and IPv6 interoperability impossible. The ability to parse a standardized header is the most fundamental first step of any shared interaction between hosts. A mismatch or incompatibility between the headers of two versions of a protocol will make that first step impossible, rendering the packets unreadable. This will often have the impact of preventing mutual compatibility between versions of a protocol with different header definitions.

There were certainly security improvements with TLS, however. The first of which was that in TLS, no single part of its cryptographic algorithms relied entirely on a hashing algorithm with known collisions. Any key that was generated was always done so with at least some inputs from a cryptographically secure hash algorithm.

It also introduced added protection against lost or modified data during the handshake phase of a connection attempt. It did this by sending a secure hash of every message that was transmitted from both parties during the final step of connection negotiation. This way, the client and the server can both check the result against their own hashes and validate that each host perceived the same interactions, eliminating the possibility of a man-in-the-middle attack modifying any part of their exchange. However, this still didn't guarantee that a man-in-the-middle attack wasn't successful in attempting to read packets—only that none were successfully modified.

Forward secrecy

One of the most important features that was introduced by TLS was the notion of forward secrecy. This is a concept in secured communication where, by using a unique session key over the course of each interaction, two hosts can guarantee that even if a secret is exposed through some attack, previous interactions will remain secure, even if they were recorded and stored by the attacker. This is because the unique session key is used as an additional input to the encryption mechanism for securing messages. Thus, private keys alone are insufficient to decrypt messages previously sent.

For perfect secrecy to work, the session key must be randomly generated via a non-deterministic function. For those not aware, in the context of computer science, a function is considered non-deterministic if and only if it could return two distinct results given the exact same inputs. Typically, this non-determinism is achieved by use of a random number generator, and some other temporary external state. So, if I had, for example, the `GetNextPrime(startingIndex)` method, then we would expect it to be deterministic. For any number, *n*, there is only one next prime after it. Every attempt to call the method with `GetNextPrime(n)` would result in the same output. Meanwhile, if I had a method called `RollDie(sides)` then I would reasonably expect that to be non-deterministic. I could pass in the same `sides`, parameter five times and get five completely distinct results. That's a non-deterministic algorithm in a nutshell.

This concept of non-determinism is important when generating a session key because it ensures that subsequent attempts to generate the same session key would fail. Thus, when an attacker gains access to the private keys of a server, they would still be missing a critical component that's necessary to decode messages from previous sessions. That missing piece of the puzzle would be much easier to find if session keys were persisted beyond the lifetime of the session, though. For that reason, it's critical to ensure for forward secrecy that a session key is destroyed as soon as a session is terminated.

Reliability of secured messages

The integrity of the data in a packet is critical to its successful delivery and decryption by the recipient host. If even one bit is out of place, the value of the decrypted message would become wholly unreadable. This property of secure encryption that even minor changes in a message will result in drastic changes to its encrypted counterpart, and vice versa, which means it is far more difficult to recover from errors occurring in transit than with unsecured messages. For that reason, TLS leverages what are called **message authentication codes (MACs)**.

These MACs are used to validate both that the data that's been transmitted has not been modified in any way, and that it was sent by the host that the recipient is expecting. In TLS, these codes are generated using sequential packet ID numbers as an added security measure. This sequential tag provides an additional level of verification on a message, thus increasing the complexity of the work a malicious actor would have to perform to successfully modify both a payload and its corresponding MAC for successful fraudulent packet delivery.

This additional security measure, along with the session ID that's used for forward secrecy, and the multilayered secure hash algorithms that's used to generate shared keys for encryption and decryption provide a robust foundation for TLS, and have allowed its reliable use across a small number of versions for nearly two decades.

Configuring TLS in .NET Core

While we've explored the nature of the interactions between hosts that want to establish secure communications in depth, we've kept the discussion to a fairly high level so far. There's a reason for this, though. In .NET Core, you'll never be coding the specific steps of the TLS protocol directly. As a high-level language executed on a portable runtime, .NET Core is not the ideal environment for attempting to implement those operations on your own. And, as you have probably already figured out, the ASP.NET Core libraries that are used to facilitate low-level socket interactions between hosts already implement TLS for us. We just have to know how to configure it and enforce its use. So, while the step-by-step interactions of TLS are important for any network engineer to understand, the low-level details are well beyond the scope of this book.

For the purposes of this demonstration, though, we'll write a simple Web API project that simulates the interactions of a TLS handshake. Hopefully, this will cement some of the more abstract ideas in your mind by giving them a concrete in-code representation. We'll also configure our application to leverage HTTPS so that you can see the steps you'll be taking in your own projects to provide this feature.

Enabling HTTPS in .NET Core

The first thing we'll do is set up our project as a new Web API project using the .NET CLI command:

```
dotnet new webapi -n DemoTLS
```

Now, we want to allow clients to interact with our services using TLS. Thankfully, to enable this, we don't actually have to do anything! Astute readers will remember that in my previous demo application in `Chapter 9`, *HTTP in .NET*, in the *Using launchSettings.json* section, I had you remove the following line of code from the `Startup.cs` file of our application:

```
app.UseHttpsRedirection();
```

Well, it turns out that by not removing that, our application's web server will respond to any standard HTTP requests with a `307 - Temporary Redirect` status code, directing the client to the appropriate port for HTTPS interactions. We took that out of our previous demo to simplify our discussion of the specifics of HTTP in `Chapter 9`, *HTTP in .NET*, but now let's leave it in and see it in action.

Simply run your application, and when your default browser opens up, you should notice that it's routed to the `https://localhost:5001/api/values` launch URL that is configured for every new Web API project. There's nothing particularly interesting about that, but now open up your browser developer tools, and navigate to the tab that displays the request traffic. I'm using Chrome, myself, and can access the developer tools by navigating through the settings or simply hitting *F12*. Once in the **Network** tab, there's an option to preserve the network logs for a browser session, as shown in the following screenshot:

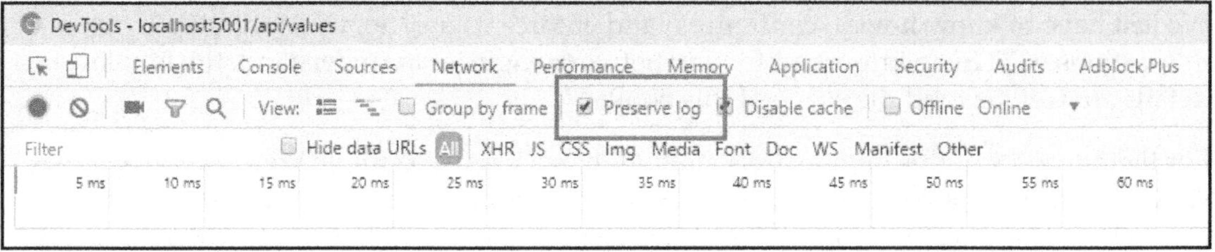

After choosing that setting, attempt to navigate directly to the unsecured URL for your API at `http://localhost:5000/api/values` and then look at the response you get in your **Network** tab. You should see your browser automatically reload the page to the secure URL again, and the following response in your **Network** tab:

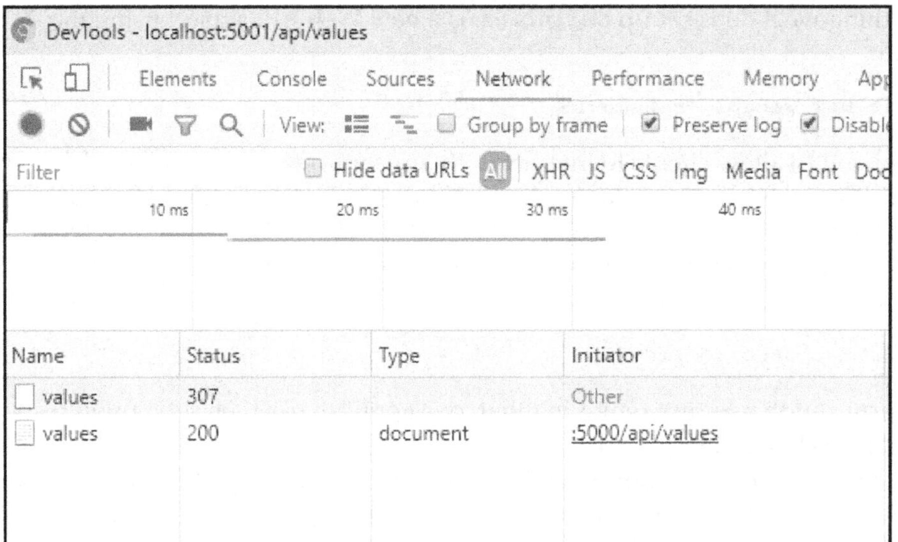

This is the behavior that your web server provides when you enable HTTPS with the `UseHttpsRedirection` middleware configuration. The initial request for the unsecured URL was not satisfied, and instead the browser was given a directive to use the secured URL. That's what the second line in our log is. It's telling us that the navigation to the secured URL (the one that returned a **200** response) was initiated by the server when we tried to navigate to the unsecured URL (the **Initiator** field of our log). That's a lot of power and reliability to get from a web server without any work on our part!

Enforcing HTTPS with HSTS

Now, if we want to notify our clients that they should be using HTTPS at all times, instead of simply trusting them to follow our redirect messages, we can do so by leveraging **HTTP Strict Transport Security** (**HSTS**). This is an interaction mechanism whereby a web server can notify any client interacting with it over an HTTPS connection that all subsequent interactions should happen over HTTPS. It delivers this notification by way of an HSTS header with a `Strict-Transport-Security` key and some arbitrary value, such as an expiration timestamp, after which the client can resume attempts to connect using unsecured URLs.

If the client complies with HSTS, it will respond to the header by updating any cached links that hold references to the unsecured URL to now hold references to the secured URL. It will also prevent any user interaction with the unsecured URL, even when a connection to the secure URL cannot be made.

Now, you might be curious how we can enable this feature in our web server, and begin returning that header in our responses. Well, hopefully you won't be surprised that it's just as simple as enabling HTTPS redirection in the first place. If you look inside the conditional `if/else` statement that checks if your application is currently running in a development environment, you'll see the following:

```
if (env.IsDevelopment()) {
  app.UseDeveloperExceptionPage();
} else {
  // The default HSTS value is 30 days. You may want to change this for
production scenarios, see https://aka.ms/aspnetcore-hsts.
  app.UseHsts();
}
```

As you can see, we're already leveraging HSTS. We just can't see as much because we're running our application locally using development settings. This is very much by design. It's strongly recommended that you don't use HSTS in development because the header value and its corresponding expiration are considered highly cacheable by browsers. This could make debugging and troubleshooting especially difficult during development. On your local environment, the setting isn't even available out of the box because the local loopback address is excluded by the middleware by default.

HTTPS port configuration

It's important to note that the only reason our application successfully redirects to our HTTPS URL is because we are listening on a distinct port for incoming HTTPS requests by default. The `launchSettings.json` file for a new Web API project is always configured to listen on both an HTTP and an HTTPS port. That same port is leveraged by the `UseHttpsRedirection` middleware when it's invoked on our application. Without configuring an HTTPS port for our application to listen on, the redirection middleware will simply fail to resolve, and requests that are made of the unsecured HTTP URLs will be processed and responded to accordingly.

There are a number of ways to configure the port that your middleware should redirect users to, but in each case you still have to make sure you're also configuring your web server to listen over that port. This includes registering `HttpsRedirectionOptions` in your application's service resolver, with the following code segment inside your `ConfigureServices(IServiceCollection services)` method, as shown here:

```
services.AddHttpsRedirection(options => {
    options.RedirectStatusCode = StatusCodes.Status307TemporaryRedirect;
    options.HttpsPort = 443;
});
```

Alternatively, you can set a secure scheme in the `UseUrls()` method of the `IWebHostBuilder` object when you're configuring your web server in your `Program.cs` file. This has the added bonus of simultaneously configuring your web server to listen on a secure port, while also configuring the `UseHttpsRedirection()` middleware to redirect users to it.

As you can hopefully see by now, though, the default support for HTTPS and secure interactions provided by .NET Core will make your life substantially easier. This is especially the case when you have to implement any sort of confidential interactions, as we'll be doing in the next chapter when we discuss authentication and authorization in web applications.

Trusting your development certificate

As we discussed at length in the section of this chapter about CA, any attempt to interact with a resource via HTTPS through a typical browser will result in a warning if the browser cannot verify the identity of the server with a trusted certificate authority. Since our applications will typically be hosted and run locally while we're developing and debugging them, we won't have access to a certificate signed by a trusted CA. Instead, we'll be using what's called a self-signed certificate. This is exactly the kind of certificate I warned you about being untrustworthy, since you can't trust the signature of a server until you can trust that you know who the server is. However, in this case, where we're developing an application locally and testing responses through our browser or REST client, we know *exactly* who the server is. It's us!

Since this scenario is common, Microsoft and Windows provide a simple one-time mechanism for getting past the untrusted certificate issue when testing HTTPS locally. Every time you install the .NET Core SDK, it includes an HTTPS development certificate that is issued by your web server whenever it is being hosted by the `dotnet` runtime application. To configure your local web browsers and other clients to trust this self-signed certificate, you only need to register it with your OS using the following CLI command:

```
dotnet dev-certs https --trust
```

Running this command will add the self-signed certificate that was included in your .NET SDK into the trusted root certificates store of your operating system. This store is then used by any application that needs to validate that an external host is who they claim to be. By storing our development certificate in this store with that CLI command, we can eliminate the warnings and alerts from our browsers any time we want to test an application that is configured to use HTTPS. And just like that, you're all set to leverage TLS within your .NET Core application.

The TLS handshake simulation

To keep things simple and to clarify the contents of this chapter, the actual implementation of the demo API we wrote will highlight each step in the TLS handshake. I've renamed my one controller to `TlsController`, and have implemented each step as its own controller action. The purpose of this is to reflect the conceptual steps taken by your web server whenever a user connects with your application over TLS.

Identity verification

As you may recall, the first step of the TLS protocol is to establish the identity of the server. In that step, the client simply initiates a secure connection by sending a request to a secure endpoint (an endpoint leveraging HTTPS) and the server responds with an X.509 certificate. To that end, we've created a simple `GET` method named `initiate-connection`, which returns a certificate, which here is just a string:

```
[HttpGet("initiate-connection")]
public ActionResult<string> GetCertificate() {
    return "SSL_CERTIFICATE";
}
```

As you may recall, the responsibility for interacting with a trusted CA falls on the client. So, at this point, we merely wait for them to confirm that we are who we say we are. Once they notify us that the certificate has been verified, we can send over our public encryption key, which they can use to encrypt their subsequent requests in the handshake protocol. For that interaction, we have the following `certificate-verified` method:

```
[HttpGet("certificate-verified")]
public ActionResult<string> GetVerification() {
    return "PUBLIC_KEY_FOR_ENCRYPTING_HANDSHAKE";
}
```

And just like that, we're ready to start negotiating our encryption scheme.

Negotiating the encryption scheme

Now that we've given them a public encryption key, we're waiting on our client to encrypt their next message with it. Both hosts must establish which encryption algorithms they support so that a mutual strong algorithm can be agreed upon. For that, we give our clients an endpoint named hash-algorithms, which will return all of the secure algorithms we support, and allow them to choose one they also support for use:

```
[HttpGet("hash-algorithms-requested")]
public ActionResult<IEnumerable<string>> GetAlgorithms() {
    return new string[] {
        "SHA-256",
        "AES",
        "RSA"
    };
}
```

Once they've determined which algorithm is most suitable for their needs and purposes, they'll notify us. So, we have another method configured to handle that response from our client. However, once this one is done, we can use the algorithm they've selected, along with our private keys, to generate a session key that will serve as the shared secret between us for the data-transfer segment of the communication session. So, the last method of our simulation API uses a static `SessionService` class to store the selected algorithm, and then uses it to return a shared key, generated from our private keys and a random session key:

```
[HttpPost("hash-algorithm-selected")]
public ActionResult<string> Post([FromBody] string sharedAlgorithm) {
    SessionService.CurrentAlgorithm = sharedAlgorithm;
    return
SessionService.GenerateSharedKeyWithPrivateKeyAndRandomSessionKey();
}
```

With that method, our session is established, and data transfer can proceed safely. Hopefully, by breaking it down into it's most basic, high-level steps like that, it's a bit more clear what's going on every time you navigate to a website with the `https://` schema. More importantly, now you know how to configure and enforce HTTPS and TLS from within your .NET Core projects going forward.

Summary

We covered a lot in this chapter, while managing to focus on a rather narrow subject. We started by taking a high-level view of the necessary steps to secure communications between two hosts over an open network. Then, we looked at how each of those steps is implemented (conceptually, at least). First, we looked at the process of verifying the identity of the host you want to interact with. We learned about trusted certificate authorities, and learned how they are leveraged by web clients to validate the identity of a server by examining a signed, cryptographic certificate.

In exploring this topic, we also considered how much trust must be placed in these CAs, and how that level of trust opens the wider public up to an incredibly high level of risk if it is ever violated. We also learned why a CA is necessary to validate a server identity, but is not necessary to validate the identity of a client in a mutual authentication scenario.

Next, we looked at how two hosts, whose identities have been sufficiently verified, can proceed to secure their communications over the course of a session. We saw how symmetric and asymmetric encryption is used to make sure that interactions are encrypted well before even a single byte of application data is transmitted.

Next, we looked at how these high-level steps for securing a communication session have been standardized and leveraged by secure protocols over the years. We saw how frequently security vulnerabilities can render a protocol functionally insecure, and how subsequent versions or standards can leverage ever-increasing tool sets to stay ahead of vulnerabilities and evolve over time.

Finally, we looked at how all of this is handled in the .NET Core framework. We saw how to configure our web services to support and rely on TLS, and how to avoid some of the additional overhead of using a CA while we're still in the development phase of a project. All of this has positioned us well to consider how to leverage this to allow for authentication and authorization in an application, which we'll be exploring in the next chapter.

Questions

1. What does HTTPS stand for? How is it distinct from HTTP?
2. What is a trusted certificate authority? What is their role in verifying the identity of a server?
3. What is the difference between simple and mutual authentication?
4. What is the difference between symmetric and asymmetric cryptography?
5. What is forward secrecy? How is it provided?
6. What is a non-deterministic function? Why is it important for securing a communication session?
7. What are message authentication codes? How are they used to provide reliability in TLS?

Further reading

For more information about establishing secure software practices and the principles underlying SSL, TLS, and all things concerning network security, I recommend *Cybersecurity – Attack and Defense Strategies, Yuri Diogenes, Dr. Erdal Ozkaya, Packt Publishing*. It's an illuminating guide to the daily considerations of the engineers who design secure protocols like TLS. It's available through Packt Publishing, here: `https://www.packtpub.com/networking-and-servers/cybersecurity-attack-and-defense-strategies`.

To understand just how much risk you assume whenever you expose your software to an open network, I'd also recommend *Network Vulnerability Assessment, Sagar Rahalkar, Packt Publishing*. It approaches the problem more from the perspective of a DevOps engineer or systems engineer than that of a software engineer, but I think it's important to have that kind of big-picture understanding. And this book is a great resource for that. It's also available through Packt, here: `https://www.packtpub.com/networking-and-servers/network-vulnerability-assessment`.

14
Authentication and Authorization on Networks

In the previous chapter, we gave serious consideration to the transport layer solutions for ensuring secure connections. With that knowledge, we'll be spending this chapter exploring the kinds of host-to-host interactions that demand that transport-level security. We'll be taking a step back up the tiers of the network stack, into the application layer, to look at how authentication and authorization is handled in .NET Core. We'll look at the various standards supported by the authorization header of HTTP. Then, we'll look at some widely used and widely supported open source tools for authentication. Finally, we'll look at how to manage access control within a C# application.

The following topics will be covered in this chapter:

- The various authentication schemes supported by valid authorization header values in HTTP requests
- Understanding OAuth tokens and how they can be leveraged for user authentication and authorization
- Strategies and settings for implementing authorization schemes in a .NET Core application

Technical requirements

In this chapter, as in the previous chapters, you'll need your IDE or source code editor of choice, as well as the sample code for this chapter `https://github.com/PacktPublishing/Hands-On-Network-Programming-with-C-and-.NET-Core/tree/master/Chapter 14`.

Check out the following video to see the code in action: `http://bit.ly/2HY64XC`

We'll also be relying heavily on a REST client to initiate requests against our demo API, so make sure you've installed one. My two recommendations stand with either Postman, which can be found at: `https://www.getpostman.com/downloads/`, or the Insomnia REST client, which can be found at: `https://insomnia.rest/`.

The authorization header

If you've ever used your browser tools to inspect an outbound request to a website you've logged on to, you will likely have noticed, in the request header segment of your network inspector, a header titled `Authorization`. This standard header in the HTTP protocol can be used to specify a variety of schemes used to authenticate and authorize a user to access content at the requested URL. If you're not familiar with it, though, you might be surprised at the sheer variety of options at your disposal for providing those basic functions in your software. So, let's look at what those authorization schemes are and how we can use them in our own projects.

Authorization versus authentication

The first thing we'll want to consider as we explore the `Authorization` header is the two functions of web security that it can enable. While it is explicitly titled an `Authorization` header, often times, in practice, it's actually a misnomer. In reality, it can be both an `Authorization` header and an `Authentication` header, and frequently it functions as both.

Now, if you're not quite clear on the distinction between these two operations, this may all sound like I'm just splitting hairs. However, they each provide fundamentally different, and fundamentally necessary, features for a robust system of access control. And when we're talking about the `Authorization` header, we are explicitly talking about controlling access to the resources of our software. So, what exactly are these operations, and how can they facilitate an access controlled architecture?

Authentication

Put simply, authentication is the process of verifying a user's claim about who they are. Your user is making a claim about their identity, and you want to make sure that the identity is authentic. This is typically done by having the user provide some information that only they could be reasonably expected to have. In access-controlled software, that information is typically a set of credentials, such as a username and password combination, but it could be any number of things, such as knowledge of previous addresses or familial ties.

Authentication credentials could be anything that the user in question should reasonably be expected to know, and which no one else could reasonably be expected to know. Once these credentials are provided, the authenticity of the user's claim can be verified. So, authentication is about verifying a user's identity.

Authorization

On the other side of the access-control coin is authorization. This is about determining what a user should be allowed to do within a system, from modifying or adding information stored by a system to even accessing it in the first place. Just as the name suggests, authorization is a precaution of not allowing a user to perform an action until the system knows that the user is authorized to do so.

In almost all access-controlled systems, authorization is dependent on authentication. You can't determine if a user is authorized to perform an action until you can first authenticate that the user is who they claim to be. Authorization has the potential to be a substantially more complex step in the access-control process, though. The authentication step is fairly straightforward, with only two possible results. Either the user is who they claimed to be, in which case authentication succeeds, or they are not, in which case authentication fails. With authorization, though, the permissions that are returned for a given user could be determined by any number of underlying rules, procedures, or conditions. So, while authentication is about verifying a user's identity, authorization is about determining the actions a user is permitted to perform.

So, now that we understand the roles authentication and authorization play in access control, let's look at the HTTP mechanisms that enable those roles.

Authorization header values

When a user attempts to access a site that is access-controlled, they might be prompted to provide an `Authorization` header from the server. For a client to authorize themselves with the server, they must do so using an authorization mechanism the server is prepared to handle. If the server is only set up for basic authentication, but the client tries to pass a bearer token, the server won't be able to parse the `Authorization` header, and will return a **401-Unauthorized** status code, regardless of the validity of the token sent by the client.

The client (who, in this case, doesn't have prior knowledge of the valid authorization schemes supported by the server) must first be told exactly which authorization mechanism it should use to authenticate with the server. This is done with a `WWW-Authenticate` response header, which is applied to the initial response from the server. This header is used to indicate to the client exactly which `Authorization` protocol the server expects. So what exactly are the `Authorization` protocols defined by HTTP, and how do they work?

Basic authentication

This specific schema is our first example of the `Authorization` header being used for an authentication task. In an HTTP interaction, the **basic authentication** (**BA**) schema is used for simple transmission of a username and password from the client to the server for authentication and authorization. It's known as the Basic, because when it is requested by a server, the client simply passes along credentials with no additional session keys or cookies and no additional handshaking between services to set the header appropriately.

With BA, the server indicates the authentication scheme by passing back a `WWW-Authenticate` header with the following structure:

```
WWW-Authenticate: Basic realm="{description of the access-controlled
area}", charset="UTF-8"
```

Here, the `realm` and `charset` parameters are technically optional, but can provide useful guidance for the client with respect to how or why they must pass their credentials. Upon receiving this header, the client is responsible for delivering their credentials via the Authorization header in subsequent requests.

The user information URL segment

We've actually seen the first method before, back in `Chapter 2`, *DNS and Resource Location*, in the *URLs, domain names, and device addresses* section. If a server supports the Basic authentication mechanism, clients can bypass the `Authorization` header altogether and simply transmit their credentials in the URL itself.

As you may remember, the first segment of a URL, after the schema specification, is actually an optional segment used for access credentials. So, let's imagine we have a user that has valid access to a remote resource. For this example, let's say their username is `aesop_rock`, and their password `A3h4s9f0cjeC`. Upon receiving the `WWW-Authenticate` method specifying Basic authentication, the client could simply redirect themselves to the access-controlled URL with the following credentials prefixed:

```
https://aesop_rock:A3hw4s9f0cjeC@test-domain.com/test/url
```

While this format meets the standards for a valid URL, and will allow for basic authentication mechanisms without passing the authentication header, it should be avoided at all costs. Transmitting passwords in plain text as part of your destination URL poses a substantial security risk. For that reason, the use of this `username:password` format is considered deprecated, and often unsupported by modern web browsers. However, the high volume of services that continue to support this URI-based authentication technique makes it worth your effort to understand and consider. As a rule, though, you should never support access with this credential mechanism. Whenever possible, you should scrub URLs of any content in the user information segment that comes after the first colon before transmitting requests over the wire to prevent accidentally persisting plain-text records of user passwords.

Basic authentication with header values

When transmitting the credentials in the request header, however, a client would transmit all subsequent requests with the `Authorization` header, configured as follows:

```
Authorization: Basic <base64-encoded-credentials>
```

Here, the credentials are first formatted with a username and password separated by a single colon, just as in the URL format, then the `base64` character encoded.

For credentials that are passed using this Basic authentication format, the first colon is always parsed as the delimiter between the username and password fields. Because of this, the username in a Basic authenticated system can never contain a colon.

So, if we have our user from the previous example, with the username of `aesop_rock` and a password of `A3h4s9f0cjeC`, then we would first format the credentials as follows:

```
j_public:A3r9f0cjeC
```

And then we would `base-64` encode the characters. Applying this to our `Authorization` header, we would have a header value that's as follows:

```
Authorization: Basic al9wdWJsaWM6QTNyOWYwY2plQw==
```

Now, we have a Basic authentication `Authorization` header that, when transmitted to the server, the server will be able to validate by decoding the value of the `base-64` encoded access credentials.

Encryption versus encoding

It's important to note that when we modify our credentials, we are merely encoding them, and not actually encrypting them. The difference here is that a user can go from the `base-64` encoding to plain text and then back to the `base-64` encoding, all without access to any sort of cryptographic key to transition from one format to another. Encoding is simply a matter of character representation. It's almost like translating a basic noun from English to Spanish, and then back from Spanish to English. The meaning isn't obscured; it's just how the words are represented. Meanwhile, encryption is about deriving a new, secret value for an input string based on an additional, secret input, to obscure the meaning of the original message entirely.

At this point, I'll just go ahead and point out the obvious—any interaction that involves an `Authorization` header must take place over a secured connection using HTTPS. Though it might not always be feasible, the simplest best practice for enforcing this more secure behavior is to simply not configure your application to listen for HTTP requests. We'll see in just a bit what other options we have for preventing privileged information from being transmitted, unencrypted, and unsecured over a network. For now, though, if you can avoid supporting HTTP altogether, I'd strongly recommend doing so.

Bearer token authorization

While Basic authentication simply provided a raw username and password credentials, the bearer authentication deals in what is known as **bearer tokens**. A bearer token is simply a security token that notifies the server that the user presenting the token (the bearer) has the credentials and permissions granted by the token.

Since, from the server's perspective, this token is used to authenticate a specific user, a bearer token can be thought of as simply a different kind of access credential. For this to be the case, though, the server must operate on the assumption that the bearer of a given security token wouldn't have it unless they were authorized to have it. For that reason, protecting the value of a given bearer token from eavesdropping or unauthorized access is just as important as protecting the value of a user password. Extra care should be taken to ensure that a token is never persisted on your server in an unsecured format.

Within the context of the `Authorization` header, the bearer authentication scheme is used specifically to support what are known as **OAuth tokens**. **Open Authentication** (**OAuth**) is a standard that was designed explicitly to support token-based authentication mechanisms for access-control of web-based resources. It's incredibly common across the internet.

OAuth basics

If you've ever logged on to a website with your Google account, Facebook, or Twitter, you've used OAuth before. It's an access control mechanism that's designed to allow a delegate service to authenticate and authorize a user for the access-controlled resource. So, when you enter a new website for the first time, and it allows you to access it with your Google account, that new website is delegating the responsibility of authenticating you to Google. Google requests your credentials and authenticates you, and you are implicitly notifying Google to provide the new website with a token which the new website will consider sufficient for *authorization*.

It's not entirely dissimilar to the **trusted certificate authority** (**CA**) system we learned about in `Chapter 13`, *Transport Layer Security*. In this context, Google would be analogous to a CA, and the users, or bearers of the token, are essentially the holders of the security certificate. So systems which support OAuth access are trusting the OAuth providers (Google, Facebook, and so on) as reliable sources for authentication.

Authorizing with bearer tokens

When a bearer token is supported, the syntax for delivering the token in your `Authorization` header is almost identical to that of Basic authentication. The format for doing so is as follows:

```
Authorization: Bearer <token>
```

The main difference here is that while the Basic authentication credentials were merely `base64` encoded, the token in a bearer authentication scheme can be cryptographically secured, providing some measure of protection if a client attempts to deliver the token over an unsecured transport mechanism. Moreover, Basic authentication credentials will only ever contain the user's access credentials, whereas bearer tokens can be far more robust in the information or context they contain.

While merely passing access credentials in a Basic authentication scheme is sufficient for authenticating a user, it leaves the task of determining any permissions that user might have up to the server. With a bearer token, though, the token might contain information for both, authentication of a user's identity as well as an assertion of the permissions granted to the user. In this way, the bearer authentication mechanism can be substantially more versatile, when implemented properly.

Digest authentication

With the Digest authentication scheme, the designers explicitly sought to provide a more secure authentication implementation than is provided by the unencrypted Basic authentication scheme. In actuality, though, it only ends up providing a set of security trade-offs, and is reliant on an outdated hashing algorithm for its encryption. It still has a number of advantages, though, and is worth considering for implementation in certain circumstances. To understand the advantages and disadvantages it introduces, and when you might want to use it, let's look at how it works.

The Digest authentication WWW-Authenticate header

When a user attempts to access a system that leverages Digest authentication, they are still prompted to use an `Authorization` header with the `WWW-Authenticate` response header. However, unlike the simple scheme specification returned with Basic and Bearer authentication schemes, the `WWW-Authenticate` header in a Digest authentication scheme contains a series of values the client will use to generate its authentication request.

These header values include the `realm` parameter that we saw as an optional parameter in Basic authentication schemes, and serves the same purpose, describing the authenticated space. There is also a required `nonce` value (nonce just means something that is only meant to be used once; in this case, for one authenticated session), which is used by the client to generate their digested credentials. This essentially serves as a shared secret or session key. In addition to these two required header parameters, there are several additional optional parameters.

The first of these optional parameters is `qop`, or quality of protection—a specification which, if included, dictates an additional set of steps the user must take in building their authenticated response. The values specified by this optional field can ensure a higher degree of security for the credentials being transmitted by the client. When left unspecified by the server, the default operations used by the client are the least secure for transit. Interestingly, the **Remote Function Call** (**RFC**), which standardized Digest authentication (RFC 7616), specifies the `qop` field as being required, but its support and implementation vary for different application servers.

The server can also specify a `domain` field, which can include a space-separated list of URIs that define the protection space. When this field is provided, the client can use the value to determine all of the URIs for which the same authentication information will be considered valid. This is useful in a distributed system wherein one resource is responsible for authenticating, but the user must forward authentication information to a separate server to access its restricted content.

The server can specify the specific hashing algorithm the client must use for its digested response with the `algorithm` parameter. When not specified, the algorithm is expected to default to MD5, which is known to be insecure in many contexts. Because of this, if you ever find yourself implementing the Digest authentication scheme, I would strongly encourage you to enforce a secure hashing algorithm using the `algorithm` parameter of your response header.

Additionally, the server can provide an `opaque` value, which is meant to be echoed exactly by the client. This is a useful mechanism by which a server can transmit state information from one resource to another through the authenticated client. So, for example, if server A is responsible for authenticating the client for access to resources on server B, then server A could transmit access details to server B, through the opaque field. When implemented properly, the client would simply echo whatever values are sent by server A in its subsequent requests to server B.

Finally, there are entirely optional parameters for minor details of the authentication interaction, such as `charset`, which is used to specify the supported encoding schemes that the client may use. There is also a `userhash` parameter, which notifies the client that the server supports hashing the username in addition to the password component of their credentials.

Taken together, each of these required and optional parameters will produce a `WWW-Authenticate` header that looks like the following sample, as presented in the original RFC for Digest authentication:

```
WWW-Authenticate: Digest
    realm="http-auth@example.org",
    qop="auth, auth-int",
    algorithm=SHA-256,
    nonce="7ypf/xlj9XXwfDPEoM4URrv/xwf94BcCAzFZH4GiTo0v",
    opaque="FQhe/qaU925kfnzjCev0ciny7QMkPqMAFRtzCUYo5tdS"
```

Now, to understand how these header values are used to create a digested credential, let's look at the client's role in this process.

Digest authentication's authorization header

Once the client has received the `WWW-Authenticate` header from the server, they are responsible for building out their Digest response using the hashing algorithm that's specified (or the default MD5, if unspecified) by the server. To do so, they follow a series of procedures for one-way hashing their passwords using the hashing algorithm, and then hashing a combination of their username, the nonce value returned by the server, and their password.

The user creates a hash value with their username, the realm, and their password, with each separated by a colon. Assuming the server specified `SHA-256`, this creates a value designated as `HA1`, as shown here:

```
HA1 = SHA256(username:realm:password)
```

Then they generate a secondary hash value, dubbed `HA2`, which is composed of the HTTP method, to access the restricted resource, and the designated URI, separated by a colon and hashed with the specified algorithm:

```
HA2 = SHA256(method:resourceURI)
```

Finally, both of these values are hashed again in combination with the `nonce` value sent over by the server to produce the `response` parameter of the `Authorization` header:

```
response = SHA256(HA1:nonce:HA2)
```

There are variations of the specific inputs for each of these three values, depending on the qop value specified by the server, but overall the interactions are the same. Once all of this is done, the client returns an Authorization header to the server that includes the response value as well as its own array of optional parameters (and the echoed opaque parameter, if the server sent one in the first place) back to the server, as shown here:

```
Authorization: Digest username="Mufasa",
    realm="testrealm@host.com",
    uri="/dir/secured.html",
    response="6629fae49393a05397450978507c4ef1",
    nonce="7ypf/xlj9XXwfDPEoM4URrv/xwf94BcCAzFZH4GiTo0v",
    opaque="FQhe/qaU925kfnzjCev0ciny7QMkPqMAFRtzCUYo5tdS"
```

The advantage to this is that the user never sends their password in plain text. The reason for this is that, since the server should know the user password, it can reproduce the same hashing algorithms, using the same inputs, and confirm the result against the response parameter of the Authorization header.

Of course, you can probably already see the risk inherent with such an implementation. For the server to reproduce the same response parameter, it must have access to the user password stored somewhere in plain text. Since this is universally a bad idea, more modern implementations will typically store the entirety of the HA1 value in a secured database the first time a user creates a new set of credentials. This technique still allows the server to produce the response calculation of SHA256(HA1:nonce:HA2) while eliminating the need for the plain-text inputs of HA1. However, that also means that any time the realm value is changed, HA1 needs to be recalculated for each user on the system.

Furthermore, even storing the HA1 value should be considered relatively insecure, since it's used to create a new response by the client and access to the database still compromises the underlying system. A malicious actor would still be able to generate a fraudulent request, even without the plain-text password of the victim. The biggest benefit to using the HA1 is that, in the event of the server being compromised, it at least protects the user's raw password from exposure, minimizing risk to users in the event of a security breach.

Although the Digest authentication scheme is intended to provide higher levels of security for the authentication step of system access, it introduces its own complications and security concerns. For this reason, it's much less used.

HTTP origin-bound access

While not a fully-realized standard, the **HTTP origin-bound access** (**HOBA**) authentication scheme represents an exciting paradigm shift in the design of access-control mechanisms. Each of the previous forms of authentication we've discussed all revolved around users providing credentials (usually in the form of a username and password) to gain access to a system. With HOBA, no credentials are ever transmitted. Instead, a client (usually a specific web browser) persists a digital signature, which is given to the server in a challenge-response scheme.

Under the HOBA mechanism, the first time a client attempts to access a system, that specific client must register with the server. During this registration, once the client has been authenticated through traditional means, the client creates a **client public key** (**CPK**) and a private key registered to the specific origin/realm for the restricted resource. The CPK is then provided to the server, which assigns the CPK as the digital signature of the client. It's this CPK that is used to authenticate and authorize subsequent requests by the user to access restricted resources within the specified realm.

This provides the major security benefit of not having to store a record of the user credentials on the server, even in a securely hashed format. The downside to this practice, though, is that the CPK is typically stored in local storage by the browser on the client's machine. This means that any time a user accesses the server from a different machine (or indeed even a different web browser on the same machine) the client will have to register the new user-agent with the server again. Though, thankfully, the RFC draft, which defines the HOBA specification, explicitly allows for servers to register multiple CPKs to a single client account. As support for this authentication scheme grows and the specification is formally standardized, I would expect to see the other modes of authentication become very quickly deprecated in favor of HOBA.

Authorization tokens

One of the most commonly leveraged mechanisms for authorization is a bearer token. The most common mechanism for issuing these tokens is by using OAuth. However, while bearer tokens are typically referred to as OAuth tokens, in reality, they are merely provisioned by OAuth. The token itself can be defined by any standard, or no standard at all. Let's see how this relationship between token and token issuer can play out.

OAuth token provisioning

As I mentioned before, OAuth is a standard for providing clients with valid authentication tokens. The formal standard for how this is done is actually relatively brief and high level, and allows for a lot of flexibility in specific implementations. It was originally designed as a way to allow third-party applications to access a target application on a user's behalf.

In the OAuth interaction scheme, a client must first register as a consumer of a resource server. In this context, a resource server is simply any server that contains access-restricted resources and relies on a delegate server to handle access control for it. During this registration process, the resource server grants the relevant permissions to the client to access the restricted resources in the future.

Once a client has been registered, whenever that client attempts to access the resource server in the future, it is prompted to acquire an **access token**. The client must then request an access token from an **authorization server**. An authorization server is a server that the resource server has registered as its delegate, and which implements the OAuth interaction standard. The client provides the authorization server any access credentials it was given by the resource server during the registration step.

Upon validating the access credentials, the authorization server returns an access token. The access token response of OAuth 2.0 forms the backbone of most users' day-to-day interactions with the standard. Whenever a valid user successfully requests a token, they will get a response body with the following properties:

- **access_token**: This property is required, for obvious reasons. It's the value of the token string that will be returned to the resource server.
- **token_type**: This indicates the specific token authorization mechanism the resource server will expect. In almost all cases, this will simply have a value of bearer.
- **expires_in**: This property, while not required, is strongly recommended. Access tokens should be short-lived, with the OAuth specification recommending a maximum lifespan of only 10 minutes for most tokens. This is a security precaution to reduce the risk of an exposed access token being used by a malicious actor.
- **refresh_token**: This property is only used if the access token has an expiration, and even then it's optional. It specifies a refresh token that can be used by the client to request a new access token from the authorization server.

- **scope**: This field is used to notify a user if their set of granted permissions are less permissive than the set of permissions they initially requested. For example, if I request an access token with read, write, and update permissions, but the server restricts my access to only read permissions, this field would be used to specify the read permissions.

Finally, the client sends a request to the resource server with the access token as its `Authorization` bearer token.

Token generation

While OAuth specifies the interactions between a client and the corresponding resource and authorization servers, it says nothing about how the `access_token` field is actually generated. Instead, that detail is left up to each server that implements or relies on OAuth. So, how are tokens generated and validated?

Persisted tokens

It's not uncommon for a token to be nothing more than a randomly generated string. In this token generation mechanism, there is a database shared by both the authorization server and the resource server, which contains all of the relevant user access credentials and permissions. On some predetermined schedule, tokens are randomly generated and then associated with each user in the database. Then, upon successful authentication, the authorization server looks up the current token for a given user and returns it as the access token. Upon authorization, the resource server then looks up the user in the database with that same token value and validates their access, and can look up any permissions they may have.

The obvious downside to this approach is the need for a shared database and concurrency within that database across both the authentication and resource server. This approach doesn't lend itself especially well to cloud-deployed systems that might have dozens of concurrently running instances of the resource or authorization server, with multiple database instances. It's also not particularly well-suited to extremely high-volume applications, since the multiple database lookups can be extremely costly in terms of an application's responsiveness. If your system is relatively centralized and handles a reasonably small volume, though, it's certainly not a terrible choice for implementing your access token system. So, what's the alternative?

Self-encoded tokens

Perhaps one of the most robust and useful token generation mechanisms is the self-encoded token. Self-encoded tokens are tokens whose bodies contain all of the information that's necessary for the resource server to authorize the bearer. So, when a user is authenticated to a system and granted a token by an authorization server, the resource server can simply inspect the body of the token to determine the success of the authorization request and any permissions or claims the user has. With the context contained entirely in the token, the resource server never has to access a shared database to validate the user or their permissions, thus saving on the orchestration of resources in a distributed environment.

Perhaps the most widely used, and widely supported, self-encoded token scheme is the **JSON Web Token** (**JWT**). A JWT implements the self-encoded token mechanism by providing a set of claims the bearer has as properties in an encoded JSON object. The structure of a JWT token consists of three separate components, which are concatenated together and separated by a period.

The first of these components is a header, which is a `base-64` encoded string with well-known header parameters represented as a JSON object. This specifies the algorithm that's used for the signature (which we'll look at in just a moment) and the token type, which is typically just JWT.

Next is the body, which is a `base-64` encoded JSON object containing the complete list of claims the bearer of the token has. There are a few required parameters in this object, such as sub (subject, or the name of the bearer) and iat (issued at). However, since the specification of the token body is done entirely at the discretion of the resource server, any number of claims can be added with any given values.

The final piece of a JWT is the verification signature. This is how your resource server will know the token came from its associated authorization server. The verify signature is an encrypted **hashed message authentication code** (**HMAC**), which is derived from the `base-64` encoded strings of the previous two sections combined with a secret key. If any part of the body of the token or the header of the token was modified, then the verification step of token authorization won't produce the same HMAC, and the resource server can find out whether the token was tampered with and is invalid. For this to work though, the resource server and authorization server must share the secret key between the two of them and use it to sign and subsequently verify any tokens passed between the two.

Whether the token has been determined to be valid or not, the first two components of the token are simply `base-64` encoded. As such, they can easily be decoded and read by any interested party. For this reason, it's important to never send private information in the body of a JWT in plain text. If confidential information or access credentials must be sent, they should be sent in a securely encrypted format, with a one-way hash when possible and secure reversible encryption otherwise.

Authorization in .NET Core

Now that we've explored the ins and outs of authorization on the application layer of the OSI stack, it's time to look at how we can leverage these features in our own applications. Thankfully, as was the case with enforcing SSL, enabling an authorization scheme on our web APIs is mostly a matter of configuration more than anything. For the purposes of this demo, we'll be creating an application which will serve as both our resource server and our authentication server. And as always, we'll be taking some shortcuts with respect to error-handling and robust application design, for simplicity's sake.

The AuthorizeAttribute

The first thing we'll want to do is designate which resources we will need the authorization to access. We'll deal with the actual process of authorizing a user later. To designate restricted resources, we apply `AuthorizeAttribute`. This attribute is designated as suitable for methods or classes. This means we can apply it directly to our application's restricted endpoint or to the entire controller. So, let's look at the impact of each approach. First, let's create our application with the CLI command:

```
dotnet new webapi -n AuthSample
```

Then, we'll navigate to the `ValuesController.cs` file, rename it `AuthController.cs`, and then modify it to the following:

```
[Route("api/[controller]")]
[ApiController]
public class AuthController : ControllerBase {

  [HttpGet("secret")]
  public ActionResult<string> GetRestrictedResource() {
    return "This message is top secret!";
  }

  [HttpPost("authenticate")]
```

```
    public void AuthenticateUser([FromBody] Credentials creds) {
    }
}
```

We want to allow users to `POST` their credentials when they authenticate, but they'll simply `GET` our top secret message. Here, I've created a simple `Credentials` class to serve as the message body of our `POST` request. This is just for the convenience of encapsulating both the `username` and `password` strings in a single container class. Now, let's look at different approaches for applying the `Authorize` attribute. One approach would be to explicitly flag a given endpoint as needing authorization. In this case, this would be the `GetRestrictedResource()` method. So, we can apply the attribute above or below the `[HttpGet]` attribute and then that's that! Lets, have a look at the following code:

```
[Authorize]
[HttpGet("secret")]
public ActionResult<string> GetRestrictedResource() {
    return "This message is top secret!";
}
```

However, I'm sure you could imagine a scenario where a controller has dozens of endpoints, each of which requiring authorization. In that scenario, you could simply apply the `Authorize` attribute to the controller class itself, like so:

```
[Route("api/[controller]")]
[ApiController]
[Authorize]
public class AuthController : ControllerBase {
```

By applying the attribute to the controller, it is automatically applied to every endpoint defined in that controller. Of course, in our current controller, we'll need some way of designating our `AuthenticateUser()` method as not needing authorization (after all, how would a user become authorized if they must first be authorized?). To do this, we can override the `Authorize` attribute that's applied at the controller level with the `AllowAnonymous` attribute applied at the method level:

```
[HttpPost]
[AllowAnonymous]
public void AuthenticateUser([FromBody] Credentials creds) {
}
```

This attribute will always override any `Authorize` attributes that would otherwise apply to the current method. For that reason, it's always important to make sure you are only ever applying the `AllowAnonymous` attribute where it is absolutely necessary.

Authorization middleware

Now that we've designated which of our resources require to use authorization to be accessed, it's time to see what that authorization step looks like in our code. For this application, we'll be taking advantage of JWT bearer token authentication. To leverage this, we will be going to our `Startup.cs` file and modifying the services we've configured to use the appropriate authentication scheme.

Thanks to its open source distribution and wide support, the `Microsoft.AspNetCore` and `Microsoft.IdentityModel` namespaces support JWT token libraries right out of the box. This will make defining our authentication behavior much easier. We'll invoke the `AddAuthentication()` method on `IServicesCollection` and apply the default JWT bearer authentication scheme using the `JwtBeareDefaults` library class. Let's have a look at the following code:

```
services.AddAuthentication(JwtBearerDefaults.AuthenticationScheme)
```

This `AddAuthentication()` method is where you can define any custom access policies you want to apply to a given `Authorize` endpoint. For example, if you wanted to define a policy for a role-based authentication scheme, you could define a policy as requiring the `Manager` privileges by adding it as an option to your `AddAuthentication()` middleware:

```
services.AddAuthorization(options => {
  options.AddPolicy("RequireManagerRole",
    policy => policy.RequireRole("Manager"));
});
```

Then, for any endpoints for which you wanted to restrict access to managers, simply define that access policy in the `Authorize` attribute, like so:

```
[Authorize(Policy = "RequireManagerRole")]
```

This can be cumbersome when you have a wide variety of access policies and need many to be applied at once. In that case, you'll often find yourself writing your own extension methods to the `IServicesCollection` class, and invoking them directly. For this example, though, we've already got an extension method to customize our authorization, provided by the `Microsoft.AspNetCore.Authentication.JwtBearer` namespace.

Simply defining our authentication scheme to the JWT default means that any endpoint with an `Authorize` directive will invoke .NET's JWT validation code. We don't have to write anything else for our application to pull the token value out of the `Authorization` header, validate its signature against our own record of the private key, and then either approve the request and continue to the method, or reject it with a **401** response. This is all done by defining `JwtBearerDefaults.AuthenticationScheme` in our `AddAuthentication()` method.

The only remaining step we have to take to enable our authentication is to define what should be considered a valid token. We'll do that by using the `AddJwtBearer()` extension method. This method allows us to define an action delegate to configure the options we want our `Authentication` code to use when validating tokens. For this sample code, I've moved the definition of a signing key, token issuer, and token audience to a static utility class called `SecurityService`. This is just to make it easier to get the same values for our token validation options and our token generation code, which we'll look at in just a moment. But if you're curious, all that class is doing is returning consistent values for some key components of our token:

```
public static class SecurityService {
  public static SymmetricSecurityKey GetSecurityKey() {
      string key = "0125eb1b-0251-4a86-8d43-8ebeeeb39d9a";
      return new SymmetricSecurityKey(Encoding.ASCII.GetBytes(key));
  }

  public static string GetIssuer() {
      return "https://our-issuer.com/oauth";
  }

  public static string GetAudience() {
      return "we_the_audience";
  }
}
```

So, by using this class for our shared symmetric key, issuer, and audience generation, we can configure those aspects of our token as being necessary for authorizing a valid user. Simply apply them to the `TokenValidationParameters` class of `JwtBearerOptions`, as follows:

```
services.AddAuthentication(JwtBearerDefaults.AuthenticationScheme)
  .AddJwtBearer(options => {
    options.TokenValidationParameters = new TokenValidationParameters {
      IssuerSigningKey = SecurityService.GetSecurityKey(),
      RequireSignedTokens = true,
      ValidateActor = false,
      ValidateAudience = true,
```

```
            ValidAudience = SecurityService.GetAudience(),
            ValidateIssuer = true,
            ValidIssuer = SecurityService.GetIssuer()
        };
    });
```

With this configuration, you can see that our application is responsible for determining the validity of a bearer token based on the claims it contains. But thanks to the extensions available in the JWT utility libraries, defining those parameters becomes very easy!

Finally, as with any middleware configured in the `ConfigureServices` method, we'll need to tell our application to leverage it by adding the following line to our `Configure` method:

```
app.UseAuthentication();
```

And now, if you run the application and attempt to access the `/auth/secret` endpoint, you'll be given a **401** response, with the `WWW-Authenticate` message indicating the expected authentication scheme:

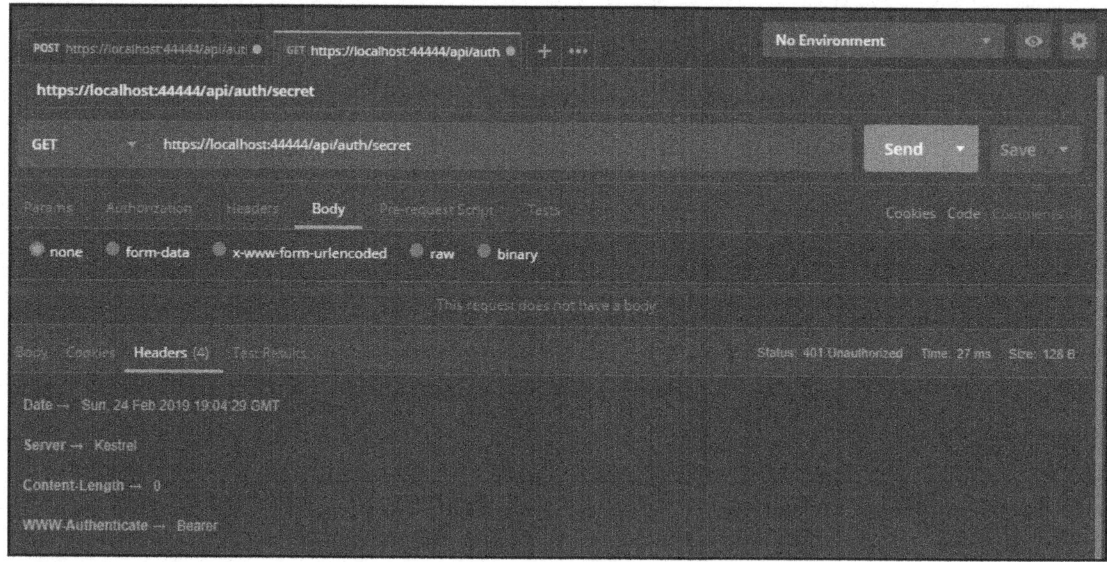

Now, all that's left is giving our users a token. Let's look at how to do that in our `AuthController` class using the JWT libraries for .NET.

Generating a token

With our /auth/secret endpoint safely locked away behind the authorize attribute, we need some way of authenticating and authorizing a user. For that, we'll use the AuthenticateUser() method, which is configured with the AllowAnonymous attribute to enable anyone to attempt to log in. The first thing we'll need is a list of users. For this, I've created a simple dictionary of username:password combinations in a user_vault.json file, which we can access with a static UserVault class. The UserVault class then exposes a simple method for checking whether a username:password combination exists in our user database. So, let's let user_vault.json be defined as follows:

```
{
    "aladdin": "open_sesame",
    "dr_suess": "green_eggs_and_ham",
    "jack_skellington": "halloween"
}
```

This gives us three valid users that we can test with. Our corresponding UserVault class allows us to check that by first being initialized with a static constructor:

```
private static Dictionary<string, string> _users { get; set; }
static UserVault() {
  try {
    using (var sr = new StreamReader("user_vault.json")) {
      var json = sr.ReadToEnd();
      _users = JsonConvert.DeserializeObject<Dictionary<string,
string>>(json);
    }
  } catch (Exception e) {
    throw e;
  }
}
```

Then, with an in-memory representation of our user_vault.json file, we can check against our private dictionary for any username:password pair with a ContainsCredentials() method:

```
public static bool ContainsCredentials(string userName, string password) {
  if (_users.ContainsKey(userName)) {
    string storedPassword;
    if(_users.TryGetValue(userName, out storedPassword)){
      return storedPassword.Equals(password);
    }
  }
  return false;
}
```

So, now that we can check for a user's presence in our user database, let's go ahead and define the authentication for our application. The first thing we'll need to do is build the key details that our authorization code will be expecting from any tokens we've issued. So, we'll need to use the same security key that we've configured our authentication middleware to expect. We'll also give the user a basic `Identity` using the `ClaimsIdentity` class:

```
[HttpPost]
[AllowAnonymous]
public ActionResult<string> AuthenticateUser([FromBody] Credentials creds)
{
  if (UserVault.ContainsCredentials(creds.UserName, creds.Password)) {
    var key = SecurityService.GetSecurityKey();
    var signingCredentials = new SigningCredentials(key,
SecurityAlgorithms.HmacSha256);
    var identity = new ClaimsIdentity(new GenericIdentity(creds.UserName,
"username"));
```

The `SigningCredentials` class in this code is a simple wrapper class that handles the details of hashing a given security key using the designated hash algorithm (in this case, HMAC SHA-256). This class is then used to generate the signature key component of the resulting JWT token. Once we've got that, we're ready to build our JWT token. To do that, we'll be using an instance of the `JwtSecurityTokenHandler` class. This is essentially a factory class that is used to produce well-formed JWT tokens with the configuration details passed to it.

Applying user claims

For the sake of demonstration, we'll be applying a few arbitrary claims to our token, just so we can inspect the result and see how those claims are applied and displayed in a well-formed token. We've got a simple helper class for that which returns a list of basic `Claim` instances:

```
private IEnumerable<Claim> GetClaims() {
  return new List<Claim>() {
    new Claim("secret_access", "true"),
    new Claim("excellent_code", "true")
  };
}
```

So, now that we've got all of our claims defined, we can apply them to the `ClaimsIdentity` that we create for the user with the following line of code:

```
identity.AddClaims(GetClaims());
```

This will give us the flexibility of restricting access to individual resources based on the permissions a user has on a case-by-case basis. The `User` property of `HttpContext` for any given request is an instance of a `ClaimsPrinciple`. Thus, we can inspect a user's claims through the `HttpContext.User.Claims` property.

When we secure an endpoint behind an authorize filter, any user claims specified by the authentication mechanism (in this case, JWT) will be applied to the `HttpContext.User.Claims` property. With that in mind, we can restrict access to our secret endpoint by inspecting our user's `Claims` property and confirming that they contain the claims we're looking for. Simply modify your `GetRestrictedResource` method to examine the `Type` parameter of your user claims, and confirm that the user has at least one claim of the valid claim types returned by `GetClaims`, as shown here:

```
[HttpGet("secret")]
public ActionResult<string> GetRestrictedResource() {
    var validClaims = GetClaims().Select(x => x.Type);
    var userClaims = HttpContext.User.Claims.Select(x => x.Type);
    if (validClaims.Intersect(userClaims).Count() < 1) {
        return StatusCode(403);
    }
    return "This message is top secret!";
}
```

With that, our user is defined, their claims are specified, and our resource is restricted to users who have those claims. And since our signing credentials are configured to use the same symmetric key as the resource server, we're ready to build out our token. This is easily done with the `JwtSecurityTokenHandler`, and `SecurityTokenDescriptor` classes:

```
var handler = new JwtSecurityTokenHandler();
var token = handler.CreateToken(new SecurityTokenDescriptor() {
  Issuer = SecurityService.GetIssuer(),
  Audience = SecurityService.GetAudience(),
  SigningCredentials = signingCredentials,
  Subject = identity,
  Expires = DateTime.Now.AddMinutes(10),
  NotBefore = DateTime.Now
});
```

Now, all that's left to do is write the token to our output for our users to apply to their subsequent requests. If you want to implement a fully compliant OAuth server, your response body and exception handling would need to adhere to the standard defined by OAuth 2.0, with your token returned as a part of a larger response body. Since we're just demonstrating the high-level workflow though, I'll leave that additional research to you. Instead, our output will just be the raw JWT token. So, with everything we've just done to fill in the blanks, the shell of our authentication method should look like this:

```
[HttpPost]
[AllowAnonymous]
public ActionResult<string> AuthenticateUser([FromBody] Credentials creds)
{
  if (UserVault.ContainsCredentials(creds.UserName, creds.Password)) {
    ... // Build and generate JWT token
    return handler.WriteToken(token);
  } else {
    return StatusCode(401);
}
```

Now, we're ready to put it all together. Run the application, post a request to the auth endpoint with any of the credentials in `user_vault.json`, and you should be greeted with a token:

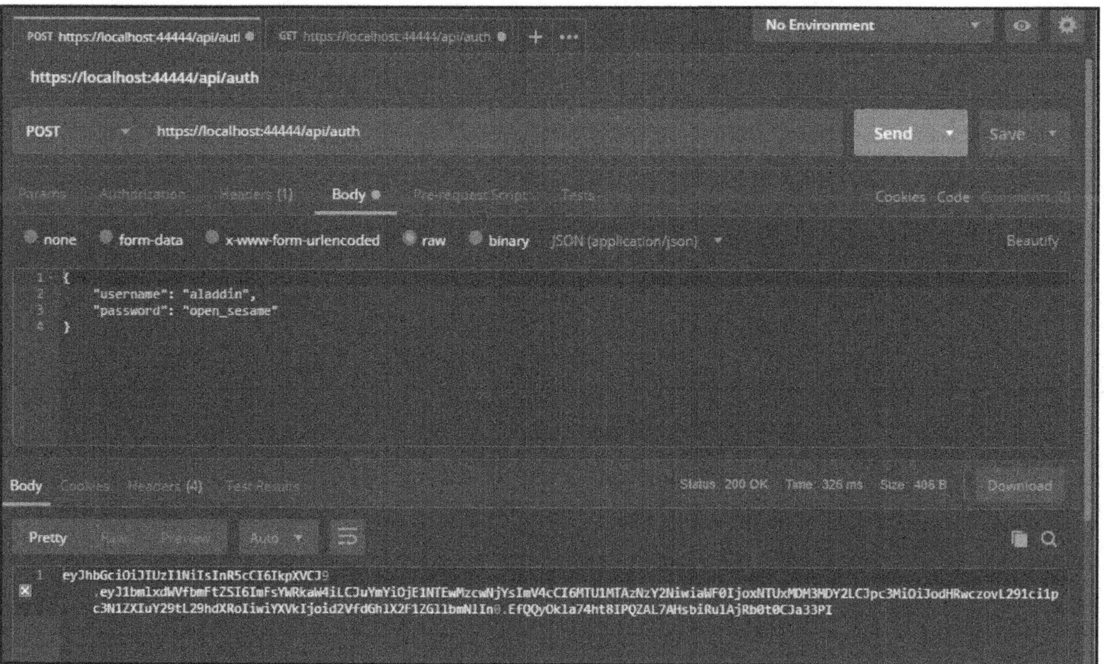

Next, make a request to the secret endpoint, supplying your newly retrieved token. To do this, go to the **Authorization** tab of Postman (or Insomnia) and set the **Authorization Type** in the drop-down list to the **Bearer Token** option. Then, paste in your newly acquired token into the input box, and send your request. If you followed all the steps here, you should get our secret message returned with a **200** status code:

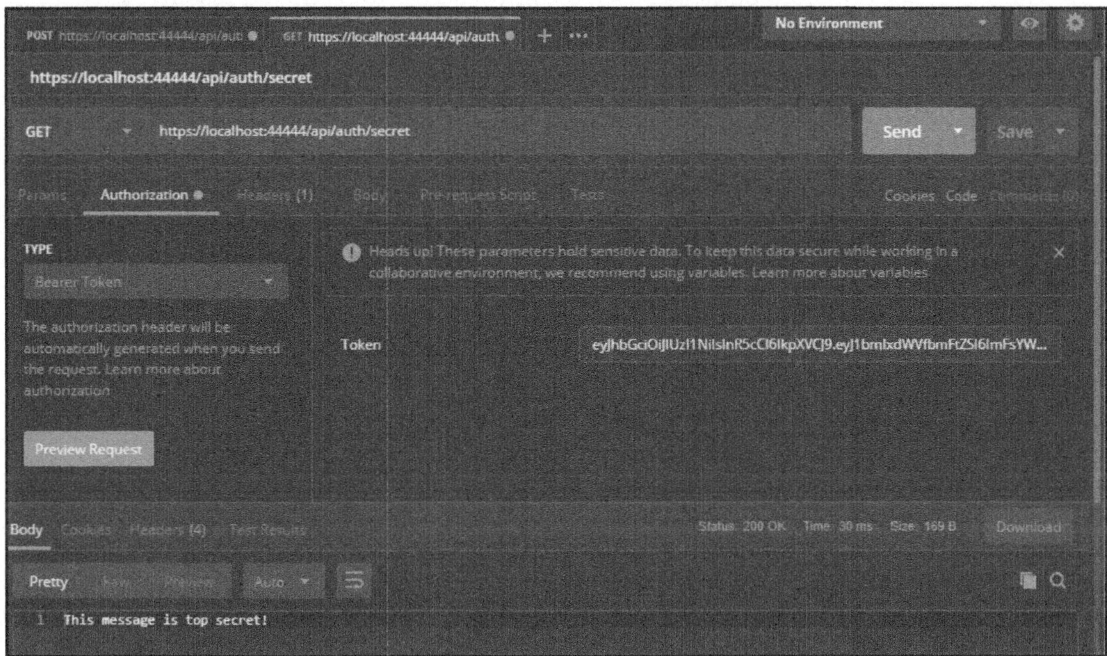

And just like that, you've implemented and applied a complete authentication and authorization scheme within .NET core, which it required a minimum amount of custom code on your part.

Before we move on, however, I would like to firmly establish that the coding practices used here are for demonstration purposes only. My goal was simply to illustrate the conceptual flow and basic patterns for an authentication/authorization framework in .NET Core. If you find yourself implementing user access in any of your applications, you have a strong responsibility to ensure the security of their private access credentials, and that should never be taken lightly.

With that said, we're now in a position to look at other ways we can improve the performance and versatility of our application layer network code. In the next chapter, we'll be taking a close look at caching strategies and patterns in .NET Core.

Summary

In this chapter, we covered every aspect of authentication and authorization at the application layer. First, we learned about the key but subtle distinction between authentication and authorization. We looked at the HTTP standard header that allows applications to perform both of those tasks to control access to restricted resources. Then, we learned about each of the valid authentication schemes supported by the standard `Authorization` header.

We saw the security risks and ease of implementation that come along with basic authentication. We looked at how a bearer token authentication could alleviate some of the security risks associated with basic authentication without necessarily adding much more in the way of complexity. Finally, we learned about the complexities and nuances of the Digest authentication mechanism. Before moving on, we also took the time to consider how authorization might be handled in the future with something like the HOBA scheme.

Next, we took a deep dive into bearer tokens. We saw how the OAuth standard defines an interaction mechanism for accessing and provisioning tokens. Then, we looked at how those tokens can be generated and leveraged by a resource server. Finally, we tied this all together by learning how to implement these features in .NET Core. Now, we're ready to look at performance improvements and resiliency strategies through caching, which we'll be exploring in the next chapter.

Questions

1. What is the difference between authentication and authorization? How do they apply to access control for web-based resources?
2. What are the valid authentication mechanisms for the authorize HTTP header?
3. What is HOBA? What is the primary advantage it has over other authentication schemes?
4. What is a bearer token? How is it used for authentication or authorization?
5. What is OAuth? How does it relate to standard authorization techniques?
6. What is a self-encoded token?
7. What is a JWT? How is it used?

Further reading

For more information about modern authentication techniques, I would strongly recommend reading *Mastering OAuth 2.0* by *Charles Bihis*. It's a relatively short read, but provides an extensive exploration of the standard. You can find it through Packt, here: `https://www.packtpub.com/application-development/mastering-oauth-2`.

Alternatively, if you have designs to leverage an OAuth system within your own software and want a more hands-on approach to the subject, I would recommend the *OAuth 2.0 Cookbook* by *Adolfo Eloy Nascimento*. It's also available through Packt, here: `https://www.packtpub.com/virtualization-and-cloud/oauth-20-cookbook`.

15
Caching Strategies for Distributed Systems

In the previous chapter, we learned all about common patterns for applying security to a network-hosted application. In this chapter, we will look at various ways to improve the performance of our network software by establishing intermediate caches. We'll see how using a cache to persist frequently accessed highly available data can grant us those performance improvements. We'll look at what a cache is and some of the various ways it can be used. Then, we'll undertake a thorough examination of one of the most common and complex architectural patterns for network caches. Finally, we'll demonstrate how to use caching at various levels of the application architecture to achieve our goals with a reasonable balance of developer effort and latency reduction.

The following topics will be covered in this chapter:

- The potential performance improvements to be gained by caching the results of common requests
- Basic patterns for caching session data to enable reliable interactions with parallel deployments of an application
- Understanding out to leverage caches within our .NET Core applications
- The strengths and weaknesses of various cache providers, including distributed network-hosted caches, memory caches, and database caches

Technical requirements

This chapter will have sample code to demonstrate each of the caching strategies we discuss. To work with that code, you'll need your trusty IDE (Visual Studio) or code editor (Visual Studio Code). You can download the sample code to work directly with it from this book's GitHub repository: `https://github.com/PacktPublishing/Hands-On-Network-Programming-with-C-and-.NET-Core/tree/master/Chapter 15`.

Check out the following video to see the code in action: `http://bit.ly/2HY67CM`

We'll also be using the Windows Subsystem for Linux to host the Linux-based Redis cache server on our local machine. Of course, if you're already running on a *nix system such as OS X or a Linux distribution, you don't have to worry about this. Alternatively, when you're running the application locally, if you don't have admin privileges or don't have any interest in learning the Redis cache server, you can modify the sample code slightly to use a different cache provider, which you'll learn about as we move through this chapter. However, I would recommend familiarizing yourself with the Redis cache since it is widely used and is an excellent choice for most circumstances. If you choose to do so, you can find instructions for installing the Linux Subsystem here: `https://docs.microsoft.com/en-us/windows/wsl/install-win10`.

Once that's done, you can find the instructions for installing and running Redis here: `https://redislabs.com/blog/redis-on-windows-10/`.

Why cache at all?

While it introduces additional complexity for the developers who are responsible for implementing it, a well-designed caching strategy can improve application performance significantly. If your software relies heavily on network resources, maximizing your use of caches can save your users time in the form of faster performance, and your company money in the form of lower network overhead. However, knowing when to cache data, and when it would be inappropriate to do so, is not always intuitive for developers. So, when should you be leveraging a caching strategy, and why?

An ideal caching scenario

Suppose you have an application that builds reports based on quarterly sales numbers. Imagine it has to pull hundreds of thousands of records from a handful of different databases, each with variable response times. Once it's acquired all of that data, it has to run extensive aggregation calculations on the records returned to produce the statistics that are displayed in the report output. Moreover, these reports are generated by dozens or even hundreds of different business analysts in a given day. Each report aggregates, for the most part, the same information, but some reports are structured to highlight different aspects of the data for different business concerns of the analysts. A naive approach to this problem would simply be to access the requested data on demand and return the results, reliably, with terrible response times. But does that necessarily have to be the case?

What I've just described is actually an ideal scenario for designing and implementing a caching strategy. What I've described is a system reliant on data owned by an external resource or process, which means that round-trip latency can be eliminated. I also noted that it is quarterly sales data, which means that it is presumably only ever updated, at most, once every three months. Finally, I mentioned that there are users generating reports with this remotely accessed data dozens to hundreds of times a day. For a distributed system, there is an almost no more obvious circumstance for pre-caching the remote data for faster and more reliable access in your on-demand application operations.

The contexts that motivate cache usage won't always be so cut and dried, but in general these three criteria will be a strong guide for when you should consider it. Just always ask yourself if any of them are met:

- Accessing resources external to your application's hosted context
- Accessing resources that are infrequently updated
- Accessing resources that are frequently used by your application

If any of those circumstances are met, you should start to think about what benefits you might reap by caching. If all of them are met, you would need to make a strong case for why you wouldn't implement a caching strategy. Of course, to understand why these criteria make caching necessary, you must first understand exactly what caching is and, just as importantly, what it isn't.

The principles of a data cache

Put simply, a cache is nothing more than an intermediary data store that can serve its data faster than the source from which the cached data originated. There are a number of reasons a cache could provide these speed improvements, and each of them requires their own consideration, so let's look at a few.

Caching long-running queries

If you have any formal database design experience, you likely know that relational databases tend toward highly normalized designs to eliminate duplicate data storage, and increase stability and data integrity. This normalization breaks out data records into various tables with highly atomic field definitions, and cross-reference tables for aggregating hierarchical data structures. And if you're not familiar with those principles of database design, then it's sufficient to say that it typically improves the usage of space at the cost of access time for a record lookup.

If you have a well-normalized relational database storing information that you would like to access as de-normalized flat records representing their application models, the queries that are used to flatten those records are often time-consuming and redundant. In this case, you might have a cache that stores flattened records, whose design is optimized for use by your application. This means that whenever a record needs to be updated, the process of de-normalizing the data can happen exactly once, sending the flattened structure to your cache. Thus, your application's interaction with the underlying data store can be reduced from a potentially beefy aggregation query against multiple tables to a simple lookup against a single application-specific table.

In this scenario, simply adding an intermediary cache for the long-running data-access operations can guarantee a performance improvement, even if the actual data storage system for the cache is the same as the origin. The primary performance bottleneck being mitigated by the cache is the query operation itself, so even if there is no reduction in network latency, you could still expect to reap some meaningful benefits.

It should be mentioned that this strategy can be applied to any long-running operations in your application flow. I used the example of slow database queries simply because those are the most commonly encountered bottlenecks with larger enterprise systems. However, in your work, you may find it beneficial to cache the results of computationally intensive operations executed within your application's host process. In this case, you'd likely be using an in-memory cache or a cache hosted on your own system, so there would be no possibility of improving your latency. But imagine deploying your application to a cloud hosting provider that's charging you by your application's uptime. In that scenario, cutting out a multi-second calculation from your application's most frequently used workflow could save thousands in compute costs over time. When you're caching the results of a method call or calculation local to your system, this is called **memoization.**

Caching high-latency network requests

Another common motivating factor for caching is high-latency network requests. In this scenario, your software would be dependent on a network resource, but some aspect of the network infrastructure makes accessing that resource unacceptably slow. It could be that your application is hosted behind a firewall, and the request validation protocols for an incoming or outgoing request introduce high latency. Or, it might just be a matter of locality, with your application server hosted in a separate physical region from your nearest data center.

Whatever the reason, a common solution to this problem is to minimize the impact of the network latency by caching the results in a more local data store. Let's suppose, for instance, the issue is a gateway or firewall introducing unacceptable latency to your data access requests. In that case, you could stand up a cache behind the firewall to eliminate the latency it introduces. With this sort of caching strategy, your objective is to store your cached data on some host that introduces less latency than the source. Even if the time to look up a record in your cache is no faster than the time to look up the same record at the source, the minimized latency is the objective.

Caching to preserve state

The last strategy for caching data is to facilitate state management. In cloud-deployed application architectures, you might have a user interacting with multiple instances of your application, running in parallel containers on different servers. However, if their interaction with your application depends on persisting any sort of session state, you'll need to share that state across all instances of your application that might service an individual request over the course of that session. When this is the case, you'll likely use a shared cache that all of the instances of your application can access and read from to determine if a request from a user relies on the state that was determined by another instance.

When to write to a cache

As I've described it so far, a cache might just sound like a duplicated data store that is optimized for your application. In some sense, that's true, but it's not technically correct, since a cache should never mirror its source system perfectly. After all, if you can store a complete copy of the underlying data store in a higher performance cache, what value is there in the underlying data store in the first place?

Instead, a cache will typically only contain a very small subset of the underlying data store. In most cases, the small size of a cache is necessary for its performance benefits, since even a simple query will scale linearly over the size of the set being queried. But if our data cache is not a perfect mirror of the source system, then we must determine which data makes it into our cache and when.

Pre-caching data

One simple but effective strategy for writing data to a cache is called **pre-caching**. In a system that pre-caches it's data, the developers will determine what is likely to be the lowest-performing or most-frequently requested data access operations, whose results are least likely to change over the lifetime of the application. Once that determination is made, those operations are performed once, usually in the initialization of the application, and loaded into the cache before any requests are received or processed by the application.

The example I mentioned earlier, involving frequently requested reports of quarterly sales data, is an ideal scenario for pre-cached data. In this case, we could request the sales data and run all of the statistical operations necessary for the output of the reports at the startup of our application. Then, we could cache the finished view models for each kind of report the application serviced. Upon receiving a request for a report, our application could reliably query the cache for the view model, and then populate the report template accordingly, saving time and compute costs over the course of the lifetime of the application.

The downside to this approach, though, is that it requires synchronization of any updates to the underlying data with refreshes of the application's cache. In cases where the application and the underlying data store are owned and managed by the same team of engineers, this synchronization is trivial. However, if the data store is owned by a different team from the engineers responsible for the application, the coordination introduces a risk. One failure to synchronize updates could result in stale data being served to customers. To mitigate this risk, you should establish a clear and resilient strategy for refreshing your cache, and automate the task as much as is possible.

On-demand cache writing

Most implementations of a caching system will be designed to write data to the cache on demand. In an on-demand system, the application will have a need for some piece of data that it can be certain is stored in the underlying database. However, prior to making the slower data access request all the way back to the underlying database, the application will first check for the requested data in the cache. If the data is found, it's called a **cache hit**. With a cache hit, the cache entry is used, and no additional call is made back to the dataset, thus improving the performance of the application.

In the alternative situation, where the requested data hasn't been written to the cache, the application has what's called a **cache miss**. With a miss, the application must make the slower call to the underlying data store. At this point, though, the cost of accessing the requested data from the lower-performing system has been paid. So now, the application can use whatever heuristics have been set for it to determine if the retrieved data should then be written to the cache, thus saving time on subsequent requests for the same piece of data.

Cache replacement strategies

If your cache is of a fixed limited size, you may find yourself needing to define a cache replacement policy. A cache replacement policy is how you determine when to replace older records with newer, potentially more relevant, ones. This will generally happen when your application experiences a cache miss. Once the data is retrieved, the application will determine whether or not to write it to the cache. If it does end up writing a record to the cache, it will need to determine which record to remove. The trouble, though, is that it is very difficult to determine a consistent heuristic for identifying which records won't be needed again soon.

You might have come up with a seemingly obvious answer in your own head just thinking about it; I certainly did when I first learned about this problem. But most of the obvious solutions don't hold up to scrutiny. For example, a fairly popular replacement policy involves eliminating the record that was least recently used. This just means replacing the entry that hasn't generated a cache hit for the longest series of cache queries. However, it may be the case that the longer it's been since a record has been used, the more likely it is that it will be the next record used, with records looked up in a cyclical order. In that case, eliminating the least recently used record would increase the chances of another cache miss in subsequent requests.

Alternatively, you could try the least frequently used replacement policy. This would drop the record with the fewest cache hits out of all records on the system, regardless of how recently those hits occurred. Of course, the drawback for this approach is that, without accounting for recency, you ignore the possibility that a recently used record might have been queried recently because it will become relevant for a series of subsequent operations the user intends to perform with it. By eliminating it due to its low hit rate, and ignoring the recency of the hit, you increase the chances of a cache miss in the future.

Each cache replacement policy has its own drawbacks and should be considered within the context of your application. However, there is a key metric by which you might determine the relative success of your replacement policy. Once your initial heuristic is designed and deployed, you can track your cache's hit ratio. A cache's hit ratio is, quite simply, the number of cache hits divided by the number of cache misses. The closer that number is to 1.0, the better your cache replacement policy is.

Cache invalidation

As you consider your cache replacement strategies, you may find that a piece of information stored in your cache will only be relevant to your application for a short period of time. When that's the case, instead of waiting for a new cache miss to overwrite the irrelevant data, you may want to expire the entry after a certain timeout. This is what's known as **cache invalidation**. Put simply, cache invalidation is the process of determining that a record in your cache should no longer be used to service subsequent requests.

In cases, as I've described, where you have a known time-to-live for any given record written to your cache, invalidating those records is as simple as setting and enforcing an expiration on the record as it's being written. However, there are other cases where it might not be so obvious that a cached record should be invalidated. Consider a web browser caching a response from the server. Without a predetermined expiration date, the browser can't know for sure that the cached response still represents the current state of the server without first checking the server, thus eliminating the performance benefit of the cache.

Since you should never be serving stale or invalid data to your users, you should always design some mechanism for invalidating your cached records. I've just discussed the two most common, and you'd be hard-pressed to find a reason not to implement at least one of them. So, if you have control over the cache itself, as in the case of a cache contained within your application architecture, you should always be diligent to invalidate cache records whenever the underlying data store is updated. And for the cases when you're not in control of your responses being cached, make sure you're always setting a reasonable cache expiration on your responses.

At this point, we've learned about what a cache is, why you might implement one in your software architecture, and what sort of strategies are at your disposal for optimizing its performance. So, now it's time to look at one of the most common caching strategies in modern cloud-deployed network architectures.

Distributed caching systems

In the previous section, I discussed using a cache for the purpose of preserving application state between parallel deployments of the same application. This is one of the most common use cases for caching in modern cloud-based architectures. However, useful as it may be, this sort of distributed session cache can introduce a whole host of challenges to the application design.

A cache-friendly architecture

Caches have historically been used to improve performance by reducing latency or operation times. With a session cache for distributed architecture, however, the cache itself is not intended to provide any specific performance improvement on a given operation. Instead, it's designed to facilitate a necessary interaction between multiple instances of an application. Its design is to facilitate state management that would otherwise involve complicated orchestration of multiple hosts. To understand how this is done, let's consider an example.

Suppose you have a cloud-hosted API that is responsible for verifying a user's identity and age. To do so, it requests various pieces of information that, taken together, could serve as verification of the user. In an effort to design your user experience to be as non-intrusive as possible, you start by asking only a few questions about their birth date and current address, which are most likely to successfully verify their age and identity. Once they've submitted their answers, your application would attempt to verify them. If it succeeds, your user can proceed, but if the initial set of questions is unsuccessful, your application follows up with a handful more questions that, when combined with the answers from the first set, are highly likely to verify the user's identity. The user submits their answers, and you continue again with failure, resulting in one final question requesting the last four digits of the user's social security number. Upon submission, the user is either successfully verified or rendered permanently unable to access your system.

That process is relatively straightforward from a business-logic perspective, but how would you implement it on a network process that is meant to remain entirely stateless between network requests? And as a cloud-hosted application, how would you maintain the current state of the user's position in that workflow across multiple possible instances of your app server processing a given request?

The case for a distributed cache

There are a handful of techniques available in this particular case, each with their own advantages and drawbacks. You could use sticky sessions to force subsequent requests from a particular host in a given session to be serviced by the same app server that processed the initial request. This would allow for some minor local state management over the course of a session. The downside to this is that it eliminates the performance benefits of horizontal scaling in a cloud-hosted system. If a user is always forced to interact with a single server over the course of a session, regardless of the traffic to that server or the availability of other servers, they may as well be interacting with a single-instance monolithic application architecture. Moreover, you would no longer be staying true to the architectural ideal of a "stateless" service, as you would be implementing some mechanism for preserving a user's position in the workflow over the course of interaction on your active service.

Alternatively, you could use the same principle we saw in the *Self-encoded tokens* section of `Chapter 14`, *Authentication and Authorization on Networks*. In this case, you'd be self-encoding the user's current state in the response from your server, and your user would be responsible for returning that self-encoded state back to the server in subsequent requests. This allows each request body to serve as a breadcrumb trail leading back to the first interaction with the client, from which the server could rebuild the state that was created in previous interactions with each subsequent interaction.

This approach will increase the complexity of your request/response models, though. It will also introduce the added risk of unenforceable limits on verification attempts. Suppose, for security purposes, your business rules dictate that a user should only be allowed to attempt each round of questions once. If you self-encode the state of the user session in your request/response models, you're relying on your users to return an accurate representation of each previous attempt with each of their requests. It would be easy for a dedicated malicious actor to make as many attempts as they please by simply scrubbing the workflow state from their subsequent requests.

In this scenario, I would argue that the most reliable solution for maintaining state across requests is a distributed cache shared by each app server in your cloud environment. This prevents you from maintaining state across your app servers, thus preserving the stateless principle of cloud-deployed service architecture, while still allowing your services to maintain full control over a user's progression through your verification workflow.

To implement this, you would host the cache provider on its own server, independently of any instances of your application servers in your cloud. Any server that successfully processes a given step in the workflow would refuse to fully resolve the interaction and provide a response to the client unless and until the result of that step was successfully written back to your data cache. In this way, the current app server instance could do the following:

- Verify that no other instances have successfully processed the same request already by confirming that no record of the workflow step exists for the user in the cache
- Notify other instances of the application that the step had been processed so that they would cease to duplicate the transaction

The benefits of a distributed cache

The system I've described has the benefit of ensuring the consistency of the user state throughout their interaction across all deployed instances of your application, with only the minor orchestration of reading from and writing to a cache. This data consistency, is key even when your distributed cache is not used for state management. It can prevent multiple instances of an application from trying to perform two incompatible modifications to the same piece of data, or allow synchronization of transactions across multiple app servers prior to committing them to the underlying database. And most importantly, from the developer's perspective, it can eliminate difficult to reproduce and difficult to track down bugs caused by race conditions between services.

Hosting the cache server independently of all other applications also provides it with a measure of resilience against app restarts or crashes. By isolating your data store, you can isolate costs associated with higher availability and resiliency guarantees from your cloud provider. It can also help to minimize the memory footprint of your application containers living on your app servers. If you pay for RAM usage, this can save you thousands as your cache scales out. So, how exactly do we reap these benefits in our code?

Working with caches in code

To see how we can benefit from the various caching mechanisms supported by .NET Core, we'll be setting up a somewhat complicated demo application structure. The first thing we'll do is create a remote data store that has long-running operations to return results from queries. Once that's done, we'll set up an application dependent on that data, and provide it a caching strategy to mitigate the impact of our artificially slowed down remote data storage.

Writing our backing data system

We'll be creating our backing data system as a simple Web API project. The goal is to expose a couple of endpoints on a single controller that expose data of different types to demonstrate how we can write the values to our cache regardless of the type discrepancy between the records. First, let's create our project with the .NET Core CLI. Let's look at the following command:

```
dotnet new webapi -n DataSimulation
```

Next, since we'll be hosting this project at the same time as our cache-ready application, we'll want to configure it to use its own port, instead of the default settings. Within your `Program.cs` file, modify your `CreateWebHostBuilder(string[] args)` method to use whatever custom URLs you want this application to listen on:

```
public static IWebHostBuilder CreateWebHostBuilder(string[] args) =>
  WebHost.CreateDefaultBuilder(args)
    .UseUrls("https://[::]:33333")
    .UseStartup<Startup>();
```

Then, we'll modify the `ValuesController.cs` class to serve up our data. First, we'll change the name of the class to `DataController` so that our routing is a bit more intuitive. We'll be getting rid of all of the preconfigured endpoints and replacing them with three new endpoints, each returning a unique data type. First, though, let's create a new data type for us to return. It will be a simple model with an ID and two arbitrary properties; one will be of the `string` type, and the other will be a `List<string>`:

```
public class OutputRecord {
  public int Id { get; set; }
  public string SimpleString { get; set; }
  public List<string> StringList { get; set; } = new List<string>();
}
```

With this model set up, we can define the endpoints we'll be exposing. For this demonstration, we'll return a simple `List<string>` string, a single `OutputRecord` instance, and a `List<OutputRecord>` method. So, by the time we've defined a lookup endpoint for each data type, we'll have methods returning simple strings, lists of strings, complex records, and lists of complex records. Let's look at the following code:

```
public class DataController : ControllerBase {

  [HttpGet("value/{id}")]
  public ActionResult<string> GetString(int id) {
    return $"{id}: some data";
  }

  [HttpGet("values/{id}")]
  public ActionResult<IEnumerable<string>> GetStrings(int id) {
    return new string[] { $"{id}: value1", $"{id + 1}: value2" };
  }
```

These define our simple string responses, and will be relatively straightforward to test with our cache. For our `OutputRecord` endpoints, though, we'll want to apply unique data to each property so that we can confirm that the full object is properly cached. So, the endpoint returning a single `OutputRecord` instance will look like this:

```
[HttpGet("record/{id}")]
public ActionResult<OutputRecord> GetRecord(int id) {
  return new OutputRecord() {
    Id = id,
    SimpleString = $"{id}: value 1",
    StringList = new List<string> {
      $"{id}:value 2",
      $"{id}:value 3"
    }
  };
}
```

This gives us an object with distinct property values, tied together by the same ID, which will make it easy for us to validate the behavior of our cache. Finally, we'll define an endpoint to return a list of the `OutputRecord` instances:

```
[HttpGet("records/{id}")]
public ActionResult<IEnumerable<OutputRecord>> GetRecords(int id) {
  return new List<OutputRecord>(){
    new OutputRecord() {
      Id = id,
      SimpleString = $"{id}: value 1",
      StringList = new List<string> {
        $"{id}:value 2",
        $"{id}:value 3"
      }
    }, new OutputRecord() {
      Id = id + 1,
      SimpleString = $"{id + 1}: value 4",
      StringList = new List<string> {
        $"{id + 1}:value 5",
        $"{id + 1}:value 6"
      }
    }
  };
}
```

Each of these endpoints returns some trivial object or string with the provided ID that's used in the response objects, but this will just be a way of distinguishing one response from the next. The important aspect of our responses will be the perceivable delay we'll be applying. For that, we'll a five second delay to each method prior to returning their result. This will give us an obvious way to identify when the backing data store has been hit versus when our user-facing application has a successful cache hit.

To simulate this delay, we'll sleep the current thread for five seconds, and then return some arbitrary string that incorporates the given ID:

```
[HttpGet("value/{id}")]
public ActionResult<string> GetString(int id) {
    Thread.Sleep(5000);
    return $"{id}: some data";
}
```

Each additional method will do the same thing, applying the delay and then initializing its expected return type with its arbitrary values. Now, if you run the application and ping your `/data/value/1234` endpoint, you should see the result come back after five seconds:

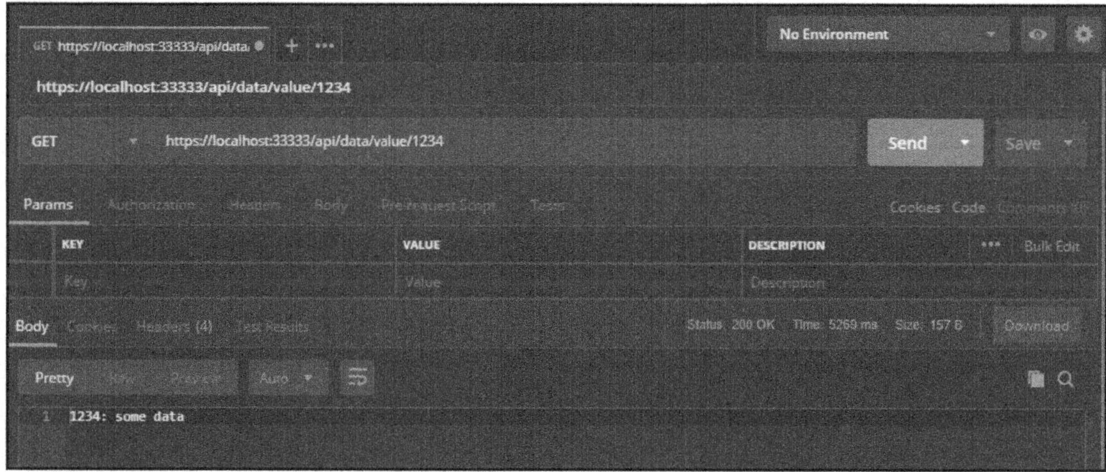

Note the response time of **5269ms**. This delay will be our indication of a cache miss, going forward. And with our data store ready, we can build our application and define its caching strategy.

Leveraging a cache

To start working with our cache, we'll first install and run a local instance of a Redis server. Redis is an open source, in-memory data store. It's frequently used in enterprise deployments as a simple key-value data store or cache. It's also supported out of the box by Azure cloud hosting environments, making it very popular for .NET based microservices and cloud-based applications.

To install it, follow the instructions in the *Technical requirements* section of this chapter. Once you've done so, you'll have your local instance running. If you've already installed the server, make sure it's up and running by opening your Windows Subsystem for Linux interface, and enter the following commands to verify its listening port:

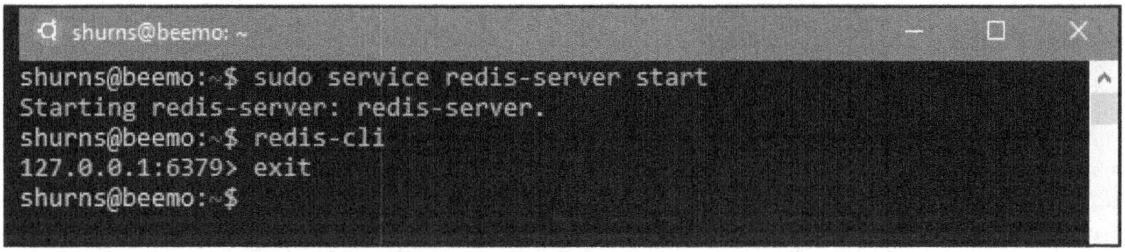

```
shurns@beemo: ~
shurns@beemo:~$ sudo service redis-server start
Starting redis-server: redis-server.
shurns@beemo:~$ redis-cli
127.0.0.1:6379> exit
shurns@beemo:~$
```

Once you've got your Redis instance running, you'll be ready to implement your sample microservice. Since we'll be loading cache misses from our backend API, we'll want to configure `HttpClient` for that particular application in our `Startup.cs` file. For this, I've created a static `Constants` class just to avoid magic strings used in my code, and used a `DATA_CLIENT` property to register a named instance of `HttpClient` inside my `ConfigureServices(IServiceCollection services)` method:

```
services.AddHttpClient(Constants.DATA_CLIENT, options => {
  options.BaseAddress = new Uri("https://localhost:33333");
  options.DefaultRequestHeaders.Add("Accept", "application/json");
});
```

Next, we'll create a service client to abstract the details of the HTTP requests we'll be making behind a clean data-access interface, using the same patterns we established in Chapter 9, *HTTP in .NET*. Our interface definition will provide the following simple methods:

```
public interface IDataService{
  Task<string> GetStringValueById(string id);
  Task<IEnumerable<string>> GetStringListById(string id);
  Task<DataRecord> GetRecordById(string id);
  Task<IEnumerable<DataRecord>> GetRecordListById(string id);
}
```

Within the implementing class for this interface, we'll have a private instance of `IHttpClientFactory`, and we'll be using our named `HttpClient` instance to access our backend data store. This common task is isolated to a private method for the actual HTTP interaction:

```
private async Task<string> GetResponseString(string path) {
    var client = _httpFactory.CreateClient(Constants.DATA_CLIENT);
    var request = new HttpRequestMessage(HttpMethod.Get, path);
    var response = await client.SendAsync(request);
    return await response.Content.ReadAsStringAsync();
}
```

Then, each of the public interface methods implements an endpoint-specific variation of the general pattern established here:

```
public async Task<DataRecord> GetRecordById(string id) {
    var respStr = await GetResponseString($"api/data/record/{id}");
    return JsonConvert.DeserializeObject<DataRecord>(respStr);
}
```

Extending this logic for all four of our access methods, we'll complete our backend data client. At this point, we should modify our controller to expose each of the backend API endpoints, and use them to test our data-access service. We'll expose the same service contract we had in our backend API, with four endpoints for each type of record we could look up. Instead of renaming our file, we'll just redefine our controller's route, and define a public constructor to allow the dependency injection framework to provide our `DataService` instance (just don't forget to register the concrete implementation in your `Startup.cs`). Lets, look at the following code:

```
[Route("api/cache-client")]
[ApiController]
public class ValuesController : ControllerBase {

    private IDataService _dataService;

    public ValuesController(IDataService data) {
        _dataService = data;
    }
    ...
```

Once we have our data service, we can use our API endpoints to call into each requested object from our backend system:

```
[HttpGet("value/{id}")]
public async Task<ActionResult<string>> GetValue(string id) {
    return await _dataService.GetStringValueById(id);
}

[HttpGet("values/{id}")]
public async Task<IEnumerable<string>> GetValues(string id) {
    return await _dataService.GetStringListById(id);
}

[HttpGet("record/{id}")]
public async Task<ActionResult<DataRecord>> GetRecord(string id) {
    return await _dataService.GetRecordById(id);
}

[HttpGet("records/{id}")]
public async Task<IEnumerable<DataRecord>> Get(string id) {
    return await _dataService.GetRecordListById(id);
}
```

At this point, by running both your backend API and your cache service API, you should be able to request the same values from your cache service, with the same five second delay. So, now that our application is fully wired up to request data from our backend service, let's improve its performance with caching.

The distributed cache client in .NET

One of the major benefits of using Redis for our distributed caching solution is that it's supported by .NET Core out of the box. There's even an extension method on the `IServicesCollection` class specifically for registering a Redis cache for use within your application. Simply install the `Microsoft.Extensions.Caching.Redis` NuGet package for your current project, and then add the following code:

```
services.AddDistributedRedisCache(options => {
    options.Configuration = "localhost";
    options.InstanceName = "local";
});
```

This will automatically register an instance of the `RedisCache` class as the concrete implementation for any instances of `IDistributedCache` you inject into any of your services. The localhost configuration setting will use the default configurations for a local deployment of the Redis client, so there's no need to specify an IP address and port unless you explicitly change it on your local deployment. Meanwhile, the `InstanceName` field will give the entries stored in the cache that were set by this application an application-specific prefix. So, in this example, if I set a record with the `1234` key with my setting of local, that key will be stored in the cache as `local1234`. The `RedisCache` instance that is registered by the `AddDistributedRedisCache()` method will automatically look for keys with the `InstanceName` prefix that we've specified in our options. We'll see this later when we inspect our cache instance.

With our Redis cache running, and our `IDistributedCache` instance configured and registered with our dependency injection container, we can write a `CacheService` class. This will follow a similar pattern to our `DataService` class, where it exposes only a small number of logical operations as public methods, hiding the details of the cache interactions. Our interface for this `CacheService` class is as follow:

```
public interface ICacheService {
    Task<bool> HasCacheRecord(string id);
    Task<string> FetchString(string id);
    Task<T> FetchRecord<T>(string id);
    Task WriteString(string id, string value);
    Task WriteRecord<T>(string id, T record);
}
```

Here, we're making the distinction between writing a single string and writing a more complex record to distinguish between the need to serialize and deserialize our entries in each method implementation.

Getting and setting cache records

The `IDistributedCache` class provides a simple mechanism for interacting with our cached data. It operates on a dumb get/set pattern whereby attempts to get a record will either return the cached byte array or string based on the given ID, or return null if no record exists. There's no error handling or state checking. The speed of the cache is dependent on this simple interaction mechanism and fail state.

Likewise, setting a record is equally easy. Simply define your ID for the record, and then provide some serialized representation of the record for storage. This serialized format can be either a string with the `SetString(string id, string value)` method, or a byte array using the `Set(string id, byte[] value)` method.

Additionally, when you write a value to the cache, you can set additional options for your cache record to specify expiration time spans. The kinds of expiration settings you can apply are as follows:

- **AbsoluteExpiration**: This sets the expiration to a specific moment in time at which point the record will be invalidated, no matter how recently it has been used.
- **AbosluteExpirationRelativeToNow**: This sets a fixed moment at which the record will be invalidated no matter how recently it has been used. The only difference with this and AbsoluteExpiration is that the expiration time is expressed in terms of some length of time from the moment the record is set in the cache.
- **SlidingExpiration**: This sets an expiration time relative to the last time the record was accessed. So, if the sliding expiration is set for 60 minutes, and the record isn't accessed again for 62 minutes, it will have expired. However, if the record is accessed again in 58 minutes, the expiration is reset for 60 minutes from that second access.

So, let's look at how we'll implement this cache. First, we've got to inject the `IDistributedCache` instance that was registered in our `Startup.cs` class:

```
public class CacheService : ICacheService {
    IDistributedCache _cache;

    public CacheService(IDistributedCache cache) {
        _cache = cache;
    }
```

Then, we'll implement the methods of our interface. The first method is fairly straightforward and only notifies our consumers if there has been a cache hit:

```
public async Task<bool> HasCacheRecord(string id) {
    var record = await _cache.GetStringAsync(id);
    return record != null;
}
```

Next, we'll implement our record retrieval methods. The only difference with each of these is that retrieval of complex data types (records and lists of strings) will require an extra step of deserialization. Other than that, though, our `Fetch...()` methods should look fairly straightforward:

```
public async Task<string> FetchString(string id) {
    return await _cache.GetStringAsync(id);
}

public async Task<T> FetchRecord<T>(string id) {
    var record = await _cache.GetStringAsync(id);
    T result = JsonConvert.DeserializeObject<T>(record);
    return result;
}
```

Finally, we'll need to implement the write methods. For the sake of demonstration, we'll write all of our records with a 60-minute sliding expiration time using the `DistributedCacheEntryOptions` class. After that, we can simply pass in our key to the cache, along with a serialized value (we'll be using JSON here, to take advantage of the `Newtonsoft.Json` libraries) and our expiration options:

```
public async Task WriteString(string id, string value) {
    DistributedCacheEntryOptions opts = new DistributedCacheEntryOptions()
{
        SlidingExpiration = TimeSpan.FromMinutes(60)
    };
    await _cache.SetStringAsync(id, value, opts);
}

public async Task WriteRecord<T>(string id, T record) {
    var value = JsonConvert.SerializeObject(record);
    DistributedCacheEntryOptions opts = new DistributedCacheEntryOptions()
{
        SlidingExpiration = TimeSpan.FromMinutes(60)
    };

    await _cache.SetStringAsync(id, value, opts);
}
```

And with that, our cache should be ready to use. Now, it's time to pull it all together in our controller endpoints. For this, the interaction pattern will be the same across each method, with the only difference being the type of read/write operation we perform on our cache. So Let's look at how we'll implement our cache strategy:

```
[HttpGet("record/{id}")]
public async Task<ActionResult<DataRecord>> GetRecord(string id) {
    var key = $"{id}record";
```

```
        if (await _cache.HasCacheRecord(key)) {
            return await _cache.FetchRecord<DataRecord>(key);
        }
        var value = await _dataService.GetRecordById(id);
        await _cache.WriteRecord(key, value);
        return value;
    }
```

The first thing you'll notice is that I apply a suffix to our given ID that matches my route. This is to allow duplicate IDs in my cache for each distinct data type. Next, we check our `HasCacheRecord` (key) method to determine whether we have a cache hit. If we do, we simply fetch the cache record and return the result. When we have a miss, though, we have to fetch the data from our underlying data store. Once we have it, we write it to our cache for faster retrieval in any subsequent requests, and then return the value.

After applying this pattern with the appropriate modifications to each of our endpoints, we're ready to test. To confirm the behavior of our cache, first run the same query against any endpoint with a new ID, twice in a row. If everything's working properly, you should have a five second delay on your first request, and almost zero delays on your subsequent request.

Once you have at least a record or two stored in your cache, you can observe the values with your redis-cli in your Windows Subsystem for Linux console. The `RedisCache` class will store the entries as hash types in the underlying cache, so you'll need to look for the key values using those commands. The operations I performed to look up the records I wrote while testing the app are as follows:

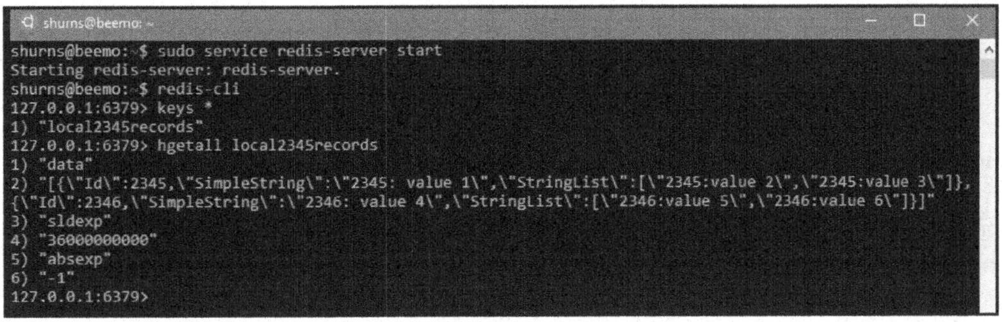

```
shurns@beemo:~$ sudo service redis-server start
Starting redis-server: redis-server.
shurns@beemo:~$ redis-cli
127.0.0.1:6379> keys *
1) "local2345records"
127.0.0.1:6379> hgetall local2345records
1) "data"
2) "[{\"Id\":2345,\"SimpleString\":\"2345: value 1\",\"StringList\":[\"2345:value 2\",\"2345:value 3\"]},
{\"Id\":2346,\"SimpleString\":\"2346: value 4\",\"StringList\":[\"2346:value 5\",\"2346:value 6\"]}]"
3) "sldexp"
4) "36000000000"
5) "absexp"
6) "-1"
127.0.0.1:6379>
```

The first command, `keys *`, simply searches all active keys that match the given pattern (* is the wildcard, so `keys *` matches all keys). Then, I used the `hgetall [key]` command to get each property in my entry's hash. In that output, you can clearly see the JSON written to the cache from my application, demonstrating the successful and expected interactions between my app and my cache.

I'd also like to point out the key structure. As I mentioned before, the keys I set (in this case, 2345 records) are prefixed with `InstanceName` of `RedisCacheOptions`, with which I configured `RedisCache` in the `Startup.cs` file. And with that output, you've seen the full interaction pattern established by Microsoft for working with a Redis cache instance.

Cache providers

While we demonstrated the use of a data cache with an instance of the `IDistributedCache` class in our sample code, that is hardly the only cache provider we have access to with .NET Core. Before we close out the subject of caches, I just want to briefly discuss the other two most common providers in the framework.

The SqlServerCache provider

Redis is certainly popular among engineers as being a high-performance cache implementation. However, it's hardly the only distributed provider out there. In fact, Microsoft's own SQL Server can serve as a cache when the situation calls for it, and they've defined a similar implementation for the `IDistributedCache` class to expose it.

One of the biggest differences with the `SqlServerCache` provider and the `RedisCache` instance is in the configuration it requires. Where Redis is a simple key-value store, `SqlServer` remains a full-featured relational database. Thus, to provide the lightweight interactions necessary for a high performing cache, you'll have to specify the precise schema, table, and database connection you intend to leverage when you set it as your `IDistributedCache` provider. And since SQL Server doesn't support the hash tables that Redis does, the table to which your application connects for caching should implement the expected structure of an `IDistributedCache` record. Thankfully, the .NET Core CLI provides a utility command for establishing just such a table: the `sql-cache create` command. And notably, since your application should only ever be interacting with injected instances of `IDistributedCache`, you won't even notice the difference, except perhaps in performance. However, for the sake of performance, I would recommend using Redis wherever possible. It is quickly becoming the industry standard and its speed is truly unmatched by SQL Server.

The MemoryCache provider

Finally, if your application either doesn't have the need, or doesn't have the means, to support a standalone cache instance, you can always leverage an in-memory caching strategy. The `MemoryCache` class of the `System.Runtime.Caching` namespace will provide exactly that. Configuring it is as simple as invoking the `services.AddMemoryCache()` method in `Startup.cs`, and it provides a similar interface to the `IDistributedCache` class we've already looked at.

It does bring some major caveats with it, however. Since you're hosting the cache within your application's own process, memory becomes a much more valuable resource. Disciplined use of a cache replacement policy, and an aggressive expiration time, becomes much more important with an in-memory caching solution. Additionally, since any state that must persist over the lifetime of a session will only be persisted within a single instance of your application, you'll need to implement sticky sessions. This will ensure that users will always interact with the app server that has their data cached in its memory.

Ultimately, your business needs and environmental constraints will play a large role in determining what sort of caching policies and strategies you should be taking advantage of in your application. However, with the information in this chapter, you should be well-suited to making the best possible decisions for your circumstances. Meanwhile, we'll be continuing our consideration of performance optimization in the next chapter as we consider performance monitoring and data tracing in a network-hosted application.

Summary

In this chapter, we took an extensive tour of the motivations for, and use cases of, data caches in a distributed network application. We started by exploring some common business and design problems that would likely reap the benefits of a caching strategy. In doing so, we identified some of the basic considerations you can make when determining if the complexity of introducing a cache management system is the right decision for your application. Then, we looked at exactly which benefits could be gained from caching, and precisely how caching can provide them.

Once we learned why we might use a cache, we looked at some of the common problems that must be solved for when implementing a cache. First, we tackled the tactics of pre-caching data and caching results on demand. Then, we looked at how to determine which data or resources should be cache. We learned about establishing a cache replacement policy that is well-suited to your application's most common data interactions, and how to invalidate records in your cache to make sure you're never returning stale results.

Finally, we saw how we could use a cache in our applications. We learned how to run a distributed cache, and we saw how to write to and read from that cache within the code. We saw that a cache record could be an arbitrary data structure with an arbitrary key, and how to detect hits within our cache instance. Finally, we looked at alternative caching mechanisms available with C# and .NET Core.

In the next chapter, we'll continue with our focus on optimizing our application performance for a network, and look at the tools available to us for monitoring our application's performance and identifying any bottlenecks in our network.

Questions

1. What are three criteria that should motivate a caching strategy?
2. What are three common pain points caches can help resolve?
3. What is a cache hit? What is a cache miss?
4. What is a cache replacement policy? What are some common cache replacement policies?
5. What is a hit ratio, and how does it relate to a replacement strategy?
6. What is cache invalidation?
7. What are some of the benefits of using a distributed cache?

Further reading

For even more hands-on guidance for building caches in a modern .NET context, I recommend the book *The Modern C# Challenge*, by *Rod Stephens*. It takes a deep dive into the same sorts of patterns and practices we discussed in this chapter with an incredibly approachable presentation. It can be found through Packt publishing, here: `https://www.packtpub.com/application-development/modern-c-challenge-0`.

Alternatively, if you want to consider other challenges inherent to distributed, horizontally scaled application architectures, you should check out *Microservice Patterns and Best Practices* by *Vinicius Feitosa Pacheco*. It's also available from Packt, and you can get it here: `https://www.packtpub.com/application-development/microservice-patterns-and-best-practices`.

16
Performance Analysis and Monitoring

As you continue to develop your knowledge of building network software, we cannot overlook the key tasks of monitoring and performance tuning. Those two responsibilities will be the focus of this chapter, as we look at the tools that are available in .NET Core applications for monitoring and testing the performance and stability of your application. We'll be looking at the tools that are available to developers for putting your application under heavy load in controlled environments and observing its stability over time. We'll look at some naive logging and monitoring approaches, and consider how we can strengthen those approaches using some of the features of .NET Core.

The following topics will be covered in this chapter:

- Identifying performance bottlenecks in your network architecture, and designing to minimize them
- Identifying end-to-end performance testing and reporting strategies
- Establishing robust and resilient performance monitoring with C#

Technical requirements

In this chapter, we'll be writing a number of samples to demonstrate various aspects of performance tracing and monitoring, all of which can be found here: `https://github.com/PacktPublishing/Hands-On-Network-Programming-with-CSharp-and-.NET-Core`/tree/master/Chapter 16.

Check out the following video to see the code in action: `http://bit.ly/2HYmD5r`

To work with this code, you'll want to use either of our trusty code editors: Visual Studio or Visual Studio Code. We'll also be using the REST clients you've come to know and love, so make sure you've got either PostMan installed (`https://www.getpostman.com/downloads/`) or the Insomnia REST client (`https://insomnia.rest/`).

Network performance analysis

As you start to build more complicated distributed software systems, you begin to lose the granular control and fine-tuning you had over smaller, more isolated software projects. Each new network interaction introduces higher chances of systemic failure, reduces visibility on the source of bugs, and muddies the waters when searching for performance bottlenecks. The best way to mitigate these impacts is to get ahead of them, and design your distributed system with performance monitoring in mind from the start. So, how do you do that? What are the key metrics and interactions with which you should be concerned? What support does .NET Core provide to you?

End-to-end performance impacts

Imagine, if you will, that you're responsible for a cloud-hosted application suite. It includes a half-dozen microservices, each with a dependency on a half-dozen more. On top of that, each parallel resource is deployed behind a load-balancing network gateway responsible for routing requests to the server with the lowest current load.

Now, imagine that each component of that system was written almost entirely in isolation from the rest of the components. Your team of engineers was focused on the design principle of the separation of concerns, and so they thoroughly separated those concerns. Every data store was given its own, limited public API, and no other system was permitted direct access to its underlying database. All of the aggregation APIs are responsible for accessing each system of record to produce domain models relevant to your business use case. There's almost no overlap in responsibility.

Now, we'll generously imagine that your engineers were also disciplined in their testing strategies. Each service included a full suite of unit tests with nearly 100% code coverage. Every unit test was fully isolated with well-defined mocks for each of its dependencies. Your engineers were so disciplined and thorough that those mocks were configured to return every possible permutation of valid and exceptional responses that the service they were mocking might return in the live system. The data contracts for each service in your ecosystem was well-defined, and all changes were well tracked and accounted for by any dependent systems.

With all of this work diligently documented, maintained, and tested, you're finally ready to deploy version 1 of your application. Now, I want you to imagine that the first time someone tries to query your application, the entire ecosystem slows to a crawl, and the response doesn't return for a full 25 seconds.

This may seem like an absurd case, but I have seen almost this exact scenario actually happen with a team of inexperienced cloud architects deploying their first fully distributed microservice-based applications. So, what went wrong in this imagined scenario of ours, and how can we avoid it in practice?

Compounding latency

It should be obvious at this point, but in this particular scenario, the primary culprit for the under-performance was isolation. With each service developed and tested entirely in a silo, there was no way that any engineers could measure the full impact of all of their backend dependencies. By always assuming a best-case scenario of near-zero latency with their upstream dependencies, the developers created unrealistic testing scenarios for their unit tests.

Integration and end-to-end testing are absolutely pivotal to designing a system that can withstand the strains and inconsistencies of a network-based hosting environment. With every new feature or microservice developed, the developers in our not-so-hypothetical development scenario should have deployed their solutions to an environment as close to their production configuration as possible. They should have been identifying bottlenecks in performance as they were implemented and mitigated those impacts.

One of the more challenging aspects of optimizing network software is that your single application is almost never the last stop for a user's interactions with it. Typically, your .NET Core services are being called by a user's browser, or another application service, at the least. Moreover, it's not uncommon for them to also rely on other services accessed through network protocols such as HTTP or TCP. What the developers in this scenario didn't realize, and what you should always be mindful of as you build more and more complicated distributed systems, is that each network hop in your chain of dependencies introduces latency and risk of failure.

With each upstream dependency, your application's latency is increased by the total average latency of your upstream dependency. Likewise, if your upstream dependency has an upstream dependency of its own, *its* latency will be whatever operational latency its own operations create, increased by the total average latency of *its* upstream dependency. This attribute of compounding the latency of networked systems is incredibly important to keep in mind whenever you're writing a network service that depends on another network service. This is why it's common with more experienced cloud architects to see strict enforcement of a three-tiered architectural model for the flow of request resolution.

A three-tiered architecture

To minimize the impact of compounding latency, it's not uncommon to minimize vertical dependencies in an architecture. For our purposes, we can think of horizontal dependencies as being the full suite of upstream dependencies that originate from the same source. Meanwhile, vertical dependencies describe any upstream dependencies that, themselves, have additional upstream dependencies:

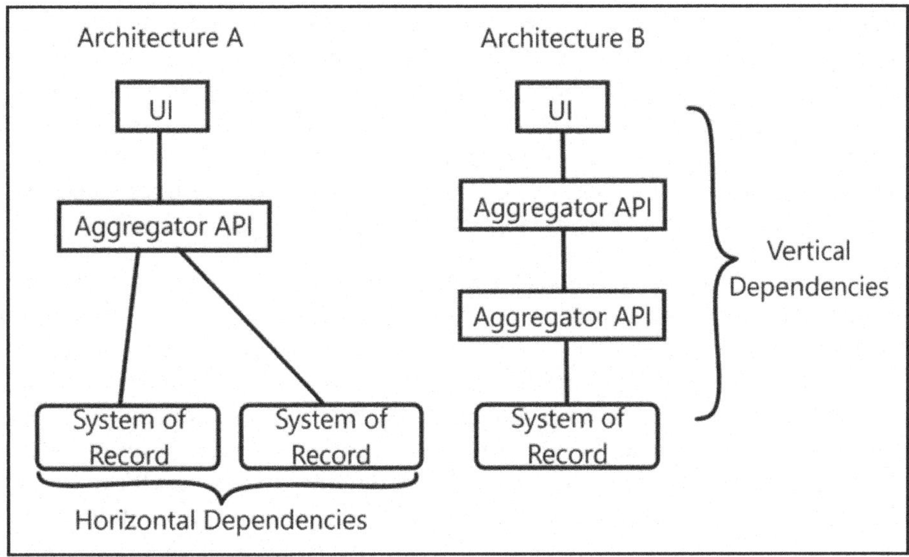

In this diagram, Architecture A has what we would call a three-tiered architecture. That is to say that there are at most three tiers of services encapsulating the entire vertical dependency graph of application interactions. This is an ideal organizational structure for cloud-hosted services. Since most hosting contexts (and, indeed, .NET Core itself) support a broad number of parallel requests being processed, the latency increase of horizontal dependencies within a given system will only ever be as large as the slowest of all of the horizontal dependencies. This is not entirely dissimilar from the benefits gained by parallelizing asynchronous operations, as we discussed in the section *Picking up the pace - multithreading data processing*, section of `Chapter 6`, *Streams, Threads, and Asynchronous Data Transfer*.

In a strict three-tiered architecture, there can only be at most two network hops between a user and any piece of data that is ultimately presented to them. The three tiers are easily conceptualized, and should be familiar to you after our discussion of the MVC design paradigm back in `Chapter 9`, *HTTP in .NET*. The first tier is the user-interaction layer, which just defines any system or mechanism with which an external user is able to access the data or processes contained within your ecosystem. Next is the aggregation tier, or the domain tier. This is where all of the business logic of the parent user-interaction is performed on any data the user is interested in seeing. Last, but not least, is the data tier. In modern cloud systems, these are typically HTTP-based APIs that expose an internal database that serves as the system of record for an enterprise dataset.

When the three-tiered paradigm is well enforced, no system is allowed to interact with a database except through its well-defined APIs. Meanwhile, if a UI needs the business logic defined in multiple aggregation services, it must either access all aggregation-tier systems itself, thus increasing its horizontal dependency map (which is considered acceptable) or a new aggregation service must be written that duplicates the work of the others. No aggregation system should ever call any other aggregation system. Doing so increases the vertical dependencies of that workflow and violates the three-tiered paradigm.

With this in mind, it should be easy to see why one of the most reliable ways to ensure high performance in your applications and implement a manageable monitoring system is by minimizing your vertical dependencies. If we can limit our search for bottlenecks to as few vertical tiers as possible, our ability to identify issues and resolve them can become almost trivial. And these compounding latency interactions only become more relevant as your software gets lower and lower in the network stack. Implementing a series of gateways or firewalls for any traffic moving between your local network and the wider internet will impact all traffic moving through your enterprise. Minimizing the vertical dependencies of such a system would need to be your first priority if you're to have any hope of success at minimizing the latency your gateway will introduce.

Performance under stress

Another common issue that arises when an insufficiently tested system is first deployed to a production environment is the application's inability to handle the load placed upon it. Even a strictly enforced three-tiered architecture can't minimize the impact of multiple responses left unprocessed due to an extremely high network load. The capacity for high volumes of network requests to utterly cripple a network resource is so great that it's actually the basis of an extremely well-known software attack known as a **Dedicated Denial of Service** (**DDoS**) attacks. In these sorts of attack, a distributed network of malware sends out a coordinated barrage of simple network requests to a single host. The volume of incoming requests absolutely destroys the host's ability to continue responding to them, locking up the resource for legitimate users, and even destabilizing the host's OS and physical infrastructure.

While a DDoS attack might be an extreme and relatively rare example, the same effects can be felt on a system with insufficient bandwidth and horizontal scalability for handling a high volume of legitimate simultaneous requests. The challenge here is that it's not always possible to know ahead of time what kind of traffic your system will encounter when it's deployed.

If you're writing an enterprise web service for a specific set of internal business users, you can probably define your operational parameters pretty clearly. Conducting a simple headcount, combined with user interviews to determine how frequently a given user will interact with your system, can give you a high degree of confidence that you know exactly how much traffic you can reasonably anticipate in a given day. However, if your application is being written for a general release to the broader public, then it could be impossible to know beforehand just how many users will hit your service in a given day.

In the sorts of scenarios where you can't reasonably determine your maximum potential network traffic prior to experiencing high volumes of requests, then you will at least want to know roughly how much traffic your application can handle. This is where load testing comes in. With load testing, you should be targeting your best guess at the worst-case scenario for network traffic against your system.

Once you determine that maximum potential load, you execute a series of tests that generate as many interactions as possible with your system, up to and including your pre-determined maximum. To be truly valuable, your tests should be run on an instance of your software that's deployed as near to your production configuration as possible. Over the course of the tests, you should be logging and monitoring response times, and any exception responses. By the time the tests are complete, if they were designed well, you should have a robust set of metrics for how much traffic your current infrastructure can reasonably handle before it fails, and just what it looks like when that failure does finally occur.

Performance monitoring

Each of the performance bottlenecks and risks I've just discussed can be mitigated with good design and robust testing strategies. However, on distributed systems, failure is inevitable. As such, the risk of failure we seek to minimize with the testing and design of your system can never fully be eliminated. However, by using the results of our performance tests as a guide, we can minimize the impact of that inevitable failure. To do this, we'll need to implement a robust system of monitoring the health and availability of our services.

Naive monitoring strategies

It's not uncommon for developers to confuse the concept of application monitoring with that of logging. And this is not an entirely unreasonable mistake. When done properly, a good logging strategy can serve as a relatively low-visibility monitoring system. The problem with that approach, though, is that logs are often incredibly *noisy*.

Overuse of logging

Think for a second of what your initial approach is when catching an exception in your code. I'd be willing to bet that a fair number of you start with a basic **log and throw** approach. You simply log that an error occurred (usually without much else in the way of details or context) and then re-throw the same error, or perhaps throw a new error of a type the calling code might be configured to respond to.

Meanwhile, I'm sure at least a few of my readers have worked in an environment where every change in scope was logged. Enter a new method? Log it. Exit the current method? Log it. Send out a TCP packet to a host? Log it. Receive a TCP packet? Log it. I could keep going, but I'll spare you the frustration.

This log everything approach is surprisingly common in large scale enterprises. What most people don't often consider, though, is that the more information you log, the less useful those logs become. As your log file grows with messages logging trivial changes in scope or context, it becomes increasingly harder to find the logs that are actually important. And, believe me, those are the logs you will be looking for when you find yourself going through a 200,000 line-long log file.

The term for this, if you've never heard of it, is the **signal-to-noise** ratio of your logs. The signal, in this ratio, describes the information that has meaning to you at the current moment. The noise, on the other hand, describes the information surrounding and obscuring your signal, which has no meaning to you at the current moment. Disciplined logging is not about logging everything diligently. Disciplined logging is about always logging only important things. This discipline should be applied to your logs, and any performance or health monitors you use in your software.

Delayed alerting

Another common shortcoming with logging approaches is that the information we want to know about our applications isn't presented to us until it's too late. Typically, with a logging strategy for performance and health monitoring, the logs are written after the failure has occurred. While this is certainly more useful than no alerting system at all (when you're only notified about a system failure by receiving an angry phone call from a user), it's far from ideal.

You should know about a system outage before anyone else can encounter it. However, that kind of visibility is impossible if you're only ever writing to a passive log file, and only when an exception has been thrown. With network software, your application is likely leveraged by a wide array of other resources in such a way that system outages could propagate outward across your network and cripple the businesses your software was written to support. So, how can you get out in front of those inevitable outages and respond before any of your users can feel an impact?

Establishing proactive monitoring

The best way to minimize the impact of an outage to your users is to identify when an outage has occurred, or is likely to occur, proactively. To do so, you'll need to define a policy for establishing health checks against your system. That strategy will have to determine a reasonable frequency for sending requests to your system. The frequency you determine will have to strike a balance between being frequent enough to have a high probability of detecting an outage before the outage could impact a customer, while being infrequent enough to not negatively impact the performance of your system under its heaviest load. On top of that, you'll need to identify all of the possible signals for an unhealthy system so that your monitors are well targeted for the most relevant aspects of your software's performance.

Defining thresholds

When defining a performance monitoring strategy, the first thing you should do is define your application's performance thresholds. These will tell you the traffic load, or resource demands, beyond which your application is likely to experience failure. For instance, if you've done extensive load testing on your application, you will likely have a deep pool of metrics about how much traffic your application server can handle. By using network tracing, which will provide a record of every request against a listening network application, you can identify when your traffic is experiencing a spike, sending alerts before the failure threshold is reached.

Additionally, if you have upstream dependencies, you should take note of their performance over time, identifying any instance in which your dependencies are the source of your system failures. You should seek to leverage the same strategy of identifying signals in the content or latency of your dependency responses that are likely to result in a system failure for your user. Once you have that information, you are well positioned to respond to it.

Proactive health checks

Once you get to know the potential points or conditions of failure are within your system, the robust monitoring strategy tests those points and conditions frequently. Services that are designed to actively monitor your system are commonly called **watchdogs**. Most cloud-hosting orchestrators or CI/CD software will allow you to configure a health-check access point into your software so that they can identify when an application has crashed using their own watchdog implementations. If your hosting solution provides these features, such as the Azure health verification tool, then you should leverage them to their fullest. If your host doesn't provide a reliable, regularly scheduled (or configurable schedule) health-check mechanism, then I would strongly advise you to roll your own. The impact on your development process is minimal, but the benefits are incredible.

We'll look at this in our sample code in just a moment, but the typical pattern for this kind of proactive health and performance monitoring is to expose an endpoint that can be pinged by your hosting provider. That endpoint will then run a series of self-diagnostic checks against key potential points of failure, and return with either a success (healthy application, no likely failures imminent) or a failure (a system is down, or will soon be taken down).

Active messaging and active recovery

A proactive health monitoring system requires a proactive response. For any error state detected by your health-monitoring system, you'll want to define a reasonable approach for responding to it. For instance, if your network traffic is spiking, a proactive approach may be configuring your health check system to automatically provision an additional parallel app server to respond to the additional request load. Meanwhile, if your health-check indicates that an upstream dependency has come offline, the active recovery system may attempt to restart the app server hosting that dependency in an effort to resolve the issue.

Regardless of what your system does to respond (though it should define at least some kind of response to a failure), it should absolutely notify any engineers who are working on the application. Specifically, it should actively notify engineers. While the event should certainly be logged to whatever audit system you use to track the reliability of your application, remember that **a log is not an alert**. Logs are inherently passive. For an engineer responsible for a system to learn that it's failed from a logged message, that engineer who's has to take it upon themself to seek out and check the logs. Meanwhile, with an active messaging response, your monitoring platform can be configured to take the contact information of any engineers that should know about outages. Then, when an outage has occurred, the active monitor can push out notifications to the contact information for every engineer that it is configured to notify.

Performance and health monitoring in C#

So, we should have a pretty clear understanding of what a robust and resilient performance and health-monitoring system looks like. It should be configured to respond to well-defined thresholds, so that potential outages can be spotted and mitigated before they occur. It should actively check the state of the application instead of passively waiting for user interactions to trigger a system failure. Finally, it should proactively respond to a failure once it has been identified, notifying anyone who might respond to it, and taking steps to bring the system back to a healthy state. So, what does this look like in .NET Core?

An unstable distributed architecture

To demonstrate how we can use performance monitoring to remain aware of the health of an unstable system, we'll first have to build an unstable system. For this example, we'll be using a three-tiered architecture, with PostMan (or Insomnia) as our interaction tier, and then two different web APIs to simulate our aggregation tier and our data tier. First, we'll create our aggregation service:

```
dotnet new webapi -n AggregatorDemo
```

We'll be looking at this later, since this aggregator will be the application whose performance we monitor. For now, though, we'll need to define an upstream dependency. This will be designed to have a negative impact on our aggregation service's performance over time:

```
dotnet new webapi -n DataAccessDemo
```

We'll be focusing on the `DataAccessDemo` application to begin with. Here, our objective will be to create a destabilized system that contains a mechanism for its own recovery. We'll use this in our Aggregator application, when poor performance is detected, to proactively recover from degrading system performance. To that end, our `DataAccessDemo` application will be relatively straightforward. We'll provide two endpoints: one will be used as an upstream dependency for our aggregator application, and one will be used to recover from degrading performance.

In practice, it's not uncommon to provide an endpoint that serves as a performance management access-point to a live application. It might reinitialize a cache, force garbage collection, or dispose of any lingering threads in its thread pool. In our case, we'll simply reset a counter to restabilize our application's performance. That counter will then be used by our dependency endpoint to enforce an ever-increasing latency in the application.

To initiate this, we'll first define our listening ports to avoid a collision with our aggregator API:

```
public static IWebHostBuilder CreateWebHostBuilder(string[] args) =>
    WebHost.CreateDefaultBuilder(args)
        .UseUrls("https://[::]:33333")
        .UseStartup<Startup>();
```

Now, we'll define a static class to hold on to our latency counter. This will be designed so that every time it's accessed, it increases the latency for the next call. Additionally, to facilitate our recovery endpoint, we'll provide a mechanism for resetting the counter to its initial state, as follows:

```
public static class Latency {
    private static int initialLatency = 1;
    private static int counter = 1;

    public static int GetLatency() {
        //milliseconds of latency. increase by .5 second per request
        return counter++ * 500;
    }

    public static void ResetLatency() {
        counter = initialLatency;
    }
}
```

Finally, from within our controller, we'll set a delay to our dependency request, after which we'll return an arbitrary value. Then, we'll expose a reset endpoint to stabilize our application, as follows:

```
[Route("api/[controller]")]
[ApiController]
public class DependencyController : ControllerBase {
    [HttpGet("new-data")]
    public ActionResult<string> GetDependentValue() {
        Thread.Sleep(Latency.GetLatency());
        return $"requested data: {new Random().Next() }";
    }
    [HttpGet("reset")]
    public ActionResult<string> Reset() {
        Latency.ResetLatency();
        return "success";
    }
}
```

This controller signature will define the vertical dependency of our aggregator API. So, Now, let's look at how we'll monitor the degrading performance of this application over time.

Performance-monitoring middleware

To monitor the health of specific aspects of our application, we'll be creating an instance of the `IHealthCheck` **middleware**. This middleware is used to define the operations that are necessary for determining the relative health of your system. For our purposes, we'll want to define a health-check that confirms that the response time for our dependent data service is below two seconds. Once that threshold has been hit, we'll consider the system to be degraded. This will allow our watchdog to notify us that a restart may be necessary. However, if the service response time increases to five seconds, we'll consider it unhealthy, notifying our watchdog to initiate a reset.

This instance of the `IHealthCheck` middleware will be registered by our system in startup, when we add health-checks to our application. And, as with all things in .NET Core, adding a health-check is as easy as registering a service and configuring your app. So, first, within your `ConfigureServices(IServicesCollection services)` method, simply add the following line of code to set up all of the supporting classes and extensions that are necessary for using health checks:

```
services.AddHealthChecks();
```

Then, within your Configure(IApplicationBuilder app, IHostingEnvironment env) method, add the following code:

```
app.UseHealthChecks("/health");
```

This simple registration pattern sets your application up to provide the results of all configured health-check middleware whenever a user sends a request to the path specified in UseHealthChecks(<path>). Because we haven't specified any specific system checks in our middleware, this endpoint will return nothing of interest. To test it, simply navigate to your application's root host, and append the /health path. You should see the following output:

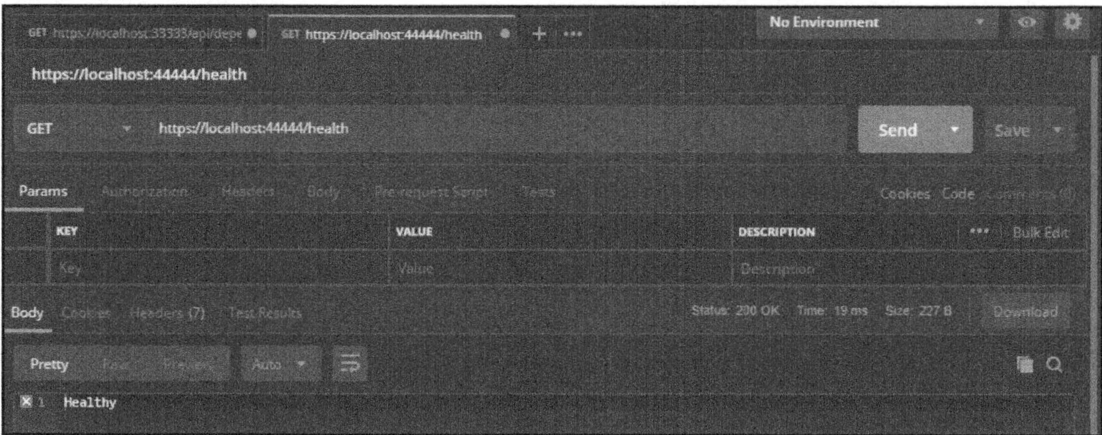

This confirms that our application is responding to health-checks. So, now, we need to define the specific check we want to use when validating the health of our system by defining our middleware. We'll start by creating an implementation for the IHealthCheck interface, which we'll call DependencyHealthCheck for simplicity's sake. This class will contain the definitions for our response thresholds, measured in milliseconds, as shown in the following code:

```
public class DependencyHealthCheck : IHealthCheck {
    private readonly int DEGRADING_THRESHOLD = 2000;
    private readonly int UNHEALTHY_THRESHOLD = 5000;
```

Now, we'll need to implement the public CheckHealthAsync() method to satisfy the requirements of the IHealthCheck interface. For this method, we'll be sending a request to our upstream dependency, and tracking the time it takes to resolve it using the Stopwatch class from the System.Diagnostics namespace.

The signature for the `CheckHealthAsync()` method accepts a `HealthCheckContext` instance that will provide our class with registration information, as well as a cancellation token. We'll be ignoring those, but they are still required to satisfy the interface signature. Then, we'll be creating our `HttpClient` instance (using the `HttpClientFactory` we discussed in `Chapter 9`, *HTTP in .NET*) and building a request to the endpoint whose stability we want to validate. So, the first part of our `CheckHealthAsync()` method should look like this:

```
public async Task<HealthCheckResult> CheckHealthAsync(
    HealthCheckContext context,
    CancellationToken token = default(CancellationToken)
) {
    var httpClient = HttpClientFactory.Create();
    httpClient.BaseAddress = new Uri("https://localhost:33333");
    var request = new HttpRequestMessage(HttpMethod.Get,
"/api/dependency/new-data");
```

At this point, we'll want to set up our stopwatch to track how long a request takes so that we can confirm whether it falls beneath our designated thresholds:

```
Stopwatch sw = Stopwatch.StartNew();
var response = await httpClient.SendAsync(request);
sw.Stop();
var responseTime = sw.ElapsedMilliseconds;
```

And, finally, we'll check the value of the response time against our thresholds, returning an instance of the `HealthCheckResult` according to the stability of our external dependency, as follows:

```
if (responseTime < DEGRADING_THRESHOLD) {
    return HealthCheckResult.Healthy("The dependent system is performing
within acceptable parameters");
} else if (responseTime < UNHEALTHY_THRESHOLD) {
    return HealthCheckResult.Degraded("The dependent system is degrading
and likely to fail soon");
} else {
    return HealthCheckResult.Unhealthy("The dependent system is
unacceptably degraded. Restart.");
}
```

This completes our implementation of the `IHealthCheck` middleware, so now all that's left is to register it with our application services as a health-check. To do so, simply call the `AddCheck()` method of the `IHealthChecksBuilder` class that's returned by the `AddHealthChecks()` method in your `Startup.cs` file. This method takes a name, and an explicit instance of your `IHealthCheck` middleware implementation.

Adding this, your `Startup.cs` file should have the following code:

```
services.AddHealthChecks()
    .AddCheck("DataDependencyCheck", new DependencyHealthCheck());
```

And, with that, we've got a custom health check that will notify any monitors of instability in our system caused by failure of an upstream dependency! To confirm that it's returning the appropriate response, simply ping your `/health` endpoint 5 to 10 times to increase the latency counter on your dependency service, and watch as the health status changes past the two- and five-second threshold.

Here, you can see that the response from my service comes back as `Degraded` when the response time has broken the two-second threshold:

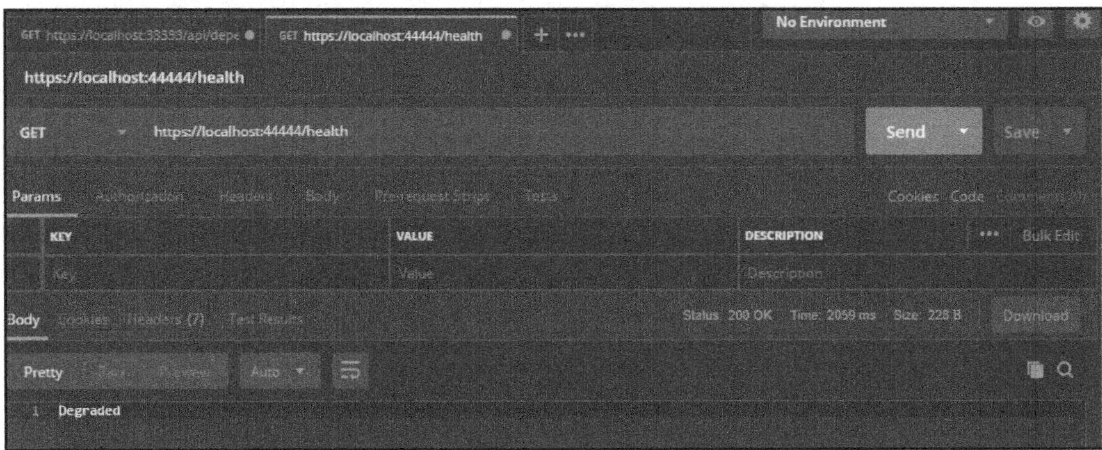

And after only a few more requests, the response decays to `Unhealthy`:

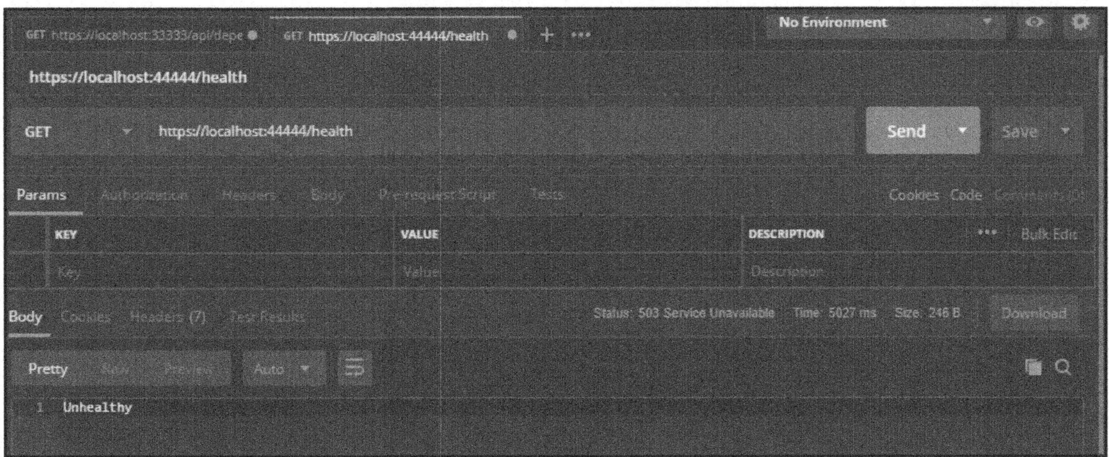

So, now you've seen how, with only a few lines of code, you can implement an extensible system for monitoring your complete system health.

Implementing a watchdog

The final piece of our proactive monitoring solution is to implement a watchdog service of our own. Since we've configured an external hook for resetting the performance of our unstable API, we'll want to define a proactive recovery mechanism that takes advantage of it. So, for this service, we'll set up a loop that pings the `/health` endpoint of our aggregator API at regular intervals, and then resets the data dependency API whenever the system comes back as `Degraded` or `Unhealthy`. Since this is a fairly trivial exercise in this case, we can keep our watchdog simple. We'll start with a console app, created with our CLI:

```
dotnet new console -n WatchdogDemo
```

We'll only be adding a few lines to our project. First, we'll set up our `HttpClient` instance. Since the scope of our application never leaves the `Main()` method, we can safely create a private, static, single instance of the `HttpClient` class without needing to rely on an `HttpClientFactory` to manage multiple instances of our clients and prevent thread starvation. We'll also assign our `Healthy` status code to a `private readonly` variable:

```
public class Program {
    private static readonly HttpClient client = new HttpClient();
    private static readonly string HEALTHY_STATUS = "Healthy";
```

Once that's in place, our `Main()` method amounts to a dozen lines of relatively trivial code. First, we create an infinite loop so that our service runs until explicitly stopped. Then, we send a request to get the health status response from our aggregator API:

```
static async Task Main(string[] args) {
  while(true) {
    var healthRequest = new HttpRequestMessage(HttpMethod.Get,
"https://localhost:44444/health");
    var healthResponse = await client.SendAsync(healthRequest);
    var healthStatus = await healthResponse.Content.ReadAsStringAsync();
```

Once we've got the response back, we can confirm that it's come back healthy. If it hasn't, we simply send another request to the `/reset` endpoint of our data service. Meanwhile, if it has come back healthy, we can simply log the request and continue processing:

```
if (healthStatus != HEALTHY_STATUS) {
  Console.WriteLine($"{ DateTime.Now.ToLocalTime().ToLongTimeString()} :
Unhealthy API. Restarting Dependency");
  var resetRequest = new HttpRequestMessage(HttpMethod.Get,
"https://localhost:33333/api/dependency/reset");
  var resetResponse = await client.SendAsync(resetRequest);
} else {
  Console.WriteLine($"{DateTime.Now.ToLocalTime().ToLongTimeString()} :
Healthy API");
}
Thread.Sleep(15000);
```

Note that, for this example, I've determined that our health-check intervals should be 15 seconds. In our case, I've chosen this value mostly at random. However, as you configure or implement watchdog solutions in your own applications, you would do well to consider the impact of too-frequent or too-infrequent intervals, and configure your system accordingly. With all three of our applications up and running, you can see here that my watchdog system is performing according to expectations, resetting my data service whenever the response times have become unacceptably slow:

```
C:\Program Files\dotnet\dotnet.exe
1:31:50 AM :  Healthy API
1:32:07 AM : Unhealthy API. Restarting Dependency
1:32:22 AM :  Healthy API
1:32:38 AM :  Healthy API
1:32:55 AM :  Healthy API
1:33:12 AM : Unhealthy API. Restarting Dependency
1:33:27 AM :  Healthy API
1:33:43 AM :  Healthy API
1:34:00 AM :  Healthy API
```

And, with that, our proactive monitoring system is complete. While we had to manufacture instability in this sample code, the strategies we devised to monitor and mitigate that instability will scale with any project you might have to write in the future.

Summary

This chapter opened up with an unfortunately common example of a naively implemented distributed architecture. Using that as a touchstone, we considered the impact that architectural design decisions can have on an application's performance. We learned about vertical dependencies in our distributed architectures, and how we can mitigate their impact with a strictly-adhered-to three-tiered design.

Next, we looked at how bad logging practices can make it untenable to use logging as a performance monitoring solution. We discussed the concept of a logging solution's signal-to-noise ratio, and we examined the practices we should all apply to our own logging strategies to maximize the effectiveness of our logs.

Once we fully examined why logging constitutes an insufficient monitoring strategy, we dove into the attributes of a truly robust approach. We saw that a well-designed monitoring strategy should take advantage of the various unit and load tests you've performed, and the information they've provided. We learned that a robust strategy involves active monitoring, and should seek to identify problems systematically before a user ever encounters an issue. Finally, we saw how such a solution could, and should, take a proactive approach to try to resolve any health or performance issues, and notify the relevant engineers of the issues.

Last, but not least, we looked at precisely how to implement just such a monitoring strategy in .NET Core. Implementing our own monitoring middleware in an ASP.NET Core application, we saw the power and flexibility of the built-in monitoring solutions available from the framework. With this piece of the architectural puzzle in place, we're ready to start exploring some more advanced subjects. With that in mind, we'll use the next chapter to explore how we might devise our own application layer protocol using the concept of pluggable protocols in .NET Core.

Questions

1. What is the difference between horizontal dependencies and vertical dependencies? How do they impact performance?
2. What is a three-tiered architecture?
3. What is a signal-to-noise ration? Why is it important in logging?
4. What are some of the reasons logging is insufficient for performance monitoring?
5. What are the key attributes of a robust monitoring strategy?
6. What is load testing? What information can it provide?
7. What does it mean to have a disciplined logging strategy?

Further reading

For an additional resource on leveraging health checks and performance monitoring in your ASP.NET Core applications, I'd recommend *Learning ASP.NET Core 2.0* by Jason de Oliveira and Michel Bruchet, and I particular, the chapter entitled *Managing and Supervising ASP.NET Core 2.0 Applications*. It's an exceptionally good read and will provide a wealth of skills that are laterally transferable to any number of different contexts. It can be found from Packt, here: `https://www.packtpub.com/application-development/learning-aspnet-core-20`.

Additionally, if you'd like to continue down the path of learning architectural design, with a focus on microservices-based ecosystems, I'd recommend *Enterprise Application Architecture with .NET Core* by Ganesan Senthilvel, Ovais Mehboob Ahmed Khan, and Habib Ahmed Qureshi. The depth with which they cover a multi-layered architecture in a cloud environment is illuminating. It can be found, as always, through Packt: `https://www.packtpub.com/application-development/enterprise-application-architecture-net-core`.

5

Section 5: Advanced Subjects

In this brief final part of the book, we'll be exploring more advanced topics, and consider how to move past the network programming features .NET Core provides directly out of the box. In the first chapter, we'll look at how to extend functionality and expected behavior with Microsoft's *Pluggable Protocols* pattern. Next, we'll think about how to examine the traffic over our networks, and determine its performance and stability. Finally, we'll look at implementing an SSH client and remote access between machines.

The following chapters will be covered in this section:

`Chapter 17`, *Pluggable Protocols in .NET Core*

`Chapter 18`, *Network Analysis and Packet Inspection*

`Chapter 19`, *Remote Logins and SSH*

17
Pluggable Protocols in .NET Core

In the previous chapters, we covered a wide breadth of topics related to general network programming concepts, challenges, and patterns. With this chapter, we'll see how to work on that knowledge to define our own application layer protocols within .NET Core. We'll learn about the concept of a **pluggable protocol**. We'll see how .NET Core gives you the ability to extend the `WebRequest` class to define your own standards and expectations for network interactions. We'll look at how to register your new protocol for use by the `WebRequest` factory methods. Finally, we'll discuss the advantages of doing so, and when you should consider using it.

The following topics will be covered in this chapter:

- Understanding pluggable protocols
- How to implement a sub-class of the `WebRequest` class from the `System.Net` namespace
- The support infrastructure, which allows custom communication protocols to be leveraged in .NET Core

Technical requirements

To follow along with the code samples in this chapter, or open them up and modify them for your own purposes, you'll need an IDE or code editor (Visual Studio or Visual Studio Code, of course) as well as the source code, which can be found here: `https://github.com/PacktPublishing/Hands-On-Network-Programming-with-C-and-.NET-Core/tree/master/Chapter 17`.

Additionally, we'll continue to take advantage of our preferred REST client, so be ready with either PostMan (`https://www.getpostman.com/downloads/`) or the Insomnia REST client `(https://insomnia.rest/)`.

Understanding pluggable protocols

To understand how best to leverage pluggable protocols, and when they might be valuable in your software, we first have to understand what they are. We need to know the problems they were designed to solve and how they seek to solve them. So, we'll start with a simple definition of what pluggable protocols are, and then look at why we might want to use them.

What exactly is a pluggable protocol?

A **pluggable protocol** is an implementation of a custom, application-layer communication protocol, written to be integrated with the .NET Core `WebRequest` model for processing network interactions. Or, put more simply, it's a how .NET Core supports non-standard communication protocols. That's it.

In `Chapter 5`, *Generating Network Requests with C#*, we saw how powerful the simple request/response pattern can be for facilitating source-agnostic network communications in our app. Moreover, we saw how well the .NET Core framework reduces the complexity of those kinds of interactions by supporting out-of-the-box `WebRequest` sub-classes to support the most common application-layer protocols in our source code. However, where the framework itself provides us with out-of-the-box implementations of common protocols, the pluggable protocols implementation pattern gives us an entry point through which we can extend that system for less-common, or custom, protocols. It gives us the ability to define our own implementations and configure them to be used just as easily and reliably as the framework classes.

Why use pluggable protocols?

Let's imagine for a second that you want to streamline communication between two critical resources in your software ecosystem. To facilitate this, you've devised a highly optimized packet structure and interaction mechanism. The headers are only exactly as large as is necessary to communicate details about the proprietary application packets. Let's also assume that this protocol uses a brief negotiation phase that takes place between hosts to facilitate data transfer.

Since this is proprietary, you could just hand-roll your interactions between the two hosts in each of their respective applications. However, this approach doesn't exactly scale with the potential growth of users of your protocol. What if another team decides that they also want to leverage your optimized protocol? You'd be responsible for communicating the specific details of your program's interactions with them, introducing a time and productivity cost to anyone involved in the knowledge transfer process.

Alternatively, how durable would such an approach be against turnover on your own teams? If you lose original members of your team that had intimate knowledge of your protocol's design and use, you'll need to on-board new team members to fill the gaps. Having to code a proprietary interaction mechanism between two network hosts increases the time to on-board new members.

What if, instead of requiring the use of bespoke interaction mechanisms for any consumers of your protocol, you could encapsulate it behind a pattern with which new users are already familiar? With pluggable protocols, you can do exactly that. The only prerequisite to leveraging the conventions and simplicity of the `WebRequest` and `WebResponse` classes is that the interactions of your protocol can be reduced, at their most basic conceptual level, to the well-understood request/response pattern.

By encompassing the operations of our custom protocol behind the conventions of the `WebRequest` and `WebResponse` classes, we can mitigate all of the challenges introduced by a proprietary protocol. New teams no longer have to be concerned with the intricacies of your header structure, or figure out the handshake that's necessary to initiate a data transfer. You can simply implement those components within your custom `WebRequest` subclass, and expose the resulting data stream after you've successfully acquired a response. Additionally, on-boarding new team members requires no additional overhead in learning the intricacies of your protocol.

Defining a pluggable protocol

While it may be obvious what benefits you'll reap by encapsulating custom communication protocols, behind the `WebRequest` and `WebResponse` classes, you might be surprised to learn that it's also a fairly simple goal to achieve. The biggest challenge you'll face is simply learning the methods and properties you'll need to override or implement as you create your subclass. But, at a high level, creating a pluggable protocol is fairly straightforward. Let's look at the steps you'll need to follow, and then we'll take those steps in the next section as we implement our own pluggable protocol.

Defining your schema

As I mentioned earlier in this section, pluggable protocols represent a custom application-layer protocol for web interactions. Requests that are sent between two applications over this protocol will need to be handled in a unique way. To distinguish requests that are transmitted over your custom protocol from other, more common protocols, you'll need to define the schema for it.

As you may remember from `Chapter 2`, *DNS and Resource Location*, the schema component of a URL is how routers and web hosts determine how to attempt to parse headers of request packets. Using the `http` or `https` schemas indicates to the recipient host that the message details can be derived by parsing the incoming byte stream according to the partitioning and delineating standards of an HTTP header. So, a host receiving a request with the schema specified as `http://` in the request URI will expect the first bytes of the incoming stream to specify the HTTP verb, the specific resource path, and the version, followed by a line-terminal character, like so:

```
GET /some/resource HTTP/1.1
```

However, suppose your protocol is designed to do away with those HTTP-specific message details. Let's say you're designing a message queue that accepts an arbitrary number of records with fields of a single fixed length. Now, let's say that the request messages for your protocol are formatted with a header composed of pipe-delimited values noting various details about the structure of the packet, such as the 0-indexed packet length, the number of optional details specified in the headers, and the byte-size of each field in the records of your message, so that your message header looks like this:

```
512|1|32
```

If you sent a message using the `http://` schema and its first line of incoming bytes contained those details, the consuming application would simply respond with a `401 - Bad Request` status. It wouldn't be able to parse the information in the header because it wouldn't have the proper context for doing so. That's what a schema provides to remote hosts: the initial context for parsing its messages. To that end, it's important that you define a schema that you're certain will be unique from other custom protocols or schemas (and certainly distinct from any standardized protocols, such as HTTP or FTP). Your schema will need to be uniquely identifiable so that there's no failure to parse your messages on any hosts that leverage it.

Implementing your protocol interactions

As I've alluded to at least a few times in this section, your first task for implementing your protocol as a pluggable protocol is to encapsulate its interactions into the most basic request/response pattern. You'll need to do this inside a class that defines itself as a sub-class of the `WebRequest` base class. Within this sub-class, your first order of business will be to override the `GetResponse()` and `GetResponseAsync()` methods.

These methods are where you'll be defining any protocol-specific interactions for your custom `WebRequest`, including defining the transport layer over which your messages will be sent, and any protocol header parsing that should happen prior to your clients receiving the response stream. When you intend to create a sub-class of the `WebRequest` object, writing your own implementations of these classes is the minimum required step you'll need to take in order to write a conventional pluggable protocol.

If your protocol specification has any additional features or aspects that you need to account for, such as authentication mechanisms, or response caching, you'll need to override those aspects of the `WebRequest` class as well. Additionally, anything that isn't captured by the public interface of the `WebRequest` class that is specific to your protocol will need to be exposed through some methods or properties that are specific to your protocol.

Registering your schema

Now that you understand how we can distinguish incoming messages from our protocol from those of other application-layer protocols, you'll need to notify your application context to do so. Once you've defined your schema, you can register a handler with the `WebRequest` class.

You might remember from `Chapter 5`, *Generating Network Requests in C#*, in the *The Sub-Classes of WebRequest* section, I mentioned that the `WebRequest` create method will provide default sub-class implementations for a request based on its specified schema. So, if you were to call `WebRequest.Create("http://somedomain.com")`, the `WebRequest` instance returned to you would be an instance of the `HttpWebRequest` type (though, as we already saw in that section, and throughout all of `Chapter 9`, *HTTP in .NET*, the `HttpWebRequest` class should be considered obsolete at this point).

By registering our custom sub-class of the `WebRequest` class, and specifying the schema for which it should be used, we can get that same behavior. Users wouldn't need to create a specific instance of our class to use it; they could just call `WebRequest.Create(<url>)` and pass in a URL whose schema segment identifies our protocol. At that point, the `WebRequest` class simply returns an instance of whatever class we've specified to handle that schema.

Now that we know what it takes to implement and incorporate a pluggable protocol in our .NET Core apps, it's time to see it in action.

Building our custom subclasses

The first thing we'll want to do is define the interaction mechanisms for our custom protocol. These interactions will be how we distinguish our protocol from alternative application-layer protocols. You might recall when I said in `Chapter 10`, *FTP and SMTP*, that each application-layer protocol is designed to optimize a specific business-layer application task. This principle should hold true with any custom protocols you've implemented as well. To that end, we'll define our protocol to meet a very specific business need. Of course, since this is still entirely for demonstration purposes, we won't concern ourselves with whether or not it's the most optimum design for our business need, but only that it is well-defined in its interactions. Once we have that in place, we can implement that specification within our `WebRequest` sub-class.

Defining our protocol

For the demonstrations in this chapter, we'll be using a new protocol optimized for sending a list of records to a database server. Because we can call our protocol whatever we want, and I find it amusing to do so, we'll call it the **DwayneTheRockJohnson** protocol, or just the **Rock** protocol for short, and it will use `dtrj://` as its schema specification in request URIs.

Request messages in our protocol will be sent, targeting a specific table in a database, and will have a body consisting of an arbitrary number of updates to make to that table. We'll define three verbs for requests in our protocol: DELETE, INSERT, and UPDATE. A request message that's sent with any given verb can only perform the specified update on the table, and the records in the body will consist of an array of pipe-delimited fields. For our purposes, our message header will consist of pipe-delimited fields in the following format:

- **VERB**: A 2-bit verb indicator: `00 = DELETE`, `01 = INSERT`, `10 = UPDATE.`
- **SIZE**: A 30-bit field indicating the total size of the message, including all header values, in bytes (providing for a maximum size of 134 MB messages).
- **FIELDS**: A 28-byte field indicating how many fields are in each record, allowing for a maximum field count greater than could ever possible be reached by any existing database system. We're only choosing that for a consistent alignment of our headers against the typical word length of 16 bits.
- **CHECKSUM**: A 32-byte secure hash of the message body, to prevent tampering.

After this 64-byte header, the rest of the body is presumed to be a sequence of pipe-delimited records, which our target hosts will be able to parse based on the **FIELDS** value of the header, and the convention of the pipe-delimiter. Taken together, the structure of our Rock message will look like this:

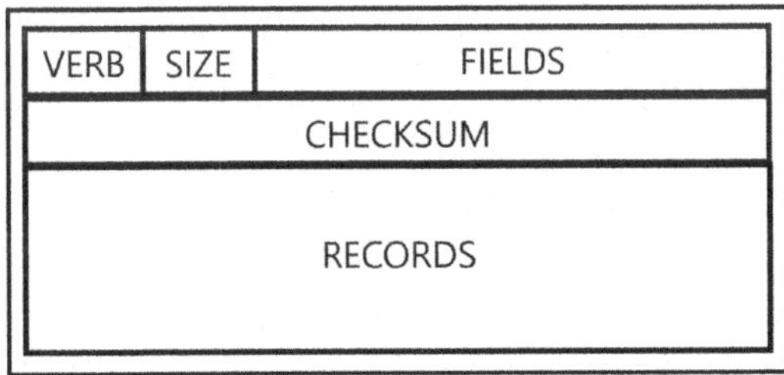

When a server has successfully received a message, its response, assuming everything was processed accordingly, will include the following headers:

- **STATUS**: A 2-bit message indicating the success of the update attempt against the data source: `00 = SUCCESS`, `01 = PARTIAL SUCCESS`, and `10 = FAILURE`
- **TIMESTAMP**: A 14-bit timestamp indicating when the updates were successfully committed to the database
- **SIZE**: A 16-bit field indicating the size of the message included, along with the rest of the response

This 32-bit header will be followed by any status message that's included along with the status code provided in the header, which may include information about which records were successfully updated, or why some or all records failed to update. With this, our response will look like this:

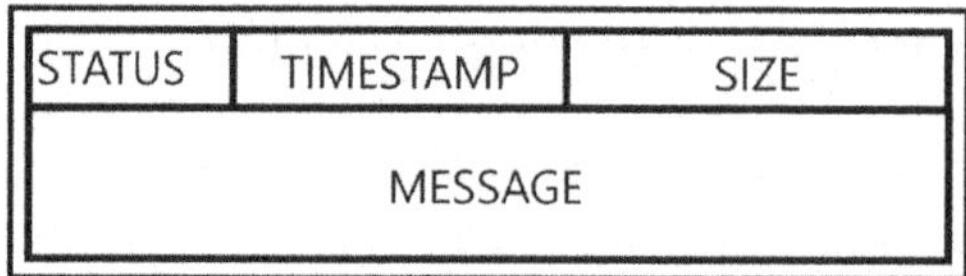

There would obviously be a lot more thought to defining a communication protocol than what we've put forth here, but this will be sufficient for the purposes of learning how to implement them in our .NET Core projects. So, now that we know what our schema definition will look like, and how our protocols should be composed and parsed, let's get to work defining our `WebRequest` sub-class.

Implementing our protocol

Our first order of business will be creating a `WebRequest` subclass with a constructor that accepts a `URI` instance, or a simple URI string as its input. This is what's used by the `WebRequest.Create()` method to instantiate our specific class whenever it is given a URI with our schema. We'll be implementing this class in a simple console app, so first create your application:

```
dotnet new console -n CustomProtocolDemo
```

Next, create a class for our `WebRequest` subclass, and define its constructors. For this example, I'll be creating a `RockWebRequest` class, with a constructor being used to set the `URI` instance that's used when sending our request out to the target host:

```
public class RockWebRequest : WebRequest {
    public override Uri RequestUri { get; }
    ...

    public RockWebRequest(Uri uri) {
        RequestUri = uri;
    }
```

Here, it's important to note that a `WebRequest` instance (or an instance of any of its subclasses) is intended to only ever be used once. Subsequent requests require additional instances of the class. This is why the `RequestUri` field (which is derived from the parent class, but must be implemented by our subclass to be used) is read-only and only ever written to upon initialization of a new instance. It won't, and shouldn't, change after the request is created.

The next thing we'll need to do is give users of our `WebRequest` class a mechanism by which they can define the records being sent over, as well as the message verb to be used on those records. This will give our users an opportunity to configure their message accordingly, prior to requesting a response. To do this, we'll define a couple of properties for our header and for our request body. We could use the `Method` property that is derived from the `WebRequest` class to define our message verb, but I'd prefer to enforce things a little more strictly in our component. We'll create a new property, whose type will be an `enum` that defines our three possible verbs. Using an `enum` will also give us the benefit of mapping the user-provided value to its underlying 2-bit representation:

```
public enum RockVerb {
    Delete = 0b00000000000000000000000000000000,
    Insert = 0b01000000000000000000000000000000,
    Update = 0b10000000000000000000000000000000
}
```

Here, we're representing our 2-bit codes as the most significant bits of a 32-bit integer value to make it especially easy to perform a bit-wise `OR` operation with our `size` header value.

Next, we'll define the corresponding property on our `RockWebRequest`. Additionally, we'll define an `IEnumerable` for the records that will be sent in any given request, with an `int` to store the number of fields in each record. Since we want our protocol to handle arbitrary record definitions, but we don't want to spend too much time writing sufficient serialization code and generic object parsers, we'll just define our records to be strings, and leave it to a consumer to generate a pipe-delimited format for their record list:

```
public RockVerb Verb { get; set; } = RockVerb.Update;
public IEnumerable<string> Records { get; set; }
public long Fields { get;set; }
```

Here, we'll default our `Verb` to `Insert`. For the purposes of this demonstration, we'll say that `Update` operations will only work if and only if there isn't an existing record with same the key as the record to be inserted. With this rule in place, `Insert` is the only operation that is safe to perform, since it can't ever incidentally override existing data. Given that, it will suit us well for our default `Verb` value. Once this is in place, however, we're ready to implement our `GetResponse()` and `GetResponseAsync()` methods. Each other property of our header can be derived without input from the user, so we'll do so in these methods.

Implementing the request pipeline

The next, and final, step to implement our pluggable protocol is to define the request and response behavior for our messages. We'll start by overriding the synchronous `GetResponse()` method. This method will be responsible for building a byte stream with the appropriate values for our header specification, and submitting over the transport protocol of our choice. For this demo, we'll be using TCP, since we've already seen how to do so in `Chapter 11`, *The Transport Layer – TCP, UDP, and Multicasting*.

Always put as much consideration and thought as you can into deciding what transport-layer protocol you'll use to support any custom application layer protocols you may write. The performance and specific use cases of any transport layer protocol can have as much of an impact on the performance of your custom protocol as any other aspect of your design. Always try to use the right tool for the job at hand.

As with all of our demonstrations, we'll be assuming that consumers of our software always use it appropriately, and so we'll forego any sort of pre-request validations. We'll just assume that we have some records configured for our message body, and that our verb has been defined appropriately.

At this point, it would serve us well to examine the high-level workflow of building and sending a message according to our protocol. Since we're assuming that we have records available prior to attempting to send a request (and that our server will assume the responsibility of validating our data), we'll build out our message body by concatenating each record (which our users have already conveniently serialized into pipe-delimited strings of all fields in each record), and separate each record with a pipe. Next, we'll convert the concatenated string into a byte array. From that, we'll build our checksum hash, as well as define the size of our message. Then, we'll build a completed byte array with our headers and message body, and write them to a `TcpClient` stream targeting the designated host URI.

Putting that into action, we'll start by generating our message byte array:

```
public override WebResponse GetResponse() {
    var messageString = ConcatenateRecords();
    var message = Encoding.ASCII.GetBytes(messageString);
```

In the following code, the actual concatenation happens in a separate, private method, to aid the readability of our code:

```
private string ConcatenateRecords() {
    StringBuilder messageBuilder = new StringBuilder();
    foreach (var record in Records) {
        if (messageBuilder.ToString().Length > 0) {
            messageBuilder.Append(Environment.NewLine);
        }
        messageBuilder.Append(record);
    }
    return messageBuilder.ToString();
}
```

As you can see, we're using the same pipe delimiter between records that we're using to separate fields in a record. We have the freedom to do this because our `fields` header notifies the server of how many individual fields should be parsed per-record. Using the same delimiter for records that we're using for fields saves the server from having to look for an exceptional case for the end of a record. It can simply look for the next instance of the delimiter character and proceed accordingly, starting a new record when the field count has been reached for the previous one.

Next, we'll compute our checksum based on our requests' body content. If you were truly defining your own protocol for a business purpose, you would likely allow clients to specify hashing algorithms from among those they have implementations for. However, for our purposes, we'll just say it's always going to be computed using SHA-256. Once we've computed our hash, we can set our `VERB` bits based on the value provided by the client. Next, we'll determine the size of our packet (the 64 byte header, plus the length of our message byte array), and write all of our bytes to a binary stream. In our `GetResponse()` method, that will simply read as follows:

```
var byteList = new List<byte>();

var checksum = SHA256.Create().ComputeHash(message);

byteList.AddRange(GetHeaderBytes(message.Length));
byteList.AddRange(checksum);
byteList.AddRange(message);
```

The `GetHeaderBytes(message.Length)` method is used to convert the binary value of our `Verb`, the given message size, and the `Fields` property, into the 32-byte header that precedes the 32 byte checksum. The method is relatively straightforward and merely applies some bit-manipulation of the appropriate values, as shown here:

```
private IEnumerable<byte> GetHeaderBytes(int messageSize) {
    var headerBytes = new List<byte>();
    int verbAndSize = (int)Verb | (messageSize >> 2);
    headerBytes.AddRange(BitConverter.GetBytes(verbAndSize));

    //Add empty byte padding in the FIELDS header
    for (var i = 0; i < 20; i++) {
        headerBytes.Add(0b00000000);
    }

    headerBytes.AddRange(BitConverter.GetBytes(Fields));
    return headerBytes;
}
```

Once that header value is computed, we can apply it, followed by the checksum, followed by the byte array of our request message, to our output byte stream. Finally, since we've declared that our protocol will use TCP as its underlying transport mechanism, we'll create our `TcpClient` instance, connecting to the host and port specified by the `RequestUri` field. Once again, we'll be making a lot of assumptions about our ability to connect to the specified URI. In realistic circumstances, you'd be implementing your `TcpClient` connections with more robust error handling and connection validation, as we did in `Chapter 11`, *The Transport Layer - TCP and UDP*. For now, though, we'll simply assume our connection succeeded, write our bytes to our `NetworkStream` instance, and then pass it along to our `RockWebResponse` instance, which we'll return from our method:

```
    TcpClient client = new TcpClient(RequestUri.Host, RequestUri.Port);
    var stream = client.GetStream();
    stream.Write(byteList.ToArray(), 0, byteList.Count);
    return new RockWebResponse(stream);
}
```

This completes our implementation of the `GetResponse()` method. Obviously, implementing the `GetResponseAsync()` method will look extremely similar in practice, but we will use the asynchronous programming patterns we established in `Chapter 6`, *Streams, Threads, and Asynchronous Data Transfer*. I'll leave it as an exercise for you to implement that specific method in our `RockWebRequest` class.

Deriving from the WebResponse class

As you may have noticed, the `GetResponse()` method of our `RockWebRequest` returns an instance of a `RockWebResponse` class. This is the other side of the implementation coin for writing a pluggable protocol. You have to define a handler that can strip away and validate any protocol specific meta-data or header information from the response stream and store them in read-only properties in your custom `WebResponse` class, prior to returning the response stream back to the method that invoked it. One of the key benefits users will expect from your pluggable protocols is that they will abstract away all of the details of parsing and manipulating that protocol-specific information out of the response byte stream.

Our implementation for this demo will be extremely simple. We're only seeking to illustrate the conceptual steps you'll need to take if you undertake this task in the future. However, because of the highly specific nature of a pluggable protocol, anything more than that high-level, conceptual approach would ultimately prove futile. Given that, our full `RockWebResponse` class is as follows:

```
public class RockWebResponse : WebResponse {
    private Stream _responseStream { get; set; }
    public DateTime TimeStamp { get; set; }
    public RockStatus Status { get; set; }
    public int Size { get; set; }
    public RockWebResponse(Stream responseStream) {
        _responseStream = responseStream;

        byte[] header = new byte[4];
        _responseStream.Read(header, 0, 4);
        var isValid = ValidateHeaders(header);
    }

    public Stream GetResponseStream() {
        return _responseStream;
    }

    private bool ValidateHeaders(byte[] header) {
        //validate headers
        return true;
    }
}
```

The first thing we do is define public properties for each of the relevant header values that a user might be concerned with. Here, we've defined a simple `RockStatus` enum to capture our three possible status states, and we represent the timestamp header value as `DateTime`.

The crux of the class definition is in the constructor for it. Here, our `RockWebResponse` instance is responsible for parsing the header values out of the response stream, and populating its instance properties with their corresponding values. Note that we read the first 4 bytes from the stream, which corresponds to our 32-bit header definition. Once that's done, we pass the byte array along to our header validation function, and return our new instance (of course, in production code, you would throw an error on validation failure, instead of returning a new instance). Since we've read the header information out of our response stream prior to returning an instance to our consumers, the call to `GetResponseStream()` will return a stream containing only the response body.

By defining this protocol-specific response handler, we've (conceptually) completed our pluggable protocol implementation. There are a number of other methods you'll have to override if you truly want to create a valid subclass of `WebRequest`, and there is substantial information in the Microsoft documentation on specifically what is required. However, following the model we've established here, you should be in the right mindset to tackle those tasks when it becomes necessary to do so. At this point, the only thing left for us to do is expose it to other engineers through the `WebRequest` factory methods, which we'll look at in the next section.

Leveraging a custom protocol

Defining our pluggable protocol is really about defining the protocol-specific interactions of our custom protocol in the context of the `WebRequest` and `WebResponse` paradigms. Now that we've done that, though, we have to notify the `WebRequest` class that we've satisfied the requirements for use by any consumers seeking to use our schema. That means we'll need to define a factory class that creates instances of our derived classes.

Implementing the IWebRequestCreate interface

We want to register our class with the `WebRequest` class so that instances of `RockWebRequest` will be returned when the `WebRequest.Create(<uri>)` method is called with the appropriate schema. To do that, though, we'll need to provide `WebRequest` with a factory class that can build well-formed instances of our `RockWebRequest` class on demand. This behavior is defined by the `IWebRequestCreate` interface, and that's the interface we'll need to implement in our factory class to register it for use with `WebRequest`.

The footprint of this interface is, thankfully, extremely simple. In fact, it's only one method. Our whole implementation is fewer than a dozen lines long:

```
public class RockWebRequestCreator : IWebRequestCreate {
    public WebRequest Create(Uri uri) {
        return new RockWebRequest(uri);
    }
}
```

With this, though, we can register our custom protocol class for use whenever our schema shows up in a URI given to the `WebRequest.Create(<uri>)` method. Simply invoke the `RegisterPrefix()` method in the startup of your application:

```
WebRequest.RegisterPrefix("dtrj", new RockWebRequestCreator());
```

Now, your custom `WebRequest` class will be freely available to respond to URIs with the designated schema.

Going beyond WebRequest

At the time of writing this book, the Microsoft documentation for the `WebRequest` class explicitly advises against using `WebRequest` or any of its subclasses. The recommendation is for developers writing new software to instead use `HttpClient`, or similar classes. So, what does that mean for the value or use of pluggable protocols?

Simply put, it means your work isn't done quite yet. As I mentioned in `Chapter 5`, *Generating Network Requests in C#*, the `WebRequest` and `WebResponse` classes still operate, in some form or other, under the hood of the `HttpClient` class. Defining your protocol interactions through these classes is still very much an essential part of implementing custom protocols in .NET Core. Deriving from these classes gives you the flexibility to parse and process application headers directly out of the `NetworkStream` of whichever transport protocol you choose to use. In fact, even the ability to specify your transport protocol is something that cannot be done with the `HttpClient` class. This sort of control over your raw protocol requests can only be leveraged with something such as `WebRequest` or `WebResponse`.

However, as new developers consistently move away from the conventions of `WebRequest` and `WebResponse`, you'll need to define more modern abstractions to keep your protocol library relevant. To that end, if you find yourself needing to define custom protocol interactions, consider defining a standardized client implementation instead. Your client can (and perhaps *should*) continue to leverage a pluggable protocol derived from the `WebRequest` and `WebResponse` classes.

However, by defining a clean abstraction for working with those requests and responses, you present an easier-to-use, and easier-to-understand, tool for your library's users. If and when you find yourself writing any custom communication protocols, keep this in mind if you want to see it adopted by a wider audience in the .NET community.

With that, we can wrap up our discussion of pluggable protocols. In the next chapter, we'll continue down the path of advanced, lower-level subjects. There, we'll explore network analysis and packet sniffing strategies for a deeper understanding of the wider context your network software exists within.

Summary

This chapter took an extremely in-depth look at the very narrow topic of pluggable protocols in .NET Core. We learned that a pluggable protocol is really just an in-framework representation of any custom, application-layer communication protocol you want to define. As we established this understanding, we considered why we should take the time to implement new communication protocols as pluggable protocols in our code. We saw how the alternative—using custom, protocol-specific code throughout our application—introduced a time and productivity cost that could be all but eliminated by simply implementing custom subclasses of the `WebRequest` and `WebResponse` classes.

After we established the case for *using* pluggable protocols, we looked at *how* we could do so in our own projects. We learned about the three core steps we would have to follow to implement a pluggable protocol. As we did, we learned how each step served to create a clean, convention-based abstraction for our custom protocols. Finally, we looked at how to implement the different protocols in our software. We designed our own test protocol, and then took the necessary steps to implement `WebRequest` and `WebResponse` subclasses that handled interactions for that test protocol.

Finally, we looked at how to incorporate our new classes directly into the `WebRequest` and `WebResponse` framework for a seamless transition for new developers, who may want to take advantage of our work. As we wrapped up, we learned about the next steps we should take to stay consistent with more modern patterns of abstracting interactions behind protocol-specific `Client` classes. In the next chapter, we'll be looking at how we can analyze the state of network interfaces and network traffic on our host machines, and what sort of applications that capability opens up for us.

Questions

1. What is a pluggable protocol?
2. What are the advantages of implementing a protocol as a pluggable protocol?
3. What steps are necessary for building a pluggable protocol in .NET Core?
4. Why is accurate schema definition important for a listening server to process a request?
5. What is the minimum footprint of `WebRequest` methods you'll have to override to implement a pluggable protocol?
6. What additional interface must you provide to register your pluggable protocol for use by the `WebRequest.Create()` method?
7. What additional steps should you take to make adoption of your pluggable protocol easier and more consistent with modern conventions?

Further reading

This being a rather niche subject in a vast framework, there isn't much to recommend in terms of further reading on the specific topic of pluggable protocols themselves. However, if you're curious to learn more about the contexts and architectures that might motivate the need for custom protocol implementation, I would recommend checking out the *Serverless Programming Cookbook* by *Heartin Kanikathottu*. Its discussion of various network interactions from cloud platform-hosted source code paints a compelling picture for new, optimized communication paradigms. It can be found from Packt, here: `https://www.packtpub.com/application-development/serverless-programming-cookbook`.

18
Network Analysis and Packet Inspection

In this chapter, we'll look at writing software and systems that allow us to explore the network they're deployed on. Whereas previously, we looked at how our software was performing in the context of the network, in this chapter, we'll be looking specifically at how the network itself is performing. We'll examine how to implement resource and device discovery from within our network software, as well as how we can collect, examine, and then pass along packets traveling over the network. We'll consider how the activity on our network can potentially negatively impact our software, and how to proactively account for those impacts and recover from or avoid them altogether.

The following topics will be covered in this chapter:

- Broadcast ports and IP addresses, and using them to identify your own software or host on a network, or learn information about other hosts on a network
- Capturing and analyzing device and traffic information for the host to which your software is deployed
- Identifying some of the risks posed by traffic on our network and how to build our applications to be resilient against those risks

Technical requirements

In this chapter, we'll be using sample code that is available from this book's GitHub repository, here: `https://github.com/PacktPublishing/Hands-On-Network-Programming-with-C-and-.NET-Core/tree/master/Chapter 18`.

Check out the following video to see the code in action: `http://bit.ly/2HUai2a`

Additionally, we'll briefly discuss the merits of using WireShark to examine and understand the breadth and volume of network requests that are interacting with our machine. If you haven't already downloaded this software for the previous chapters, it can be found here: `https://www.wireshark.org/#download`.

I strongly recommend familiarizing yourself with it, as it can prove invaluable as a tool for network software engineers.

Network resources and topography

As we discussed all the way back in `Chapter 1`, *Networks in a Nutshell*, a network is a system that is agnostic of the participants of that system. Any given network has no knowledge of the entities or hosts that are wired up to it. As such, it can give no such information to any new hosts that try to connect to it. Instead, those hosts are responsible for broadcasting information about themselves out to others. Not only that, they're responsible for listening for broadcast information coming from other hosts so that they might know what other resources or hosts are on their network. So, how exactly does this happen?

Node-to-node communication

In just about all of the host-to-host interactions we've described in this book, one host must resolve a domain name or IP address for another host by communicating over a path of routers, switches, and gateways. However, this process of address resolution through a chain of external host devices doesn't help us establish the *initial* communication with the next host on our network. If we want our host to successfully transmit information to the nearest neighbor in the network path, we need to know specifically what address it might be listening on.

While I realize you're already aware of this fact, I would wager that you don't often think about the fact that when you establish a connection between two hosts, that connection is purely *logical*. The expectation is that each router or switch along the network path between your hosts will simply forward your packets along to their target, creating an unbroken chain of physical connections. Taken together, that chain of connections constitutes a single, logical connection. However, for that to work, your host must first connect to the next-nearest neighbor in that connection chain.

Every time we want to establish a higher-level connection with a remote host over something such as TCP or HTTP, the software that operates at the device and network level must determine the path for us. It does so by sending a message to its nearest neighbor and, essentially, asking if that neighbor can resolve a path. Then, that network device will forward the request to any of its neighbors, asking the same thing. As long as one of them responds affirmatively, your nearest neighbor will also respond affirmatively. If we consider our network as a tree, with our host as the root, we can think of this process in terms of a recursive tree-traversal algorithm. This recursive algorithm continues until one of two possible determinations is made. In the event that a path cannot be established, every leaf node of the network tree responds negatively, shown in the following diagram:

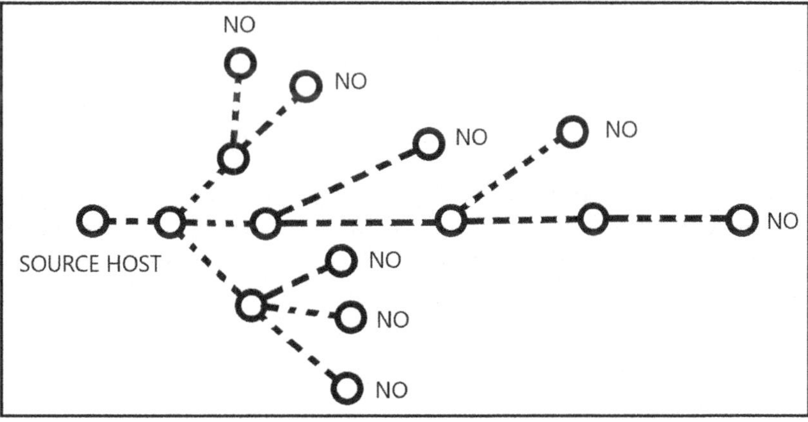

Meanwhile, in the event of a successful path determination, the target host is eventually reached by some path through our network tree. In that case, *any* node in our tree that can connect directly with our destination host will respond affirmatively, and the affirmative responses will propagate all the way back to our source host, notifying it that a connection can be made, shown in the following diagram:

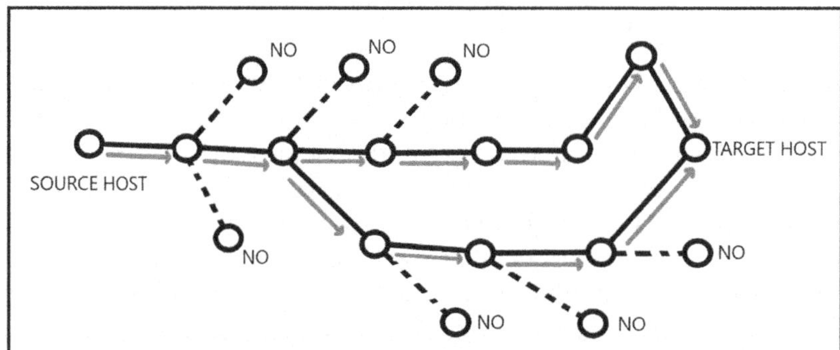

Note, though, that the source only learns that a path *can* be established. Even in the best cases, if multiple paths can be established between two hosts, there is no guarantee that any given packet will travel along the optimal path (if there even is an optimal path). In fact, there's no guarantee that all the packets of a given request will even travel along the *same* path. This is what causes the out-of-order packet delivery that we discussed in `Chapter 11`, *The Transport Layer – TCP, UDP, and Multicasting*.

So far, we've only considered connections as being established between two hosts over a transport or application layer protocol. With that as our context, there hasn't been any need for us to *identify* anything but our target host, using an IP address or domain name and the designated listening port. Using only these identifying details, network and device layer protocols have done the work of establishing a path on our network and forwarding our requests packets along that path. Our software simply receives an open line of communication between the two hosts.

What you may not realize, though, is that the software running at the network layer has to explicitly identify the nearest neighbor in our network by *its* network address. Moreover, our host has to communicate with its nearest neighbor through a port and communication mechanism that the neighbor is configured to listen for. This leaves us with the sort of chicken-and-egg problem that is so common when trying to solve communication over an agnostic network. How can a source host identify the address and protocol with which to communicate with a destination host, without first communicating with the destination host to learn of those details? The answer is with a broadcast address.

Broadcast addressing

When you first connect a device to a network, there are a number of things that must be coordinated between the new device and any other devices on the network before it can effectively communicate over that network. Your device must be assigned a local IP address, and it must be informed of the IP addresses and listening ports or sockets for any devices to which it has a direct connection. Additionally, any gateways into your subnetwork must be made aware of the new device so that, if any host outside your subnetwork wants to establish a connection, the gateways will respond affirmatively to any pathing requests they receive while attempting to establish a connection.

To establish the initial identity of a new host on a network, every standard network device will have what's known as a **broadcast address.** A broadcast address is simply any address on which every device on a given network or subnetwork is expected to be listening. With this standard universally established, any new host attempting to connect to a network can establish its presence for any devices that may need to know about it by sending out basic identifying information to a broadcast address. Once a message is broadcast, routers, switches, and gateways can use whatever conventions or protocols they've been configured with to mutually agree on a new network address to provision for the new host.

In the initial broadcast message, a new host won't have been assigned an IP address from its network. However, it still needs to establish a unique identifier by which other devices can communicate *back* to it. To give its nearest physical neighbor some identifier by that to return configuration information, a new host will typically send a **media access control address**, or **MAC address,** as part of its initial broadcast message. A MAC address is a globally unique identifier that's given to every single physical **network interface card (NIC)**.

The MAC address is occasionally called the **burned-in** address, since it is configured and fixed at the hardware level at the time the network card was fabricated, and cannot be changed by any means. A MAC address consists of six hexadecimal digits, separated by a colon, hyphen, or no separator at all. And because there is a unique MAC address per network card, any host which is configured with multiple network cards is going to have multiple MAC addresses, identifying each physical interface it has available to it. If you've ever opened up your command Terminal and run this command, you'll have seen your MAC address for any network card installed on your machine:

```
ipconfig /all
```

In the following command terminal, it's the property labeled **Physical Address**:

```
Select C:\WINDOWS\system32\cmd.exe
C:\Users\shurns>ipconfig /all

Windows IP Configuration

   Host Name . . . . . . . . . . . . : beemo
   Primary Dns Suffix  . . . . . . . :
   Node Type . . . . . . . . . . . . : Hybrid
   IP Routing Enabled. . . . . . . . : No
   WINS Proxy Enabled. . . . . . . . : No
   DNS Suffix Search List. . . . . . : fios-router.home

Ethernet adapter Ethernet:

   Connection-specific DNS Suffix  . : fios-router.home
   Description . . . . . . . . . . . : Intel(R) Ethernet Connection (2) I219-V
   Physical Address. . . . . . . . . : 34-97-F6-85-9D-35
   DHCP Enabled. . . . . . . . . . . : Yes
   Autoconfiguration Enabled . . . . : Yes
   Link-local IPv6 Address . . . . . : fe80::5584:7902:d228:6f0e%11(Preferred)
   IPv4 Address. . . . . . . . . . . : 192.168.1.181(Preferred)
   Subnet Mask . . . . . . . . . . . : 255.255.255.0
   Lease Obtained. . . . . . . . . . : Friday, March 1, 2019 8:43:08 PM
   Lease Expires . . . . . . . . . . : Tuesday, March 5, 2019 8:11:59 PM
   Default Gateway . . . . . . . . . : 192.168.1.1
   DHCP Server . . . . . . . . . . . : 192.168.1.1
   DHCPv6 IAID . . . . . . . . . . . : 355768310
   DHCPv6 Client DUID. . . . . . . . : 00-01-00-01-1F-01-3E-7F-34-97-F6-85-9D-35
   DNS Servers . . . . . . . . . . . : 192.168.1.1
   NetBIOS over Tcpip. . . . . . . . : Enabled

Ethernet adapter Ethernet 2:

   Media State . . . . . . . . . . . : Media disconnected
   Connection-specific DNS Suffix  . :
   Description . . . . . . . . . . . : TAP-Windows Adapter V9
   Physical Address. . . . . . . . . : 00-FF-5C-13-11-21
   DHCP Enabled. . . . . . . . . . . : Yes
   Autoconfiguration Enabled . . . . : Yes
```

Since a MAC address cannot be changed and is known to be globally unique, a new host may broadcast it out to its network and hope for network configuration details, including IP address assignment and subnet mask specification, in response.

By using the broadcast information from each connection host, network servers and routers can build an internal representation of the logical topology of their network. This topology and registry of device configuration are used to control and monitor the flow of inter-network communication. So, now, the question is, how can we leverage these broadcasts and other information when we need to establish the same knowledge about the networks our software is hosted on?

Network analysis

Now that we have a basic picture of how network information is communicated between arbitrary nodes across our network, we can start to leverage that information to implement lower-level network software from within our .NET Core projects. So, what information are we looking for and how can we use it in code?

Understanding the NetworkInformation namespace

Many of the details and network interactions we discussed in the previous section exist and are managed by software and devices lower in the network stack than .NET Core libraries can provide access to. There is, however, a wealth of information about the transport layer traffic that moves through your application's listening network sockets and interfaces. For that information, the .NET Standard provides the `System.Net.NetworkInformation` namespace.

The `NetworkInformation` namespace provides an array of utility classes and interfaces that can be used to build a comprehensive picture of the ways in which your software interacts with the network it's connected to. Using the classes in this namespace, you can learn about packet traffic, device addresses, including the registered IP addresses for routers and gateways on your current sub-network, and utilities for identifying the availability of remote devices in your network.

What's especially interesting about this namespace and its use case is that it can be used to investigate *all* connections and traffic moving across your host machine. This gives you the ability to analyze how network requests targeting a different process co-located on your machine could potentially impact the performance and behavior of your own network software. Additionally, leveraging this class gives your code the information that's necessary to manage connections and sockets for more internal processes, allowing for such applications as writing your own application server or a request management solution. So, what kind of information can we glean from the classes in this namespace?

Querying physical device information

Suppose for a moment that you want to write an application that provides detailed information about the network devices on the host computer. Certainly, you could use something such as Powershell scripting or simple batch processes to run terminal commands such as `ipconfig /all` or the `netsh dump` command, writing the results to a text file. But what if you want more information about your system? What if you want to deploy this software to multiple hosts with incompatible terminals? A scripting solution, while relatively simple, is incredibly inflexible and limited in its potential scope.

Instead, using the `NetworkInterface` class and its subclasses, you could access information about your network devices directly from within your software solution. Using the `NetworkInterface` abstract class, we can access every physical network device detectable from our software's host operating system and display information about the current active status, interface type, physical MAC address, current operational status, and more. To see that in action, let's write our network information display software. We'll start by creating a console application for our demo code for this chapter:

```
dotnet new console -n NetworkAnalysisDemo
```

Then, from within our `Main()` method, we'll get a list of all network adapters that are currently detectable by our operating system using the `GetAllNetworkInterfaces()` static method on the `NetworkInterface` class. This will return an array of subclasses of the `NetworkInterface` abstract class, with each instance in the array representing exactly one physical device on your system. Once we have the list of devices, we'll loop through them and see what information we can discover about them using this interface:

```
private static void DisplayDeviceInformation() {
  var adapters = NetworkInterface.GetAllNetworkInterfaces();
  Console.WriteLine($"There were {adapters.Length} devices detected on your
machine");
  Console.WriteLine();
```

The `NetworkInterface` class is actually an abstract base class. The resulting instances that are returned to our adapters container will be instances of a `SystemNetworkInterface`. Now, let's find out what information we can glean from these adapter instances. We'll just use a basic loop through our adapters to print out some of the more interesting properties and find out just what kind of details we can learn about:

```
Console.WriteLine("Device Details");
foreach (NetworkInterface adapter in adapters) {
Console.WriteLine("=========================================================
=================");
  Console.WriteLine();
  Console.WriteLine($"Device ID: ----------------- {adapter.Id}");
  Console.WriteLine($"Device Name: --------------- {adapter.Name}");
  Console.WriteLine($"Description: --------------- {adapter.Description}");
  Console.WriteLine($"Interface type: ------------
{adapter.NetworkInterfaceType}");
  Console.WriteLine($"Physical Address: ----------
{adapter.GetPhysicalAddress().ToString()}");
  Console.WriteLine($"Operational status: --------
{adapter.OperationalStatus}");
  Console.WriteLine($"Adapter Speed: ------------- {adapter.Speed}");
  Console.WriteLine($"Multicast Support: ---------
{adapter.SupportsMulticast}");
}

Thread.Sleep(20000);
```

As you can see by the properties, through this class, we can gather just about the same level of detail about our host machine as we might gather from a terminal command querying our NIC. In fact, we can confirm as much by running an `ipconig /all` command, and comparing the device details that are returned against the output of our program. Doing so on my own machine, we can compare my program output against the terminal output I showed you in the previous section of this chapter:

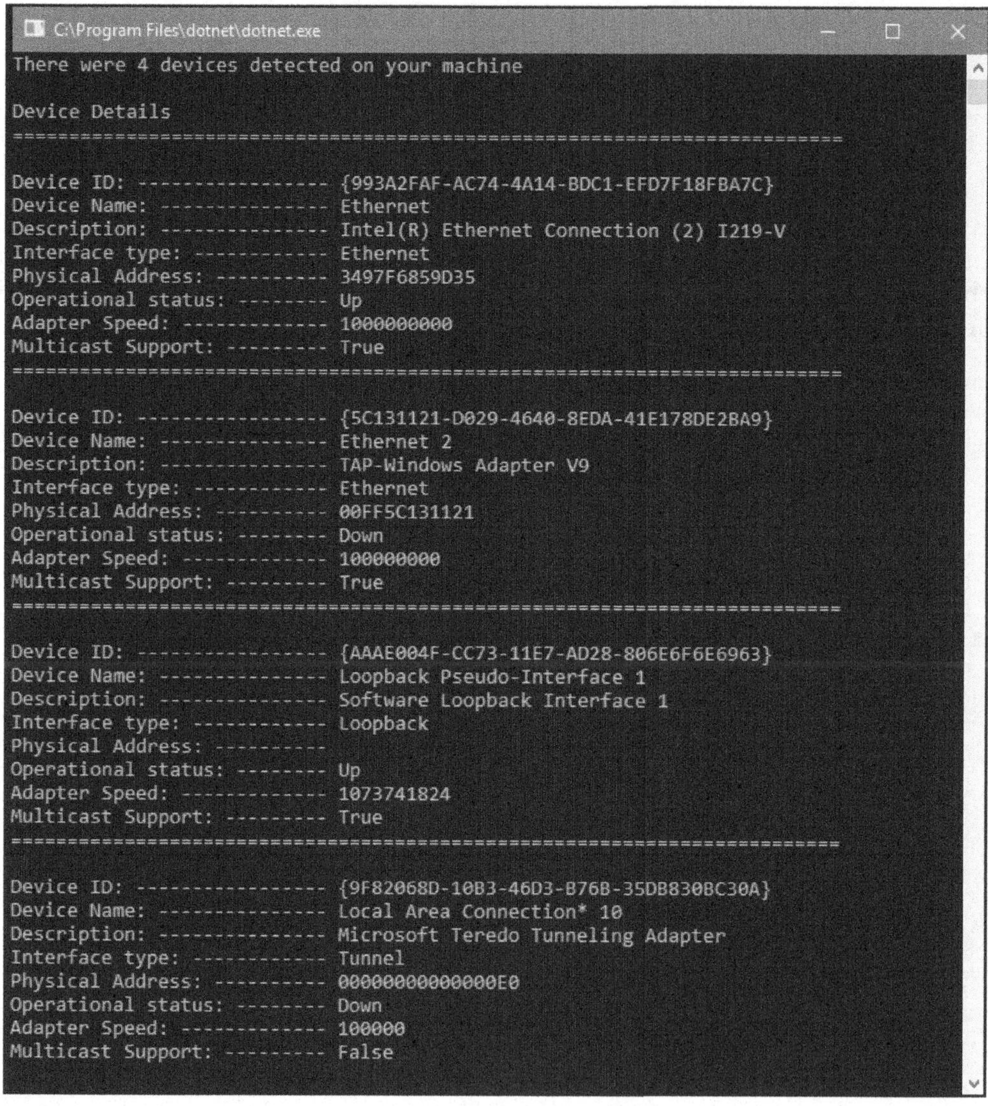

Here, we can see that we can access much of the information returned by our `ipconfig /all` call from the previous section. While the hex digits aren't grouped into dash-delimited pairs, the `PhysicalAddress` property obviously maps directly to the MAC address for your adapter, and the `OperationalStatus` property gives an accurate representation of the availability of the device for network requests. We can also see that my operating system is configured to use a Teredo tunneling adapter to allow IPv4 communication over IPv6 sub-networks, just as we discussed in `Chapter 12`, *The Internet Protocol*.

Exploring the `NetworkInterface` class more, you can find information about the devices your network adapters are connected to. By requesting information that's through the `GetIPProperties()` method, you have access to details about the network configuration information currently set for each adapter. This includes the IP addresses for DHCP servers, DNS servers, and your sub-networks gateway device, as well as any registered multicast or unicast addresses registered on your machine for other devices on your network.

The depth of information we can learn about our physical adapters from this class is considerably more extensive than what we can learn from our terminal commands. Especially when we consider the information retrieved by the `GetIPProperties()` method. The benefit of using this class over a simple terminal command, though, is that it gives us access to all of this information from inside our software. We can implement conditional behavior based on device availability, or provide meaningful statistics and information to a system health report all without having to rely on host-specific terminal commands and external load modules.

With this information, we could feasibly implement our own software for broadcasting our MAC address and requesting addressing, as well as configuration information from our network. Even if you don't ever find a need for implementing that code yourself, this hopefully paints a clear picture of the kind of features opened up to you with this class. This provides a host-agnostic mechanism for low-level network details and programming. So, what other information can we learn from the classes in the `System.Net.NetworkInformation` namespace?

Querying connection information

While learning information about the status and availability of our own network interfaces is useful (and, indeed, even critical in many contexts), it doesn't paint the complete picture. For that, we'll need to examine the incoming and outgoing network traffic our adapters are being exposed to. Thankfully, as was the case with information about our network adapters, the .NET standard provides a set of classes that can display and monitor this information through clean and easy-to-use abstractions.

Instead of interacting with a `NetworkInterface` method, we'll want to look at our TCP connections, so for this next segment, we'll be looking at the `IPGlobalProperties` abstract base class. In much the same way that we examined the network interface information by calling the `GetAllNetworkInterfaces()` method, we can collect a wealth of IP traffic information using the `GetIpGlobalProperties()` static method. Once we have that, we can get everything from a list of all the active TCP connections (useful for determining the current load on your device), to statistics about incoming and outgoing IP packets. You can even sort your IP traffic statistics by the transport protocol that facilitated their delivery, with distinct methods targeting TCP statistics and UDP statistics.

Let's see what sort of information we can learn about using these classes and their queries. We'll start by learning about what active TCP connections we have running against our machine at the current moment. First, we'll get our global properties, and then we'll request our active TCP connection information:

```
private static void DisplayActiveTcpConnections() {
  var ipStats = IPGlobalProperties.GetIPGlobalProperties();
  var tcpConnections = ipStats.GetActiveTcpConnections();

  Console.WriteLine($"There are {tcpConnections.Length} active TCP
connections on this machine");
  Console.WriteLine();
```

Now that we have our active connections, we can loop through them to determine who is connected to who, and what state the connection is in:

```
foreach(var connection in tcpConnections) {
    Console.WriteLine("============================================");
    Console.WriteLine($"Local host:");
    Console.WriteLine($" Connected On Address:
{connection.LocalEndPoint.Address.ToString()}");
    Console.WriteLine($" Over Port Number:
{connection.LocalEndPoint.Port}");
    Console.WriteLine($"Remote host: {connection.RemoteEndPoint.Address}");
    Console.WriteLine($" Connected On Address:
{connection.RemoteEndPoint.Address.ToString()}");
```

```
    Console.WriteLine($" Over Port Number:
{connection.RemoteEndPoint.Port}");
    Console.WriteLine($"Connection State: {connection.State.ToString()}");
}
```

By running this, you should see some variation of your localhost address (either `192.168.1.XXX`, or `127.0.0.1`) as the local address for every connection, and it might not seem entirely obvious why you might want access to that information. However, consider a scenario where you've got multiple IP addresses registered to a single host, and each address is mapped to a single, distinct application process. Let's say you've configured these distinct listening patterns through the `UsingUrls(...)` method of your kestrel `IWebHostBuilder`, as we discussed in `Chapter 9`, *HTTP in .NET*. If that's the case, you could use the local address information to distinguish between connections to different applications on your host. This could give you insight into application traffic and resource usage. I expect by now you've got an intuitive idea of how that could be immensely useful in a number of contexts.

Monitoring traffic and remote device information

Finally, let's wrap up our discussion about the `System.Net.NetworkInterface` namespace by looking at some of the traffic statistics and information made available through its classes. This will give us statistical information that's about the total number of packets we've received at a given point in time, fragmentation failures, dropped outbound packets, and much more. We can request these statistics based on IP version, with distinct methods for `GetIPv4GlobalStatistics()` and `GetIPv6GlobalStatistics()`, as well as filtering those statistics by transport protocol with `GetTcpIPv4Statistics()` and `GetUdpIPv4Statistics()`.

Taking a look at some of the properties made available through instances of the `IPGlobalStatistics` class, we can see the kind of valuable information we can draw out of our traffic. Let's look at just a few examples of this in some sample code:

```
private static void DisplayIPv4TrafficStatistics() {
    var ipProperties = IPGlobalProperties.GetIPGlobalProperties();
    var ipStats = ipProperties.GetIPv4GlobalStatistics();
    Console.WriteLine($"Incoming Packets: {ipStats.ReceivedPackets}");
    Console.WriteLine($"Outgoing Packets: {ipStats.OutputPacketRequests}");
    Console.WriteLine($"Discareded Incoming Packets:
{ipStats.ReceivedPacketsDiscarded}");
    Console.WriteLine($"Discarded Outgoing Packets:
{ipStats.OutputPacketsDiscarded}");
    Console.WriteLine($"Fragmentation Failures:
{ipStats.PacketFragmentFailures}");
```

```
    Console.WriteLine($"Reassembly Failures:
{ipStats.PacketReassemblyFailures}");
}
```

Here, you can see the kind of picture you can paint about your network's overall health and stability. We have access to information about fragmentation and reassembly failure, dropped packets, and the overall incoming and outgoing traffic. In this case, we were looking at our global IP traffic, but we could have just as easily sorted this by TCP and UDP for more meaningful breakdowns of our network interactions.

Not all properties of the `IpGlobalStatistics` are supported on all platforms. Some information about discarded packets and fragment failures will only be available on Windows hosts. Make sure to validate that the statistical information you want access to is supported by the platform your software will be deployed to, and always write your code to degrade gracefully when host support may be limited.

While I hope this has provided a clear understanding of just what sort of information you can learn about the broader network context surrounding your hosted software, I've only begun to scratch the service of the information that's available through the `System.Net.NetworkInformation` namespace. I'd strongly encourage you to read through the Microsoft docs yourself to see what other tools are at your disposal.

Additional tools and analysis

While the information we can capture with the `System.Net.NetworkInformation` namespace provides a very clear picture of the state of our network, it does have one major shortcoming when it comes to network analysis: it cannot provide any insight into the content of any traffic or requests in real time. The only way to access that information in code is to actively register a listener on an open port and process the incoming traffic accordingly. So, for network and DevOps engineers who need to monitor the content of their network traffic as well as the volume and context, what other tools are available?

Using Wireshark for packet inspection

As we saw back in `Chapter 4`, *Packets and Streams*, Wireshark can be a powerful tool for performing network analysis and what's called **packet sniffing**. Put simply, packet sniffing is inspecting the content of packets outside the context of their intended recipient. So, for example, if I've requested a web page in my browser, but then investigate the packet stream that makes up that web page with a tool such as Wireshark, that would constitute packet sniffing. The packets were intended for receipt and use by my browser, not Wireshark. It doesn't actually matter whether I was the one who requested them through the browser in the first place.

In some contexts, this can be a dangerous tool for malicious actors to gain access to other internet traffic. However, in the hands of a network engineer behaving ethically, it can be a wonderful way to identify unintended or undesirable activity on your network. So, how can we use this to our advantage?

Consider a case where you've got software running that uses the `System.Net.NetworkInformation` classes to provide real-time health information about your hosting environment. If you've designed your alerting mechanism well (as discussed in `Chapter 16`, *Performance Analysis and Monitoring*), you would quickly be made aware of any unanticipated spikes in network traffic beyond a given threshold. If that happens, the information that's available to you from your health monitoring software is limited by what's provided by the `System.Net.NetworkInformation` library.

With the resources we've discussed in this chapter, you can devise a sound strategy for detecting and responding to those kinds of critical network events. Simply use the statistical information that's available through the `System.Net.NetworkInformation` classes as your alert system, and a more robust inspection tool, such as Wireshark, for deeper analysis when alerts arise. This can give you deeper insight into what information is being conveyed to your host in that high-volume spike of packets.

The basics of using Wireshark for rudimentary packet sniffing were discussed in `Chapter 4`, *Packets and Streams*, in the *The Anatomy of a Packet section*. With that in mind, I won't belabor the point, as more advanced use cases for Wireshark are well beyond the scope of this book. However, I felt it was important to address it in this chapter, since anyone who's serious about network programming and all it entails should have as deep of a set of tools at their disposal as possible. To that end, I'd highly encourage you to set aside time at your job, or even in your free time, to learn and practice using Wireshark and other packet inspection tools for deep network analysis.

With that out of the way, we're ready to tackle our final topic. In the next chapter, we'll be exploring the SSH interaction scheme. We'll learn how it came about, how it's evolved over time, and how we can use it for remote process invocation and host access.

Summary

In this chapter, we explored the very niche, but extremely powerful, subject of network device analysis using .NET Core libraries. We started by learning about how network devices communicate information about themselves across device-agnostic connections to establish an internal registry of nearby device addresses and interaction mechanisms. In doing so, we learned about the use of broadcasting, and broadcast addresses for transmitting messages reliably, even without any connection information about the devices you intend to communicate with. Finally, we learned how uniquely addressing hardware interfaces can facilitate device identification even in the absence of a registered network address.

Once we learned about the features and interactions that are necessary to facilitate more typical interactions between hosts on a network, we looked at how we can access that low-level network information from within our .NET applications. We explored various classes within the `System.Net.NetworkInformation` namespace, and saw how we could use them to access valuable information about our network adapters, and the devices to which they were connected. We saw how we could access critical operational information about our physical network adapters programmatically, giving us access to a wide range of diagnostic and statistical information. We also looked at how we could examine and monitor IP traffic against each of our network interfaces to perform packet inspection and network health analysis. Finally, we considered additional tools available that could provide greater context and detail about network traffic, and how we could use all of this information to identify and respond to an unstable network. Going into our final chapter, we'll look at how computers can control and operate hosts remotely over a network using SSH.

Questions

1. Describe the process of address resolution, as it occurs at the network layer.
2. What is a broadcast address? How is it used?
3. What is a MAC address? How is it distinct from other network addresses?
4. What sort of information can be learned from instances of the `NetworkInterface` class?
5. What is packet sniffing? How is it useful in network analysis?
6. What sort of traffic information can we query using the `NetworkInformation` classes?
7. How can we use traffic statistics to detect and respond to unstable network conditions?

Further reading

Once again, we've covered a relatively niche topic in this chapter, and the additional resources for learning more are few and far between. I'd certainly recommend you explore the Microsoft documentation for the `System.Net.NetworkInformation` namespace, which can be found here: `https://docs.microsoft.com/en-us/dotnet/api/system.net.networkinformation?view=netcore-3.0`

Additionally, if you have any interest in continuing down the path of network traffic analysis and packet inspection, I'd recommend the book *Packet Analysis with Wireshark* by Anish Nath. This book provides an extensive how-to for investigating and understanding the nature of the raw network packets that come into contact with your network adapters moment to moment. It's available through Packt, here: `https://www.packtpub.com/networking-and-servers/packet-analysis-wireshark`.

19
Remote Logins and SSH

In this final chapter, we'll look at how we can implement remote host access and control in .NET Core. Here, we'll create a **Secure Shell** (**SSH**) client for remotely accessing computing resources over a network. We'll look at how the SSH.NET library supports making calls to known external resources and explore the underlying source code for the SSH.NET library to understand how it supports SSH in .NET Core. Finally, we'll look at how we can leverage it to perform a variety of operations on external machines over a network.

The following topics will be covered in this chapter:

- The Secure Shell protocol for remote device access and process execution
- Establishing SSH connections using .NET Core
- Executing remote commands on external machines through the SSH connections

Technical requirements

In this final chapter, we'll be using our trusty source code editor, whether that's Visual Studio or Visual Studio Code, and we'll be developing and discussing the source code found in this book's GitHub repository, here: `https://github.com/PacktPublishing/Hands-On-Network-Programming-with-C-and-.NET-Core/tree/master/Chapter 19`.

We'll also be using the free (as in gratis) virtual machine host VirtualBox to set up a false remote host for us to interact with through our SSH software. You can use whatever virtualization software you may already have on your own machine if you want to follow along with the demonstrations in this chapter, though. The important thing is just to have a virtual host to interact with. The installer for VirtualBox can be found here: `https://www.virtualbox.org/wiki/Downloads`.

Finally, we'll be using an installation of the Ubuntu operating system to load onto our virtual machine. Ubuntu is free and open source, and a disk image for the OS can be found here: `https://www.ubuntu.com/download/desktop`.

Check out the following video to see the code in action: `http://bit.ly/2HYQMSu`

What is SSH?

Starting from the beginning, the first step to understanding how we can leverage SSH in our software is to understand what SSH is, and how it works. Put simply, SSH is a network protocol for securely logging into a remote host. Once that remote login has been established, the protocol supports executing and operating remote resources over an otherwise unsecured network. As with all of the protocols we've explored throughout this book, its design is intentionally generalized for use in a wide variety of contexts. So, how did it begin, and how, specifically, does it work?

The origin of SSH

Originally created in 1995 by Finnish researcher Tatu Ylönen, SSH was created to provide a secure channel over which remote terminal access could be established. Ylönen was motivated by a recent password-sniffing attack that struck the network of the Helsinki University of Technology, where he was working at the time. Recognizing the inherent insecurity of more common (or at least, more common at the time) text-based remote terminal protocols, such as Telnet, rlogin, and FTP, his primary objective was to create sufficiently strong authentication and encryption to ensure the privacy of network communications. Through his work, users could remotely log into machines, and access and operate the remote machine's terminal through their own SSH interface.

The original version, and subsequent minor releases of version 1, was developed by the SSH Communications Security, a privately held cybersecurity company founded by Ylönen. However, as of version 2.0, an IETF working group known as **Secsh** has been responsible for defining and refining the protocol. The Secsh team's work was formalized and accepted as a standard, dubbed **SSH-2**, in 2006.

With the release of SSH-2, the team improved the security and feature set of SSH-1 through the use of improved key-exchange algorithms for establishing symmetric keys for communication. The new version also introduced securely hashed message authentication codes (HMAC codes, not to be confused with the MAC address we discussed in `Chapter 18`, *Network Analysis and Packet Inspection*). Among the features that were introduced with SSH-2 was support for multiple parallel terminal sessions over a single SSH connection.

While it was originally built on top of, and released as, free software throughout its earliest releases, the protocol has since fragmented and exists in various open and proprietary implementations and versions. However, developers across the globe continued to have a need for open sourced implementations of the protocol. To solve this, new, open source implementations have been developed and established a strong foothold. This includes the OpenSSH implementation, which was developed by the community of developers behind OpenBSD, and first released in 1999. Today, OpenSSH is the most widely used implementation of the suite of protocols and features, and it is the only implementation used by modern Windows machines.

If you've ever used GitHub or BitBucket as a remote Git repository, you've likely used OpenSSH already and may not have even realized it. Many Git clients, including Atlassian's source tree, and even the default client, leverage SSH to establish and maintain access credentials between your machine and the remote repository for your code base. The single-sign on mechanism supported by something such as SourceTree is built entirely on OpenSSH. In fact, whenever you start SourceTree, the startup process also starts an instance of the PuTTY SSH client, which SourceTree uses to establish its own connections with your remote repositories. But now that you know what SSH is, we should take a moment to look at how it works.

The SSH protocol design

The SSH protocol leverages a client-server architecture, not entirely dissimilar from the application-layer protocols we've examined all throughout this book, such as FTP and HTTP. The basic interaction mechanism actually looks very similar to the handshake and security negotiation that takes place in a TLS handshake. The basic interactions are as follows:

- The client establishes a connection with the server, notifying the server of a desire to communicate via SSH
- The server acknowledges the request, and responds with public encryption key information with which the client can secure its own subsequent responses until a symmetric encryption scheme can be established
- The server and the client negotiate the security structure for the connection, transmit any necessary keys, and establish a secure, symmetric encryption mechanism for use over the lifetime of the SSH session
- The client is free to securely log on to the remote host, transmitting and executing commands for which their credentials have permissions

The primary distinction between SSH and something such as TLS is that SSH is explicitly designed to be general purpose and connection agnostic.

This interaction scheme is supported by an architecture, defined by a series of RFCs by the IETF (4251-4256, if you're interested), as a three-tiered system of components with distinct responsibilities. Each tier supports a specific task in the process of establishing and maintaining an SSH session between a client and a server, and they're all well-documented by their respective standards.

The transport tier

The first of these tiers is the transport layer protocol, or **SSH-TRANS**, which provides secure delivery of messages with all of the functionality you've come to expect from TLS. Since SSH is all about secure communication, it's important that the transport layer provides a strong authentication and encryption mechanism. This should include server authentication (usually through an X.509, or similar certificate validation mechanism), public key encryption, and message verification.

While RFC 4251 notes that the transport layer is likely to be implemented over TCP/IP in most cases, it does leave room for new or alternative protocols. The only aspect of a transport layer protocol that must be in place for SSH is reliability of transport. This rules out UDP and other connectionless protocols as viable transport mechanisms, since connectionless datagram delivery is considered inherently unreliable.

The user authentication tier

The next, and perhaps most critical, tier of the SSH-2 architecture is the **authentication protocol layer**, or **SSH-USERAUTH**. This is the layer that's responsible for establishing and maintaining a validated identity for any client seeking to connect to an SSH server. According to RFC 4252, the server is responsible for establishing the valid set of authentication methods that the client may use to authenticate themselves. From that set of authentication methods, the client is free to use any available method, and is free to attempt them in any order. According to the RFC, there are three valid authentication methods that a server might list for a client to attempt to authenticate by.

The public key authentication mode

The first of these and the only one that an SSH-2 server is actually required to support, according to the standard is the `publickey` authentication scheme. However, while there is a requirement that all servers support the ability to use public key authentication, there is no requirement that all clients actually have public keys. The public key scheme behaves very similarly to what we saw in `Chapter 13`, *Transport Layer Security*. When the `publickey` method is specified, the SSH client will send a signature, which has been generated from a private key, to the server. Once received, the server validates the signature as being generated with the user's private key, and upon successful validation, the authentication succeeds for the client.

Client software will typically store a registered private key as an encrypted value on the local system, and restrict access to it from external processes. The SSH client will also, typically, use some form of password authentication prior to generate a public key signature to transmit over the server, though this is not always a requirement.

The password authentication mode

The next valid authentication mechanism that a server might specify for use by a client is the **password authentication scheme**. While support for the password scheme is not explicitly required by the standard, it is strongly recommended that implementations should support password authentication. In this authentication mechanism, much as the name suggests, the connecting client provides a plain text password to the server over a series of packet negotiations.

Since the user authentication layer of the SSH-2 architecture rests on top of the transport layer, the fact that the password is transmitted as plain-text should be mitigated by the secure encryption of the underlying transport protocol. However, RFC 4252 does specify that it is the responsibility of both the server and the client to confirm the confidentiality of the transport layer's encryption mechanism prior to sending the password in plain-text. If either the client or the server determines that there is no encryption, or insufficient encryption, being used by the transport protocol, the password authentication mode should be disabled by both the client and the server.

Whenever a server implements the password authentication scheme, it should also provide a mechanism whereby a user can change or update their password through the SSH connection establishment mechanism, in the event that a user's password has expired. This enables users who would be prompted to enter and update their passage upon authentication to do so through the remote terminal. However, in much the same way that the client and server should validate that the transport layer provides sufficient security prior to allowing the password authentication mode, they must also determine whether there is sufficient support for data integrity prior to supporting a password update mechanism. This is because, if the data was mutated or modified in transit, neither the server nor the client would have knowledge of the discrepancy without some form of integrity check.

Thus, the server would assign the new, mutated password for the user's future authentication attempts, but the client would have no knowledge of the mutation, and would subsequently fail to authenticate with the original, unmodified password. Therefore, if there is no assurance of data integrity provided by either a MAC or HMAC as part of the packets delivered by the transport layer, then the server must disable any password update functionality.

The host-based authentication mode

The final authentication mode is the `hostbased` mode. This is the only mode that's explicitly noted in the standard as being optional, and it allows users to be authenticated based on the host machine they are connecting from (hence the name). This mode relies on a designated host machine having a private key that's provisioned for a specific individual host machine. The host then generates a signature from that private key, which can be validated by the server using the host's public key. This signature is then validated against the public key and the specific host name. As long as the host name provided with the signature matches the origin of the request, and the server's registry of valid hosts, the authentication succeeds.

The connection tier

Designed and intended to run on top of both the transport tier and the user authentication tier, the connection tier of the SSH-2 architecture defines the systems that support the various operations and interactions that are available over an SSH connection. Defined in RFC 4254, the connection tier of the stack is described as providing **connection channels** over which SSH features can be executed. This includes any remote terminal sessions over which the client can execute remote commands, and port-forwarding sessions, which allow a client to directly access a network connection port on the remote host and listen for incoming requests, and any remote login sessions for navigating within and interacting with the remote host.

According to the RFC, a single SSH connection should implement support for multiplexing multiple channels over the course of a session. These channels are uniquely identified on both ends of the connection, though the identifiers may be different from server to client. Once a channel is opened, though, data can flow between hosts in what's known as a **window**. A window is simply a designated maximum number of bytes that one host can transmit to the other before further data is blocked. Once the window-size is reached, the transmitting host must wait for the window to be adjusted by the recipient host. In this way, windows are used to control the flow of traffic over a given SSH connection channel.

A series of channels provisioned over a given SSH connection establish what is known as an **interactive session**. According to the standard, an interactive session is simply any remote execution of a program by the client, on the server. This can include port or authentication forwarding, session data transfer, or any number of other jobs, tasks, and activities.

The versatility of SSH

Since SSH is primarily concerned with establishing secure connections over insecure networks, the range of applications for it is quite extensive. It can, of course, provide the remote terminal interaction mechanisms that were part and parcel of the protocols it was designed to replace. It can be used as a passwordless authentication mechanism when established with public/private keys between a client and a server, as is the case with OpenSSH in GitHub and BitBucket.

Use with FTP

While FTP can provide a reliable client-server interaction mechanism for transferring files between hosts, it doesn't typically do so in a secure way. To that end, SSH is leveraged heavily whenever security is required for securely copying or transferring files between hosts. In fact, the secure protocol specification for FTP relies on SSH, and is explicitly entitled **SSH File Transfer Protocol,** or **SFTP**. The shells provided by SSH can even allow the **secure copy** (**scp**) Linux program to execute over a remote connection.

As you may recall from `Chapter 10`, *FTP and SMTP*, FTP leverages two separate and distinct connections for its file transfer interactions: the control connection and the data transfer connection. Interestingly, since FTP leverages these two separate connections, you can optionally apply SSH to either of the two connections, independent of whether or not you've also leveraged SSH on the other connection. This exact interaction mechanism is used by the **Fast and Secure Protocol** (**FASP**).

Use as a network tunnel

When properly configured for it, a remote SSH server could provide a number of network security features and functions for the client's interactions with the wider internet, with the ability to facilitate port forwarding, where a client establishes a listening network port and then connects it directly to the input stream for a listening network port on the remote host. In this mechanism, any traffic sent to the port on the remote host will be received and processed by the listening port on the client host. This could allow a client device that is hosted behind a firewall or restricted gateway to establish an SSH connection with a remote device hosted outside the restriction boundaries, and begin listening for unrestricted network access.

Taking that idea further, **OpenSSH** even offers support for a fully encrypted VPN service to operate between the client and the server. This provides fully encrypted interactions between the two hosts by bypassing any gateways, switches, or bridges between the two hosts, thus creating a logical "local" network with secure interactions and restricted access.

While it would be hyperbolic to describe the possible applications of SSH as being endless, they are certainly extensive. So much so as to be worth your curiosity and exploration. With that in mind, let's look at how we can start taking advantage of SSH within our software.

Establishing SSH connections

While .NET Core lacks native support for establishing SSH sessions in its own libraries, there are a number of third-party libraries and NuGet packages that can fill that gap. We'll be looking at one of the most popular of those packages, SSH.NET, and seeing how we can use it to connect to a remote machine and start interacting with it through a virtual terminal.

Setting up a remote host

For the purposes of this demonstration, we'll need to set up a remote host for us to SSH into. For this, we'll be using an Ubuntu virtual machine, configured on our system with **VirtualBox**. We'll be installing and operating on an Ubuntu image within our machine. To set this up, you'll want to create a new VM within VirtualBox by clicking the **New** button and following the wizard. Within the wizard, you'll be given the option to name your machine and select the OS type (Windows, Linux, macOS X, and so on) and the specific version. For this, we'll want to select Linux as our type, and Ubuntu 64-bit as our version, as shown here:

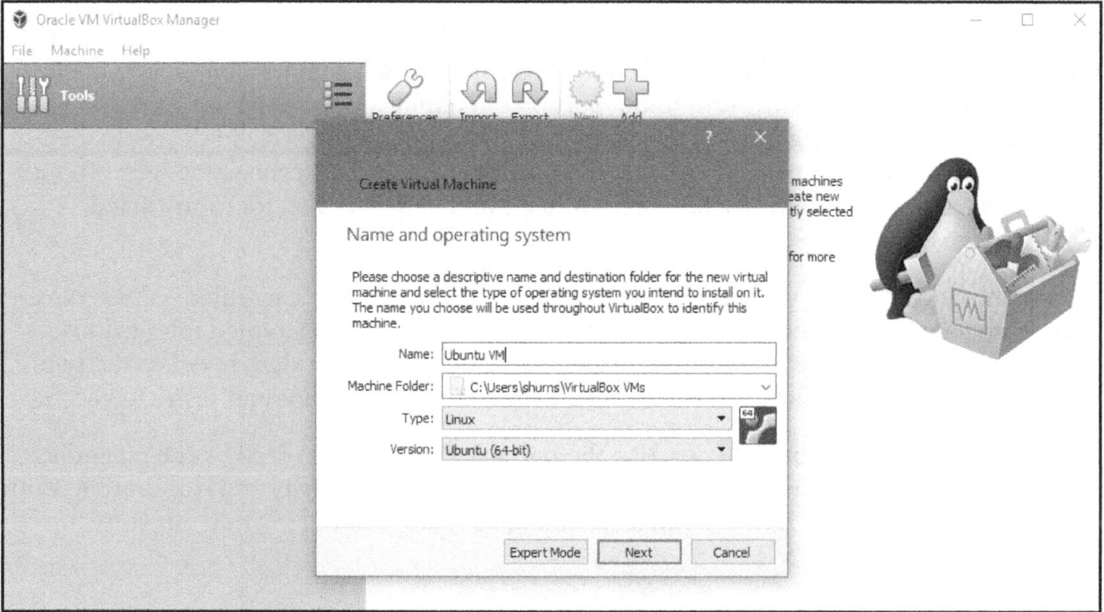

While setting up your VM, make sure to provision at least enough resources to meet the minimum installation requirements for Ubuntu, including 8 GB of virtual disk space and 2 GB of memory. Once we've got our machine set up, we'll need to install Ubuntu on it. Using the image I referenced in the technical requirements, install Ubuntu on your newly provisioned virtual machine. While you're installing the operating system, make sure that when you're prompted to create a user account, you require a password to login. This will allow us to demonstrate the use of SSH for remote logins.

Once you've installed Ubuntu on to the virtual machine you've provisioned, you'll need to enable SSH on the box. To do that, open up the machine's Terminal and run the following commands:

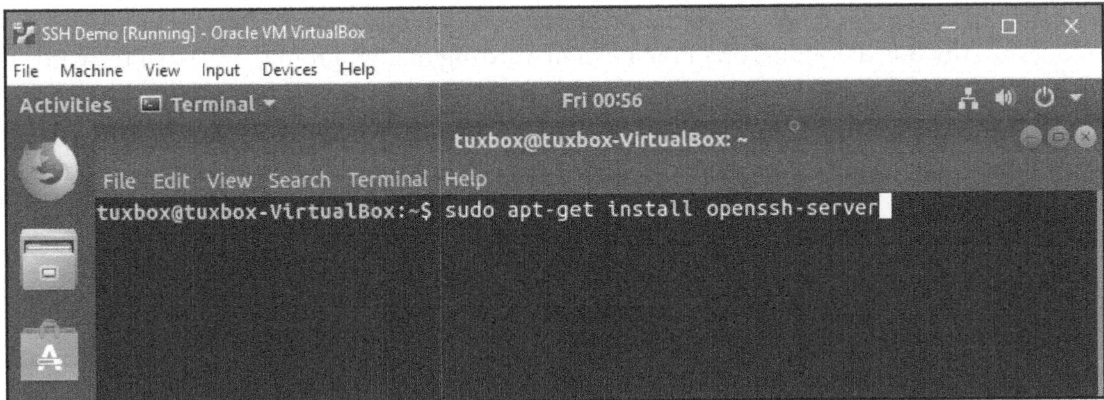

Once you run that, you should see a long run of installation scripts, after which your SSH server will have been installed. You can check the status of the SSH server by running following commands:

```
tuxbox@tuxbox-VirtualBox:~$ sudo systemctl status ssh.service
● ssh.service - OpenBSD Secure Shell server
   Loaded: loaded (/lib/systemd/system/ssh.service; enabled; vendor preset: ena
   Active: active (running) since Fri 2019-03-08 00:56:28 EST; 1min 27s ago
 Main PID: 4213 (sshd)
    Tasks: 1 (limit: 2316)
   CGroup: /system.slice/ssh.service
           └─4213 /usr/sbin/sshd -D

Mar 08 00:56:28 tuxbox-VirtualBox systemd[1]: Starting OpenBSD Secure Shell ser
Mar 08 00:56:28 tuxbox-VirtualBox sshd[4213]: Server listening on 0.0.0.0 port
Mar 08 00:56:28 tuxbox-VirtualBox sshd[4213]: Server listening on :: port 22.
Mar 08 00:56:28 tuxbox-VirtualBox systemd[1]: Started OpenBSD Secure Shell serv
lines 1-12/12 (END)
```

With that done, there are a couple things I want to note about our setup. First, notice that the virtual box is wholly distinct from my own machine, with a unique user and a unique host name. Second, note that the port is listening on port `22`. This is the default port for SSH servers to listen on, and we'll be using this detail when we establish our connection with the remote machine in our C# project.

Finally, we'll need to know how to interact with our virtual host from our own machine. For that, we'll be setting up port-forwarding on our virtual machine, so that requests that target the designated port on our host will be forwarded along as requests targeting the designated host in our VM. This will make our lives easier when we want to establish a connection. To do that, you'll open up the **Network** settings on your running instance and under the **Advanced** options, open the **PortForwarding** dialog. From there, we'll forward along all of our SSH connection attempts, which will always go to port `22`, to the listening SSH port on our guest host (the virtual machine):

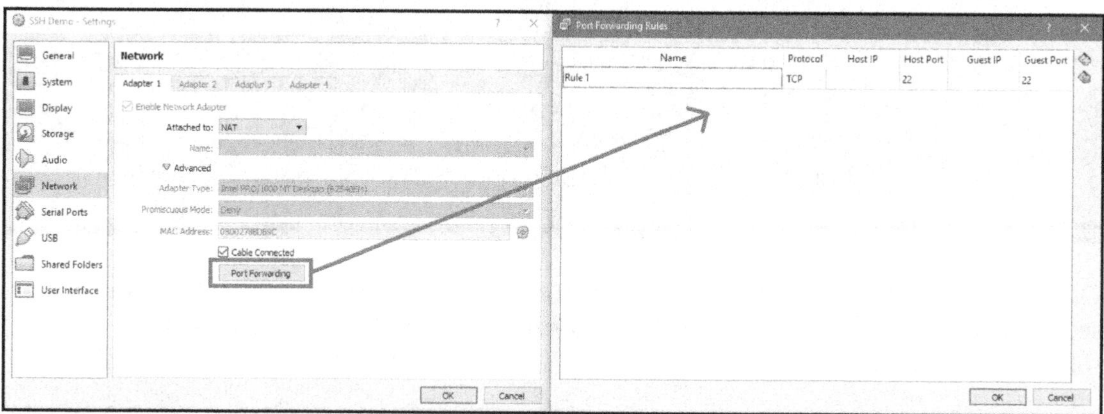

Once we have that configured, we'll be able to connect to our virtual machine just by sending a request to our localhost IP address of `127.0.0.1`, and because it's an SSH request targeting port `22`, the request will be forwarded. And, with that, it's time for us to wire up SSH.NET and connect.

Connecting to an SSH server with SSH.NET

As with all of our projects, our first order of business is to create it with the CLI. We'll be using another console app for this demonstration, so navigate to your target directory and run the following in your command prompt:

```
dotnet new console -n SshDemo
```

Since SSH.NET is not an out-of-the-box library with .NET Core, we'll need to add the package. You can do this with either the NuGet package manager from within Visual Studio, or by using the .NET Core CLI to install the desired package from within your project file's directory folder. The CLI command for the latter approach will be as follows:

```
dotnet add package SSH.NET --version 2016.1.0
```

Now, when you open up your `Program.cs` file, you can include the reference by adding the following `using` directive:

```
using Renci.SshNet;
```

And, with that, we're ready to establish our connection. The SSH.NET library provides a wealth of abstractions for interacting with your SSH server according to the standard. This includes classes that encapsulate authentication modes, connection information, and, of course, an `SshClient` that we can work with just as simply as the `TcpClient` and `HttpClient` classes.

For this initial demo, we just want to establish an SSH connection using the login credentials for our remote machine. The purpose is to show you how you can establish remote access to a host using your credentials for that host. We'll be using the password authentication mode, and passing in the username and password we created for our Ubuntu instance when we installed it on VirtualBox. Then, we'll create a new `SshClient` and attempt to connect. The code for that is as follows:

```
public static async Task Main(string[] args) {
    AuthenticationMethod method = new
PasswordAuthenticationMethod("tuxbox", "xobxut");
    ConnectionInfo connection = new ConnectionInfo("127.0.0.1", "tuxbox",
method);
    var client = new SshClient(connection);
    client.Connect();
    if (!client.IsConnected) {
        Console.WriteLine("There was an error establishing the
connection!");
    } else {
    Console.WriteLine("We've connected!");
    Thread.Sleep(10000);
}
```

In our first line, you can see we're creating an instance of the `PasswordAuthenticationMethod` class, providing our username and password. There are classes for each of the authentication modes we've discussed, including one that we didn't, called the `KeyboardInteractiveAuthenticationMode` class. This class simply provides a way for users to directly authenticate through an open connection terminal, as opposed to passing the credentials back and forth between the client and server.

Once we have our `AuthenticationMethod` class created, we pass it into an instance of the `ConnectionInfo` class. This class simply encapsulates the host, username, authentication method, and optional port specification (defaulting to `22`, of course) to be used when establishing an SSH connection. Finally, that connection information is passed to our `SshClient`. The `SshClient` instance is only initialized with the connection information as an instance property, however. Thus, we still have to explicitly connect to our remote server.

If you've configured your virtual machine as I showed you, and you run the application, you should see the **We've connected!** message in your application's output. The question, though, is how can we verify that we actually did connect? By looking at the status of our listening SSH server in our Linux VM, we should see that the authentication credentials were accepted:

```
tuxbox@tuxbox-VirtualBox:~$ sudo systemctl status ssh.service
● ssh.service - OpenBSD Secure Shell server
   Loaded: loaded (/lib/systemd/system/ssh.service; enabled; vendor preset: ena
   Active: active (running) since Fri 2019-03-08 02:20:28 EST; 13min ago
  Process: 6171 ExecStartPre=/usr/sbin/sshd -t (code=exited, status=0/SUCCESS)
 Main PID: 6172 (sshd)
    Tasks: 1 (limit: 2316)
   CGroup: /system.slice/ssh.service
           └─6172 /usr/sbin/sshd -D

Mar 08 02:20:28 tuxbox-VirtualBox systemd[1]: Starting OpenBSD Secure Shell ser
Mar 08 02:20:28 tuxbox-VirtualBox sshd[6172]: Server listening on 0.0.0.0 port
Mar 08 02:20:28 tuxbox-VirtualBox sshd[6172]: Server listening on :: port 22.
Mar 08 02:20:28 tuxbox-VirtualBox systemd[1]: Started OpenBSD Secure Shell serv
Mar 08 02:34:21 tuxbox-VirtualBox sshd[6209]: Accepted password for tuxbox from
Mar 08 02:34:21 tuxbox-VirtualBox sshd[6209]: pam_unix(sshd:session): session o
lines 1-15/15 (END)
```

And, just like that, we've remotely logged on to a host over an SSH connection. So, now that we know we can establish a connection, what can we actually do once we're logged on?

Remote execution with SSH

The SSH.NET library exposes operations on its `SshClient` class to perform everything from a simple command to opening up a shell terminal linked to the remote host. One of the core aspects of SSH, though, is that it is only intended to serve as a communication tunnel to a remote host. Therefore, the connections you can execute and the resources you can take advantage of will always be constrained by the remote host you're interacting with. In our example, we're working with an Ubuntu Linux host, so we're restricted to the commands and features supported by `OpenSSH` servers hosted on Ubuntu. With that in mind, let's look at how we can execute the operations available to us using SSH.NET.

Creating commands in SSH.NET

Now that we've successfully connected with our remote host using the `SshClient` class, we can use that client to start executing commands on that host. The pattern for this, as defined by SSH.NET, is to create a command, invoke its execution, and then observe its results. Alternatively, if you are executing exceptionally simple commands (as we'll be doing in this demo), you can create and invoke your command in a single step. The result of invoking a command will always be an instance of the command, which will contain a handle to any output streams returned by the client, as well as the result you obtained when the command was executed. To see what that looks like in code, we'll be using the Linux `uname` command, which simply returns information about the hardware and operating system kernel for the current host. I chose this because there's no `uname` command in Windows, so by viewing our result, we can be sure we're executing the calls against our remote host:

```
var command = client.RunCommand("uname -mrs");
Console.WriteLine(command.Result);
```

It's relatively straightforward, but it demonstrates the pattern of executing a command, and then using the returned instance of the `Command` class to view the result. By applying those lines of code to our program and then running it, we should see the following result returned from our VM:

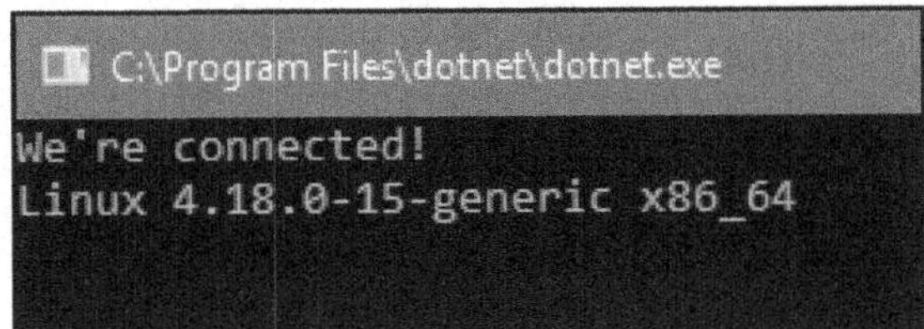

As if it wasn't clear from the operating system listed in our result, we are definitely connecting to our Ubuntu VM.

Modifying our remote host

To validate that we have the full permissions we should expect when logged in with our administrator accounts, let's add an additional command to modify the directories on our VM. Then, we can confirm our full user access by confirming the presence of our new directory in our Ubuntu instance. To do this, we'll add the following line of code to our project:

```
var writeCommand = client.RunCommand("mkdir
\"/home/tuxbox/Desktop/ssh_output\"");
```

If you're not familiar with the Linux filesystem standards, the `/home/tuxbox` root directory is the same as navigating to the `C:\Users\tuxbox\` directory in a Windows system. You can see that with this line of code, I intend to create a new directory on my remote machine, directly on the desktop, called `ssh_output`. After running it, I can open up my desktop directly in my VM, and I see the following result:

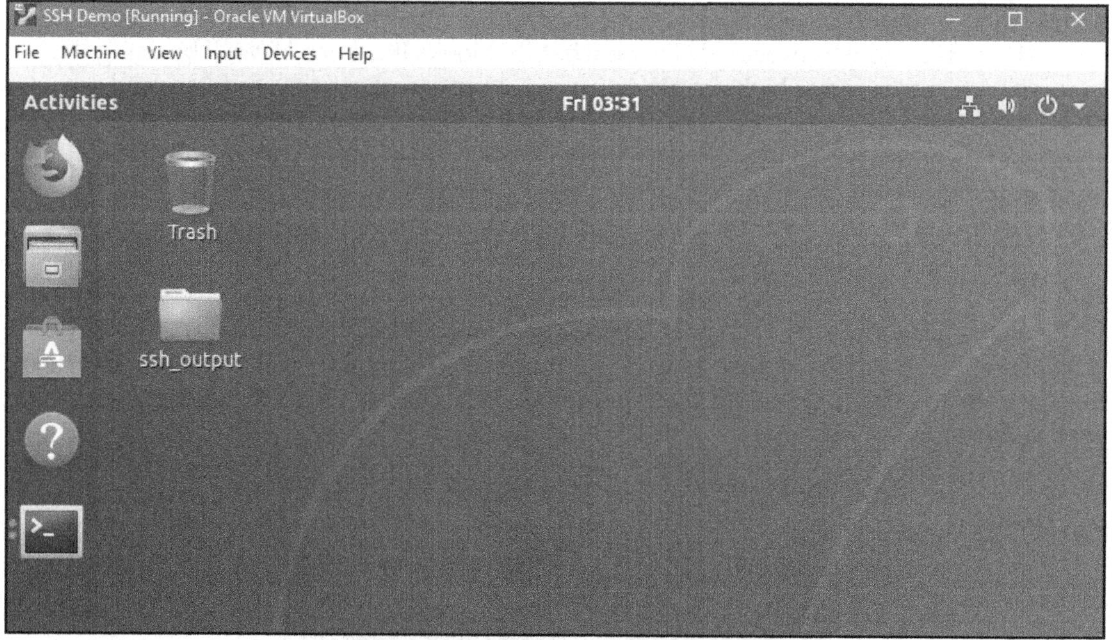

And, just like that, we've established a channel of secure communication from our software to a designated remote host.

If you take a little bit of time to explore the documentation, or even just the IntelliSense code suggestions for the SSH.NET library, you'll quickly see that it offers substantially more than we've looked at here. You can quickly and easily designate a port to forward to your remote host's listening ports, or create an entire shell, within a single line of code. The full breadth of features for it are certainly outside the scope of this book, but I'd strongly encourage you to take the features for a spin as you continue to learn and grow in the network programming space. I truly cannot overstate the value of simple, secure access to any remote resource you have configured to provide that kind of access.

For our purposes, though, I'm certain that your newfound understanding of the foundations of SSH, its design principles, and its implementation standards will give you all the tools you need to continue with your own learning. Ultimately, I hope that's what I've done throughout this whole book. My objective was to cover the foundational concepts of network programming and present them in an approachable and engaging way, viewed through the scope of C# development using the .NET Core framework. I sincerely hope I succeeded.

Summary

For our final chapter, we took another extremely deep dive into an extremely focused topic. We learned just about everything there is to know about SSH and its use. We spent a fair bit of time learning about the origins and development history of the protocol, as well as some of the features and applications it allows. Next, we took a tour of the various RFCs that define the architecture of SSH.

We learned about each of the three tiers in the architectural design of the protocol, starting with the transport tier and the requirements for security and data integrity that are demanded by the standard. After that, we saw how user authentication was accomplished, looking at how each of the standard authentication modes are defined and typically implemented. Finally, we learned about the connection tier, and how the SSH standard characterizes the multiple, distinct interactions that can be happening simultaneously between two hosts connected over SSH.

With that perspective in place, we were able to explore how we could leverage and interact with SSH in our C# projects. We discovered the SSH.NET library and took it for a spin, interacting with our own remote host. We saw how the library provides clean and intuitively defined abstractions for each of the architectural concepts we discussed earlier in this chapter. Finally, we looked at how we could act on behalf of our users, over SSH, to execute commands on a remote host.

And, with that, we have completed our comprehensive overview of the world of network programming, as seen through the lens of C# and the .NET Core framework. I sincerely hope it was as illuminating and informative and enjoyable for you to read as it was for me to research and write.

Questions

1. Why was SSH originally created? What problems did it seek to solve?
2. What are some of the more broadly used applications of SSH?
3. What are the three tiers of the SSH application architecture?
4. What are the three standard authentication modes that are supported by SSH?
5. What is a connection channel in the context of SSH?
6. What is a window? How is it used?
7. What is an interactive session?

Further reading

As we wrap up this book, hopefully you've taken many of my suggestions for further reading. This chapter focused, once again, on an advanced and extremely niche topic, for which there isn't much in the way of additional resources. However, if you are still interested in the subject of secure network tunneling, I would recommend the book *Understanding SSL VPN*, by Joseph Steinberg and Tim Speed. It gives a comprehensive look at the ins and outs of how secured VPNs work, and how they are administered. It's certainly something that will be of interest as you carry your new knowledge forward and plumb the depths of network programming. The book is available through Packt Publishing Ltd., and you can find a copy here: `https://www.packtpub.com/networking-and-servers/ssl-vpn-understanding-evaluating-and-planning-secure-web-based-remote-access`.

Other Books You May Enjoy

If you enjoyed this book, you may be interested in these other books by Packt:

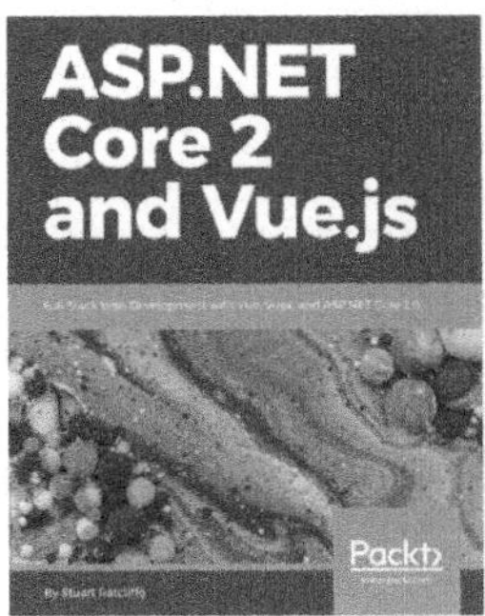

ASP.NET Core 2 and Vue.js
Stuart Ratcliffe

ISBN: 9781788839464

- Setup a modern development environment for building both client-side and server-side code
- Use Vue CLI to scaffold front-end applications
- Build and compose a set of Vue.js components
- Setup and configure client-side routing to introduce multiple pages into a SPA
- Integrate popular CSS frameworks with Vue.js to build a product catalogue
- Build a functioning shopping cart that persists its contents across browser sessions
- Build client-side forms with immediate validation feedback using an open-source library dedicated to Vue.js form validation
- Refactor backend application to use the OpenIddict library

If you enjoyed this book, you may be interested in these other books by Packt:

Hands-On TypeScript for C# and .NET Core Developers
Francesco Abbruzzese

ISBN: 9781789130287

- Organize, test, and package large TypeScript code base
- Add TypeScript to projects using TypeScript declaration files
- Perform DOM manipulation with TypeScript
- Develop Angular projects with the Visual Studio Angular project template
- Define and use inheritance, abstract classes, and methods
- Leverage TypeScript-type compatibility rules
- Use WebPack to bundle JavaScript and other resources such as CSS to improve performance
- Build custom directives and attributes, and learn about animations

Leave a review - let other readers know what you think

Please share your thoughts on this book with others by leaving a review on the site that you bought it from. If you purchased the book from Amazon, please leave us an honest review on this book's Amazon page. This is vital so that other potential readers can see and use your unbiased opinion to make purchasing decisions, we can understand what our customers think about our products, and our authors can see your feedback on the title that they have worked with Packt to create. It will only take a few minutes of your time, but is valuable to other potential customers, our authors, and Packt. Thank you!

Index

E

F

G

H

I

J

K

L

M

N

O

P

Q

R

S

T

U

V

W

Made in the USA
Coppell, TX
03 January 2020

14066797R00269